THE TSAR'S COLONELS

THE TSAR'S COLONELS

Professionalism, Strategy, and Subversion in Late Imperial Russia

David Alan Rich

HARVARD UNIVERSITY PRESS

Cambridge, Massachusetts
London, England   1998

Copyright © 1998 by the President and Fellows of Harvard College
All rights reserved
Printed in the United States of America

Library of Congress Cataloging-in-Publication Data

Rich, David Alan.
    The Tsar's colonels : professionalism, strategy, and subversion in
late Imperial Russia / David Alan Rich.
        p.   cm.
    Includes bibliographical references and index.
    ISBN 0-674-91111-3
    1. Russia. Armiía. Glavnyĭ shtab—History.
2. Russia. General 'nyĭ shtab—History.
3. Russia—History, Military—1801–1917. I. Title.
UB225.R9R53 1998
355'.033547'09034—dc21   98-19400

Contents

Maps, Figures, and Tables

Preface

This book began with a close study of the activities of Russian general
staff officers during the months before the 1877–1878 Russo-Turkish
War, and it grew decades outward from there. I had wanted to see for
myself whether the Russian general staff was, as others who looked at
the staff had argued, an apolitical remnant of aristocratic privilege,
disengaged from issues of state policy and even from professional bearing. If so, then Russia's abysmal performance on the battlefields of
Bulgaria and Anatolia in 1877 would be at least comprehensible (as
would the events of 1904–1905 and 1914–1916). However, any comparative examination of the development of a *new* technology, such as
the general staff was in the latter nineteenth century, would entail review of the whole gamut of social and political developments in late
imperial Russia. It would have to begin with Russia's professions and
encompass military technology, the elite's culture and social milieus,
midcentury intellectual and radical ideologies, and finally the myth of
autocracy itself. The results of this extended investigation are the meat
of what follows.

To locate Russia's general staff comfortably in its military, governmental, cultural, and social contexts, however, necessitated doing some
damage to received ideas of professions—in Russia and in general—and
challenging in a rather explicit way autocracy's claim to coherence as a
political system. All this, in the half century preceding the revolutionary

challenges of 1905. The findings on the general staff presented here come not so much as a surprise as a relief. While this study will argue in favor of Russian exceptionalism on the path to modernization (in contemporaneous terms), Russia was not alone among authoritarian, imperial powers that based their security and international standing on general staffing mechanisms. Remarkably homologous characteristics described both Russia's and Prusso-Germany's staffs as they confronted innovation and reform in the 1860s and 1870s. How was it possible that Russia's supreme military planning body could have failed to develop methods, practices, and even philosophies—and politically independent interests—similar to Germany's? Had not the nature of modern warfare in post-Crimean Europe changed the role and labors of the military staff to such a degree that the staff had emerged as a potential challenger to any government, in the absence of institutional counterweights or patterns of oversight? What I discovered brought me to the conclusions presented herein.

THE CORPS OF individuals and institutions that lent a hand in the research and preparation of this book eclipses the space even my generous Harvard University Press editor, Jeff Kehoe, could offer for acknowledgment. My research prospered thanks, initially, to a long-term research (and rumination) grant from the Finnish-U.S. Educational Exchange Commission (FUSEEC) and the IIE Fulbright Commission, which ensconced me in comfort for a productive winter in Helsinki. In Moscow my archival diggings flowered under the sponsorship of the American Professional Schools of International Affairs (APSIA) and the Diplomatic Academy of the former Soviet Ministry of Foreign Affairs, and later aided by Arch Getty's research exchange program. The staff of the Military-Historical Archive (RGVIA) in particular opened up a torrent of unexploited materials for examination in the Dvorets Lefortovo. My kind reading room hosts in the imperial foreign ministry archives (AVPR) provided me one of the real historical documentary gems for which researchers are constantly alert. In the United States I received support from the Harry Frank Guggenheim Foundation, the Graduate School of Georgetown University and the Piepho Fund of its History Department, and the University of Illinois at Urbana-Champaign Summer Russian and East European Institute. Crowning the research, a long-term research scholarship at the Kennan Institute for Advanced Russian Studies allowed me to temper sophomoric arguments and the worst of plebeian prose; Blair Ruble and his staff provided the sort of environment that is simply unattainable elsewhere. Under the Kennan Institute's auspices I produced an essay based on materials drafted from chapters 2, 3, and 4 of *The Tsar's Colonels* entitled "Imperialism, Reform and Strategy: Russian Military statistics, 1840–1880," which subsequently appeared in the University of London's *Slavonic and East European Review* in October 1996. To the editors of the *Review* I am grateful for permission to include in expanded form those arguments in this monograph.

Two men served as midwives (husbands?) to my infant manuscript: David M. Goldfrank and Richard Stites. If this work accrues any laurels, I hope they might believe their decade of patience and advice worthwhile. Michael Smith (Purdue University) saw shape and potential in the study's claylike texture before anyone else. To him in particular go my thanks for unflagging encouragement and assistance. In addition, my good friend, MacGregor Knox, Stevenson Professor at the London School of Economics, has unwittingly mentored this work since 1975. Various readers helped bring the project to its final form with penetrating and nuanced appreciations of the draft. Bruce Menning of the U.S. Army's Command and General Staff College in Fort Leavenworth sharpened my arguments on strategic developments, challenged my views on military professionalism, and introduced me to the latest research on General Nikolai Obruchev shortly before I delivered this manuscript to Harvard University Press. Willis Brooks at Chapel Hill has shared my enthusiasm for jettisoning the "liberal" label in reference to military reformers—even those "progressive" enough to throw bombs. I owe him special thanks for his reflections on Miliutin's place in this story, a topic about which he knows more than anyone. I owe David MacLaren McDonald, University of Wisconsin–Madison, thanks for the most encouraging comments a young historian could receive from a referee. His thoughts reaffirmed the significance of what I'd found in the literature of autocracy's political crisis and the place of professions in that crisis. Richard Wortman's reading of chapters 2 and 3 alerted me, in a generous letter, to various pitfalls worth avoiding. Finally, Dr. William C. Fuller, Jr., phoned an enthusiastic verbal endorsement of an early draft one gloomy Sunday afternoon, during a jobless summer that saw little else encouraging. My sincere thanks go to all of these people.

Without domestic sustenance, though, none of the work that preceded this would have mattered. Mary and Sena have endured much; separations, penury, and my periodic crankiness accompanied the work on this study. Mary's good nature and level head reminded me that typhoons in teacups cannot replace the nurture of family. Thanks, and my promise that the next one will not bring with it similar hardships!

The views contained in this study in no way reflect those of my current employer, the U.S. Department of Justice, nor was the work on this study performed with government resources or time.

Note on Translation and Transliteration

$\mathcal{S}$ome diversity has crept into the translation of Russian military organization titles. *Upravlenie* is often rendered "Administration," and there are variations that seem to make no attempt at acceptable translation of *Glavnyi shtab* or *Glavnoe upravlenie* (sometimes rendered "General Staff" and "Supreme Administration," respectively). Likewise, some organs of the war ministry present almost limitless possibility for confusion: *Voenno-uchenyi komitet* and *Voenno-uchebnyi komitet* have been erroneously and interchangeably called the "Military Education Committee" and "Military Scholarly Committee," probably from simple confusion of the two organizations (despite their completely different functions, composition, characteristics, and historical importance). I have usually followed the translations used in the English-language edition of *Bol'shaia sovetskaia entsiklopediia* because of their sensibility and resonance with more recent institutional manifestations.

On the problem of names—personal and place—I have accepted a Western equivalent principally for individuals of extraordinary notoriety (for instance, the emperors), or in rendering names firmly established by convention (Witte, Lieven). Thus, I have retained the Russian family names of some individuals of German background, even when the original family name closely approximates the Russian form. Thus,

General Kotsebu (not Kotzebue, from the German); but Reutern instead of Reitern because the finance minister was German-born and returned to his homeland after retirement from Russian service. For locations in Poland I have retained the Russian name (reflecting the documentary evidence and an imperial perspective) but have added for clarity the Polish form to some (for instance, Sedlets [*Siedlec*]). Transliteration in general follows the modified Library of Congress system, sans diacritics.

THE TSAR'S COLONELS

Introduction

Over a five decade span, a group of Russian general staff officers—never more than a few dozen men at any time—learned to work and act in ways that inflamed the fear of the only potential menace to Russia, Germany. War plans hatched in the general staff building on Palace Square in the Russian capital were the staff's response to threats on its western borders; they were the product of the staff's decades of learned behavior, acquired professional convictions, and vision of its leaders. The general staff in St. Petersburg then orchestrated an alliance to quiet its own strategic anxieties, without concern for unified foreign policy or the state's larger international interests. The staff's plans directly challenged the voice and will of the tsar-autocrat even in matters of *ultima ratio regum*.

General staff culture rested on the matrix of positivist scientism. Before the 1870s, that culture manifested itself in theories of warfare and critical histories of Russia's wars, crafted by instructors at the general staff academy. During the reign of Nicholas I, those men also participated in every sphere of imperial science, striking out across international borders to explore the outside world. Over the course of three generations, habits of information collection and learning led general staff officers gradually away from traditional tropisms in their work and loyalty to the dynastic regime. The quest for knowledge also carried them on mapping and intelligence expeditions, eventually plac-

1

ing at risk Russia's international relations. Leading each generation
of staff officers between 1840 and 1890 stood a succession of young
generals, each of whom reflected the particular spirit of his milieu as
much as a permanent impulse to military effectiveness. Those officers,
in turn, led the staff through its three phases of evolution, from inception through maturity to cultural implosion. Generals Dmitrii Miliutin
(1816–1912), Nikolai Obruchev (1830–1904), and Aleksei Kuropatkin
(1848–1925) were as united in their concern for Russia's international
position as they were different in temperament and partiality. They
moved the empire's highest strategic planning staff onto a rarefied plane
of professional expertise from which it came to assert authority beyond
its legitimate realm.

Dmitrii Alekseevich Miliutin is best known as the reform-minded
war minister from 1861 and the confidant of Alexander II. His invention of Russian military statistical theory and its military practice—
what today would be termed *military intelligence*—preceded all his other
works. Formally recognized as creator of this new branch of statistical
work, Miliutin used it to rationalize general staff work during his tenure
at the general staff academy in the 1840s. There, he established the
military statistical discipline as the matrix that bound together all new
general staff officers and set them apart from the rest of the officer
corps. As Obruchev's mentor and sometime protector, Miliutin discovered in the young colonel the protégé through whom he could also
remake Russian strategic tradition and practice from the 1860s onward.

Nikolai Nikolaevich Obruchev, a barely known general staff officer
though no less important than Miliutin, touched every aspect of strategic activity from the early 1860s until his resignation in 1898 as chief of
Main Staff. Mystery still surrounds Obruchev, who began his military
career with involvement in midcentury radical activity. The climax of
his service came in 1892 when he privately carried through the discussions that produced the French alliance a year later, unsanctioned by
the autocrat. In between, Obruchev molded the strategic acculturation
of two generations of Russian staff officers and thus changed the course
of the balance of power in Europe, a legacy recognizable today. Yet he
left virtually no trace on the historiography of the era.

Aleksei Nikolaevich Kuropatkin lacked Miliutin's intellectual vigor
and creativity and Obruchev's strategic vision and organizational
authority. But he had the disposition of the quintessential staff officer, a

technician of the highest capability and patience. Taking Obruchev's vision and goals, Kuropatkin built an organization to mate Russia's limited resources to his mentor's objectives. As Obruchev's right hand for most of the 1880s, Kuropatkin installed in the general staff all the components for effective mobilization planning and in the process became the Russian Schlieffen. His uninspiring personality might have rendered him yet another anonymous war planner in the mobilization section of the general staff but for his unexpected elevation to the war minister's seat at the end of the 1890s. The demands his emperor placed on him there were well beyond his narrow technical background and limited strategic capability. Behind these three officers worked the anonymous staff officers, the captains and colonels selected for mobilization planning work, who carried rationalization into the cerebrum of the Russian imperial army.

After the Crimean War (1853–1856), the shock of defeat did not shake the conviction among military reformers that deliverance of the empire lay in knowledge. This certitude figured behind the efforts of the officers who gathered around Miliutin. Those men played out the military mandate for fundamental change in the 1860s, simultaneously in organizational reform, a necessary antecedent to all strategic rejuvenation, and in renewal of routine general staff work — military statistics. By the 1860s, the positivist and scientist attitudes of younger general staff officers, including some of radical background, elevated the energy of staff work and prepared those lieutenant colonels and colonels to act as experts in any matter within the staff's purview or reach. Military statistical expertise also created a shared cultural experience that bound even the youngest staff captain to the chief of Main Staff—and sharply distinguished them from the rest of the officer corps, including the aristocratic Guards officer corps to which most belonged. Their otherwise mundane labors formed the basis for decisive changes in Russia's strategic direction in the 1870s and 1880s.

The Franco-Prussian War (1870–1871) was the watershed of Russia's strategic relations with western Europe. The tactical and operational lessons of that war held the interest of most Russian officers into the mid-1870s. The war's architects, General Helmut von Moltke (1800–1891) and his Prussian staff officers, however, confronted Russia's general staff with an emphatic example for emulation. The German also confirmed Obruchev's already polarized evaluation of the Continent's strategic landscape, and injected vitality and direction into staff statistical work and war planning. Prussian mobilization in 1870 demonstrated the potential of railroads to revolutionize warfare through mechanization of army concentration. Russian staff officers already possessed the wherewithal to master planning techniques essential for exploitation of strategic railroads in Russia. Most important for Russia, the war created for the first time in sixty years a single potential enemy who could destroy the tsarist state: unified Germany. The "mobilization gap," an economic but especially military-technological differential distinguishing the two empires, animated the secret strategic conference convened by Alexander II in February 1873, which led directly to the introduction of universal military service nine months later. The attention of military planners in St. Petersburg shifted toward the five western military districts to an extraordinary degree after 1870, in frantic preparation of the means to defend the Polish salient against Germany's military potential, even as other Russian officers carved out new acquisitions in Central Asia or cultivated appetites for the Turkish Straits. The general staff's rationalization shortly paid dividends, but not against the power it feared most.

Russian planning for war against Turkey began almost a year and a half before declaration of hostilities in April 1877. The process started as a simple staff exercise in late 1875: How would Russia fight and win a war with Turkey in Europe? But in April 1876 the Main Staff commenced mobilization preparations in earnest. As the war plan matured, those preparations took on a momentum of purely military character that quickly outran the political and diplomatic considerations on which they were based. Not until the emperor intervened in October to *slow* the military timetable did the Main Staff realize it would not have its war until 1877. The divergence of military and political considerations that characterized 1876 established a pattern for Russia's foreign relations into the 1880s and up to the French alliance of the 1890s. War planning resulted in an efficient and rapid mobilization of forces that stunned the closely observing General Moltke in Berlin. Obruchev's offensive plan also anticipated maneuver and rapid decision, not a war of annihilation or attrition, equally surprising to the Prussian general. In an early 1877 memorandum, Moltke observed for the first time that in the next war with France, Russia's ability to mobilize successfully would change the balance of power on the continent.

In early January 1880, after a year's reflection on the recent Turkish war's outcome, Obruchev composed for Miliutin and the tsar a brief memorandum evaluating Russia's strategic position in Europe and focusing on the German threat. After the tsar approved the memo's conclusions, it became the cornerstone of all Russian strategic planning and mobilization preparations until the Russo-Japanese War (1904–1905). Obruchev's evaluation of the Russo-German and Russo-Austrian relationships, which he drafted after two decades of intimate personal ties with France, served as a strategic road map for his mobilization planners. One of Obruchev's young staff officers, Kuropatkin, would do the planning that realized Obruchev's vision. Kuropatkin's place in history as later war minister and the loser during the Russo-Japanese War has displaced attention to his work in the 1880s and his relationship to the general staff. During that earlier decade, Kuropatkin was Obruchev's protégé par excellence and heir apparent, a careful, calculating staff officer who distilled war preparations to their finest degree, technically. More than any other planner, Kuropatkin saw to the crafting of a mobilization plan that would be practicable *and* credible even though in a war it could not save Russia but by suspension of disbelief. His success in that work was reflected in the growing desperation of General Moltke's plans for war against Russia and France. After Kuropatkin drafted Russia's first viable war plan (1887), he attempted to manipulate the remaining factor over which the staff had no control: the interference of amateurs, such as the tsar's brothers and uncles, in the business of war-fighting. Technical military considerations finally eclipsed the prerogatives and traditions of the dynastic regime. Military specialists objectified the sovereign they served as they had objectified Russia and its neighbors through military-statistical work.

Two decades of professional development culminated in Obruchev's commandeering of Franco-Russian rapprochement from foreign ministry control and his imposition of a formal military agreement in its place. The Main Staff's interpretation of Russia's strategic interests, at once pledging Russian policy to full coordination with France's while illicitly spurning any limitations on Russia's strategy, was a most practical and bloody-minded way to salvage its own unworkable strategy. The staff's view of the new alliance was the fullest imaginable expression of staff professionalization, in that the "authority of experts" eclipsed broader state interests and dynastic prerogative—Nicholas II's subsequent confirmation of the arrangement notwithstanding. The agreement also established the principle that purely "military considerations" not only would define Russia's field regulations (where Kuropatkin had left his mark) but also might presume to govern the empire's political and diplomatic policy. Like their German counterparts, Russian general staffers turned Clausewitz on his head.

French interest in the agreement was unaffected by Russia's weak economic condition, dangerously unstable domestic situation, and pathetically underdeveloped strategic railroad network, all important ingredients of a credible military alliance. What the French saw, instead, was a staff mechanism of a sophistication second only to Germany's. Russia's ability to *conceptualize* and plan the mobilization of a million-man army counted for more than all the existing material impediments that would prevent a successful mobilization. That gamble alone explains Franco-Russian strategic relations from 1892 to 1914.

The memoirs of general staff officers assigned in St. Petersburg in the mid-1890s evince a growing lethargy, preoccupation with appearance, and boredom—even as they remark the limits on autocratic choice they were all helping construct. Work, of course, continued on the plan for mobilization against the Central Powers, but staff officers seemed, in their own minds, to believe the French alliance had relieved them of their principal burden. The strategic problem had been solved, and, after Obruchev's retirement, staff officers no longer felt impelled to scramble for solutions to myriad other problems. From that time, Obruchev's alliance locked the tsar into a strategy that would survive until the collapse of the Provisional Government in 1917.

Strategic planning habits became an imperative that detracted from the dynasty's exercise of power and ran contrary to real interests of state. Only in their dynastic myths was the Russian tsar (and the German kaiser) a charismatic warlord (*Glavnokomanduiushchii, Feldherr*), a military leader who guided his state's strategy and led it on the battlefield. Instead, both were rationalized *objects* of rationalized, professionalized systems of state. Statistical knowledge empowered Russian state servants to act willfully, yet from motives at once more self-serving and bureaucratically defensible than traditional arbitrariness (*proizvol*). The general staff, however, led the rest of Russia's government on this path of rationalization. Russia's educated strata—or, more precisely, its well-educated noble officials—laid the path to state modernization and in the process wandered upon the uncharted consequences that none consciously intended or anticipated. The general staff's place in the center of both dynastic myth and state power rendered it an extraordinary example of these developments. The general staff was indispensable to the state's mediation of any notion of autocracy by the middle of the nineteenth century, and to the symbol of autocracy's coercive power and martial strength. Its capacity to remake itself in an era of rapidly changing warfare, however, rendered it perhaps the most subversive institution of all in late imperial Russia.

War Plans and Strategy: Nineteenth-Century General Staffs

Professionalization is comprehensible only comparatively, that is, against the best technique of any group of active practitioners. In the mid–nineteenth century Prussia emerged as the leading practitioner of the general staff art. Yet stereoscopic examination of the Russian and German staffs seems to accentuate their dissimilarities. When static social and organizational forms are applied to the comparison, they prove themselves least useful to understanding the general staff's significance. Where general staffs were similar was in a common tropism: in response to imperial interests and anxieties, they planned for wartime mobilization during peacetime. What every general staff did was examine military options it could place at the disposal of policy, and prepare the documents (plans) necessary for the army to carry out one or more of those options. Before the era of Moltke (chief of Prussia's and then Germany's general staff, 1857–1888), staff strategic planning consisted of logistical support for the course of action chosen by the supreme warlord and his counselors. That was, essentially, the Russian staff's experience on the eve of the Crimean War in 1853. In Russia, the convergence of technological changes and increasing political and economic tensions permanently subordinated intendancy (logistical) concerns to "higher planning" by the end of the 1860s. Staffs became the only bodies in which the state could concentrate the expertise necessary to *imagine* a war still lying somewhere off in the future. Strategical imagination, "deep future–oriented" thinking, as Arden Bucholz calls it,[1] became a quintessential characteristic of the rationalized general staff, perhaps the modern world's first institutional example of "global" thinking. A war plan was the principal expression of that vision.

Organizational structures attributable to the Prussian staff system did not inspire competing Continental staffs; no European power shared more than approximate bureaucratic similarity with the Prusso-German staff. In fact, Russia's staff organization and operation remained particularly unstable, even ad hoc, until 1903. The flexibility of Russia's strategic administration (a characteristic notably absent from Germany's system) allowed the center of gravity in strategic deliberation to shift repeatedly. It rested first with the Military-Scientific Committee (*Voenno-Uchenyi komitet*, or VUK), which Obruchev dominated for three decades until 1898. Subsequently, under war minister Kuropatkin it gravitated to his office. The staff professionalization Obruchev oversaw, in part abetted by institutional flexibility, also coincided with deepening strategic anarchy at the highest levels of the government. In the wake of Obruchev's departure, the offices that planned Russia's wars underwent disruptive reorganizations that cast the system into confusion on the eve of the Russo-Japanese War. Following Kuropatkin's fall in 1905, something approaching chaos ruled within the war-planning and strategy-making organs until the outbreak of the Great War. As its professional behavior disintegrated, the staff's planning work continued without interruption for the empire's final two decades. The unique Russian route to staff rationalization—taking advantage of organizational irrationality—unraveled in the hands of men of lesser capability and willpower than Nikolai Obruchev.

War planning was a facet of state security that mirrored the international system in which staffs operated. Between 1859 and 1861 Prussia, under a king of bolder ambition than his predecessor, expanded the royal army by 40 percent. The wars Prussia fought in the 1860s accelerated the army's growth. Prussia's aggressive but limited policy preoccupied central European states; it dominated the considerations of Russia's general staff. Russia lay militarily prostrate and diplomatically isolated after its Crimean War defeat, and it was paralyzed by social debate on the eve of the emancipation. It was the defensive party in central Europe (though not without ambitions). And as Prussia's army grew, Russia's shrank and dispersed across European Russia and western Siberia, as the government searched for more affordable ways to organize its strength. The staff in St. Petersburg attached itself to the challenge of simply plumbing the vastness of the empire in those bleak years, rather then struggle with offensive and defensive plans for its next wars. Indeed, the very first, primitive mobilization schedule did not emerge from the staff until the year Prussia tackled France.

Strategy framed in the general staff on narrowly "military considerations" sprang from a *static* view of the world. One set of states represented friends and another set opponents. Only the British, with no higher military planning apparatus until the start of the next century, could comfortably declare that they had no "eternal friends, only eternal interests," in Gladstone's memorable words. For military planners the problem was not, foremost, the divination of other powers' intentions but knowledge of their capabilities. Capability, usually a most slowly changing attribute, reinforced stasis in military planners' strategic views and overshadowed the politics of nuance, balance, and relative advantage. Prussia's surge in military strength in the early 1860s boded ill for all its neighbors, as Russian planners understood immediately.

As the Prusso-Danish and Prusso-Austrian wars had portended, the defeat of France in 1870 galvanized all of Europe. Russian general staff officers who took seriously their role in the empire's security were startled not only by Prussian tactical and operational success but also by the military effectiveness of the new entity that arose in central Europe. Although foreign policy remained the province of the foreign ministry, the Main Staff (*Glavnyi shtab*, or *Glavshtab*) by default or hubris drew its own conclusions about the implications of German unification. Some Russian staff officers followed reports of Moltke's army and of his general staff from St. Petersburg, while others accompanied the Prussians into eastern France. The success, to many of them, was plainly due to superior staff preparations. Russian war planners then had to face the prospect of a powerful new neighbor whose army had redefined, among other things, the objectives and standards of general staff work. As Russians learned to do the same sort of planning, they inevitably affected Europe's military balance and international relations, not least by the impression they made on their counterparts in Berlin.

Russia's military and diplomatic policy-making apparatus was severely dysfunctional. There was no supreme council of state to frame unified, interministerial policy. Not even the emperor's signature could impose coherence on self-interested ministries that vied for influence over state security and, more important, for control of resources.[2] Without a unified policy, such as Prussia-Germany had to a much larger degree until Prince Bismarck's fall, Russian military planners operated from crisis to crisis without coherent higher objectives that state policy would have provided. Each ministry analyzed international relations from its own narrow geostrategic—and bureaucratic—perspective, and planners framed Russia's interests as they saw them. Policy "vacuum" alone, however, cannot account for the Main Staff's bold intrusion into the realm of international relations. The emergence of a new "expert" element,[3] the army's mobilization planners, threw policy formulation even further from its traditional foreign ministry center of gravity.

Until 1914 the war plan of a European power was in essence a complex, systematic program for rapid army mobilization and concentration for battle; it was not necessarily a coherent expression of strategic thinking. The grand strategic concepts from which a staff derived an excruciatingly detailed mobilization schedule were not a part of modern staff work per se, even though they claimed to embody the highest political and military view of international conditions. Individuals, not committees, performed the work of conceptualization, usually in extrabureaucratic channels, away from the light of oversight. Miscasting a statement of concepts as a "war plan" illustrates the difficulty of writing strategic history from conceptual documents.[4] Finished mobilization schedules illustrated little of the policy or prejudices from which they arose. More often than not, the final schedule relied so heavily on purely military (i.e., technical) considerations that policy took a decided backseat. To technical aspects of army organization, matériel technology and manpower, the staff added considerations of time and space: the imperative for compression of both became, after 1870, a source of chronic anxiety and an impetus for perfectionism. On the contrary, war planners did not consciously consider state policy while they labored to produce mobilization documents. In principle, therefore, there is no reason to assume that a mobilization schedule was the one best, "rational" solution to an articulated security problem, regardless of the rationality of the system that produced it. Nor did strategy necessarily unfold in so many deduced successive approximations and improvements, from one plan to the next. Positivist taxonomies and scientific "objectivity" notwithstanding, Russia's mobilization plans now seem less the encapsulated essence of a political and strategic arithmetic than planners' best guesses about how they hoped their next war would go, or worse, merely paperwork exercises with little connection to the militarily possible.

Russia's formulation of strategic consensus was awkward at best, and thus like most bureaucratic decision making during the late imperial period. A strategic thinker first floated a new proposition (as happened in important memoranda in 1868, 1872–1873, and 1880, for instance), or put it forward at high-level gatherings (such as those of 1873, 1876, 1881, 1887, and 1892). The war plan (or, to be precise, the mobilization schedule) provided the technical elaboration of strategic policy as later received or perceived by lower-level specialists. Few of the experts had more than glancing knowledge of the conceptual documentation that gave birth to their labors. The challenges were entirely issues of detail, and only rarely did flickers of larger strategic context appear through the papers they left behind. One or two men usually produced conceptual statements of strategy in imperial Russia; on the other hand, dozens of general staff officers contributed to a mobilization schedule.

With little variation, states typically invested *political* actors, that is, individuals with de facto political responsibility, with the authority to conceptualize the state's strategic interests—to make strategy. In Russia, as in Germany, that power formally resided in, and only in, the supreme warlord. Yet with the problematic exception of Emperor Nicholas I, Russia had no emperor equipped and inclined to exercise that responsibility. Instead, Russia's political culture since the reign of Alexander I had settled on the mechanism that Witte came to describe so well at the end of the nineteenth century: "The tsar is autocrat because it depends on him to impart action to the machine, but since he is a man, he needs the machine for the administration . . . as his human strength cannot replace the machine."[5]

With Nicholas I's death, Russian strategy making returned to patterns recalled from Alexander I's reign. Divergent bureaucratic interests maneuvered for the autocrat's ear, and strategic disunity and confusion were the order of the day. In practice, institutions that retained the emperor's confidence (*doverie*) were free to do as they deemed fit. They arrogated to themselves that authority—power—that properly rested in autocratic hands, even in issues as central to imperial self-identity as war making. It then fell to individuals of no extraordinary position to thus exercise responsibility for strategic choices; no emperor after

Nicholas I challenged their competence. Paradoxically, it was precisely the emperor's confidence in his generals and colonels that relieved him of the need to acknowledge his own role in setting the empire's strategic course. Nikolai Nikolaevich Obruchev was the figure after 1865 who relieved Russia's emperors of strategic leadership. He assumed the role of strategic thinker in the absence of anyone else suitably positioned with the necessary temperament and training. His articulation of Russia's "interests" is therefore of fundamental importance to the study of Russian strategy, foreign policy, and autocracy from the 1860s onward. Although Obruchev never ascended to the war ministryship, his protégé Kuropatkin did.

From the early 1860s, four activities constituted general staff work. Three of these—mobilization planning, survey and statistical work, and intelligence gathering—defined *war preparations*. The fourth, dissemination of military knowledge ("military science") to general staff officers and the forces—a necessary precondition to all professionalization—accounted for the staff's *educational preparation*. Most Continental armies formalized the distinction between the preparational and educational spheres through maintenance of general staff academies. As in Prussia, Russia's staff fused practical and theoretical activities by a continuous exchange of ideas and individuals between the staff, the academy, and the line, the so-called open general staff system. Staff officer recruitment and training could not have satisfied the army's demand for specialists: on the eve of the general staff's most rapid expansion, its academy produced too few new staff officers even to fill all positions within its walls. Low graduation rates before 1855—low enough to alarm even the antistaff inclinations of Nicholas I, who in fact induced them—resulted in almost three decades of undermanning and staff officer shortages. Those that acquired the General Staff designation had to be well trained if they were to perform the variety of functions demanded of them.

The complexity of staff work comes from its fusion of organizational, representational (topographic and cartographic), educational, and analytic activities.[6] The melding of a particular outlook with a new work *process* was fully expressed only in the preparation of a war plan. The elephantine organization in Russia that carried on these activities, the Main Staff, had components that did myriad other things as well. Those activities were indispensable to war preparations. But the technicians who drafted war plans came to see such business as ancillary, merely an adjunct of the staff's principal concern, the mobilization plan. Medical support, geodesic and hypsometric surveying, even the business of supply, could all be turned over to other specialists once the staff had defined the technical parameters of the plan and, more important, set up a railroad transportation schedule. Even though all of the army's geodesists and cartographers came from the general staff academy, very few of them left a personal mark on the strategic landscape they sketched and measured. Yet their presence has come down vividly to late-twentieth-century imagination through cinematic representation: Akira Kurosawa's portrayal of a military geographer in *Dersu Usala* (1976).

The staff officers who made Obruchev's and Kuropatkin's labors possible were junior, the lieutenant colonels and colonels who occupied desks in the planning apparatus. They were powerful staff *deloproizvoditely* whose labors confound recent assumptions about imperial bureaucrats. Although their position is typically translated as "clerks," *deloproizvoditely* in the Main Staff were "action officers" (to borrow from contemporary bureaucratic jargon) who operated with the encouragement of Obruchev, Kuropatkin, and planning department heads. They were not Gogol's lethargic, imbecilic minor functionaries.[7] The general staff organization saddled these men of relative youth and junior rank with vast responsibility and authority. If they did not work autonomously and with initiative, they could not have succeeded as mobilization planners, for too much other planning activity depended on their own. Their rank, age, and background are not insignificant: in the same manner after the Napoleonic Wars, privileged young staff officers carried forward serious concern for military competence and modernization that also came to impinge on traditional prerogatives of the elite leadership.

General staff reformers were both Guards officers *and* staff reformers and thinkers; notionally, they were as much a part of the Guards elite as they were Miliutin's reforming assistants. The advantages of accelerated promotion accorded to Guards officers and their access to the state's very best elite and military schools assured them of intellectual development *(nauka)* and access to the places from which they could influence army effectiveness *(deistvennost')*. Thus, unlike line regiments, the general staff was suffused with Guards lieutenant colonels and colo-

nels in their early thirties—often a decade younger than their line counterparts. The scientific character of staff work drew these young men to
the general staff during Nicholas's reign as they had been drawn to
higher military thinking during the Napoleonic era.[8]

Rationalization and Modernization in Russia

Imperatives for change existed in Russia and Germany throughout the
nineteenth century. Necessity most often had a military face, whether
it was represented by Prussian defeat at Jena and Auerstädt in 1806 or
by the embarrassment of Sevastopol in 1855. Well before midcentury,
Germany's elites had discovered that political, social, and economic
modernization by no means led necessarily to political liberalization.
After 1848 they were free to unleash modernizing forces without fear of
serious bourgeois challenge to established political and social institutions.[9] Russia's circumstances did not argue contrariwise. Rieber notes
that there was no historical imperative driving Russia to choose between the "immobility of caste and the dynamism of class," to force
development onto one track or the other. Forces for change possessed
characteristics from opposite ends of that spectrum, and elements both
in and out of state service nurtured hopes for more effective government.[10] After 1860, Russian statesmen initiated with varying degrees of
success the reform of Russia's social and economic spheres of life. Agriculture, rural administration, jurisprudence, and education underwent
reform so as to better serve the state's interests, that is to say, within or
extending traditional institutional boundaries. At the same time the
government, assisted by its entrepreneurial servants, attempted focused
stimulation of the economy (railroads, foremost), and in some ministries introduced recruitment into state elites based on merit as well as
birth. An 1860s "vanguard of reform" that guided these changes set its
own agenda to satisfy particular ministerial goals; it was not "led" by the
autocrat and the dynasty.[11] But defeat in war lay behind this reform as
surely as did Prussia's re-creation after 1806–1807.

Alexander II did not emancipate Russia's serfs as an act of "defensive
modernization," merely fighting a rearguard action against the forces
of progress. Wehler offered that problematic formulation to describe
Prussia's "special path" to modernization during the second half of the
nineteenth century, and it worked no better in explaining the peculiarities of that kingdom. Alexander (on counsel of his advisers) did it pur-

posefully, to strengthen his state in the face of external threat and to liberate the internal forces necessary to underpin state development. It was the fullest expression of those intellectual and cultural influences that had likewise gripped his father and uncle before him. By no means did all of his—or his predecessors' and successors'—servitors operate to similar compelling purposes or share the perspective that made change so compelling. Enough of Russia's state servitors, however, did; reason and knowledge were their tools. As in Prussia, Russia's technical accomplishments were the work of bureaucrats. General staff officers, few in number, set out to improve the effectiveness of their army even before the Crimean War. The resource of which they held exclusive command was knowledge. Knowledge of the specifics of a problem, they believed, would lead to clear choices among myriad routes for its solution. Through what Isaiah Berlin called a "sensational conjuring trick," such men came to believe that all knowledge was the taxonomic constituent of science and could ultimately account for the universal. These men were positivists.[12]

The assumptions behind rationalization are explicitly positivist, as are the ideas that nurture rationalization's most modern practitioners, the professionals. Russia had a history of rationalizers: Speranskii collected laws so the empire's administrators could increase their effectiveness by providing them a predictable legal framework; Count Kiselev and Nikolai Miliutin (and the youthful reformers in the ministries of state domains and internal affairs) collected data on Russia's rural and urban conditions to undergird their authority for social reforms. Simultaneously, the first generation of general staff academy graduates began the most ambitious and enduring rationalization project of all: to plumb the physical, natural, and social width and breadth of Russia and its neighbors, ultimately to acquire the key resource for securing effective defense of the realm. Reform and modernization were the endgame; information gathering was propaedeutic to that purpose but itself became an end: knowledge for knowledge's sake. In all these pursuits Russia was unexceptional among modernizing, traditional European states, including the Germanies and the Hapsburg empire.

At midcentury, however, Russia remained on at least three levels an exceptional European state. Socially, it possessed an elite of extraordinary size and with near-exclusive access to educational resources. Its elite cultivated complex, critical views through education at home or abroad. By any measure, however, the Russian nobility was unequal to the task of governing. Both in proportion to the empire's size and in political fortitude, it was deficient: bureaucratic undermanning was endemic, with the general staff a prime example, and few felt a need to challenge tsarism's political legitimacy. When the general staff began producing effective administrators, other ministries succeeded in drafting many to satisfy their own desperate need, which exacerbated the staff's shortages. Second, state reformers could never consciously escape autocracy's graceful and seductive vision of political culture, to free the government to act consistently in favor of national interests. And like their ministerial masters, bureaucrats typically did not act professional; they defended their turf against each other, without concern for (or comprehension of) state or national interests. Finally, Russia's Western-inspired metropolitanism was exceptional in its inefficacy: the organizing power of the capital, so effectively exercised by Berlin, Paris, London, even Ottawa, over their provinces, was absent in Russia. War planners, like their counterparts throughout the state structure, found themselves endlessly carping at subordinates in the provinces to get on with their work. The achievements of the few military, scientific, and technical experts underscore the narrowness of the Russian empire's basis for rationalization and regularization.

If modernization is concerned with contemporaneously accepted patterns of effectual labor (a proposition explored further in chapter 1), it does not depend on the social or political values that first spawn rationalization. Action, not ideology, drives modernization. The empire's educated elite circles imitated the patterns of governance that proved effective in the West, but Russian society's exceptional character prevented it from participating in the sort of cultural and political acculturation and transformation that in other countries made new techniques of government action effective, lasting, and thus "modern." The Russian general staff exhibited selective rationalization as well. Without Continental patterns of purposeful accumulation of knowledge, protoscientific habits that dated from the eighteenth century, the rationalization of any general staff after 1856 is unimaginable. General staff reform in Russia, as across Europe, depended on methods of scientific investigation borrowed from the natural sciences, on modes of thought characterized by precision and taxonomy, on consideration of the ultimate ends to which knowledge might be harnessed, and on centralized bureaucracies for managing knowledge. Russian general staff officers were quite capable of these patterns of modern thinking, and they acted "professionally" as they went about this work. Being modern and professional did not, however, make them liberal or democratic. As a profession, war planning was perhaps the most "modern," and it certainly was critical to continued state survival by the 1860s. At the same time, many of its practitioners were among Russia's leading "state conservatives."

Military planners had moved out of the world of aristocratic dilettantism epitomized by the swarms of aides-de-camp and adjutants that decorated the reign of Nicholas I. This was evident in all armies that underwent rapid reform and modernization. Without exception, reform of military technology and bureaucracy depended on a sophisticated understanding of new organizing techniques for complex data. Almost always reform began with the strengthening of military information structures as well. A cycle of perpetual modernization at one level or another began around midcentury. Data, information, statistics—these were the building blocks of military rationalization in Russia no less than anywhere else on the Continent. New organizations, new guns, new strategies—and new national appetites, interests, and responsibilities—all followed.

A general staff historical "strategic memory," the result of a decade of well-focused labor on mobilization issues and decades on military history, instilled some continuity in staff work by the beginning of the 1880s. It did not, however, warrant the planning process against decay when the dangers posed by Austro-German solidarity were offset by Russia's French alliance. After 1898 the mechanism itself began its slide into "de-professionalization," not least due to the departure of its guiding light. Lacking their predecessors' sense of urgency, and believing Russia had been relieved of decades-long strategic isolation, staffers fell into unsettled cycles of reorganization and experimentation with military theory. In turmoil, the war ministry was in no position (particularly after the 1905 East Asian debacle) to win even the fiscal resources necessary for minimal matériel modernization.

Consequences of Rationalism and Professionalization

Bureaucratic rationalization penetrated most parts of Russian government in the nineteenth century. The service ethic of Russian officials during the Russian empire's final century turned on their idea of "progress" or modernization. Soldiers and administrators might disagree on the pace and extent of change, constrained as they were by socially conservative ideology and dynastic loyalty, but the majority of them undoubtedly shared a concern for Russia's stature as a European power. For critics, whether they be statist, populist, or Pan-Slavist, the autocratic state's seeming inability to keep pace with its counterparts to the west cast doubt on the empire's efficacy in a rapidly changing world. Government officers were well situated to appreciate the cost of Russia's difference from its western neighbors. After Nicholas I's reign there was no doubt that difference meant backwardness, if not obviously in terms of social and political development, then unequivocally in economic and military progress and competence. Among the imperial army's general staff officers criticism was blunt and the empire's military malfunction was painfully obvious. In order to rescue Russia from disaster, these men called for a far-reaching program of modernization through rationalization.

Social scientists define modernization as a calculated process undertaken by a power-holding elite to achieve some goal. As a state group able to mobilize sufficient resources for the modernizing project, the general staff had few equals. General staff reformers had crossed Gellner's "Big Ditch" to modernity. Even before 1850 they divined that wholly new form of power that characterized modern thought systems: cognitive power. They framed it in terms of rational systems of knowledge; they perceived in it the lever with which they would transform the Russian army into a more effective instrument. In the process they would fundamentally (if unintentionally) dislocate traditional social organizations and challenge the basis of autocratic power as well. These officers were professionals.

Professional groups are the proponents of rationalization in traditional states. They possess the modern perspective inherent in their command of specialized, often technical, knowledge. In Russia's general staff, however, their rationalization agenda ultimately failed. Reformers at the ministerial level, like their counterparts within the general staff, were unable to steer between the constraint of dynastic prerogative and the devolution of ministerial government. In moments of political crisis, as in the months preceding each of the empire's last three wars, the "power" ministries (interior, war, foreign affairs, and finance) failed to cooperate successfully for Russia's interests. Even under a final reform-minded (if ruthless) premier, modernizing ministers found the passage between Scylla and Charybdis unnavigable.[13]

A touchstone of political legitimacy—the adequate discharge of national security responsibilities—proved beyond the autocratic government when it entered its final cataclysm. Its civilian political leaders, who had sought unification of policy in the Council of Ministers after 1905, ultimately found themselves hobbled by habits of insularity and by the supreme power, Tsar Nicholas II, who thought government his personal possession.[14] Professional bureaucrats, the experts whose authority might have insinuated interministerial political unity, instead settled into parochialism, and none more so than the technicians of the Russian general staff. In the end, professionals were not the potential saviors of autocracy and empire but virtual guarantors of their demise.

Those who participated in general staff professionalization were anonymous officers immersed in statistical minutiae and the perfection of their war plan. The internal dynamics of Russia's general staff, the body to which those few men belonged, forms an unimagined past to most historians of the late Russian empire. Its importance lies in three planes. It exercised rising influence far beyond its size within the Russian state and the European state system after the death in 1855 of Nicholas I; it exerted unrestrained freedom to define Russia's supreme strategic and security interests; and its members wore uniforms of the most privileged elite within Russia's omniuniformed ruling class.

By midcentury, virtually every young staff officer had participated in the army's statistical survey work, some of it on or beyond the empire's borders. Self-reliance and initiative were essential to their success. Some also flouted autocratic authority in activities inimical to the state. Among those who survived this period of moral resistance, the responsibility to science and habits of independence *(samostoiatel'nost')* continued to stand above fealty to the dynasty and emperor. As generals by the 1880s, they cultivated subordinates unschooled in their own mid-century idealism. Their protégés were experts, however, who likewise usurped political authority and dynastic prerogative, but not to overthrow the system. That later generation's intent was, rather, loyalty to professional dictates and technical military considerations. On behalf of "technical considerations" they undermined the basis for tsarism's symbolic narrative of power.

The autocrat-emperor's authority and compassion flowed, foremost, from his power. Trappings of ceremony—public, courtly, and domestic—reinforced his symbolic fatherhood of the empire. He cloaked himself and his family in the uniform of the Guards regiments (Germanic or domestic), themselves bastions of martial spirit and masculine prerogative. The emperor was the mannequin of traditionalist conservative militarism, regardless of his private repulsion at the gore and slaughter of warfare.[15] His ministers operated autonomously only to the extent that they enjoyed his confidence, which, before the late 1890s, he most often extended them. Officers of the St. Petersburg Guards and staffs projected an indispensable variation on the theme of autocratic power that flew in the face of their sovereign's impotence. These privileged officers mediated reception of autocracy's myths in nineteenth-century Russia and cloaked the dynasty's tenuous grip on an unevenly modernizing society. Writ large, the military shepherded the narrative of power to the whole empire; its general staff was the narrative's sanctum sanctorum.

The transformation and operation of Russia's imperial general staff were components of staff professionalization; the rise of the staff's influence beyond military planning was its consequence. Hence, professionalization had little to do with the corporate *social* character of officers designated "of the General Staff."[16] How those officers worked at the center of the army's planning system defined them as rationalizing professionals. The staff affected the empire's security and foreign policy through activities characteristic of all general staffs: information gathering and mobilization planning. The influence of general staff experts on Russian policy after 1870 derived from their narrowly technical work on war plans. What began as an organization's search for solutions to strategic problems developed into an obsession with a plan to save Russia's western regions, and the realm itself. By the 1880s, among the consequences of that obsession was the gravitation of key officers, led by future war minister Aleksei Nikolaevich Kuropatkin, toward a limitation on autocratic participation in the business of strategy making and war-fighting. The limitation of imperial options by staff experts—essentially the marginalization of the autocrat and the dynastic regime—presents a powerful argument for reexamination of the concept of "professions" in modernizing, tradition-bound militarized states, and as an analytic tool in Russian history as well.

The existence of a simple potential—of military rationalization through knowledge, system, and purpose—was the imagined and contingent future that existed in the minds of this small but influential group of army specialists. General staff officers—*genshtabisty*—epitomized the spirit of inquisitiveness afoot in Nicholaevan Russia. It was alive in Russia's new societies, most clearly in the Imperial Geographic Society and the Imperial Technological Society, of which army officers formed the early core membership. These young officers—geographers, cartographers, surveyors, artillerists, and statisticians—mapped and described their empire, and so prepared it for expansion southward and eastward. Through a thirst for universal knowledge they were also well situated to see military decay before anyone else, as Russia exited the Crimean War. They embraced the idea that Russia's military tradition could be salvaged and refurbished by way of knowledge in a new era of warfare, and that in so renovating Russia's ability to make war in Europe they would also save and remake the empire itself. The bureaucratic organs in which they thought about these problems were the womb of strategy: the planning and education components of the general staff.

The general staff's leaders for the first time began thinking routinely, if occasionally confusedly, in "deep future–oriented" terms. That thinking demanded a new, orderly work habit, and good control of information and sources. It rested on intellectual preparation begun in the general staff academy through a vigorous engagement with problems over *la longue durée*, inculcated through study of military history. The new outlook depended on a systematic accumulation of information and preparation of studies to assist the deliberations of planners and leaders. All these activities took place at first haphazardly in the 1840s and 1850s, and then with greater order and purpose by the 1860s and 1870s. Deep future–oriented strategy formulation—preparation of war plans based on years (if not decades) of anticipated military, social, and economic development—was an almost entirely cerebral activity. And as a system of national security planning, it was new to all European armies in the middle of the nineteenth century.

The strategy-framing process fed on vast amounts of data, the grist from which a general staff constituted a workable mobilization plan for defense or offense. That information, potentially constituting the superset of universal knowledge with no limit on range or content, had first to be conceived, imagined in the minds of those whose tool it would be. It then had to be accumulated, organized, understood, mediated. The ways in which the general staff would use information, having no precedent in Russian experience, had themselves to be invented. But first, the indispensable ingredients for exploitation of knowledge were *objects* of imperial strategy: an enemy (real or imagined) and a mission. These, too, Russian planners lacked until they divined them in the 1860s. The staff's energetically cultivated habits of scientific inquiry became the first intelligence systems on which primitive war planning rested, but the prejudices and convictions of war planners themselves acted as the lens through which military potential found its target. That target was Russia's dynastic *frère*, Germany. The wide-ranging search for effective solutions to the problem of imperial security was the impulse that drove rationalization.

Chronologically, this study brackets the greatest strategic crisis the Russian empire faced in the century before 1914. German unification, in a matter of weeks in the summer of 1870, created a potentially antagonistic power whose raw industrial and especially military might could dismember—if not, as senior Russian officers believed, *destroy*—the empire. An abortive search for strategic focus sponsored by the tsar followed German unification. However, it was the staff's perception of German perfidy after the Russo-Turkish War (1877–1878) that galvanized its activity and began the gradual circumscription of dynasty from the staff's consideration of Russia's highest interests. Planners received their first agenda in 1880 in a document, prepared by a senior staff technician and planner, that defined Russia's enemies in strategically explicit terms. It dictated a more clearly focused agenda for information collection and planning work. The search for a practicable war plan, one that encompassed the indispensable technical components of universal military service and mechanized mobilization, bore fruit in 1887. An alliance with France a few years later fulfilled the war planners' ambitions, but the solution that these specialists devised depended on two conditions that Russia did not enjoy. First, their war plan resorted to a political-military alliance that Russia could not afford (as the tsar's senior diplomat knew). Second, the plan's success depended on a level of field command agility that Russia's military tradition had never consistently demonstrated or cultivated. Retirement of the architect of the French "project," Nikolai Obruchev, relieved the staff of its directing hand. Few general staff officers attended to Russia's military problems with the vigor evident over the preceding forty years, while many retreated into theoretical ruminations or bureaucratic infighting.

Military Reform as a Historiographic Problem

Part I of this study is principally intellectual and cultural history: the story of discovery by members of Russia's most tradition-bound governmental group of philosophies of state security that promised unbounded potential for effectiveness and change. Part II explores the strategic and political consequences of this development, in the period when general staffers imposed systematic limitations on dynastic and imperial options. Staff officers subordinated imperial prerogative to strategic considerations as they fashioned improvements to deployment schemes and mobilization plans in a futile search for viable security. As international history this study searches for the connections—alarmingly tenuous—between Russian strategy and policy, and the perpetual dialogue between the two. Throughout, it is a story of the harshly disappointed expectations of rationalization's power, and the absence of philosophical and material alternatives in Russia's struggle to modernize.

The politics of thoroughgoing military reform and civil-military relations in Russia began with discussion of the emancipation program in the 1850s. Emancipation arose from military rationale—that is, the emperor made the decision principally for reasons of state security rather than in mere reaction to pressure "from below." Similar calculations drove deliberations on military questions in the 1860s and 1870s.[17] As late as the 1873 secret strategic conference, for instance, political debate between reformers and their traditionalist opponents occupied much of the invective on military issues. Documentary traces of Obruchev's and Miliutin's preparations for the showdown over universal military service at that conference, however, underline the strategic issues they saw to be at the heart of the decision and apparently irrelevant to their uncomprehending opponents.

A significant proportion of the general staff's finest minds spent their careers teaching at the Nicholas Academy of the General Staff in St. Petersburg (with periodic forays to field command, prerequisite for promotion). Two groups worked in the academy: those with permanent, full-time positions there, and those whose principal duties in the capital brought them to the academy part-time. With few exceptions, men in the former group produced the army's large bibliography of theoretical works but rarely had places in the war-planning apparatus doing mobilization work or crafting "real-world" strategy.[18] The heuristic reward supposedly arising from study of Russian military theory is not found in the body of literature produced in the academy during this era. A convincing argument for the connection between bookish writings and patterns of strategic problem solving has not been made yet. Indeed, professionalism has no necessary relationship with any occupation's "formal knowledge" (embracing its formal philosophy and theoretical systems). One historian of the professions found that often-assumed connection unequivocally tenuous: "The analysis of scientific and scholarly texts can be no substitute for the analysis of the human interaction that creates them and that transforms them in the course of using them in a practical enterprise."[19] The interaction of a small group of military men with the problems of Russian imperial security and defense from the 1860s through the 1890s—*not* pursuit of unified theories of war—defined the professional level of general staff work.

Russia's army consisted of much more than its general staff. The General Staff Corps constituted only a tiny proportion of the twenty-odd thousand officers in the army's officer corps. Mobilization planners, those at the very heart of the apparatus Miliutin, Obruchev, and Kuropatkin wielded, represented a minority in the general staff. Their labors did not touch the common peasant soldier *(muzhik-soldat)* except when their work failed: in wartime. Paradoxically, the apparent apathy among Obruchev and his assistants toward the competence of the field army, the common soldiers and their brother officers, raises serious doubt about the planners' strategic realism. It also casts their judgment of the capacity of *technique* to save Russia as fantastically optimistic. Could Obruchev and Kuropatkin, though acutely aware of Russia's transport handicaps and mobilization shortfalls, have thought their plans might also obviate the well-known incompetence of field leaders from company to army level?[20] Staff myopia and uninterrupted fascination with the problem of mobilization schedules after 1880 reinforced staff officers' preoccupation with Germany and Austria (whatever their intentions), and occurred almost always at the expense of attention to Russia's own combat preparedness. Only in the general staff academy did a few youthful officers begin to tackle that failure of Russian tactical acculturation and doctrine.

The intersection between a new general staff culture born before the 1860s and broad positivist and scholarly currents buoyed by scientific methods in educated Russian society[21] bears out the place of *genshtabisty* among modernizing elements in late imperial Russia. More interestingly, it establishes a linkage between Russia's educated culture (with its intellectual limitations) and its international relations after 1855. That intersection also underlines the exceptional absence of choices available to those who would have saved the autocratic empire.

I

The Emergence of General Staff Professionalism

1

Expert Knowledge and the
Problem of Higher Military Staffs

Autocracy's constructed dynastic myth left little room for state professionals. Partnership with the rising ranks of experts who filled the central bureaucracy—and sharing of authority with them—were beyond its defining tropes. Men in the uniform of elite army contingents, including general staff officers, were in principle not excepted. Autocracy's military regalia, borrowed heavily from petrified German practice, festooned the public autocrat for his role as absolute and unlimited authoritarian. To the Russian people, and to most army officers, he was warlord, as well as a loving but unchallengeable father. The professional men of Russia's general staff knew the images well, coming as most did from Guards regiments in the capital. Reception of the myth, however, deteriorated as professional practices crept into state circles. The distance that the autocrat placed between himself and the unpleasant business of both governing and ruling eroded the myth's grip on servants with competing dispositions and a real interest in seeing progress in the condition of the Russian state (or, at least, their small parts of it). Although the reigns of the two Alexanders witnessed a remarkable degree of delegation of authority to general staff officers, that was not enough from the planners' perspective. Each new international crisis after 1870 strengthened their inclination to limit dynastic options for the benefit of their own professional labor.

This sort of professional behavior is considerably more complicated than the pattern described by many social historians who study professions. Foremost they see the simple exercise of corporate independence as a preeminent and sufficient mark of a "professional" group, without reference to the developments that moved the group to such behavior. This definition of "professionalism" slides further toward trivialization with application of other traits not commonly found in society at large. The final shape of the label, "profession," offers few clues to what precisely separates one educated group from another in a modernizing society. It promises to explain the often contradictory behaviors of professional groups that form part of a traditionalist political system or the ambivalent attitudes of professional practitioners toward extraconstitutional political authority—but it never does. The problem of professions in Russian history centers less on their autonomy than on an understanding of professions' shared characteristics and, more important, their prejudices and ideologies. The characteristic Russia's bureaucracy needed most in its officials was *initiative*; a group like the general staff simply seized it, as it became professional.

Russian historians have been less interested in the ways some occupations appropriated formal knowledge to solve problems than in construction of a priori definitions to encompass the right professions. Without exception, practitioners of new specialities held strong convictions about progress and rationality that were not shared by traditional elites or uneducated strata of society. Those convictions either did not inhere in other occupations or simply were inappropriate or superfluous. The source of professional culture, that is, a faith in the mastery and efficacious application of systematic knowledge, is scientific positivism; in its military manifestation it may be called "staff culture." It was concerned ultimately with effectiveness.

AS WITH A SCIENTIFIC breakthrough, the origins of a profession's development are often elusive. But in the case of the professionalization of general staffs in the nineteenth century a watershed is easily divined.[1] The performance of Prussia's Great General Staff in 1866 and especially 1870–1871 rendered obsolete any higher military structure on the Continent not similarly employed. Development of a new technology—general staff work—had at least as revolutionary an impact on warfare as did the later automation of firearms or the all-big-gun battleship. The potential perfectibility of war plans became not merely an imperative but an obsession with Continental armies. It is not inappropriate to see in the development of general staffs after 1870 the same cultivation of the *new man*, the military technician, that inspired others who pursued administrative utopias. Myths of progress were indispensable to both, progress through knowledge was the promised method, and in the nineteenth century both rode squarely on scientific positivism. Croce declared the era after 1870 the real age of positivism, particularly as philosophy and politics dragooned the methods and language of natural science to diverse ends.[2] The promise of perfectibility offered by scientific methods excited the interest of general staff officers, as well as utopian bomb throwers and social Darwinists.

Unlike revolutions in the equipment of war, the staff has remained unsurpassed among military technologies to our day. Every European power except Britain, which temporized until its own disastrous war in the Cape colonies to create a unified staff, comprehended the revolution of 1866–1870. The extent to which the higher staff of any European army responded to this innovation became a good measure of its rise to the level of a professional body. Professionalization arose (in Charles McClelland's formulation) as "a 'project' carried out by the 'external' dictates of *disciplinary necessity*."[3] It was also one (in the Russian case) that bore the characteristics of its own native origins.

Rationalization and professionalization in Russia occurred over a couple of decades around midcentury, at a time of remarkable innovation in the institutions of government and in the scientific realm. The Russian army recruited its staff heavily from privileged, educated noble society, that is, from the corps of officers assigned to Guards regiments in the capital (and, to a lesser extent, in Warsaw). Guards duty was expensive, and certainly beyond the means of officers who lacked independent means. At the same time, the general staff academy admitted only the brightest officers for a general staff education. After days of examination and interviews, only a fraction of the applicants began the academy's two-year (later three-year) course. The staff developed a social and cultural character combining the elitism and affluence of the Guards and nobility, and the scientific positivism of a modern, educated upper class.[4]

Some young officers in the capital and Warsaw diverged from their social milieu during the early years of Alexander II's reign. Like other noblemen around them, they transcended the army's traditional aversion to change and assumed instead the philosophy of progress afoot in wider, educated civil society.[5] This was especially true of the general staff's officers and other technical specialists who harnessed the methods of modern sciences to do their work. Cultural differences fractured the army officer corps as a whole, but there were even graver fissures *within* the General Staff Corps that widened with the increasing specialization of work attendant to statistical work and later to mobilization preparations. Professionalization in effect drove social and cultural wedges into the distinctively elite body, the general staff, and separated "progressives" from more traditionalist officers. Education was the key prerequisite of professional development, although it neither made an officer professional nor itself constituted "professionalism." Corporate membership and education were inadequate for the definition of any nineteenth-century profession.

The historical problem is complex because the idea of "professionalism" has been burdened, inter alia, with the success or failure of Russian modernization and autocracy's twentieth-century crisis. A useful definition of the term must successfully place every professional group between its impulse toward progressive change and traditional loyalty. Social historians have devoted much thought to the question of definitions, although their categorizations spring to life without reference to the sources of the modernizing impulse. Definition is not trivial, for it would also point toward answers to the questions posed routinely in studies of late imperial Russian social and political history, and indeed, more generally of modern European history as well. What was it about Russian professions that made them, like Russian development in general, "exceptional"? Why were there never enough professionals? And why were they seemingly so ineffectual in other spheres of public and political life?[6]

Corporate social characteristics such as class, social origin, or religion are unhelpful in answering these questions or, for that matter, as sources for understanding modernization. They explain nothing about how staff officers (or engineers or doctors) did their work, or much about the work itself. They do not account for modernization undertaken by "state conservative" elements or for the political and social inactivity among nongovernmental professionals. The use of "professionalism" as an analytic tool in recent social studies of Russia is found wanting if applied to civil social development, likewise to general staff operation as well, and modernization in general.

The question of whether Russia's general staff was *professional* marks an important prism through which to refract the changes that animated the staff during the quarter century before 1870. It can also play host to an explanation of why the staff usurped the autocrat's military option, even as staffers worked loyally to assure their empire's security.

Educational breadth and exposure to the intellectual prejudices of positivism and scientism among young officers underwrote general staff adaptation to the demands of modern warfare. Prussia had itself decided that security and *Bilduing* (education in the broadest sense) were inseparable. Since Prussia's defeats in 1806, German military reformers had understood that the future belonged to the state that was able to field an army of thinkers: self-reliance, initiative, and effectiveness sprang from their precondition, education.[7] The same was true in every state where the process pertained—and, analogously, within every profession as it emerged. Positivism and scientism were conspicuous components of an ideology of inquisitiveness among bureaucrats who underwent rationalization.

A "professionalization imperative" did not exist uniformly throughout the Russian bureaucracy, as Gogal's caricatures strongly suggest, nor even among the power ministries. In contrast to war planning, for instance, nineteenth-century diplomacy was a calling that successfully resisted the pull of professional specialization until nearer the century's end. Diplomacy bore the state's highest interests to the table of negotiation, where they could be bartered to advantage with other sovereign states. But it remained the realm in which the generalist, rather than the technician, typically held the field. Diplomacy's artful character may also explain the deep distrust staff professionals had for their foreign ministry counterparts, why they were willing to rely on their own scientific work to attain Russia's interests, and why general staff officers may have expected to rescue the realm from the worst of those political dilettantes, their reigning emperors, without the cooperation of Russia's diplomats. In the end, however, the diplomats and traditionalists saw more clearly the mortal threats to empire and dynasty.

Professionalism and Its Models

The challenge that historians of imperial Russia have faced in placing general staff officers in a professional context arises from the larger problem of Russia's exceptional development; outside models of social behavior and development simply do not transfer well to the Russian case. Neither the Anglo-American notion of professions nor the Weberian model of rational bureaucracy serves analytic and explanatory ends if applied against autocratic society and government. Instead, the cloudy prejudices of early nineteenth-century positivism and scientism unite professional groups by shaping their views of knowledge, progress, and modernization. Those prejudices tempered their recourse to traditional symbols of political power, without displacing their native class thirst for privilege and proximity to power.

The corporate social traits described in the Anglo-American approach most accurately convey the way Russian general staff officers developed between the Crimean War and the end of the century. Staff officers acquired and systematized a body of specialized knowledge that empowered them to act autonomously, behavior that went unchallenged by outsiders. That model relates professional behavior to the growth of autonomy and expertise among practitioners. Because that model is subculturally oriented, it focuses on the profession's internal operation, where characteristics of the profession develop. No military staff, however, was composed of individual practitioners. General staff officers worked in highly corporate and hierarchical ways (even as individual experts on particular problems), and staffs existed as cornerstone agencies of conservative governmental and bureaucratic will. With the exception of the handful of men who guided staff operation, general staff officers were anonymous, even to their tsar and emperor.

The Weberian model, with its emphasis on rationalization of traditional institutions within a generally educated society, captures the origins of professionalized organs most precisely, because membership in those bodies depended entirely on satisfaction of advanced educational requirements; on meritorious work in related activities like research, exploration, or map making; and on an inclination toward efficacious application of knowlege to complex organizational problems.[8] Historically, the Continental and Anglo-American models are discrete.

Following the example of Duma-era critics, some historians have developed the notion of "civil society" as the context best suited for assessment of Russian modernization, and they have placed the professions squarely in that social sphere.[9] But they make civil society the *exclusive* domain of professions, and thus place Russia's professions within the Anglo-American rather than the Continental model. Furthermore, the literature on the history and sociology of Continental (and especially German) professions also repudiates the assumption that professions mediated the interests of a sphere separate from government, that is, civil society. For Russian historians the example of the general staff remains the paradox: if it was *not* (according to them) a part of civil society, then how did it attain all the formal characteristics of professional development? The answer lies in the exceptional character of Russian modernization.

Those who have worked with the civil society paradigm look for traits with which to distinguish a civil profession from specialized government employment. One scholar noted the difference thus: "The two groups [civil and bureaucratic] came from different milieux and, with few exceptions, did not mix easily."[10] Distinctiveness and separation thus resulted from their members' education, on the one hand in military academies and elite schools, and on the other in universities. The cost of this interpretation is high: civil society would have to exclude the vast majority of Russian engineers, doctors, and lawyers before 1900 who, although university-educated, *were* government employees and could not be part, professionally, of the civil society they supposedly constituted. It is not clear how the source of a man's education consigned him to one *outlook* or another, for most fundamentally, professional behavior itself constitutes a particular self-identity and outlook. Like other distinctions between government and civic spheres, this one based on education is false because until the last half of the century almost all educated Russians received their schooling either in elite governmental institutions or at home. Joining the Corps of Pages in infancy, for instance, no more consigned a boy to military or state service than home and university education assured him a civil career.[11] A more significant distinction, although one with little analytic use, was between those whose wealth allowed them to remain idle and those whose family means made some career imperative.

Since Weber's work ninety years ago, the direction of sociological examination of professions has been precisely the opposite: to explain the *intersection* of private and governmental modernization in the development of professions. It is here that the civil-bureaucratic categorization is of little relevance to the definition of professions as *expert labor.* According to Weber, *rationalization*, intimately associated with Western modernization and the rise of science, emerged first in the shape of "rational-legal bureaucracies," by definition the repositories of experts.

Russia's embrace of general staff modernization occurred within the

limits of a well-known social and cultural context: elitist privilege in a
highly educated, socially rigid society. The staff shared this ground with
other groups of specialists that grew to maturity before and after the
Crimean War. Given the achievements and changes that distinguished
the staff, the question again arises: Where did the officer-noblemen
of Russia's general staff lie in Russia's social spectrum? The question
is complicated by their loose midcentury radical philosophical roots,
their development and use of sophisticated information technology,
and their later veiled but persistent challenge to the dynastic regime's
prerogative. A redefinition of professionalism is useful to any answer to
this question.

Models aside, attributes of "professionalism" carry a variety of rhe-
torical and popular meanings (and, surprisingly, some analytic uses as
well). The most benign and universal definitions include participation
in higher education and theoretical knowledge. To this is usually added
some form of organization with a degree of autonomy from the state,
and occasionally formal accountability of the individual practitioner in
professional practice.[12] Military historians have given the term professionalism their own particular spin, reflecting popular vernacular: salaried work, human resources not based on conscription, or doing one's
job well. To them, military defeat is prima facie proof of unprofessional
effort. More nuanced approaches prescribe some sort of melding of
military theory with the study of military history as professionalism's
basis. Although reassuringly descriptive, formulations like these have
little hermeneutic value. Most of these trait clusters emerge only as a
result of a particular intellectual and cultural disposition ("professionalism"), or remain by no means necessarily connected to a concern for
effectiveness. Instead, the professional attribute should describe the
extraordinary relationship of practitioners to their work and explain
what that work does to the professional.

The use of characteristics of autonomy (in the language of sociology)
to identify professions is particularly inappropriate in the Russian case.
Autonomy, indicating the extent to which a profession's members operate independently of hierarchical social control (i.e., not under the bureaucratic authority of nonexperts), is accompanied by self-regulation
through collegial mechanisms. There is no evidence, however, that civil
organizations imposed any less conformity (i.e., control or limits on
autonomy) on an employed professional than governmental bureaucra-

cies did on their professionals.[13] In fact, the dysfunctionality of much of Russia's bureaucracy argues the reverse, that such autonomy followed professionalization rather than constituted it. The *day-to-day* exercise of discretion by practitioners in their work, based on their expertise, better described professional relations.[14] This follows Weber on the question of mutual accommodation between professionals and bureaucrats, reached in the course of professional development. While some historians think these two processes vaguely antithetical, in fact both are integral (and historically conjunctive) to modernization.[15]

In their Continental manifestation professions were important elements in the transition to mature industrial society because of their indispensability to the *functioning* of modern bureaucracies, and thus societies.[16] Professionalization occurred coincidentally to the emergence of jobs that involved state use of expert knowledge. Knowledge labor clearly was not the exclusive domain of bourgeois capitalist social and economic development, although Weber does not look far beyond that context. His bureaucratic model fails because it is tied to a social class in a society that can no longer quarantine traditional privileged elements to "appropriate" sorts of work (or, more accurately, prevent those elements from appropriating the tools of the bourgeois professions). Professions fed into a structure of industrial power by way of a special and differentiated labor function that was indispensable to the modernization and industrialization of society. What was missing from Weber's model was a special view among professionals of the potential power of knowledge and system: the positivist perspective. Professions, then as now, rest foremost on a faith in the power of taxonomic systems of "scientific" knowledge to achieve positive ends. Postmodernism and professionalism are, not surprisingly, mutually exclusive.

From the 1860s (at the latest) into the 1880s, notions of *professiia, obshchestvennost'* (society, or *Gesellschaft*), and even *burzhuaziia* had little conceptual content in Russian in comparison to western European usage.[17] Instead, what did have meaning was education and *nauka* (loosely science, but especially rigorous learning). From the middle of the nineteenth century, learning inspired successive generations of doctors, lawyers, engineers, and even some government functionaries *(chinovniki)* and privileged army officers. And if positivism came into full flower after 1870, as Croce declared, its antecedents dated back decades. The scientific positivist spirit could animate any group that, through education and labor, was exposed to the influence of *nauka*, and therein lay professionalism's origins in Russia. The history of ideas (rather than social history) is the best window on those origins. By way of metaphor, men as different as Nikolai Obruchev and the fictional medical student of *Fathers and Sons*, Evgenii Bazarov, shared closer views of man, society, and labor than they did of government and politics, and quite possibly, their similarities were more significant and interesting than their differences. One was a general staff officer and strategic planner; the other, Russia's protonihilist. However, scientific knowledge laced with a strong dose of positivism animated the views of both men, and in fact defined what little we know about each. What distinguished them from each other was their respective sense of reality. As Isaiah Berlin observed, unbridled positivism—drafting conclusions about the universal from command of the merely particular—produced the Utopian delusion.

The organs (and hence the men) of the Main Staff operated differently than most other government offices. Staff officers developed "scientific" habits of data collection and a work routine that, over time, they standardized and passed from one generation to the next. These characteristics—in the jargon of sociology, *organizational demography* and *organizational learning*—are associated with "professional" behavior.[18] The former trait influenced the bases for individual promotion: performance and ability supplemented seniority and background. Organizational learning perpetuated "collective memory," the incorporation of experience and knowledge into an organization's legacy to following generations. Groups that could evaluate and incorporate their experience and knowledge, through history writing and record keeping, adapted more successfully to modernization than those that did not. Information control and the development of flexible routines were important to that success. In the nineteenth century, the staff officer was a modern army's "master builder"—its *architekton*—not of space or structure but of information and knowledge. These ideas precisely describe the dynamics of change within the Russian professions, and especially in the general staff. Architectonics, the seamless web of universal and general knowledge, was the realm in which the planner operated, and information gathering was his basic activity.[19]

All professions arose coincidentally with new social and cultural currents, but as consequence of changes in the natural sciences.[20] Subordination of opinion to formal knowledge (i.e., to all learned, disciplinary, and systematic knowledge, by definition *elite* knowledge) was well advanced at midcentury, and it coincided with formalization of the modern scientific method. That method gradually but fundamentally changed the organization and accessibility of knowledge. Throughout Europe labor professionalization was characterized by adoption of the "power" of formal knowledge. The application of that power to human endeavors, the definition of Weber's *rationalization*, has also been called *technique:* the "intervention of reason and consciousness [that] can be described as the quest for the *one best means* in every field. And this 'one best means' is in fact the technical means."[21] The "best means" to what? To effectiveness. The domination of systematic knowledge holds right into the late twentieth century; John Kenneth Galbraith defined technology as the "systematic application of scientific and other *organized* knowledge to practical tasks,"[22] which makes explicit the conjunction of knowledge-technology and effectual activity. From the perspective of formal knowledge and technique, professionalism had much more to do with a process of *structuring and using information* than with satisfaction of a shopping list of social traits or a posteriori characteristics.

Both professionalism and professionalization must be viewed as processes rather than states for the historian of rationalization. Occupations gain professional status only *through the process of working with systematic knowledge*, although it is not that knowledge, per se, that makes them professional. Just as an unskilled worker's interaction with his task could change both his view of the job and his sense of self, so, too, with people occupied in jobs involving expert knowledge. The seduction of scientific methods and universal knowledge would be especially strong within groups involved in work on practical problems, such as engineers, and doctors—and war planners. The dynamic of professionalism denied its practitioners any hope of progressive advance, for much more militates against an organization (and especially a bureaucracy) developing institutional memory than in favor of perpetual identification of the best technical means of doing the job. From the 1840s through the 1890s, Russia's general staff perpetuated its professional ethic of knowledge under the firm hand of Dmitrii Miliutin and then Nikolai Obruchev. After 1897, however, the professional's hand left the tiller of staff professionalization, lethargy and lassitude crept in, and the Russian general staff deprofessionalized itself during the decade before the Great War.

In the last sixty-five years, only one scholar has examined imperial

Russia's strategic-military history and attempted to incorporate a nuanced concern for "professionalism" into his work on the late imperial Russian officer corps.[23] Social studies of the general staff corps have provided a clear picture of origins and background of the general staff's "everyman." The "average" *genshtabist*, in these amalgamations, is exactly the person one might expect to meet: politically conservative, reflecting his social origins, with suspected predispositions even the brightest academy graduates did not abandon. Inefficient and even unprofessional, many officers of the general staff (like those of the officer corps in general) could be no better than the stratum from which they came. Complete supplantation of privilege and seniority by standards of merit in promotion was neither attempted nor necessary; the Russian army could afford a measure of traditional stasis, just as the Prussian army could.

Aggregation of social data, of course, has the effect of trivializing the profoundly important distinctions that justify the study of history in the first place. For instance, men like Dmitrii Alekseevich Miliutin who shaped the staff and academy were unquestionably political conservatives, loyal to legitimate state policy (*gosudarstvennost'*). They did not, however, fully equate their military responsibility with unquestioning loyalty to dynasty. They mastered serious scientific method, for which they received public acclaim (membership in the Imperial Russian Academy of Sciences, to which Obruchev also rose), and they expected the same of other officers handpicked for important Main Staff positions. Obruchev and his lieutenants successfully *excluded* men who did not possess skills and attitudes that were scientific and were, implicitly, incompatible with dynastic prerogative. It was only with the ascension of a *gosudar* (overload, sovereign) who took seriously his dynastic prerogative to decide issues of state and government—rather than relying on his "machine" (in Sergei Witte's analogy)—that the military specialists finally lost control of the mechanism most important to state security, the general staff.

2

Science and Military Statistics in Nicholas's Army

Science is merely the repugnance felt by intellect in the face of chaos.
Nietzsche

The origins of staff competence are found deep in the prereform era. Like the roots of virtually all midcentury reforms, the transformations envisioned by military reformers, no matter how "progressive" or essential, contained an element of ambivalence toward state power. State conservatives in court and ministerial positions or adjutant generals commanding provinces almost all had reason to fear the optimistic and vaguely subversive implications of reform based on scientific prejudice and positivist impulse. There was little ground for compatibility between the philosophies of the two sides, although both stood explicitly and loyally behind the tsarist throne's legitimacy. Implicitly, the question would become one of whose authority inhered: the rationalist authority of experts or the autocratic myth of unbridled authority.

THE CRIMEAN CATASTROPHE that concluded the reign of Nicholas I unsaddled Russia's martial pretensions among Europe's great powers. His army proved unworthy of the reflected pomp and radiance of his reign when it met its European counterparts. Before Britain and France imposed that judgement, however, a new military ethos had begun to emerge in counterpoint to military pageantry. A culture of military administration and thinking, scientifically based and highly rational, distinguished the work of a small component of the army: the planners on its general staff. The culture matured for over a decade in the General Staff Corps and provided an innovative, even groundbreaking, answer to industrially inspired strategic changes that crept across Europe during the years before the Crimean War.

Rationalist culture shaped the work and expectations of a coterie of young instructors at the general staff academy in St. Petersburg just as surely as it stirred generally that generation of educated youth throughout Russia. Those instructors and their students carried the culture into the army's central staff. It spread there but slowly, with the growth of the General Staff Corps itself, and then rapidly with the rise after 1856 of strategic planning and an administration itself committed to rationalization. After Nicholas's reign the staff's culture of scientism dominated ministry-wide reform, even after shifting intellectual dispositions gradually attenuated widespread faith in science to solve all Russia's problems.

By the middle of the nineteenth century, Russia possessed cultured learning unexcelled in continental Europe. Under Nicholas, Russia's educated society alone possessed the attitudes that expressed the new culture, and in the army those attitudes resided principally among officers trained at the academy. The origins of military staff professionalization are not found primarily in institutions—the academy and general staff organizations. Although unquestionably the most significant sites of rationalization, these institutions were themselves objects of transformation before they assumed a role in military reform. Behind all modernizing change lay the maturation of intellectual and cultural prejudices inherent in nineteenth-century positivism; in every case, protoprofessional attitudes preceded their institutional expression, and no less so in the Russian general staff.[1]

Military reformers built a theory and an advanced practicum for systematic information management that anticipated and shaped effective centralized administration in the ministry. The modernizing project had first to build a new man, from whom new institutions and new ideas would flow. That new man was a functionary of vital importance to military reform and central staff work, the *deloproizvoditel'*, or staff action officer. He made his appearance in the war ministry in the late 1830s as a powerful, young military bureaucrat of stunningly high caliber.[2] His arrival accompanied regularization of many military administrative activities and codification of paperwork routine, both expressions of bureaucratic rationalization and essential prerequisites in an organization that soon cultivated the broadest imaginable information sources.

It was the information first gathered and systematized by its members that eventually drew the general staff's attention to Russia's uncomfortable strategic position in central Europe and offered enticing alternatives. Pursuit of knowledge was an entirely natural outgrowth of appropriated scientific attitudes, which these men had assumed. Multiple views of the outside world existed in the minds of general staff officers. Strategically, the most important portion of the empire was its western borderland, still only vaguely reconnoitered before the 1870s. The southern and eastern frontiers, however, were where Russian imagination—artistic and imperial—played out a romantic destiny.[3] Exploration, particularly by general staffers, attracted the imagination of many in the state's elite, whose gaze fell not on Russia's tenuous western frontiers but on the vast, empty field of staff officer activity: Asiatic Russia. Both the west and the east came to be known through the general staff's inclination to categorize, describe, count, and objectify.[4]

In the end, the staff divided its commitment to universal knowledge between the two—Europe and Asia. That commitment was embodied in so-called *military-scientific work*, and *military statistics* in particular. This discipline comprised topographic and geographic studies; description of population distribution, political organization, and national infrastructure; examination of agricultural and industrial production; and everything related to the armed forces. Mid-nineteenth-century Russian military statistics anticipated with exactitude late-twentieth-century military *intelligence*. General staff officers collected these data in every military district and organized them in the capital for one purpose: the quest for universal and general knowledge, pursuant to war planning.

The origins of military statistics lie in the middle of Nicholas I's reign. By the 1840s, scientific attitudes dominated the culture of the most dynamic segments of Russia's general staff. Natural science, founded on observation (data collection) and analysis, had its corollary among the social sciences in the field of "statistics." Statistics as application of probability theory to sampled data is a more recent specialization of the field. The "statistic" in the nineteenth century was a branch of political science dealing with the collection, classification, and discussion of facts bearing on the *condition of a state* or a community. In contrast to "political arithmetic," which was of numerical character and focalized on estimations and reckoning, statistics before about 1850 were primarily qualitative and descriptive. An "era of enthusiasm" for statistics gripped European countries in the middle third of the nineteenth century. The boundaries of the field stretched as the rift deepened between practitioners of the descriptive forms and mathematically oriented statisticians who rejected any role for arithmetic in adjudication of moral and political study. Both groups, however, shared the conviction that enumeration was essentially useful and that such counting of society served the higher purposes of more effective government.[5]

A transition from ancien régime political arithmetic to a newer state-centered discipline, called *Staatenkunde* by its German practitioners, began during the last half of the eighteenth century. Republican France's *departemental* administrators eagerly abandoned political arithmetic and seized upon the new descriptive tools of German academic statistics to serve the state's interests and to "inform the nation."[6] These patterns of seeing and describing the state spread rapidly across Europe with Napoleon's army and French administration. The annexation of northern Italy, re-creation of a Polish political entity, and subjugation of Germany introduced descriptive statistical practices as the "last and fascinating chapter of the eighteenth-century 'police sciences'" to the rest of Europe by 1815. Descriptive statistics would recede as the century's end approached and nonquantitative methods melded with those that searched for aggregate group behavior, predictability, the "everyman." As late as 1850, however, the two approaches remained distinct, as European writers (in particular the Germans) considered statistics both a science of the social life of man and a method of investigation. Karl G. A. Knies (1821–1898) exemplified the shift around midcentury from geopolitical description toward enumeration, and the work of Georg von Mayr (1841–1925), Max Haushofer, and Antonio Gabaglio completed the transition by the 1880s, considering statistics both a science and a method. The application of probability to "large numbers" statistics accelerated with the work of the Belgian Adolphe Quetelet (1796–1874), working in England still later, where departments of government in London adopted it only around the turn of the twentieth century.[7]

Russian government departments began systematic consolidation of information management (i.e., of their general statistical activities) around 1860, long after the war ministry. However, the Ministry of Internal Affairs (MVD, from its Russian initials) in particular was a center of statistical activity for almost two decades before institution of the Great Reforms (and emancipation in particular), but in the tradition of political arithmetic. Count Pavel Kisilev and Nikolai Miliutin (the future war minister's younger brother) labored through much of the 1840s crafting a ministerial mechanism for the collection of information on Russia's urban and rural condition—countings and quantifications—but not until 1858 did MVD create a Central Statistical Committee, an expert body empowered to regularize statistical work. General nonagricultural statistical work fell under the statistics section, headed after 1860 by the geographer Petr Petrovich Semenov, who became a driving force in Russia behind statistical enumeration of the empire, eventually culminating in its first census. Semenov's section absorbed the senior committee two years later, and he became director of the state's Central Statistics Council, composed of academicians and representatives of other ministries and departments. Governmental statistical work resisted further consolidation because of bureaucratic recalcitrance and, more important, increasing statistical specialization, so the council remained largely powerless to coordinate and promote standardized methods throughout the government.[8] In all this the general staff diverged dramatically from other branches of government. It followed closely the path trodden by German and French statists; in data and methodology the war ministry led the government in the drive to "know" the Russian empire, rather than merely tabulate it.

Positivistic, "scientistic" attitudes scripted the general staff's gradual recognition of its responsibility for Russia's strategic solvency. That intellectual and cultural matrix, however, likewise animated the worldviews of people far removed from the army. Scientific positivism, the faith in the efficacious power of scientific methods,[9] in tandem with a profound commitment to modernization and rationalization of the Russian state and society, served as culture for Russian nihilism and early populism. Those "modern" characteristics stimulated young Guards and general staff officers observing Russia's military reforms from the 1840s onward. The fine distinction between radical criticism and reform-minded labor vanished for a significant number of officers.[10]

Nikolai Nikolaevich Obruchev disturbed the norms of elite and radical society (to both of which he belonged in the early 1860s) on his rise to the pinnacle of the military establishment. Yet his life and career have escaped adequate investigation; he is among the very few pivotal figures of late imperial Russia still absent from modern historical literature. His biography also defies the persistent trivialization of the midcentury Russian army officer corps as a monolithic bastion of privilege and reaction. The history of Russian general staff modernization would be unimaginable in the absence of Obruchev, and he is incomprehensible in the context of simple statist conservatism on which he seemingly landed eventually.

Obruchev's early career seems so extraordinary merely by reason of the lofty position to which he subsequently ascended.[11] In fact, into the early 1860s neither his activities nor his career was far removed from the paths followed by many (perhaps most) young general staff officers. Particularly among officers at the academy and those assigned to forces in Poland where Obruchev was born, the imperative for military reform rested on convictions deeper than mere humiliation at the hands of modern, liberal Britain and France. Those convictions predated the unfortunate Crimean experience. Obruchev's earliest assignment, from 1848 to 1856 in the Guards-Petersburg Military District, gave him access to the most interesting salons of the capital in which like-minded men, such as his mentor and future war minister, Dmitrii Miliutin, also moved.[12] Obruchev's acquaintance with Nikolai Chernyshevskii (and later Nikolai Dobroliubov) dated from the immediate postwar years, at a time when Miliutin's own relationship with the radical thinker and journalist was in full flower, and through whom Obruchev possibly met Chernyshevskii. Of all the intellectual influences swirling around Obruchev's circle of radical friends, Dobroliubov's exaggerated scientism was most congenial to the young general staff captain's own ethic. At this time, a young mathematician and colonel at the artillery academy, Petr Lavrov (1823–1900), hovered on the fringe of an underground general staff group, through which he would have known Obruchev.[13]

Obruchev's association led to some considerable difficulty in 1857, a year after he joined the academy as an adjunct professor of military statistics. Captain Obruchev faced dismissal from the academy's faculty, the General Staff Corps, and the service.[14] His survival was due to the intervention of an unnamed, influential officer. Miliutin could not have interceded easily because he had departed St. Petersburg by the time Obruchev began work at the academy: he was on leave from June to

September 1856, then left for his third Caucasus assignment. Miliutin's longtime friend, and another close acquaintance of Chernyshevskii's, Major General A. P. Kartsev, head of the tactics department in the academy, may have intervened in Miliutin's absence. In any case, Obruchev's recovery was swift. Within three months he was promoted to colonel, made acting professor of military statistics, and became co–assistant editor (under Chernyshevskii) of Miliutin's newly established professional journal, *Voennyi sbornik*—a remarkable political resurrection.[15] The circle of men involved in *Voennyi sbornik*—Obruchev, Miliutin, Chernyshevskii, Vladimir Mikhailovich Anichkov, and Kartsev—had formed close personal friendships that predated the formal convening of the new journal's editorial group in early 1858. Thereafter, according to Brooks, the two associate editors became regular visitors to Chernyshevskii's rooms.[16]

Obruchev left St. Petersburg in May 1860 for a year of foreign study and travel in the west under the auspices of the academy. His assignment was to prepare conspectuses of military statistics courses taught in France and Britain and to gather materials for use in the academy's military-statistical curriculum. His marriage in France to Mlle Berg, whose inheritance included an attractive château and estate in the Dordogne, initiated a partnership that produced one of St. Petersburg's best-known salons. The family sojourned each autumn at the Loire estate, where Obruchev could receive his French military acquaintances in the comfort of intimate, private surroundings.[17]

In the spring of 1861 Obruchev traveled to London, where he had a brief but active involvement with exiled Russian radicals and revolutionaries, including N. P. Ogarev, A. I. Herzen, and A. A. Sleptsov. Along with writing anonymous editorials for Herzen's *Kolokol*, Obruchev coauthored and published with Ogarëv a pamphlet on the Russian army's role in maintaining internal order. The academy had approved his original excursion *(komandirovka)* for twelve months; subsequently, the director granted Obruchev's request for a six-month travel extension, which began at precisely the time he went to London and entered the Herzen-Ogarev circle. Thus, it is unlikely that underground activity was Obruchev's principal purpose for leaving Russia in 1860, for otherwise he would have made contact with the exiles sooner.[18]

During this period his views on the place of Ukraine and Poland in the Russian empire—that they should be liberated both for their own good and for the good of Russia—was anathema to Herzen's circle, although it marked a very important point on Obruchev's path to strategic maturity. His approach to the western provinces reflected a remarkably strong sense of Russian nationhood, which entered his view of the empire. For reasons of international law, economy, and justice, he argued, both Poland and Ukraine should be allowed to secede from the empire. Politically and socially they represented more than a burden for Russia: from their peasant populations would arise the next mass disorders, they were a natural target for the appetites of Russia's neighbors, and Russia could not afford to garrison them in its weakened state. He elaborated on Russia's economic condition and the economic rationale for redeployment of the army *out* of Poland after 1855 in articles in *Voennyi Sbornik* a few years later.[19] By 1860 Poland had already become an object of interest in the imagination of German colonial dreamers *(Drang nach Osten)*, an appetite that would be the Russian empire's undoing sixty years later.

The underground pamphlet *Velikoruss*, three issues of which came off the general staff printing presses surreptitiously between July and September 1861, was the idea of Obruchev and his younger cousin, Vladimir. Soviet scholars attribute much of the material in *Velikoruss* to Nikolai. Vladimir had hoped to follow in Nikolai's footsteps but, upon graduation from the academy in 1858, he was assigned to the Quartermaster Corps rather than the General Staff Corps. This disruption of his career plans prompted him to give up the army (and thus the *sanctioned* reform of empire through its institutions) and begin subversive activity. Following his arrest shortly after publication of the *Velikoruss* numbers in 1861, Vladimir was exiled to Siberia until 1877; when the Russo-Turkish War broke out, he volunteered for recall to duty, served with distinction, and continued his career until retirement as a major general. Although Nikolai was still in western Europe in 1861 when *Velikoruss* appeared, he maintained regular (and secure) communication with his cousin and other contacts in St. Petersburg, possibly by use of the diplomatic pouch that the foreign ministry had authorized in Obruchev's travel documents.[20]

Although Obruchev's earliest strategic views departed from the government's position, they also clashed with Herzen's opinion and bore little similarity to later nationalistic chauvinism. The notion that Russia's Polish and Ukrainian possessions themselves might be daggers pointed at the heart of Russia, threats to domestic order *and* national security, confounded radicals on both the right and the left, particularly when articulated years *before* the 1863 Polish uprisings. Obruchev's formulation was free of the sentimental nationalism that animated Herzen and inspired the latter's pen in late 1862. Yet Obruchev's strategic appreciation of Russia's security, without rival in the early 1860s, distinguished him from all other military men. From this position Obruchev started down a path that helps make sense of his subsequent transformation from underground radical to preeminent strategic thinker.

Obruchev returned to the academy in November 1861 as the new academic year began. Within thirty months he left the country again. Whether as a result of his London writings and acquaintances, or because he had refused orders to join his division in Vilna district in late 1862 to suppress the Polish uprising,[21] or actually for his health, in May 1864 Obruchev received four months of "sick leave" to travel in France and Germany, during which time his first son, Vladimir, was born. The leave was granted on condition that he gather new information about a French *"applikatsionnaia shkola,"* one of the advanced technical colleges such as École des Ponts et Chaussées or École du Génie Militaire. He was also to solicit the thoughts of Baron Jomini, the academy's retired founder, on a new charter for the institution, and gather recent books for its library.[22] In early 1865 Obruchev resumed his work at the academy and with the war minister's principal advisory committee, a collateral duty he received in 1863. There is no thoughtful explanation of Obruchev's early intellectual origins; most scholars have viewed his participation in radical circles in the 1850s and early 1860s as anomalous, an inexplicable youthful folly. Despite promising recent work on the issue, Obruchev's life and works over the four decades of his influence (1850s to 1890s) still await complete biographical treatment.[23]

Obruchev, of course, had not been alone in his political sympathies toward the Poles in 1863. Other Russian general staff officers in Warsaw and in St. Petersburg abetted the rebels and then attempted to escape retribution.[24] It is difficult to gauge the extent of conspiratorial activity in Russia's rising military technical elite. The evidence of illegal activity is episodic, although it is clear that the centers of action were in army staffs in St. Petersburg and Poland, and within the Guards regiments in St. Petersburg, as well as in organs of the general staff itself

and in the academy in particular. The technical branches also participated: A large number of students at the engineering academy in the
early sixties, for instance, studied disapproved ideas in the subversive
"History" circle. Count Petr Shuvalov's Third Section and the MVD
eventually undertook a sweeping investigation of military complicity
and resistance that lasted a decade.

Overlap among the centers of radicalism in the military was extensive. They had become magnets for young noblemen, many well-educated, hoping to make careers in the army. The officer corps and the
general staff in particular were not as important per se as the environment they fostered, which encouraged engagement in critical inquiry, a
scientific outlook, and rigor in research work. There is no question of
widespread participation in critical (if not radical) activities among Russia's educated strata, including military officer.[25] The academy's annual
dispatch of graduates to western Europe for further education in statistics and the sciences (although not in military subjects) exposed many
staff officers to strong doses of Comte, Saint-Simon, Feuerbach, and
Herder. At the same time, some of those who set about reforming the
army undoubtedly honed their zeal for progress through involvement
in Russia's first radical circles. If during Miliutin's years of ascendancy
the General Staff Corps was opened to men of "new ideas," and he
promoted their influence and activity, the same could not be said even a
decade later.[26]

Such intellectual habits could be cultivated outside the staff as well;
the lives of Bakunin and Kropotkin testify to the wider confluence of
scientific and knowledge-based philosophies with the military life—at
least among those of good birth and education. Although neither was
a general staff officer, both received the best technical military education and successful careers until emigration. They shared a passionate
interest in natural science and geography while in military service, and
eventually, each abandoned tsarist Russia. As a young officer Bakunin
greatly admired General N. N. Murav'ev-Amurskii as an efficacious
and progressive governor, even as the general devoured large tracts of
the Amur valley in the name of the Russian tsar. Kropotkin, who was
accepted into the academy but declined entrance, found war minister
Miliutin the only high official in St. Petersburg uncorrupted by proximity to the court and bureaucracy.[27] The homologous traits shared by
young general staff reformers and exiled or underground radicals origi-

nated in nineteenth-century positivism and scientism, buoyed by zeal, vision, and a commitment to change.

Not least because he was a colonel and an instructor at the artillery academy, Lavrov is emblematic of the nexus of service and science. He had hovered on the fringes of Obruchev's *Zemlia i volia* group, without effect, but he preferred to work out his own philosophy rather than follow others' political doctrines. In the late 1850s Lavrov began to grapple with the relationship between the individual's responsibility to science and to society, paralleling neo-Kantian concerns afoot in Germany. He was already anticipating the argument he eventually made in the *Historical Letters* (1868–1869). Even as the era of the scientifically inspired general staff officer was drawing to a close, Lavrov argued that an overweening surrender to the power of science was "infantile," and no guide in the most perplexing human problems. His words drew young Russians to consider their social responsibility, thus leading to the birth of *narodnichestvo* (Russian populism). If general staff officers heard his words, their work betrayed no loss of faith in statistics and systems to solve Russia's strategic problems.[28]

Analogous cultural developments emerged in France in the 1860s under the socially more heterogeneous Second Empire. By the collapse of Napoleon III's government, influential financiers in Paris had melded dissonant elements into a "conservative-liberal" philosophy. Similar influences colored the views held by some Russian radical military officers: anti-imperial nationalism, antidemocratic elitism, scientific positivism. Educational aspects of conservative-liberalism, which were to have far-reaching influence on policy under the Third Republic, underpinned the philosophy and curriculum of the École Libre des Sciences Politiques (Sciences-Po, for short). The school's instructors, self-anointed remediators of society's and the state's problems through science and education, arrogated leadership of the ignorant masses to those suited by virtue of their successful passage into the school.[29] The social vision of the Sciences-Po's creators found no precise homologue in Russia, although similarities between the attitudes of French conservative intellectuals and Russian general staffers remain suggestive. Yet the reconciliation of paternalistic, antidisorder elitism with antidynastic, profoundly rational and positivistic philosophy was a continent-wide phenomenon. For Russia, the historical significance of French conservative-liberalism lay in the latter's parallel with "state conservative" views of men such as the Miliutin brothers and the Obruchevs. No other framework can explain, for instance, the apparent political volte-face Obruchev had made by 1868 or his enduring suspicion of Germany, while retaining analytic usefulness on the questions of both his midcentury radicalism *and* his pact with the French military almost three decades later.[30]

There is no evidence that Miliutin foresaw the impact that technical expertise would have on strategic attitudes within two decades, a transformation to which simple structural reforms in the 1860s merely opened the door. To attribute that development to Miliutin's plans would grant the war minister degrees of foresight and influence he simply did not have.[31] Widespread cultural currents first floated the staff's and Miliutin's new approach to military administration; Miliutin's structural rationalization made the ministry a more effective and hospitable organization, particularly in the area of statistical work. The changes on which staff professionalization ultimately rested by the 1860s reflected certain officers' commitment to material and scientific progress through rationalization. Faith in progress, even in the narrow sphere of military modernization, could spill over into activities inimical to autocracy: the line separating change that was regime-sanctioned, and modernization "from below," both of which arose from a zealous confidence in the ideal of positive progress, vanished for some officers, as the records of their dismissal from the staff academy and military service attest.[32]

Dmitrii Alekseevich Miliutin is more representative than Obruchev of the links between Russia's midcentury social and scientific currents and the evolution of military reforms; his importance cannot be over-stated.[33] His impoverished *dvorianstvo* background obstructed access to an elite Cadet Corps education. Like other respected ministers later brought into government by Alexander II, Miliutin graduated in 1832 at age sixteen from Moscow University's boarding school (*universitetskii pansion*), where he studied under the renowned astronomer and mathematician D. M. Perevoshchikov. For six months he then read mathematics, mechanics, and astronomy at the university before entering the army in 1833. Miliutin had an early interest in the Institute of Lines of Communication (of the Ministry of Lines of Communication—*Ministerstvo Putei soobshchenii*—or MPS), from which he would have graduated as an engineer.[34] Instead, he entered the advanced (second-year) course at the general staff academy, which he completed with honors, and with considerable disdain for the whole process, in 1836. Like his protégé Obruchev, after graduation Miliutin combined professional military criticism with literary interests in essays and larger works while attached to the Guards staff.[35]

Fleeing an arduous year of staff work in the Caucasus (the first of three assignments there), Miliutin received a leave of absence in 1840 with little intention of continuing a military career. Before he left Russia, the intervention of a friend secured for him a position at the academy upon his return, which he found more to his liking.[36] He traveled about Europe for thirteen months before taking up the new posting. With his service background in topography and applied mathematics (which became the bases of military statistics), Miliutin would have observed with keen interest the Prussian application of scientific techniques to their "Trigonometric and Topographic Survey" of the kingdom, then entering its second phase. The young Russian certainly had an opportunity to become familiar with the cartographic product of those surveys: Prussian general staff maps were for the first time made available to the public in 1841, during Miliutin's sojourn.[37] Regrettably, his artful recollections for posterity eschewed most honest traces of professional reaction to the things he saw in Prussia. However, a decade before his visit to the west, Miliutin had written *A Guide to Map Surveying through Use of Mathematics*,[38] which established his enduring interest in the science of mapping and the military applications of cartography. It is inconceivable that he found nothing of interest in Berlin in 1841. Miliutin returned to Russia with new ideas about the proper employment of a general staff (and its academy), although this is rarely credited. The count himself later recalled his anticipation in 1840 of the journey for just such purposes.[39]

Miliutin's dissatisfaction in 1845 with the "state of the art" upon assuming responsibility for military geography instruction at the academy led to his development of Russian military statistics. He presented the new course as an amalgamation of the geographic sciences (cartography, geography, geodesy) with all other scientific and social-scientific information relevant to military affairs.[40] The longer he reflected, Miliutin wrote in his memoirs,

the more I became convinced that to create a special military "science" from purely geographic matter was unthinkable . . . From this I came to the conclusion that [geographically based] strategic analyses . . . comprised only one of the many aspects of a general study of military capacity of nations. Thus, only by more thorough research [*vsestoronnee issledovanie*] could one establish the subject and goal of scientific teaching. In this sense it would be not military *Geography*, but a special offshoot of Statistics, which might be termed "Military Statistics."[41]

In the twentieth century this military statistics program would be called *military intelligence*. Miliutin broke it into three sections: a statistical data section dealing with the state's material resources (finances, territory, national populations, state organization); analysis of the state's armed forces and of their military institutions; and territorial provisions of authority for defensive or offensive war.[42]

Miliutin's *First Experiments in Military Statistics* was both an agenda for future general staff development through training and the theoretical basis for the staff's research methodology. The work's two volumes examined, first, the "Political and Military Foundation of the North German Confederation" and, second, "Prussian Military Statistics." Van Dyke observes that Miliutin rejected historically predetermined social development as a basis for solving military problems. Instead, Miliutin insisted that the correct method (using social-scientific research and statistics) had but one aim: to elucidate the process of social change itself. Knowledge could then be used to guide one course of development or another.[43] In 1856, as a major general, Miliutin transferred to the Caucasus for duty as Prince Bariatinskii's chief of staff, where he also oversaw the mapping work in the viceregal territory. He was succeeded as professor of military statistics by two of his star pupils, Captain Obruchev and Lieutenant Colonel Aleksei Maksheev.

Virtually every general staff officer who graduated from the academy between 1848 and 1857 received instruction under Miliutin in military-statistical methods; all later graduates received it from his closest disciples (including Obruchev, Maksheev, Dmitrii Naglovskii, and Nikolai Glinoetskii, followed later by Aleksei Kuropatkin). In fact, every military instructor at the academy during the last third of the nineteenth century felt Miliutin's intellectual influence, and the same applied to every general staff officer, whether he found a place on the Main Staff or led armies in the field. Not least among Miliutin's intellectual progeny was Russia's most celebrated military historian and academic strategist, Genrikh Leer. Leer's place in the story of military professionalization in Russia is easy to miscast: although he was the army's foremost academic theorist, his work per se did not constitute professionalism, as understood here. Rather, Leer was an exemplar of the directions abstract thought took in the military sphere under the influence of mid-century scientism and positivism.

Leer's field experience began and ended with the Crimean War, after which he entered a forty-year association with the academy and taught military history, strategy, and tactics. Leer's early work offered a provocative, original interpretation of the art of war (at least, in his students' opinion).[44] Nevertheless, whether Leer's views had a fundamental and direct influence on the Main Staff's strategic work is more difficult to gauge. His concern was not the practical side of strategy formulation on the Main Staff but the development of an intellectual outlook: How could military history serve as a tool for investigating strategy and tactics? His "critical-historical" method resonated closely with Miliutin's advocacy of empirical knowledge as the building block of truth, in Leer's case, of true laws of military history and thus of strategy. As an 1854 academy graduate, Leer probably developed his appreciation of empirical precision, and the theoretical possibilities it opened, from Miliutin's instruction in military statistics during Leer's first years as a student. Furthermore, there are traces of Comtean positivism in Leer's theoretical and historical writing, an unremarkable observation given the date, and Leer introduced his new method with some curious "philosophical plumage" (as Van Dyke put it) that resonated closely with the Frenchman's thought. Like Comte, Leer envisioned history as a "process in which culture became transformed into civilization," and Leer (like many of his peers) might have believed that the army, if not Russia itself, was entering the individualistic, destructive phase that Comte called "critical thought." Comte's view of philosophy as the systematization of data of the individual sciences likewise resonated with the transdisciplinarian character of Russian military statistics.[45]

At one level, the Russian army's use of military history differed from the historical methods and aims of Prussia's general staff and its *Kriegsakademie*. Although both placed the subject on a pedestal in the pantheon of military science, the Prussians did not search for a unified theory of military history (as, for instance, Leer did) but instead insisted that history's substance serve diverse ends.[46] Schlieffen's form of military history placed accuracy and precision second to didactic usefulness. Schlieffen did not aim, Bucholz writes, for historical accuracy; "he was not trying to use the best primary sources . . . Rather he wanted a general outline as a teaching vehicle for practical military exercises and future war planning . . .—personalities and events powerfully portrayed to illustrate operational views."[47]

Military history for the Russians satisfied at least two ends. First, it served more as empirical guidance, a scientific yardstick against which planners could test their assumptions and broaden their experience. This is the service military history offers to this day. The Russians' Prussian counterparts viewed history as a pedagogical tool to be consciously manipulated in confirmation of established military axioms, especially those perceived to be Clausewitz's.[48] In both cases, history was the handmaiden of system. Second, the years of intense engagement with a systematized, supposedly coherent story of military affairs provided students a basis for framing practical problems after graduation and introduced them to the disciplining effects of deep future–oriented thinking. Historical "progress" served indispensable ends as much for mobilization planners as it did for scientific positivists and dialectical materialists.

Clearly, the Prussian intellectual influence should not be underestimated. Critical scholarship was the direction in which Leer pushed his students, and the uninterrupted emphasis on statistics (and the theory of military-statistical work) demanded solid scholarly resources for the education of future general staff officers. By the 1870s, the cornerstone of Russia's military science (or, as German academic purists considered it, *Fachwissenschaft*, a technical discipline) was military history. It provided rigor to the struggle between "opinions," and it decided "the eternal arguments" about military science. Military historical sources, thus, were the "experimental facts" that Leer wished to "more and more increase,"[49] and the holdings of the general staff academy library showed what sources the Russians found useful (Table 2.1).

The figures in the table are not analytic; another impression of the library's holdings, however, may be useful. Strong representation among studies of the Napoleonic Wars gave way to more contemporary topics (e.g., the U.S. Civil War among works in "Other Languages") after 1870. What the library held, and what the students and instructors read

Table 2.1. Holdings of the Library of the General Staff Academy by Language
(1866: total volumes; 1873 and 1887: additional volumes)

	Military History			Military Art/Science		
Language	1866	1873	1887	1866	1873	1887
Russian	133	+ 63	+ 183	110	+ 68	+ 95
French	386	+ 139	+ 238	319	+ 77	+ 183
German	281	+ 164	+ 314	384	+ 178	+ 327
Other	37	+ 117	+ 24	117	+ 5	+ 0

Condensed from: *Katalog biblioteki Nikolaevskoi akademii General'nogo shtaba, vol. 2, 1866–1873*, ed. [Colonel] Vil'k (St. Petersburg, 1873); *Sistematicheskii katalog biblioteki Nikolaevskoi akademii General'nogo shtaba* (St. Petersburg, 1879–1880/1887).

may have been two quite different things. Nevertheless, language was no barrier; all students spoke and read either German or French, and most could work in both. The great reliance on broad military-scientific knowledge, both to qualify for the academy and to succeed once there, necessitated heavy use of the library's resources. With French and German military publication industries in vigorous growth, the figures on what the general staff academy bought are suggestive of where the Russians' interests lay.

An Organization for Knowledge

Institutionally, Russia's war ministry had long maintained a close interest in questions of research and investigation that it broadened with the founding of the general staff academy. From at least 1812, the ministry's Artillery Sciences Committee, renamed the Military-Scientific Committee (*Voenno-uchenyi komitet*, or VUK), operated as the "advanced scholarly-scientific section for military art and for the diffusion of military-scientific information into the forces."[50] Although dominated in its early years by two technical specialities, artillery ballistics and military engineering, VUK took over all matters of *potential* interest to the army involving research and the sciences. Most important, VUK guided all military-statistical activity of the general staff. In Russia as in Prussia-Germany the core of general staff work was military statistics, a field in the early 1860s with decades of effort behind it but comparatively little of quality to show. Military statistics, as Russia's general staff officers actually practiced it, was foremost data accumulation: military, economic, social, foreign, domestic. Regimental officers derisively called general staff officers "chancellery clerks" (*kantseliaristy*) for their preoccupation with data accumulation, although their true sentiments, for career and social reasons, were closer to envy.[51] Statistical work not only accounted for most general staff officers' sole employment but also constituted the core of their education at the general staff academy. Furthermore, every reform Miliutin initiated rested on the data his general staff officers had collected. From this perspective the reform of military administration began first with the reform of the information compilation and analysis techniques taught in the academy.

From the academy's establishment in 1832, its curriculum served the purposes of military-statistical work by its breadth and sophistication; the opposite, a focused technical education, could not have done the same. Students studied foreign and Russian languages, political and military history, strategy and tactics, fortifications, geography, military statistics and administration, and mathematics. Central Asian languages supplemented requirements in German and French, and a separate Division of Topography and Geodesy produced many of the empire's best-trained cartographers, surveyors, and geodesists. The scientific character of academy education also improved in the late 1860s when the course in physical geography (since 1854 a part of the geodesic curriculum only) entered the general curriculum of all students. Physical geography was essential to every general staff officer, the director of the academy wrote to the Chief of Main Staff: every staff officer needed practical knowledge of the principles of horizontal and vertical measurement, and an appreciation of physical geography based on cartographic training. The request for authorization to place such training into the general curriculum for all second-year students was quickly approved.[52] Civilian faculty arrived from the universities to teach, and the most promising graduates rejoined the academy as instructors and researchers.

Every future general staff officer did not necessarily benefit from a strong command of geodesic and geographic theory and practice, or put his education at the disposal of military-statistical work. For instance, Captain Mikhail Dragomirov followed very closely the path taken by Obruchev four years earlier, spending most of 1858 and 1859 in Germany and France, with tours to Algeria, Egypt, and England, observing and writing on topics of interest to the staff and academy. Unlike Obruchev, he neither exercised his temporary political freedom while abroad nor remained interested in military statistics upon his return to the capital. Instead, in 1860 he received an appointment to teach tactics under Miliutin's confidant Kartsev, and he devoted himself to elaboration of the connection between peacetime training and wartime tactical success. After some years at the academy he commanded units at every level, participated with distinction in actions around the Shipka Pass during the Russo-Turkish War, and then served as director of the academy and later commander of forces in the Kiev Military District.[53]

Academy education served virtually no practical purpose for a certain Captain Mikhail Skobelev, who graduated in 1868 with the lowest grade in his class in geographic studies; clearly, he never intended to make his name behind a desk. Skobelev's results are instructive, although probably unusual: he excelled in strategy, military history, Russian and foreign languages, and fortifications; he was at the bottom of his class in military statistics and artillery theory (ballistics), as well as geography. Why? Perhaps because his only education before the academy had been at home, an unusual background for an academy student by the 1860s.[54] Skobelev's later fame and glory rested not on intellect but on personal dash, blind fearlessness, and an arrogance fed by near-perpetual battlefield success. Reflection, patience, and self-discipline—attributes more fitting of a general staff officer—were not his.

The partnership between civil and military institutions of learning and scholarship in the quest for imperial knowledge was nowhere of greater practical importance than on the farthest undefined frontiers of the empire. Junior general staff officers, acting as geographers, cartographers, geodesists, and trigonometric surveyors, accompanied expeditions of exploration under the auspices of the Imperial Geographic Society into the Tienshan and Altai Mountains, Tibet, and along the Amu and Syr Daria systems into Central Asia. Cartographers established the first hypsometric surveys of the Kirgiz steppe, European Russia, and the Caucasus, and officers at the academy and on field staffs conducted a bewildering variety of data collection activities throughout the empire. Although Miliutin had codified a methodology for statistical work at the academy in the 1840s, the practical aspects of data collection—that is, the fieldwork—were haphazard and the material collected remained unverifiable. The central bureaucratic organs proved insufficient to the task of managing the activities of the provinces. And although there simply were too few qualified general staff officers to go around all the district staffs, and too few even to occupy the central staff offices that would guide the fieldwork, there were endless opportunities for these men to explore and map.

By the 1850s, the annual number of new *genshtabisty* needed invariably exceeded the size of the graduating class; the number suitable by training and inclination for statistical work was fewer still. Thus, the post-Crimean staff could not correct decades of statistical error and shortfall induced by undertraining until well into the 1880s. Graduation statistics demonstrate the scale of the restriction under which the academy operated, and indicate why the shortage existed (Table 2.2).

Widening the compass of military statistics, to investigate not merely Russia's resources and potentialities but also those of its neighbors, had been an explicit part of Miliutin's work from the early 1840s. The second volume of his textbook on statistical theory glossed Prussia as its case study. Nonetheless, the personal experience of Miliutin's successors at the academy in that field was also of some importance to the impulse to carry the study beyond Russia's borders. And as military-statistical work assumed a more pronounced military character, the differentiation among purely scientific, broadly statistical, and narrowly *intelligence* goals vanished, at least insofar as neither its practitioners nor its theorists acknowledged distinctions between different categories of knowledge. This reflected their conviction that inherent taxonomies governed the seamless web of information describing the material world.[55]

Table 2.2. General Staff Academy Graduates, 1834–1860

Period	Graduates
1834–1840	118
1841–1845	74
1846–1850	75
1851–1855	99
1856–1860	238

Source: N. P. Glinoetskii, *Istoricheskii ocherk Nikolaevskoi akademii General'nogo shtaba* (St. Petersburg, 1882), *Osoboe prilozhenie*, "List of Graduates."

Geographic exploration served intrinsically as the locus for science, statistics, and intelligence. From the mid-1830s through the 1860s, academy graduates accompanied every expedition that went abroad for scientific purposes. General staff officers gathered data of scientific as well as future intelligence value and, particularly in the case of Central Asian exploration, scouted the routes taken years or decades later by Russian military detachments. The journal of the Imperial Russian Geographic Society (IRGO) brimmed with articles written by members who were general staff officers; indeed, into the 1850s the society's membership was dominated by such officers.[56] Six of the twelve members of the 1836 expedition around the eastern coastline of the Caspian Sea were from the war ministry—topographers and geographers—led by two general staff officers.[57] A more substantial journey followed a decade later. In 1847 Lieutenant Colonel A. I. Maksheev and naval Lieutenant Aleksei Butakov began a scientific expedition sponsored by IRGO to chart the northern Caspian area, the Aral Sea coastline, and the lower reaches of the Syr Daria.[58] They established a base at a fortified place near Raim on the lower Syr Daria, by order of the commander of Orenburg *krai* (district), General V. A. Obruchev (a distant relation of N. N. Obruchev). The scientific portion of their assignment proceeded at a leisurely pace for fourteen months. Some of Maksheev's extensive compilations entered the archive of IRGO; the portions of his study of a military character went to the VUK archive and the general staff academy's library, where they were used in later planning work and in pedagogical exercises. Maksheev's account of the expedition was finally published fifty years later, three years after his death—a fitting capstone to the half century of Russian exploration and expansion.[59]

Upon return to the capital, Maksheev joined the academy's faculty as an instructor in his field of specialization (applied military statistics). He drew on his experience to promote introduction of new instruction sections in Arabic, Farsi, Turkish, and Tatari. The academy also established a cash prize for the graduating officer who produced the best Persian manuscript. Most of the new academic departments *(kafedry)* began instruction during the Crimean War.[60] The academy thenceforth exercised these resources to train prospective general staff officers not only in theories of statistical analysis and compilation, but also to acculturate them with an attitude of inquisitiveness toward surrounding areas (especially if relatively unknown and uncharted): the transfrontier zone was first and foremost to be *known*.[61]

Although statistical work made its importance felt in Miliutin's organizational reform of the war ministry, institutional problems per se were not the concern of young general staff officers. The colonels and lieutenant colonels, most of them in their early to mid-thirties, carried on with their staff responsibilities largely detached from the high political tensions at Miliutin's level.[62] Their principal peacetime occupation was statistical compilations for Russia and its neighbors, and *genshtabisty* had returned to that work as soon as the Crimean War ended. In 1856 a group of military topographers and geodesists joined Petr Semenov's first expedition across the border into China and the Tienshan Mountains. They charted areas never before seen by Western men and laid the groundwork for the forays of the 1870s and 1880s by such general staff imperialists as N. M. Przheval'skii. General N. N. Murav'ev led the fourth of his "exploratory" military expeditions since 1850 down the Amur River and finally extracted Chinese recognition of Russian "discoveries" at Aigun in 1858.[63] Expeditions of exploration under IRGO auspices continued uninterrupted from the society's founding in 1845 through the Crimean War.[64]

In St. Petersburg, postwar military-statistical work returned first to the great publication project begun during the reign of Nicholas I. In 1836 Nicholas had decided to publish the *Military-Statistical Survey of the Gubernii and Oblasti of the Russian Empire*, which would encompass all of the empire's sixty-nine administrative areas. He ordered War Minister Chernyshev to compose (and then correct every three years) the survey, which was divided into a general statistical and geographic section and a part containing specialized data for war ministry use.[65] Before the Crimean War the survey appeared in three editions exclusively for use by the war ministry, its directorates, and the general staff. General staff officers began work anew on the publication collections as the war ended, apparently without guidance from St. Petersburg. For the half decade until Miliutin assumed the assistant ministryship in 1860, little innovation was introduced into the survey—or anywhere else in the war ministry. With Miliutin's elevation, however, a searching process of self-evaluation began, and the direction of statistical research changed decisively in the 1860s. With that change, Russia's general staff began to define its responsibilities in terms other than abstract dedication to science and knowledge.

Staff officers propelled science and military modernization not merely from their activities in the capital or on special expeditions but also from their permanent assignments to frontier staffs. In the early 1850s, General Quartermaster of the Main Staff General-Adjutant Baron Vil'gelm Karlovich Lieven, ordered academy-trained officers to take up duties with field units and on staffs where their presence had not been traditional. One officer so assigned was Ivan Fedorovich Babkov.[66] He participated in the 1849 and Crimean campaigns and then, following graduation from the general staff academy, commenced a thirty-year assignment to western Siberia. As a result of his blistering confidential critique of the 24th Infantry Division, his new posting, Babkov secured the esteem and confidence of his Main Staff superiors in the capital. His activity subsequently combined scientific and military dimensions of the staff professional. He made repeated inspections of combat units in the expansive southern steppe region and carried out a perpetual series of frontier cartographic surveys and expeditions. His discoveries found their way into IRGO's *Izvestiia* during the 1860s and 1870s, and supplemented his three larger studies of the Kirgizian transfrontier region.[67] As a young lieutenant colonel in 1863 he led the "Zaisan Lake expedition" aboard a river steamer up the Chernii Irtysh River, along the edge of the Kirgiz steppe to the southern edge of the Altai Mountains in western Mongolia. This opened the commercial gate to Urumqi and thence to the ancient silk route to China. From 1860 an active member of IRGO (and after 1877 the chair of its western Siberian geographic section), Babkov won a silver medal from the Geographic Society in 1866 for his exploration and border demarcation work. He also produced Russia's first topographic map of Semirechinsk oblast in the 1860s and opened the strategically vital Zungharian Gate into Sinkiang. His work inspired subsequent generations of soldier-explorers to elaborate Russia's imperial destiny in the western Chinese core area, a future battleground of the Great Game.[68] The emperor also conveyed his pleasure with Babkov's mapping work by sending him a gold ring in appreciation.

As a rationalizing general staff officer, Babkov's relationship with the region's other officers and leaders was contentious. The governors-general—most general-adjutants of traditional conservative cloth—proved particularly hostile to the aggressive officer recently arrived from the capital. Although some were personally abusive and arrogant, those general-adjutants left the young *genshtabist* to his own devices and duties, which St. Petersburg staff happily set for him. More difficult were the garrison officers with whom Babkov lived and worked. Some had served decades without promotion on the frontier, and seemed never to have left the confines of the casern. Garrison duty sapped whatever curiosity and sense of purpose they might once have possessed. A disproportionate number of them were not Russian. On the Western Siberian district staff in Omsk there was not a single officer from a Russian family, Babkov recalled, when he arrived. By the end of his life this fact struck him as the greatest folly, for it entrusted Russia's security to alien German elements. He might have considered instead the national appetites and ambitions his own work had fired, and the cost of those passions to Russia's overextended circumstances on the eve of his death in 1904.

Conclusions

Rationalism and traditional notions of authority could hardly have found a better battleground than reform of Russia's organs of war preparation. Every aspect of military reform implicitly favored that confrontation: introduction of scientific standards to statistical work and military science, history, and administration; promotion of an open corps of general staff officers; organizational reform that centralized authority under new bodies of technical experts. Most especially the mapping of the empire implicitly challenged the established order: it was general staff officers who mapped, and thus defined and discovered (in nineteenth-century terms), what "Russia" was, and therefore it was they who really conquered it. But did they do it for the tsar, or for the state, or for themselves? Ostensibly, staff rationalization promised only to place a more effective army at the state's and the emperor's disposal. In fact, in the following decades it also raised the issue of *who*—the supreme authority or his loyal experts—would decide the direction in which Russia would move strategically, militarily, and, sometimes, diplomatically.

3

Main Staff Reform between Sevastopol and Sedan

With their aggressively positivist and rationalist convictions firmly in hand by the end of the 1850s, general staff officers prepared to tackle their biggest internal fight: reform and rationalization of the general staff's structure. Nicholas's departure liberated their most innovative members from professional exile in the Caucasus. Hidden from probing imperial eyes, general staffers in the mountainous south under Prince Bariatinskii had tested numerous organizational arrangements to increase the army's effectiveness against Shamil's rebels. Those officers returned to the capital with a taste for effectiveness, acquired through rigorous experience in the empire's least forgiving theater of operations. They brought to the capital new habits and organizational ideas that actually worked, and they reshaped the central military bureaucracy while fighting off attacks by traditionalist elements uninterested in rationalization.

The 1860s did not stand still while military reformers wrestled with bureaucracy, however. Military technology changed at a logarithmic rate; railroads caught the attention of Russian and Prussian planners as industrialization went hand in hand with military reform; emancipation of Russia's rural population (the army's manpower pool) demanded reconstruction of the entire social basis for military service. A material and social complex of tasks confronted staff and ministry reformers, which made the stakes the parties fought for very high indeed. Simple resistance to change thus does not explain the traditionalists' obstruction at every step: a loss on one front foretold failure in other areas. The two sides sparred for most of the decade, blocking each other at every turn, postponing as long as possible the denouement—universal military service and strategic control of Russia's destiny.

THE MAIN STAFF (*Glavnyi shtab*) of the imperial Russian army did not exist when Miliutin became war minister in 1861. As one of the new institutions of military administration, it arose in part as a result of thirty-three years of direct imperial mismanagement and malcommand of the army. The supreme military staff fell into disuse early in the reign of Nicholas I, a victim of the martial self-realization of the new *gosudar*. Like Germany's last kaiser, Nicholas possessed a spirited sense of ultimate military responsibility, which he (unlike Wilhelm) chose to exercise. Nicholas's oldest brother, Alexander I, likewise took his own wartime responsibility too seriously, although he was repulsed by most of what he saw of warfare. Nicholas, however, played the part not only of commander in chief but also of chief of staff anytime the Imperial General Headquarters, run by his personal adjutants, assumed command of the field army. The form of the military staff was less important than the competence of those who issued orders and directed war preparations; in 1852, both those responsibilities lay in Nicholas's hands. And although higher staffs were not yet commonplace nor indispensable to military success, Russia's other insurmountable difficulties—climate, transportation and communications, organization, intelligence, victualing, armaments—militated in favor of *any* edge a modern staff could have given the empire.

That Nicholas reveled in militaria is known to the point of cliché; but he also adjudged too highly his own and his advisers' strategic competence and knowledge.[1] In 1852 and 1853 higher military staff work (including peacetime preparation for war) did not influence the emperor's military decisions. Nicholas chose the regiments he wished to mobilize from lists prepared by his adjutants, and he often communicated his orders directly to army commanders.[2] He guided his field commanders' preparations for the Crimean and Danubian campaigns: operational objectives, logistics, even loss replenishment. Nicholas, in the role of chief of staff that he was ill suited to fill, did not also provide his commanders the benefits offered by a central staff system: clear political-military objectives (i.e., war aims that articulated military objectives in the light of political goals), high-level intelligence information from sources such as attachés or spies, thoroughly elaborated contingency and logistics plans, or even the assurance of attention to any of these matters.[3] Russia had a command and staff structure before the war, but it reflected Nicholas's view of his role as warlord rather than the military problems that would affect success in the Crimean War. Effectiveness was perhaps assumed rather then worked for. Finally, diplomatic failure (again, largely the fault of Nicholas) cost Russia an unaffordable war, but archaic military administration and command authority did not ameliorate the disaster.[4] Nicholas's son and successor, Alexander, a less self-confident supreme commander, came to rely heavily on the advice of military reformers to solve the military question.

The new staff's shape and purpose were the subject of a struggle between proponents of the so-called French and Prussian models of army administration, led by Miliutin and Prince Bariatinskii, respectively.[5] As a consequence of bureaucratic struggle in the 1860s the Main Staff was firmly subordinated to the war minister, along the lines of the French model of military administration. However, within two decades the staff's statistical habits, the dynasty's meddling, and Russia's strategic constraint conditioned its gradual transformation into an agency of command, on the Prussian model. The history of that trans figuration begins properly with the reconstitution of the Main Staff in 1865, and the character it adopted as a result of the events of 1870–1871. General staff intellectual development, which began with the reform of military statistics in the general staff academy before midcentury, underpinned the birth of a staff culture in Russia. Interest in railroads accompanied renascent Russian military statistics, and even before 1870 a few general staff officers, including future Chief of Main Staff Obruchev, examined seriously the problems of railroad mobilization and grasped the disadvantage Russia would live with for years to come. Transition to a knowledge-based system of military planning signaled abandonment of Nicholas's charismatic system of command.

Reshaping a General Staff: Structural Rationalization

In retrospect, the completeness of Russia's martial failure in 1855 is clear. Among contemporaries, while all knew that something was wrong, there was little agreement on just how much could be salvaged from the wreckage of the Nicholaevan army and society. The absence of consensus accounted for Alexander II's selection of a man of mediocre talent and without a reform agenda to lead the war ministry (N. O. Sukhozanet).[6] General-Adjutant Rediger wrote the new tsar in July 1855 that the failure resulted from "the occupation by incapable people of all important posts in the army and in the military administration in general . . . [and] complete disregard of the fundamental principles of military art," a profound observation as Russia's defenses collapsed in Sevastopol and the war's end approached. Among Rediger's proposals was amalgamation of the three higher service academies (general staff, artillery, and engineering) under a Council of Imperial Military Academies. An abundance of other odd proposals (and some good ones) filled the pages of *Voennyi sbornik*, closely guided by Miliutin (assistant war minister) and under the editorship of Nikolai Chernyshevskii and the young Obruchev.[7] The failure's magnitude in almost every facet of military art and science overwhelmed the best minds, as well as the harshest critics in the army.

That the blame for Russia's Crimean catastrophe rested principally on the state's material (economic) deficiencies is more often assumed than proved. Critics in the late 1850s noted these shortcomings, but the dysfunctionality of leadership and the army's structural paralysis dominated published military discussions.[8] The most observant critics understood that much of the commentary lacked even an elementary basis in fact; knowledge of Russia's true condition had never been a goal of Nicholas's administration. Miliutin, the military's most zealous reformer and advocate, appreciated the relationship between functional administration and information far better than most other critics. His initial mandate as minister, to reduce the cost and size of the military establishment and increase its effectiveness, demanded an attack on structural decrepitude and reorganization of the army's information management. The package of reforms Miliutin laid before Alexander II on 15 January 1862 offered virtually no improvement in the army's future battlefield performance.[9] However, structural reorganization promised to disempower some and raise in authority others; it stood thus as the first, most visible symbol of army reform to supporters and opponents of change.

Following presentation to the tsar of his reform plan, Miliutin's first organizational initiative was to form an advisory group around the thirty-two-year-old Obruchev. In 1863 Miliutin established his Consultative Committee *(Soveshchatel'nyi komitet)*, to give "a more rational and systematic direction to the military-scientific activity of the general staff in connection with statistics, military history and topography." It directed "the learned [*uchenyi*] activity of [officers of] the general staff and Corps of Topographers within all branches, staffs [*sostavliaiushchie*] and specialties." The committee was nominally under Chief of Main Staff Fëdor Geiden; all of its members were general officers. Obruchev, first as head of the committee's chancellery (its *deloproizvoditel'*) and then as executive secretary *(upravliaiushchii delami)*, guided the committee's agenda, as Miliutin probably intended from the start.[10] The committee reverted to its earlier title, the Military-Scientific Committee *(Voenno-uchenyi komitet—VUK)* in 1867, once Miliutin completed the core of his structural reforms.

Between 1862 and 1864 Miliutin worked on administrative rationalization through consolidation of overlapping offices into new Main Directorates *(Glavnye upravleniia)*, first for the engineering and then for intendancy and artillery branches. By the end of the decade there were eight such organizations. The Main Inspectorate for Cavalry (under the tsar's brother, Grand Duke Nikolai Nikolaevich), however, escaped incorporation into the Main Staff in deference to the army's most tradition-bound and aristocratic branch of arms, and it remained the playground of grand dukes and Guards cavalrymen. In 1863 all administrative and clerical functions transferred to the Main Directorate of the General Staff *(Glavnoe upravlenie General'nogo shtaba—GUGSh)*, wherein also resided the Military Topographical Section *(Voenno-topograficheskaia chast')*. The heterogeneous combination of administrative activity with the highly technical business of cartography led one observer to note that Miliutin never planned GUGSh to exist as an independent organization for very long—that it was merely a halfway step. Anticipating the transitional reformation, Miliutin had written in 1861 that "at the present time it is already clear that [with sufficient numbers of officers receiving higher military education] it is possible to expand the work of the general staff and to amalgamate the quartermaster branch with the inspectorate department."[11] The army's keepers of personnel data, order-of-battle, and deployment information, the Inspectorate Department *(Inspektorskii departament,* also called the *Dezhurstvo)* was a part of the war ministry but not of the general staff.

In late 1865 Miliutin merged it with GUGSh to create the Main Staff *(Glavnyi shtab)* and placed the structure firmly under himself, effective 31 December 1865.[12] Structural reorganization then depended directly on the capacity of the general staff academy to produce sufficient officers who knew how to handle information.

The resulting leviathan had great influence on day-to-day and long-term military administrative activity. It controlled manning and personnel matters; officer assignments; strategic and economic aspects of force deployment; and the organization, servicing, allocation, training, and provisioning of forces. These duties occupied the Main Staff's six reorganized departments *(otdeleniia)* plus the newly independent Military-Topographical Department[13] and three permanent committees (Military-Scientific, Military-Topographical, and, after 1867, the Committee on Transportation of Forces by Railroad and Waterway). These organizational changes reflected Miliutin's decades of experience with administrative reform in the Caucasus and certainly brought a greater measure of rationality to the organization of work in the staff. The minister supplanted traditional use of the commander's circle of adjutants with new departments whose officers held great power within carefully circumscribed areas.

The shortcomings of the post-1865 staff were significant. Internal organizational competition and constrained individual authority remained the most serious handicaps to plague the reformed staff at a time when technical specialization of work (especially mobilization planning) placed increasingly heavy and ever-novel demands on the organization.[14] Although rationalized and consolidated, Russia's top military bureaucracy (like the government itself) operated with disunited policy and some functional overlap, even as those traditional characteristics of governing culture sapped resources and effectiveness.

Miliutin's new organization unintentionally perpetuated infighting among its ten "powerful fiefdoms"[15] for three reasons. First, there were important areas over which the chief of Main Staff had no effective control. The most prestigious branch of arms, and certainly the most extravagantly expensive, was the cavalry; yet it lay beyond either the chief's or the even war minister's direct influence until the 1870s. Second, the mammoth size of the staff unnecessarily impeded direct, rational control by any minister. Insofar as Russia's military culture did not yet count among its institutional values personal initiative or mission effectiveness, even the most perfectly rationalized organization would have resisted harmonization, absenting officers with such characteristics as Miliutin and Obruchev seem to have had. It would be years until staff officers of high caliber would occupy every significant desk on the staff. Third, the chronic budgetary difficulties of which Miliutin complained merely exacerbated the ministry's and staff's infighting. Because Russia's strategic priorities were set by individuals rather than by political consensus, the problem of rational allocation of resources to those priorities could hardly be resolved satisfactorily by isolated organizational mechanisms.

The tension these ingredients imparted also masked what was perhaps the most serious flaw of the reorganized staff: Miliutin and his assistants did not distinguish or separate the functions of intelligence collection and operational planning, that is, the collection versus the use of information. Each office decided what information it needed; it then made its own arrangements to collect that information. This led to monocular collection and thus flawed the basis for planning. Adulteration of foreign intelligence was always a potentially serious problem, of course, but the bureaucratic waste attendant to these indistinctly evolving processes was vast and likewise perpetual. Every office collected and used whatever information it deemed appropriate to its sphere of responsibility. This led to duplication of effort among war ministry offices, often with disappointing results. The staff did not finally get the two processes separated until the great reorganization of December 1900.

Along with the rapid concentration of *administrative* functions in his ministry, Miliutin put in place the military district system (1864) to decentralize authority, thus shifting the responsibility for much peacetime work. The district system stood second in importance only to introduction of universal military service (1874) among military reforms. The new district system, like other components of Miliutin's reforms, took its shape from the general's Caucasus experience. The staffs that ran each district matured in the next decade into adjuncts of the Main Staff's war-planning section and exercised considerable local authority in execution of St. Petersburg's plans. Each also developed a distinctive character, giving the empire's military staff system its own geography of talent, which complemented its emerging culture of talent.

Successful subordination of the reconstituted Main Staff to the war
minister, rather than to a chief who would serve the tsar directly (as the
Prussian monarch insisted), outlasted not only Miliutin's but also his
successors' tenures.[16] From its inception the Main Staff was shorn of
command pretensions (or, at least, command authority). The result was
firm subordination of the staff to the minister and surrender of wartime
field command to "others"—after 1870, the tsar's family, following the
inspired performance of their Prussian first cousins in the French war.
Clearly this step applied a brake to the pace of staff reform and modernization, even as it redirected the energy of general staff officers into a
new path of work. Restriction on staff field authority thus solved one
problem while creating another. The next thirty years saw a gradual
deterioration of the bridle Miliutin had placed on the staff, a deterioration that was a result of "purely military considerations." The Main
Staff never became independent, de jure, of the minister. Yet, paradoxically, the expertise that staff officers developed in their war-planning
work also guaranteed them latitude under Miliutin's successor. After
Miliutin's departure in 1881, the staff gradually instituted the de facto
command authority that Miliutin had firmly denied it in 1865.

Like the German general staff system, Russia's was an "open" corps
of officers: the General Staff Corps recruited new members from all
branches of arms after they had demonstrated some competence as
junior officers in line units (regiments). The French, in contrast, waited
until the 1880s to adopt the open system; until that time, French officers entered the *État-Major* without line experience and were never
expected to return to regimental service.[17] The goal of open general
staff recruitment was to attract specialists: work specialization, the principal transformation of general staffs after 1870, demanded well-trained
men with disparate practical experience to take on the various components of mobilization planning (although, curiously, one could not
characterize the general staff academy's curriculum as particularly specialized). An open system had strengths: intellectual depth and sophistication that could be brought to bear on planning problems. The cost of
that system: redoubled vigilance on the part of those in supreme command over the experts in war plans departments. The Main Staff's
ability to assert independence in the 1880s came from the technical
illiteracy of everyone else, most especially the war minister.

With Obruchev and his protégés in control of Russia's strategic policy by the 1880s, Miliutin's successor, Petr Semenovich Vannovskii, an officer who, in his own words, "was deficient in military theory and science,"[18] was in no position to guide or oversee mobilization work. The age in which technology necessarily ruled the work of the supreme staff had arrived. Completing Vannovskii's marginalization was his poor health. His repeated absence on sick leave in Europe liberated Obruchev from interference but handicapped the ministry's stature in councils of state. By the mid-1890s Vannovskii spent up to six months each year away from Russia for health reasons, leaving the ministry's operation in Obruchev's hands.[19] There were no other candidates for the ministryship after Miliutin, who combined technical authority with a keen sense of political responsibility to the tsar while retaining the confidence of the dynastic regime. Alexander III's dismissal of the still-vigorous Miliutin in 1881 removed the only individual who could fill that role. Evidence of the Main Staff's successful adaptation to the demands of specialization—and exploitation of its position—lies in the fact that Vannovskii (not a *genshtabist*) never challenged the technical advice or initiative of his general staff officers, even on questions of fundamental importance to the state and tsar.[20]

Reform of Military Statistics

The shape that statistical work assumed in the early 1860s presaged the ministry's abandonment of the pursuit of general information. It became increasingly apparent that an institutional commitment to accumulation of every variety of data resulted in programmatic anarchy and overextension of the staff's resources. A crisis in information management had befallen the staff. Instructors at the academy grasped this fact and attended to reorganization of the process of collection, analysis, management, and dissemination of the army's statistical material, in the hope that they might bring the data to bear on issues of military reform and strategic preparation. The very men who had managed the military's statistical work for decades became the harshest critics of what that labor had produced, a necessary step to reform of the collection and management of the army's formal knowledge.

At the beginning of Alexander II's reign, war minister Sukhozanet acted on a proposal by Lieven to make the data collected by general staff officers available to the rest of government and even society in view of its "practical use" to Russia.[21] The army had for a decade also published some of its statistical information as *The Statistical Description* (the staff's restricted-use edition was entitled *The Military Statistical Survey*).[22] Lieven, a professor of military statistics at the academy, drafted the regulation that governed this work; his coeditor, Aleksandr Lavrent'ev, prepared a new course at the academy on the surveying aspects of statistical compilation based on Miliutin's texts. That year, military-statistical survey work resumed in two-thirds of Russia's gubernias and oblasts; all the work, when published, was "open to critical examination [*glasnost'*] and the verdict of scholarly criticism."[23] By early 1860 general staff officers had produced fourteen *Statistical Descriptions* (with another ten in advanced preparation) and five volumes of the *Survey's* succeeding series, *Materials on the Geography and Statistics of Russia*.

At the same time, the general staff began a critique of all information-related work: statistical, scientific, intelligence. VUK's progenitor, the Consultative Committee, besides assisting Miliutin on organizational reforms, defined a new agenda for military data and intelligence collection. The relationship between the goals of reform and information gathering was more than casual. From its inception, the Consultative Committee considered in tandem the obstacles of maladministration and misinformation, with the former arising in part from the latter. Administrative rationalization was hobbled by a dearth of useful (and, sometimes, any) data about the Russian army and the state's resources. Military intelligence was stunted by ignorance of Russia's neighbors. The structures of the Russian state were perpetually impervious to reform as a result of self-ignorance. An earlier bureaucrat-reformer, Mikhail Speranskii, had felt the handicap of institutionalized ignorance of the empire and had decided (with the tsar's approval) "to collect as much correct data as possible" before undertaking Russia's first modern codification of laws.[24] A half century later, Miliutin's reformers would have well understood Speranskii's difficulty when they began reform.

In 1863 General-Adjutant Prince Nikolai Golitsyn described every statistical project finished from 1826 until the Crimean War as "unsatisfactory, incomplete, incorrect"—in a word, useless.[25] "Raw, fragmentary and unsatisfactory" is how Maksheev characterized the preceding twenty-seven years of work on military statistics.[26] The basic data on Russian forces gathered during that period had been "neither researched nor even formally analyzed" yet. The problem, Maksheev wrote, lay in the management and organization of the entire effort. Golitsyn, the head of the war ministry's central statistical office, agreed. He thought it logical that all statistical work should be performed within a single general staff department, but he observed that in fact almost everyone had some hand in gathering whatever data they thought fit: "[E]verything begins in the general staff academy; however, a general military statistical education should be supplemented by study of the theory and sources of military statistics. The essential step of criticism and scholarly judgment of quality must not be supplanted by reproach. At the same time, while each student must be judged equally on [his] statistical work, the judgments should also identify those of real talent for future positions in the academy."[27]

Maksheev proposed that the collation process should be organized by function, rather than according to the previous system of gathering data simply for its own sake. The staff needed information about the empire in the following five areas:

Manpower [*komplektovanie*]: on the size, movements and distribution of the population;

Population distribution [*raspolozhenie*]: in urban and rural communities;

Transportation [*peredvizhenie*]: by land and water-borne routes;

Supply or provisioning [*snabzhenie*]: on the development of general and specialized industries; and

Operations [*deistvie*]: on the country's frontiers, deserts, and seas, and their topography or characteristics.

Maksheev observed: "Such groupings of statistical information, essential for the military establishment, follow from [the war ministry's] highly specialized objectives. I believe it is most natural for the general staff's work . . . not to run contrary to generally accepted statistical systems."[28]

Furthermore, the statistics, once compiled and analyzed, had to be published in a usable form, which, Maksheev argued, would best consist of two series: one organized in conformance with the requirements of each new main directorate, and another by topic. The two series would also be cross-referenced ("as Philip II of Spain had done" with his data). Among Maksheev's recommendations he urged a reshaping of the military administration *in conformity with* the statistical requirements of the army; the adoption of a uniform system of both collection and compilation of statistics; and the formalization of foreign intelligence gathered by attachés, general staff officers, and "by other means" (presumably, covert espionage and double agents).[29] In his earlier survey of statistical work, Golitsyn had likewise proposed a more careful integration of attachés into the information- and intelligence-gathering process, particularly for collection on the *theory of military statistics*, and especially in Prussia and Austria.[30]

The Consultative Committee approved most of Maksheev's recommendations and decided to assign much of the new work to district staffs. The committee transmitted its decisions to GUGSh's III Department (the committee's principal executive arm) in April 1865. The III Department then developed prototypical formats for data collection and drafted administrative guidelines to govern staff officers' authority in collection work.[31] The care that accompanied preparation of these measures paid dividends: the new formats served the Main Staff's needs so well that two decades later district staff officers were still collecting data in essentially the same form. In the late 1880s, for instance, one collection program followed the original system by dividing the task into four categories: topography and geography; population and population centers; lines of communications; and means of provisioning forces in the theater of operations.[32]

If form changed little after the approval of Maksheev's project, the need to supplement and correct the information only increased. Decades later, looking back on the staff's work, VUK's executive secretary wrote to his predecessor, Obruchev:

> Between 1869 and 1877 military [statistical] *Surveys* of the four western border districts (Vilna, Warsaw, Kiev, Odessa) and of Finland were published in accordance with identical programs, and in 1885 for St. Petersburg by the same program. Most material was gathered by general staff officers in the 1860s. Now most of the information (except for St. Petersburg's) is obsolete. Because most of the material was gathered before officers had a keen sense of *strategic* realities, it simply did not address some key "military questions," especially concerning the conduct of military operations in the western frontier area.[33]

As well as data collection, the preparation of military maps and topo-graphic materials of the empire was in poor condition. Cartographic studies had been firmly established in general staff qualifications since the 1830s; Chief of Main Staff Geiden and his successor, Obruchev, themselves had participated in the survey of southern and western Russia. Yet not until after the Franco-Prussian War did VUK set up army map depots *(topograficheskie sklady)* in the four western military districts, near the probable theater of war. Notwithstanding even the war minister's appreciation of military cartography, many Russian military maps were useless into the mid-1870s, as the Main Staff tried to bring its cartographics up to date.[34] Again, hobbled by a desperate shortage of qualified staff officers who could do the work, the mapping of western Russia continued at a snail's pace.

Up to 1870, therefore, Russian general staff officers were involved in three areas of study—statistics, science, and intelligence—which brought them into contact with the two sorts of information that to-gether constituted military statistics: geographic/topographic and sta-tistical. The Main Staff systematized its work during the 1860s. Its officers, however, carried out the labor without reference to formal priorities of information that might have been determined by strategic consensus. Consequently, much of the data proved obsolete and neces-sitated recollection within two decades. General staff officers developed what Fedor Aleksandrovich Fel'dman called a "keen sense of strategic reality" between 1870 and 1876, first from Prussia's success and then in the course of another eastern crisis later that decade. Russia's General Staff Corps, however, brought the new strategic reality to bear on its area of responsibility only with delay.

The evolution of the Main Staff's responsibilities, from technical research bureau to war and mobilization planning staff, was a result of two developments. First, the staff acquired high technical competence from its pioneering work in data gathering and statistical analysis, often with the assistance of severe self-criticism. The labors of key staff offi-cers marked them as experts, and their near monopoly in strategic questions assured them wide influence and autonomy within their nar-row technical sphere, a realm they progressively expanded in the 1870s and 1880s. Of more dramatic and immediate significance, however, was the example that Prussia provided to Europe of the potent edge a mod-ernized, scientific general staff could give to a state's army. The medium

through which higher military planning could achieve strategic superiority was the railroad, and technical experts monopolized the manipu-
lation of that medium.

The Main Staff and Railroads

Russia's transportation handicaps are too well known to endure another
extended summary.[35] Comparative economic history, however, can dis-
tort the character of Russia's transport deficit for modern historians as
much as it did for contemporary military planners. For instance, researchers have repeatedly noted that in terms of both absolute rail
mileage and rail density, Russia trailed most European states. However,
a far larger portion of Russia's European territory than, say, Germany's
could never be under any imaginable military threat. Thus, while economic objectives might militate for uniform, intense transportation development on the empire's territory, the *strategic* imperative for uniform
network construction was weak. Only in the western half of European
Russia, and in tsarist Poland in particular, did Russia face meaningful
challenges to its security.[36]

The king of Russian railroad development, finance minister Sergei
Witte, later dismissed all preceding "strategic considerations" for railroad planning as wasteful without exception; commercial concerns
alone served both the state and the army, and did so better than any
amount of military involvement in network planning.[37] In the 1870s
and 1880s the fragmentation of policy slowed development of lines
from Russia into Poland, and, worse, disunity of state priorities hobbled
the war ministry's ability to advocate successfully for the network it
wanted. Nevertheless, Russia's European mileage increased more than
sixfold between 1861 and 1871 (the only decade during which the war
ministry had any measure of influence in construction), from, 1,580 to
10,695 kilometers. By 1875 it stood at 18,840 kilometers, an addition of
15,036 kilometers over the previous ten years. Five major lines entered
service from 1865 to 1875, of which three became key trunks for the
mobilization plans developed in the 1880s.[38]

The railroad problem was a watershed of sorts for the Main Staff's
planners. It was the first issue of acute complexity that required planners to apply fresh statistical information in order to disaggregate the
problem into its component questions. While the ultimate efficacy of

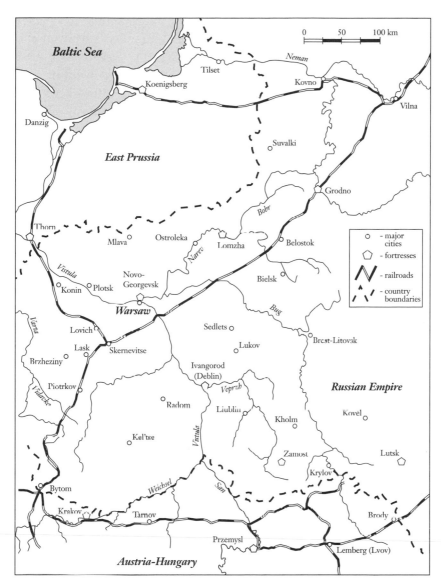

Map 1. Western Russian provinces, 1870.

their work may be in doubt, the quality of their thorough, efficient and methodical work is not, for the Main Staff required no subsequent special committees to determine its requirements for railroads. Individuals on the Main Staff and in the academy fretted over the military uses of railroads and Russia's retarded transportation network development long before Prussia demonstrated the full potential of mechanized mobilization in 1870.[39] The head of the II Department of the Main Staff wrote to the academy in February 1866 that reports from the military attachés in Berlin and especially Vienna demonstrated alarmingly the progress those states had made on exploitation of railroads for mobilization. As early as the beginning of 1864, Austria had exercised its primitive network by moving a thirty-six-thousand-man corps from Vienna to Salzburg by rail. At that time the head of the I Department had also reported on these matters (based on classified Prussian documents) and likewise recommended a conference to discuss the matter, to no avail. By 1866, however, the war minister was ready to investigate the matter;[40] he established two commissions under the auspices of MPS (Lieutenant-General P. P. Mel'nikov) to collect reliable, basic statistics on the military role and potential of railroads in Russia and elsewhere. The commissions' work, like most military statistical work undertaken during the 1860s, comprised systematic sorting of information. The survey confirmed the limited military potential of the existing rail system in Russia and dwelled on its gross inferiority to the Prussian and Austrian networks.[41]

The First Commission ("on collection of data concerning foreign railroads") tackled the question of what the rest of Europe was doing. As well as glossing the entire railroad system of western Europe (a total of fifty-three studies), commission members examined German, French, and Austrian solutions to technical problems such as water supplies, topographic obstacles to line construction, single-track versus double-track construction, development of telegraphic and signaling communications systems, and planning of network reserves (backup lines) and their infrastructure. Strategic assumptions guided the commission's inquiry: How would railroads allow Russia to assist a neighboring ally in the event of war; and how would a neighbor's railroads facilitate a hostile concentration on Russia's borders?[42]

The commission paid almost no attention to the first scenario, Russia's responsibility to an allied neighbor (the possibility being governed by recollections of 1848 and 1859, and perhaps 1866 as well). The commissioners elaborated the latter scenario, and their final report encapsulated one of the earliest formulations of Russia's strategic concerns on its western frontier. "An enemy army" would concentrate on the frontier at Krakov, Chernovtsy (in Bukhovina), or opposite

Verzhbolovo in East Prussia (due west of Vilna on the frontier). That army would consist of five corps and associated cavalry and artillery, a total of about 185,000 men, fifty-six thousand horses, and five thousand guns—considerably fewer than the armies that had participated in the recent Austro-Prussian War. An Austrian concentration at either Krakov or Chernovtsy would make use of the rolling stock of the Vienna-Krakov-Chernovtsy line only, rather than from the entire Austrian system. That limitation, the commission calculated, would retard the Hapsburg's arrival at the frontier (about thirty-six to thirty-seven days from the start of mobilization, or m + 36 or m + 37). Prussia, on the other hand, would have access to rolling stock from the entire North German Confederation, and with double-tracked lines to the border of East Prussia, it could concentrate its army in as little as twenty-two days (m + 22). Clearly, the commission concluded, Russia must follow Prussia's example. Interestingly, the group under General-Adjutant Lev Batiushkov discounted the possibility of Austro-Prussian rapprochement, and analyzed potential adversaries individually rather than as a strategic system.[43]

The Second Commission ("on the condition and resources of the railroads existing in the Empire"), under Ivanin, had the greatest difficulty meeting its objectives: it relied on MPS and the various private railroad companies for all its information. After eight months, for example, only one railroad company had deigned to respond to the requests of the Chief of the Main Staff and the commission chairman for data on their portion of the network. Among the commission's recommendations were formation of a permanent war ministry body to supervise force transportation in peacetime and wartime. Each military district staff in European Russia would designate one officer as a mobilization transportation coordinator, responsible for all local preparations.[44] In May 1868 the Main Staff formed that permanent group, the Committee on Transportation of Forces by Railroad and Waterway, through which the commission reported. The Third Desk assisted the committee's work until the Main Staff reorganization of 1877, when the Fourth Desk took over all responsibility for railway conveyance of forces during mobilization.

Aside from the committee's small circle of specialists, few army officers appreciated the magnitude of Russia's transportation disadvantage, but many felt apprehensive about Russia's mobilization speed and capability. In 1869 the governor-general of southern Russia, the elderly Pavel Kotsebu, vaguely concluded in a report to Miliutin that "Russia's European neighbors" could threaten southern Russia with railroad-based mobilization and that greater military preparation was essential.[45] He naively warned of rapprochement between the German states ("the emerging political constellation") long before there was evidence of that; but worse, he did not foresee any role for Russia's own railroads in answer to the danger he divined. By the end of 1869, Kotsebu had assumed command of Warsaw Military District—the empire's most important field command—from where he (or his chief of staff, more likely) reported to Miliutin the priorities there:

> I have always considered a rail route from Brest-Litovsk to Smolensk and Berdichev with branches from Kobrina to Pinsk to be supremely and urgently necessary. Construction of this line will take no less than three years, during which time our policy towards the central European states may so change that only a rail route linking Warsaw with the interior provinces of Russia will make it possible not only to provide timely supplies of men, horses, provisions and combat stores to the army on the Vistula, but also their very transportation along portions of this route running close to the Prussian frontier. It will be impossible to consider [this project] completed without the construction of the two ordered routes to Smolensk and Berdichev, not postponing these works until a more favorable time.[46]

Kotsebu's "evolving" opinion of the priorities for railroad construction obscured the fundamental difficulty for Russia's strategic planners. In a world of limited resources, would Russian security be better served by north-south lines, which could strengthen defenses of the Black Sea and Baltic flanks, or by radial lines into Poland along which men and supplies could be rushed to the defense of the salient? North-south orientation would better anticipate maritime (Franco-British) hostility; east-west lines would imply that central European powers were the greater threat.

One unsigned and undated report from 1867, prepared in the Main Staff, was emblematic of the shift in military thought on this question. Whereas past studies had emphasized the need for a railroad from

Moscow to the Black Sea coast, only *financial* considerations were now paramount in the arguments for that construction. From a military point of view, a line from Moscow to Warsaw was of supreme importance. "The greatest fortresses and the largest concentration of forces of the empire are located in tsarist Poland," declared the author. But their security could not be assured without "direct communications with the center of Russia." "Warsaw has the railroad to St. Petersburg, which might be connected on to Kiev. But just a glance at the map demonstrates that none of these links nor others may be securely held for the defense of Russia's western border."[47]

From a strategic perspective, Moscow—not St. Petersburg—was the hub of western Russian defense ("because of its historical, industrial, and administrative importance"). The rail line itself was necessary "to defend our ownership of Poland"; it was to be the carotid artery of imperial Russian security. Without that line first in place, any other railroad construction to Warsaw would be folly, for any other line would be vulnerable to interdiction in the event of war with Prussia-Germany or Austria.[48] This argument became axiomatic to future military pressure for railroad development in European Russia.

As a result of the Second Commission's work, the war minister authorized the establishment of a military railroad command even before receipt of Kotsebu's anxious report. The command, guided by the Committee and II Department, oversaw Russia's first experimental unit transfers by railroad. In 1866 and 1867, parts of infantry regiments and artillery batteries of the Guards-Petersburg Military District moved along the Nicholas Railroad (St. Petersburg to Moscow), and the tsar observed embarkation, transportation, and debarkation of a Guards battalion and cavalry regiment on the Peterhof line during summer maneuvers.[49] Finally, during the 1869 summer maneuvers the 37th Infantry Division (with artillery) transited by rail, river, and foot, from Kazan Military District, from embarkation at Nizhnii Novgorod through Moscow to St. Petersburg and Krasnoe Selo.[50]

Three months later, at the start of the winter work season, the Main Staff became a permanent participant in the organization and management of transportation resources. Men with some background in transportation organization, particularly those versed in western European railroad organization, assumed key positions in the Main Staff. In the future, general staff officers (not railroad employees) would oversee all transportation of forces by railroad and waterway.[51] Chief of Main Staff Geiden and his executor, VUK, apparently intended merely to have transportation experts assist other military planners. They did not yet prize military transportation as *the* governing mechanism of modern mobilization and supply.

The interrelation of security and railroads was more fully and clearly expounded in an unsigned report of enormous significance.[52] Its anonymous author, Obruchev, began his report to Miliutin with a grand tour of Russia's strategic landscape: "Russia, leaning on Asia, seems with respect to Europe the greatest of powers, invulnerable either from the rear or the flanks." The empire was, however, "conveniently accessible from the west, where the Baltic and the Black Sea coastlines are open to hostile assault by fleets and amphibious landings [*desanty*], and in the center between Lolangen and the Troianov Banks, by any land army." The frontier strip from Finland, through the Baltic area, Lithuania, Poland, Volhynia, Bessarabia, and the Crimea to the Caucasus, constituted, in Obruchev's view, a great, vulnerable zone for the empire, a tempting target for the only enemies he could imagine—the Germanic powers. The convenient concatenation of all of Russia's security concerns into a single geographic zone, however, did not reassure this officer: those very borders were the least defensible of all, geographically, and the weakest areas politically. "The center is formed by Tsarist Poland. It penetrates deepest of all into the body of Europe and contains the most inflammatory material of all [our western borders]. To inflict a *mortal blow* on Russia her enemies are presented every opportunity, foremost in Poland."[53]

Obruchev had understood for nearly a decade what others still could not imagine. With their border fortifications resting comfortably in the Sudeten, the Beskids, and the Carpathian Mountains, or mired in swampy lake lands, the Germanic powers could gaze hungrily (and with growing appetite, in the Prussian case) toward the great central Polish plain, as enticing and indefensible as they themselves were invulnerable. Obruchev's report became part of a corpus of works that guided the Russian general staff's strategic views for a quarter century. The studies that made up that corpus, most of them by Obruchev, defined the empire's enemies in geographically specific terms and described great states as if they had the characteristics of immobile regiments, with "flanks" and "rears." In Obruchev's cosmology, Russia's enemies

and interests lay foremost in central Europe, and the very act of defining the *entire* western border as a strategic weak point implied that
there would be no differentiating the two Germanic powers, Prussia
and Austria, when it came to the empire's security. He perpetuated
these perspectives to the officers who passed through the academy, thus
laying the groundwork for a strategic orthodoxy that emerged after
1870. A year before Austro-Prussian rapprochement, Obruchev had
redefined central European politics in terms explicitly hostile to Russia's security. Lagging strategic railroad construction would become the
backbone of that bleak view of the west.

More than a month before Prussia began mobilization against France
in 1870, the Main Staff's railroad section (Third Desk of the II Department) knew that the Russian army could increase still further its use of
railways in the event of war. From the time of Prusso-German mobilization onward, the staff cultivated technical transportation expertise,
and general staff specialists received assignment not only throughout
the war ministry but also in MPS and the interior ministry. The day
of the Russian military railroad specialist had arrived.[54] Throughout
the decade of most rapid railroad development, 1866–1877, most engineering and management specialists (civil and military) who ran the
system received training in the Institute of Lines of Communications
(of MPS).[55]

MPS's highest positions were in the hands of military graduates of
the institute. Yet in 1870 the minister, Count V. A. Bobrinskii, described to Witte the institute's graduates as "infected by the corporate
spirit of the engineers," unqualified for any aspect of railroad operation
except the purely technical.[56] The minister's opinion did not, however,
change the fact that specialists would thereafter dominate the profession. Bobrinskii and many of his subordinates had no interest in pro-
moting the Main Staff's technical planning goals or strategic priorities.
At times they would not even answer the mail from the war ministry
chancellery. Seven times between December 1866 and the following
May, the committee requested information from the director of railroads (Department of Railroads, MPS) about the St. Petersburg-
Warsaw railroad (the Nicholas Railroad) and the Riga-Vitebsk railroad.
MPS, Ivanin's committee feebly reported, never responded.[57]

The Main Staff's preeminent railway technical expert was Mikhail
Nikolaevich Annenkov.[58] Although he was a distinguished 1858 acad-

emy graduate, Annenkov's engineering background left him in unexceptional positions until he was assigned as the general staff's inspector
of the new railway command in 1868. He participated in the Second
Commission (1866–1868) and wrote an important essay, "Concerning
the Application of Railroads to Military Ends," while serving with the
study group.[59] His technical expertise placed him in considerable demand in St. Petersburg and with the staffs of the military districts,
which were beginning to assume responsibility for the preparation of
forces for rail-borne transportation in their areas. During the summer
of 1867 Annenkov visited each of the western military districts to in-
struct the staffs and units gathered for summer exercises on proper use
of embarkation bridges (an untrustworthy piece of equipment, developed as a stopgap until all railroad stations received raised platforms for
loading troops, horses, and equipment).[60] Annenkov and other staff
specialists understood that the pace of loading and unloading would
place an important limitation on troop transportation speed. Embarkation practice concerned mobilization planners from the late 1860s onward, and summer unit training rarely neglected at least some attention
to train embarkation exercises. Still a major, Annenkov penned the May
1870 memorandum on the future importance of military railroad use;
just eighteen months later he was promoted to major general. In the
1870s Annenkov served with the interministerial Baranov Commission
on the condition of Russia's railways,[61] and then won high praise as chief
of military railway transportation during the Russo-Turkish War. Before the end of the war he reached the rank of lieutenant general.[62] If
not yet respected or heeded in every high counsel of state and administration, the railroad expert had proved his indispensability to Russian
strategic planning, and received recognition of his work.

Conclusions

Had 1870 not confronted Russia's military leaders with a new, potentially threatening power in central Europe, the tensions generated during the 1860s might have remained a curious footnote to the military
reforms of Miliutin's first decade. Those tensions—between minister
and his staff; between a corps of experts and charismatic state authority;
between the opinions of specialists and the unresponsiveness of bureaucratic bodies—might otherwise have stood as merely petty structural

inefficiencies and inconveniences to the orderly development of the Russian state. But a contrary course of events rocked Europe in mid-1870, and those tensions cast into sharp relief the charade of autocracy's capacity for self-mobilization or even for administration sufficient to assure its own survival. Miliutin's new staff organs had a demanding task—preparation for general mobilization in the event of war with Germany—which left Russia the choice of virtually inventing a *professional* general staff or of slipping into the economic and political orbit of the German empire.

General staff officers read a variety of lessons into the German campaign up to Sedan, but the staff did not have a unified understanding of that war to internalize until Obruchev placed the new European order in a strategic context for Miliutin and the tsar two years later. Introduction of universal military service paralleled the rapid accommodation of German practices into Russian general staff work habits, none of which took place in the academy. The staff's leaders attempted to convert very well trained generalists into mobilization planning specialists. Finally, the Main Staff groaned through another round of ad hoc structural change as it searched for an effective organizational arrangement in which to plan Russia's next war. And these measures were taken without reference to dynastic prerogative or autocratic authority.

4

Mortal Danger as
Strategic Rebirth

"It seems to me that on 2 September the first stone was laid for a future Franco-Russian alliance," the Russian minister in Brussels, Prince Nikolai Orlov, wrote imperial chancellor and foreign minister Gorchakov on 4 September 1870. The French army had capitulated at Sedan two days earlier.[1] Orlov's observation was nothing more than a lucky guess, for there was nothing inevitable about the military arrangement in which republican France and autocratic Russia found themselves a quarter century later. Almost every phase of the two states' relations during the nineteenth century militated against Orlov's prediction. Russia's close political and dynastic affinity to Prussia presented no excuse for the tsar to wish an alliance against his imperial German relations. In fact, Germany and Russia would sign three defensive alliances, each a cornerstone of Bismarck's interlocking Continental system, before the German chancellor's worst nightmare finally became a reality in the early 1890s. And apart from a million-man army, which Russia could not mobilize and was barely able to feed and arm, what could a Russian alliance possibly offer France after the unification of Germany? In a word, nothing—but a potential.

Russian general staff officers observed the lightning-quick Prussian victories in 1870 with admiration, and probably with more apprehension than their regimental brethren. Aside from the political implications of Germany's unification (principally by force of arms, in the opinion of Russian military men), the Main Staff confronted two questions about its own competency and future. First, how precisely would Russia's higher military staff go about the work of preparing for a war like that? And then, how would its General Staff Corps reshape itself, to be assured of a perpetual stream of young officers with the knowledge and skills necessary to do such work? Members of the Military-Scientific Committee, for whom Obruchev nominally worked, felt their way around these questions between 1871 and 1876 as their leaders (principally war minister Miliutin) brought the loftier question of Russia's strategic direction before the tsar and his ministers.

Besides fending off another onslaught from conservative opponents, Miliutin also secured imperial recognition of the strategic and military costs of Russia's proximity to Germany (first coherently articulated by Obruchev) and sanction of the Main Staff's new course in response to that challenge. With assistance of the staffs of the most important military districts—Warsaw, Vilna, Kiev, and Odessa—Obruchev and his colonels introduced Prussian practices into general staff officer training: staff rides, war games, strategic studies. These activities usefully distracted the general staff from most outside concerns after 1870, with Obruchev and VUK taking barely any notice of Kaufman's imposition of a protectorate over Khiva (1873), the Turkomans uprising against Russia's puppet khan there (1874),[2] or the "war in sight" crisis between France and Germany (1875).

In consequence of a compounding of the planning staff's responsibilities, itself a reflection of the rapid pace of work rationalization, Obruchev led yet another round of reorganizations. Miliutin's reforms in the mid-1860s had given the staff its essential shape and determined the lines of authority; when Obruchev took charge of strategic work in 1872 he revitalized military statistics but turned it explicitly toward intelligence collection in support of mobilization planning. Maturation of the staff, reflected in function- and information-driven rationalization, marked the beginning of a golden age of the Main Staff. The staff's structure did not equilibrate until Obruchev's men produced Russia's first viable, fully elaborated "modern" war plan in 1887, and during the intervening fifteen years formal organization perpetually fell short of the tangled and transitory internal modus operandi. Thus, 1870 did not produce an immediate or direct effect on the staff, or even in the government as a whole. Prussia's victory allowed sides in Russia to define battle lines and gave the reformers their agenda. Before any other activity could begin, Miliutin and Obruchev needed a mandate for action; they wasted no time seeking it from the tsar.

The Inspiration of 1870

The technique of modern general staff operation, defined under Field Marshall von Moltke's influence, demonstrably continues today. While the problems which that phase of the military revolution posed to political leaders eluded straightforward solution, the *purely military* importance of higher staff organs was unquestioned after 1870. Given war's increasingly technical character, no power with imperial or great-power ambitions could expect *less* than technical competence of its military administration in post-1870 Europe, and no land power could offer an alternative to the Prussian system of war preparation and planning, as even the French finally discovered in the 1870s. The Warsaw Military District staff wrote in December 1873: "The necessity of adoption of a similar procedure [for mobilization and concentration] is acknowledged now not only throughout Germany but in fact by Austria and *every other first-rate power* [*pervostepennaia derzhava*]." Kings had to begin to trust their military experts in ways they had not before. Of course Prussia did not hold an uninterrupted claim on modern general staff excellence: its system was only a generation old in 1870 and, like Russia's, had emerged from well-deserved disrepute. As recently as the 1848 revolutionary crisis a general staff officer described the Prussian chief of General Staff's performance as "dilettantish wheezing."[3]

If Prussian performance in 1864 and 1866 aroused the attention of some Russian officers, German mobilization and the trouncing of France's army in 1870 propelled even the tsar off his throne into conference with his advisers. Military thinkers published hundreds of pages of analysis of the events around Sedan and Metz, their industry unslaked even into the 1890s. The regiments of the tsar's army were also alive with the latest reports from the front. Like their contemporaries in line regiments or at the academy, officers of the general staff (*genshtabisty*) within the bureaucracy followed the war but with more than the debating-point mentality or dilettantish distraction of their brethren. To at least a few, the strategic problem was clear: How could the army possibly protect the empire from its western neighbor if the Hohenzollerns embraced larger eastern ambitions?[4]

Strategically and politically, the army was naive. It had undertaken its security responsibilities after the Crimean War in an "*ad hoc*, poorly coordinated, and badly planned" way.[5] That order of things underlined the aridity of Russia's strategic tradition and the aimlessness of planning at the highest levels of the war ministry and the government. The leadership was preoccupied with internal restructuring and the complicated international aftermath of the Paris Peace. At the same time, rogue generals carved out new territories in Central Asia, either in the absence of unified national policy or oblivious to St. Petersburg's commands to the contrary. Foreign minister Gorchakov's assurances could not assuage British anxiety, and the war ministry in St. Petersburg was unable to curb the tsar's generals who operated happily incommunicado.[6] Russia's masters, marooned on the eastern periphery of Europe's fragmented system and largely blind to the diplomatic costs of General Cherniaev's and later General Skobelev's glorious insubordination, stumbled from one policy crisis to another for most of the fifteen years leading up to 1870.

Pan-Slavic agitation grew in acrimony and forced the government's attention toward the southeast; although it was of questionable direct influence on Russian policy, the agitation alarmed Austria and hence compelled Russia to shift its focus as well. In a happier vein, France's projected triple alliance against Prussia-Russia failed thanks to Napoleon's inability to end the occupation of the capital of his prospective ally, Italy. Russian policy resonated with the aimless drift that characterized relations among the other great powers; military adventurism along the distant southern periphery of the empire scarcely even raised the risk of confrontation with Britain, sitting in self-limiting isolation.[7]

The day France delivered its declaration of war in Berlin, the Russian chief of Main Staff General-Adjutant Geiden (prompted by his most important subordinate, Obruchev) ordered general staff officers to the Prussian and French armies as observers. Many Russian officers expressed low expectations of Prussia's prospects. Like most Europeans they held France's army in high esteem and believed that this time Bismarck and Moltke would meet their match.[8] Russia's elite was culturally and by tradition Francophile, and since the early 1830s the Russian general staff had warmly embraced the French method in military science and administration. It was a Swiss-born Francophone, General Henri Jomini, to whom Nicholas I had turned to create Russia's general staff academy in 1832. These prejudices likewise moved important indi-

viduals: Kennan observes that both war minister Miliutin and his rising
protégé, Obruchev, maintained long-standing family, official, and professional ties to the French.[9]

Russia's officer corps received news of the unfolding campaign
through army journals such as *Voennyi sbornik*; the academy library and
most regiments also received French and German military journals
with yet more information. The Russian press likewise followed events
closely.[10] Witte recounted in his memoirs the scene each evening in the
palace of the governor-general in Odessa: "Military men would gather
at Count Kotsebu's to plot the course of the war and engage in armchair
strategy. Most, including my uncle [General R. A. Fadeev], let sympathy for France cloud their judgment, but Kotsebu, a Russian German,
took a more realistic view of the war."[11] General Login Zeddeler, one of
the officers ordered to the Prussian field headquarters, captivated military and court audiences with colorful descriptions of operations following the war.[12] Despite sympathy for Emperor Napoleon's plight,
most Russian military men came to admire the apparent precision with
which Moltke's army dispatched MacMahon and the other French field
commanders.

Leer produced the army's first critical description of the 1870–1871
war in twelve articles, republished under one cover, which he began
shortly before the end of hostilities. He identified a number of questions the war raised, among which the future role of railroad operations
(as lines of communications) struck him as being of the highest technical complexity and importance.[13] The essays on the Franco-Prussian
War cemented his reputation as the army's most influential theoretician
because the topic showcased the power of his "critical-historical" research method. Leer's study appeared so thorough and compellingly
argued that his essays subsequently defined the army's official view of
that war's lessons (certainly reflected in an uncritical preoccupation
with geometrically arranged lines of communications), and stood
largely unchallenged for the next two decades.[14] Leer's interest lay not
with political-strategic issues but with the tactical innovations that 1870
produced. Another officer, Staff Captain Nikolai Ivanovich Mau, who
had recently graduated from Leer's institution, published a study on the
tactical importance of railroads that came to the attention of VUK. Yet
neither Leer's nor Mau's work betrayed a grasp of the military revolution promised by the marriage of transportation technology and mass

armies, a revolution that had Prussia's General Staff thoroughly in its grip by the 1860s.

Beyond what must have been typical martial interest in a great war, how did Russian officers comprehend those features of Prussian combat performance that made history in 1870? Few officers in line regiments felt more threatened after German unification than they had before. Among military technicians on the Main Staff and on the western district staffs in Warsaw, Vilna, Kiev, and Odessa, news of what the *Grosser Generalstab* had achieved inspired both admiration and concern. Not only did Prussia-Germany have qualitative organizational advantage over Russia in new military technologies like railroad systems and all sorts of armaments, but its central planning body had demonstrated that it could use its material advantages, and had accumulated unrivaled experience in three recent wars. In the autumn of 1871 the chief of staff in Warsaw urgently inquired after any information St. Petersburg held on the mobilization capacity of Russia's new western neighbor. The Committee on Transportation of Forces by Railroad confirmed Warsaw's fears with simple raw data that was testimony to St. Petersburg's own grim evaluation of the situation (Table 4.1).

After working inconspicuously through the 1860s, VUK's executive secretary, Obruchev, stepped forward with Miliutin's blessing to present a closely argued appreciation of the war's strategic importance for Russia. His unadorned, Manichaean assessment of Russia's Continental position had three advantages. First, its geographic specificity answered the most pressing questions that faced the general staff regarding the empire's international direction. Russia would follow Obruchev's lead and fix its strategic gaze on the Germanies. Second, it pointed the staff toward the path of rapid expansion into the fields of war plan-

Table 4.1. Great Power Rolling Stock, Central Europe, 1871

	Locomotives	Passenger Wagons	Baggage Wagons	Freight Wagons
Germany	5,012	9,441	2,026	88,315
Austria	1,656	3,180	883	37,016
Russia	1,986	2,733	510	39,610

Source: RGVIA, F. 400, op. 3, d. 1878, ll. 1–2: COS Warsaw [Prince Imeretinskii] to Chief of Main Staff (II Dept/2 Desk), 23 October 1871.

ning, mobilization planning, and intelligence gathering, areas that the central and district staffs had dealt with among a variety of other activities that dissipated their efforts. And third, it offered the state unambiguous but misleading alternatives for its strategic future because continental European political reality was not nearly as clear-cut as narrow military thinkers believed. Miliutin's influential patronage of Obruchev, in spite of the well-known fact of the latter's youthful radical associations, was undoubtedly the most important assistance he gave to the Main Staff in his capacity as war minister during the 1860s. Obruchev subsequently molded and directed Russia's strategic policy under two war ministers, without peer, oversight, or challenge, until near the end of the century.

The 1873 Secret Conference

The secret strategic conference of 1873 was possibly the most important deliberative gathering to take place during the reign of Alexander II, yet its origins, course, and outcome have escaped the attention of all but a small number of specialists. Knowledge of the meeting remains poor because of the disappearance from the archives of important files concerning the conference's sessions.[15] P. A. Zaionchkovskii left us various accounts of the five sessions[16] between 28 February to 31 March 1873, but questions remain unanswerable without the minutes. Although Miliutin proposed the conference to the tsar as a consequence of German unification—that is, for military and strategic reasons—the gathering devolved into a forum for counterreform elements in the military again to do battle with the war minister.[17] Zaionchkovskii's accounts reflect his interest in the internal politics of military reform rather than in the conference's original purpose, Russia's strategic dilemmas. Of all the literature on Russian military history before 1992, only one observer fathomed the strong early influence of Obruchev in preparing for the conference. In a penetrating but entirely too brief summary of the meeting, A. M. Zaionchkovskii saw a connection between the 1870–1871 war and the subsequent conference, and was familiar with the role played by Obruchev's 1872 and 1873 memoranda, not only for the 1873 meeting but also for all subsequent Main Staff strategic planning through 1909.[18]

In October 1870 Alexander II approved Miliutin's request to present a report on Russia's position and military capabilities as a basis for an imperial decision on the reorganization of the army. In October the Main Staff (specifically, Chief of Main Staff Geiden and Generals Obruchev and Grigorii Vasil'evich Meshcherinov) combed through reports from district staffs to draft two memoranda that Miliutin presented to the tsar on 7 November.[19] The broad questions of manpower and reorganization posed by Miliutin's memoranda could not be answered absenting consensus on strategic priorities from the very highest levels of state. To precipitate such decisions Obruchev composed his "Considerations Concerning the Defense of Russia," based on surveys prepared by military district staffs, in late 1872.[20] Its immediate purpose was to assist the deliberations of a special commission that was planning army reorganization and examining the bases for military service. For historians, however, it is a unique document on the Main Staff's perspective of Russia's strategic future following unification of Germany. Russian *genshtabisty* later viewed the memorandum that way: subsequent Main Staff strategic documents into the 1880s began with reference to Obruchev's 1872 study.[21]

"We must take measures urgently for the security of the empire, especially since now, the transition from peace to war is accomplished, so to speak, instantaneously." Army mobilization, Obruchev wrote, was terra incognita for the Russian staff. "For us this business is completely new." Russia lacked the trained manpower, the transportation system, or even the horses to match Germany alone, much less if it stood in alliance with Austria. And the solution to these problems could not be found in the war ministry; these were issues for "general governmental action," especially regarding the transportation problem. First Obruchev scrutinized the problem of mobilization, that is, the call-up of men from yet-to-be created reserve and replacement cohorts. Once universal military service was enacted, the challenge would be strictly for the *kantseliaristy:* the men of the Main Staff would "work out in the finest detail . . . the obligations of all men acting according to the call-up . . . from the moment the districts receive the [declaration of mobilization] telegram." That plan, however, would merely get men to their mustering camps; they would still need transportation to assembly points when their units reached war strength.[22]

In the section entitled "The Concentration of the Army" Obruchev described in bleak detail Russia's transportation (and thus mobilization) disadvantage, an underdeveloped rail system of no comparison to the networks of its neighbors. In terms of line density, double or quadruple tracking, routes to the border area, and between the frontier zone and the state's center, Russia trailed Germany so distantly that Obruchev's estimates of army concentration offered not the least reason for hope. In war with Germany, Russia could mobilize and concentrate in fifty-four to fifty-eight days, while Germany could do the same in twenty-three days or better. In an Austrian war, Russia could mobilize and concentrate in nine to ten weeks, while Austria could do the same in thirty to thirty-three days.[23] The Germanic states each had more rail lines to the frontier than Russia: Germany had ten lines and Austria six, while Russia had five lines to Germany's border and three to Austria's. The specter of an Austro-German compact against Russia promised military disadvantage so insurmountable that they defied imagination: Obruchev refused to broach the possibility in his study, even though the central European empires were in fact already moving toward each other.

Russia had two choices in a European war. It could either join battle with an aggressor at the frontier, but before it completed mobilization and concentration of its army, or it might wait for completion of concentration in secure areas far to the rear so as to enter battle at full wartime strength—a course that would risk the loss of large portions of Poland. In the latter scenario, Obruchev calculated, Germany would have seized most of northern and western Poland and parts of Lithuania by the thirtieth day of mobilization; Austria could take northwestern Volhynia and parts of southern Poland.[24] To secure Poland—that part of Russia of "unwavering historical importance," the very "head of European Russia"[25]—the army needed between 820 and 840 battalions, a number "absolutely *essential* and *the very minimum* for defense" of the state.

Since 4 November 1870, when an imperial announcement in the government's official register *(Pravitel'stvennyi vestnik)* declared that at some time in the future Russia's army would be based on universal military service and trained reserves,[26] the military establishment had debated the appropriate basis of military manpower. Obruchev's figures (and, in fact, his entire strategy) forced the decision on German-style conscription, as the French general staff and government were likewise contemplating at that very same time.[27] His principal concerns rested on the successful movement of very large numbers of troops. Russia needed railroads—lots of railroads—into and within Poland. Initially, Obruchev insisted on four lines (see Map 1):

- Lukov to Ivangorod fortress (60 versts/64 kilometers);

- Novogeorgevsk fortress to Ivangorod then eastward to Zamost [Zamosc], with a branch to Piaska, through Kholm [Chelm] to Kovel (to connect to the Kiev-Brest line) (395 versts/419 kilometers);

- Ivangorod to Radom and to the border at Krakov [Cracow], with branches for coal transport (255 versts/270 kilometers);

- Liublin [Lublin] to Koliushka station (Lodz railway line) (235 versts/249 kilometers).[28]

These lines would interconnect the army's three routes from the heartland to the Vistula with the three secure Transvistulean bridge-heads (Warsaw, Ivangorod, Iozefov [Jósefów]). The empire would also gain a second operational line toward Krakov (in addition to the Chenstokhov [Czestochowa] line). Obruchev noted the vulnerability of two of the three main trunks into Poland (the St. Petersburg and Kiev lines), and argued vigorously for one more artery from central Russia into the salient (Briansk-Gomel-Mozyr-Pinsk-Brest, with end branches to Grodno and Rovno).[29] Finally, Obruchev advocated construction of secondary lines that would interconnect existing trunks: Vitebsk-Gomel (290 versts/315 kilometers), a Black Sea line (Perekop-Kherson-Odessa: 320 versts/350 kilometers), and three central Russian lines (Kursk-Voronezh, Khar'kov-Borisoglebsk, Nikitovka-Tsaritsyn, a total of 1,000 versts/1,090 kilometers). The minimum strategic railroad network that Obruchev proposed comprised 6,780 versts of additional construction (7,390 km), to be built over five years. His detailed elaboration of the army's railroad construction requirements served a number of purposes. As a reflection of his comprehensive argument on Russia's strategic position it mirrored his views on where and how the army would fight Germany and Austria. Indirectly, he hoped to use the study as a way to overcome extraministerial resistance to the minimal strategic railroad construction program drafted by the railroad commissions and committees in the 1860s. Finance minister Michael Reutern had worked hard to block expenditures since 1870.[30] Reutern thought that Poland, with its four main lines, was "in an incomparably more advantageous condition" than other areas of the empire. He felt that the fifty-three million rubles that the war ministry wanted for Polish development, a network that could not serve the Russian interior, was unjustifiable because the interior was "more important in economic terms and inevitably of strategic importance."[31] Obruchev was wise to seek directly the tsar's endorsement of his grander program, although he had yet to be disabused of his faith in the efficacy or permanence of any decision Alexander might make.

The question facing the government in the early 1870s was not one of limited construction capacity, but of the purpose that railroad construction would serve. Russia, in fact, was able to build an average of 7,900 versts (8,610 kilometers) each half decade between 1865 and 1875, so Obruchev was accurate to state that his plan fell within Russia's economic grasp.[32] As long as European Russia remained primarily an agricultural region, its western and southwestern provinces would generate the dominant portion of its foreign revenues. Furthermore, since the Crimean War, shifting trade patterns and transportation technology had supplanted the Mediterranean seaborne route with potentially far cheaper and swifter overland rail transportation. Development of the rail network in western Russia and Poland would thus have generated economic returns in the short term more rapidly than expenditure on interior infrastructure, although, as Reutern knew, the latter remained the sine qua non for any modern, industrial development of the state.[33]

Obruchev's final desideratum was fortress construction, again in Poland. Obruchev's (and Miliutin's) strategy for a future European conflict finally emerged in this section. Main Staff planners knew Russia could not close the technological lead that Germany held in mobilization (at least, not at a price the state could afford, and perhaps not ever). They also knew that the empire could not afford (and the tsar would not allow them) to trade most of tsarist Poland for the time necessary to complete mobilization, and their strategy had to reflect that imperative. Obruchev believed that construction of a semiporous system of frontier forts and rear citadels could break the momentum of an enemy assault. Russia would gain time to complete mobilization in secure areas, and then smash an exhausted invader hung up in the defensive works north and south of Warsaw.[34] Obruchev based the empire's salvation on three conditions: a massive army in Poland (dependent on universal military service), large-scale railroad construction (dependent on the tsar's generosity and patience with the construction program), and a strengthened fortress system (dependent on the finance ministry's largess for construction and reinforcement of those strategic points).

Miliutin anticipated the challenge that his staff's plan would encounter in the conference. Conference participants submitted numerous papers on various aspects of the agenda during the weeks before the meeting convened; without exception, their arguments missed the mark entirely concerning the questionable strategic solvency of the western borderlands. Grand Duke Nikolai Nikolaevich senior, commander of Guards units in the capital, submitted a verbose study which claimed that the problems of mobilization and deployment during a transition to war were simply a reflection of underdeveloped railroads. There was no reason to do away with the standing army or to introduce universal military service. In any case, he argued, the key to mobilization and concentration of the army was speed, which demanded that the mass of the army be kept on the Vistula.[35] Comments also came from General-Adjutant N. P. Ignat'ev (minister to the Porte) and from the western military district commanders. Absent from all these submissions was consideration of Russia's strategic, or even economic, condition. Absent also was any activity in the foreign ministry.

Neither Chancellor Gorchakov nor his more competent and energetic aides had bothered, by late January 1873, to make preparation for the conference. Miliutin, perhaps sensing the foreign minister's openness to suggestion, began to brief his colleague by highly classified correspondence, passing letters and reports from 23 January onward. The foreign minister was quite content to follow Miliutin's lead. To firmly establish in Gorchakov's and other participant's minds the war ministry's perspective, Miliutin transmitted copies of Obruchev's "Considerations" and noted that the concern of the tsar would be, first, "the measures necessary to strengthen our military posture" and, second, the sort of organization to give to the armed forces. Information contained in the Obruchev strategic study had to be kept "absolutely secret" and was only for the participants' "personal knowledge"; each recipient had to return his numbered copy to Miliutin for destruction.[36] A week later Miliutin fed the foreign minister a report from the Special Commission on Reorganization of Forces, which recommended adoption of universal military service for strategic and economic reasons, and from mid-

February until the start of the conference Gorchakov received a steady stream of Main Staff and war ministry information. How much of it he read is questionable; Gorchakov did not subsequently attend all sessions of the conference, and his presence left no mark on the meetings.[37] Miliutin sent along new estimates of the strategic situation in the Caucasus, bleak 1871 statistical tables of economic and military data demonstrating the comparative gaps between Russia and the North German Confederation, and reports on the Austrian threat to southwestern Russia.[38] Miliutin cultivated not only the foreign minister but also finance minister Reutern, who knew only too well the economic burden of the standing army.

Miliutin spent most of conference sessions defending the first decade of reform and ultimately secured the tsar's agreement to universal military service. There is no evidence to show how the meeting's other participants judged Obruchev's strategic memorandum, or whether they were even given it. Reutern, although a firm ally of Miliutin on the need for a conscript army, did not subsequently join the consensus on accelerated spending for railroad construction.[39] He overturned that consensus on strategic priorities immediately after the conference adjourned by appropriating the same tactic Obruchev had used. He argued directly to Alexander that Russia could not afford *even* the railroad program, much less Obruchev's program for fortresses, highways, and modernized small arms and artillery. Reutern secured the emperor's agreement to cap war ministry budgets for the first time since the beginning of the reforms. Strategic railroad construction immediately slowed as Alexander displayed the same lack of perseverance in his economic commitment to the strategic problem as he had shown toward tradition when he chose Obruchev's and Miliutin's strategic arguments over the more congenial and conservative advice of his uncle. Fuller argues that the conference approved the Obruchev/Miliutin strategic plan, while Zaionchkovskii's account indicates debate focused on army organization, the quality of its manpower, and the cost of its reorganization.[40] What was the significance of these two decisions, and what was the impact of subsequent fiscal constraints on each?

The process of *preparation* for the conference gave Obruchev (through his work with VUK) an opportunity to choose Russia's strategic priorities as he saw them. The tsar validated those priorities and also, all would have assumed, supported the steps necessary to put them into effect for the defense of Poland and western Russia. Within months, however, Reutern's argument in favor of budgetary restraint convinced the staff's strategic visionaries that they would never see their strategic plan realized. The war ministry instead struggled *inter pares* for every kopec it thought it needed for rearmament and railroad construction. Withdrawal of budgetary support at the moment of nascent Russian strategic imagination underlined two facts for Obruchev and Miliutin. First, Russia alone would never find the resources to defend itself against united Germany; neither its economy nor its unstable policy apparatus could sustain decades-long commitment to a single, essential purpose. Second, no one in government—not in the other ministries nor among the most senior officers around the throne, nor even the tsar—had the capacity to appreciate Russia's desperate strategic position and act to salvage the empire's position in Europe. The fate of the decision on universal military service was somewhat happier. Insofar as the tsar's approval of the war ministry proposal apparently required merely a new law, the road was essentially open to implement the decision. The summer saw further subaltern struggle around the content of the imperial *ustav* for conscription, but fiscal expense would subsequently affect only the *size* of the new army, not the structure or its recruitment.[41]

The conference, despite its usefulness to military reform in general, became the first occasion for Obruchev to consider an "arrangement" with France. Obruchev's plan had depended on railroad development in western Russia and Poland, so he was without question disappointed by the exchequer's (and the tsar's) unwillingness to shore up the empire's security. Russia's "window of vulnerability," however, existed merely within the context of its neighbors' *potential*, not their intentions. Forty years later, after most of Obruchev's plan was either in place or superseded, Russia went to war with Germany and Austria. Yet, at the moment when Russia was most vulnerable and Germany at its greatest relative advantage, there existed almost no possibility of conflict between the two imperial powers. Only in the minds of specialists who examined potential instead of intentions did the possibility exist.

Another alternative to careful strategic planning and rational investment in the empire's security was to act in the face of political and strategical reality, or, as one scholar put it, to resort to "magic." Russia's military "technologists," who relied on modern systems to solve their strategic problems, were distinct from its "magicians," those who saw the answers to basic military troubles in the esprit of sturdy, long-enduring *muzhiki-soldat*. Every state, of course, invested its soldiery with the spiritual, transcendent superiority that was part of the esprit that senior officers also shared.[42] Other descriptions of this distinction, such as Von Wahlde's "academics" (i.e., Westernizers) and "nationalists" (Slavophiles),[43] are not without merit. That distinction, by 1873 already a decade in development, was between those who found salvation in the martial spirit ("nationalists") and those who embraced science ("academics"). In any case, the existence of some philosophical cleavage is unchallengeable even if its character is unclear.

How do we know that the conference fundamentally interrupted the direction of the staff's strategic philosophy? First, because after March 1873 there were organizational changes that made the Main Staff look and operate like a strategic planning body instead of merely a collection of military information bureaus. General staff specialists threw themselves into new lines of planning activity, and the Main Staff's planning sections underwent rapid growth and reorganization. These changes marked the staff's adaptation to the dictates of scientific work and rising labor specialization. The changes were also consistent with an organizational shift toward "deep future–oriented" strategic thinking in accord with Obruchev's agenda. Yet even in early 1873 this new thinking remained restricted to a small circle of officers. Within two months of the conference, the tsar's close friend General-Adjutant Count F. F. Berg, the commander of Warsaw Military District, accompanied his master to Berlin, where he and Moltke promptly crafted an agreement that promised significant military assistance if one or the other party were attacked. Berg, a participant in the secret strategic conference, certainly knew the organizational objections to his "pet project," a Russo-German dynastic and military alignment. His agreement with Moltke, had it not been defanged by Bismarck, also might have forestalled Obruchev's reshaping of Russian strategic orientation. Without doubt, Berg's initiative began decades of divergence among St. Petersburg war planners, the foreign policy establishment, and the dynasty on the control of Russia's security.[44]

Beyond the politics of diplomacy, the 1870s witnessed Russian staff officers *for the first time* displaying real direction in their activity, and particularly of the strategic basis of their works. Internal vision of men like Obruchev had been alloyed with external influences. The work demonstrated this consciousness routinely in the introductory background to their planning studies. Russia had emerged from its self-imposed international isolation during the 1870–1873 crisis of direction. The planners' consciousness of purpose converged with development of an institutional memory in political-strategic matters. General staff planners began to share a common work culture, of ways of doing work and thinking about basic problems, that materialized clearly after the 1873 conference. German unification, coupled with evolution of a scientific attitude among younger general staff officers, established hospitable conditions for a fuller maturation of strategic thought and planning after the emperor accepted Obruchev's "Considerations." The key remained, as before, accurate information—statistics, but increasingly also espionage—to move the planning process forward. Obruchev's system then lacked only some basic tools that would be of German origin to fulfill the potential of the new staff and make a mark on Russia's military problems.

Reading a Gentlemen's Mail: Strategic Intelligence

Elevation of unified Germany to a place of honor in the Main Staff's survey of Russia's strategic landscape, on the basis of its imputed capacity to do Russia harm, imposed on military planners an imperative to acquire knowledge of foreign *intentions* rather than simply capabilities and potential. In certain instances, the Military-Scientific Committee (which directed military intelligence within the ministry) developed its own sources: before the Russo-Turkish war in 1876, general staff officers were particularly active and effective in clandestine reconnaissance of the theater of operations, as well as in foreign capitals from Vienna southward. Typically, though, Miliutin relied on the foreign ministry's remarkably sophisticated cryptoanalytic capabilities to stay apprised of the most sensitive foreign developments.[45]

By 1868 at the latest, the war and foreign ministries routinely exchanged reports and documents of mutual interest. Russian military attachés (almost all of whom were General Staff-designees) answered to the war ministry (to Miliutin, by way of the ministry chancellery), and political reports from ambassadors went to Nikolai K. Giers in the foreign ministry. The war ministry itself possessed no routine channels for communications with its diplomatic agents; its requests to overseas missions seem inevitably to have passed through the foreign ministry.[46]

The foreign ministry's code-breaking capability during these decades was surely unrivaled in Europe. The Germans were bitterly aware of it: Bismarck's fulminations in 1876 against the kaiser's special envoy to Alexander for his incautious use of enciphered telegrams from the Crimea is well known. In fact, foreign ministry code breakers read almost all foreign diplomatic traffic *into and out of St. Petersburg*, as well as almost everything that passed over wires crossing Russian territory to third states. The ministry's agents occasionally picked through embassy garbage cans (in Russia and in foreign capitals) to pilfer working copies of documents from their foreign originators.[47] British and German communications appear to have been particularly susceptible to compromise, while Austria's and Sweden's rarely appeared before Giers. Foreign communications to Constantinople yielded perhaps a half dozen intercepts daily by the early 1870s, and Russians routinely read London's messages to its mission in Beijing. Foreign powers understood, of course, the importance of cable security; some changed their ciphers as frequently as monthly, an occurrence the foreign ministry's cryptographic technicians duly noted on the first communiqué in the newly broken code!

The foreign and war ministries appreciated Britain's isolation from November 1873 onward during the heightening Khivan crisis. Absenting local observers, foreign secretary Granville in London had to rely on Loftus, his minister in Petersburg, for information on the crisis. Like Gorchakov and Giers, Loftus depended on Russian press reports for information of the massacres by Turkoman insurgents and the refugees flooding into Orenburg. St. Petersburg's simultaneous insight into Europe's detachment from Britain's Central Asian dilemma did nothing to slow General Kaufman's advance over the next two years.[48]

The difficulty of using secret knowledge is only too apparent from the history of foreign ministry bumbling and disengagement. A state whose diplomatic establishment was more activist and purposeful might have found far greater advantage in such knowledge, as in fact the Asiatic Desk of the foreign ministry inevitably did, when left to its own devices. Giers alone selected which data should be shared with the war ministry, and he made his selections in a somewhat haphazard way. The absence of established patterns of information sharing renders judgment of the influence on military planning of Russia's strategic intelligence successes problematic. In any case, during Miliutin's tenure (until 1881) probably he alone consumed these foreign ministry reports rather than sharing them routinely with his planners or VUK. Insofar as the minister had arrogated strategic planning virtually entirely to VUK, Obruchev's ignorance of international diplomatic developments must be considered the single greatest failure of the Russian strategic planning apparatus after 1870. In fairness to Obruchev, however, without a sufficiently large and competent body of assistants on which to rely, he could not have taken on the added duty of senior political-military intelligence analyst for the Russian empire. His day-to-day preoccupations were far more mundane, but from a military point of view they were indispensable.

Coup d'Oeil Afoot: Staff Rides

Staff rides occupied an intermediary place in the spectrum of staff readiness training, somewhere between a staff exercise *en cabinet* and a field war game with participating forces; they were also part of the advanced practicum of staff officer training, a component of advanced military education.[49] In character, as an extension of three decades of military statistical practice, they also occupied a special place in the general staff's transition from an information-processing organization to an intelligence-processing body. The ride was quintessentially a Prussian institution, crucial to the development of war plans, the selection and promotion of "rising stars" among young general staff officers, and the qualification of all staff officers for their duties. All of this was clear enough to Obruchev by 1873[50] for him to prescribe annual rides for Main Staff officers and to participate annually as a leader. Those rides took place in the western provinces, and involved groups of general staff officers from St. Petersburg and the district staffs, students from the academy, and selected line officers who showed talent for higher military planning work.[51] Russian rides were never a part of the war game *(Kriegspiel)* system, as Prussia's were, which integrated staff solutions of real and hypothetical problems with horseback fieldwork and examination of historical battlefields for their tactical significance. Obruchev's rides consistently had objectives of both scientific (cartographic and topographic) and strategic (reconnaissance) importance.

This *applied* approach to exercises paralleled Obruchev's advice to Miliutin (contra Leer) to press the technical and practical aspects of general staff academy curriculum rather than the universalist, tertiary syllabus that would have turned the academy into a "military university."[52]

Obruchev led the first of 1875's three strategic reconnaissances, and district staffs carried out numerous other local reconnaissances.[53] The three strategic rides had parties of eighteen to forty officers: the "General Staff" group under Obruchev; the Warsaw Military District party under chief of staff Prince Imeretinskii; and the Odessa Military District officers under chief of staff Major General Iakov Semenovich Krzhivoblotskii and the commander of the Fourteenth Infantry Division, Major-General Mikhail Dragomirov. Each ride followed a pattern of preparation, reconnaissance, and evaluation. The pattern rather than the detail of those rides remains of interest because it was thereafter repeated annually up to the Great War.

The preparation phase in 1875 involved strategic and military studies by the rides' participants, and examination of the cartographic data (especially for any lacunae in the records), that lasted two to four weeks. Reconnaissances organized by a district included preparatory excursions of small groups to review particular military sites (bivouac, forage, etc.) or potential march routes. Districts might also review the *Military-Statistical Survey* data for their area and prepare new studies to update the information on hand. After the 1875 rides the leaders all recommended that preparatory work start during the preceding autumn *at the latest*. Otherwise, shortages of satisfactory maps and want of existing information (surveys, strategic studies, deployment inventories) could not be made up during the short time before a ride began.[54]

The ride occurred in phases. For district staffs the first stage might be a local war game: the district staff presented a scenario reflecting actual resources and enemy intentions within the assigned area. The participants examined their mobilization plans in light of the scenario and made modifications to account for the exercise's unexpected circumstances. A couple weeks of tactical and operational analysis and planning allowed participants to calculate troop march rates and prepare schedules for force concentration at the best sites for initial engagement with the enemy. The ride leaders and their assistants, acting as referees, drafted the party's route for fieldwork, and the groups then took to horseback.[55] In the field the parties examined sequentially the routes and sites of battles that they had considered during the war game, over the course of a week and a half or more. The fieldwork concluded with another week and a half of tactical exercises under the direct supervision of the officer leading the staff reconnaissance ride.

Obruchev's party, made up of officers from the Main Staff and the Artillery and Engineering Main Directorates, was somewhat different. Its objective was simply to familiarize itself with the area in which the most important battles of the "next war" would first occur. Between 25 May and 20 June, Obruchev's group examined the entire front area between the Novogeorgevsk citadel, north of Warsaw, and Grodno, a vulnerable railroad hub to the northeast. These were not pleasant day trips, punctuated by jolly evenings in tavern or casern. For the first half of the period, the party split into two groups, which scouted each side of the Narev River and its tributaries. Obruchev then personally led his entire detachment (eighteen officers, including two general officers) into and around the swamps in the vicinity of Shafranka and at the confluence of the Bobr (Biebrza) and Netta Rivers.[56]

In general, staff rides resulted in three sorts of documents. First, and least often, the leader might compose an important strategic reevaluation of the area reconnoitered. Obruchev drafted three such reports after his ride, and those ended on the war minister's desk. More often, the party would identify major errors in the district's statistical (intelligence) resources, or in maps that could be turned over to the district staff or the Military-Topographical Section for resolution. The problem of representational data—maps, geodesic data, information on roadways and railroad routes—plagued Russian military work well into the 1880s, and the annual staff rides went a long way toward identifying where the gaps lay. Finally, the ride leader's evaluation of the party's performance affected the way the staff conducted subsequent rides and reconnaissances. The first year, for instance, it was clear that logistics officers gained nothing from participation in the ride; they were subsequently dropped from the field portion.

Rides organized for line officers by district staffs generally included no period of preparatory or staff work, such as examination of existing strategic studies and mobilization plans. The parties were usually much larger (thirty to fifty officers, mainly from infantry regiments), and they lasted only ten days to two weeks.[57] These rides, if less rigorous in their preparation, nevertheless gave a select group of line officer (few from

Guards regiments) a useful dose of tactical training, and the leaders of the group were always general staff–qualified district staff officers. It is impossible to say whether those participants, who usually were junior captains and senior lieutenants, were already in line to enter the general staff academy, although that might be a reasonable assumption. Their number *did* include officers of the academy who, during their summers, were assigned to line regiments for just this sort of training.

Obruchev considered the annual rides of such importance that, even in the midst of preparation for war during the summer of 1876, he led another reconnaissance of the right flank of the Polish salient in May.[58] Apparently 1877 was not a good year for staff rides (almost the entire Main Staff was supporting operations in the Balkans, either in theater or from St. Petersburg), but the following year, even as the army began demobilization, the rides resumed.[59] The rides in 1878 and 1879, however, were limited in scope and participation. The most surprising conclusion of those postwar rides was that officers, many recently returned from Bulgarian battlefields, had no idea about how a staff officer should read a map or use cartographic materials for orientation or navigation. One evaluator wrote that most of the fieldwork was of barely any use.[60] Russia's combat-experienced junior officers were clearly of low technical or professional competence; their platoon and company leadership abilities could hardly have inspired much confidence among the ranks. But the real problem with Russia's system of rides was their limited reach: perhaps one hundred officers a year might sharpen their tactical and operational coup d'oeil, out of an officer corps that numbered more than twenty thousand,[61] and the "tsar's colonels" were few and far between.

Maneuvers and Field Exercises

The Russian imperial army's practice of field maneuvers and tactical exercise had a more direct influence on the army's combat readiness than any other factor. Only peacetime practice of the activity of war could give unit leaders and troops some expectation of success in the unfavorable circumstances of battle. With pathetically few exceptions, however, Russia's army occupied itself with economic pursuits, controlling civil unrest, drunkenness, and card games; practice of tactical doctrine was an afterthought. A variety of field exercises did occur, if aperiodically, at most levels of command. The multiplicity of forms in orchestration, purpose, and extent defied systematic regulation even by the Main Staff. Like much else in Russia's army after 1870, the philosophy and practice of field exercises were under close scrutiny and criticism. Some Main Staff officers took the problem of tactical incompetence seriously, as an adjunct to the activities of both the academy and the staff, and proposed or introduced innovations to raise tactical consciousness in the field army.[62]

Before 1855, the "Emperor" (or "Great") maneuvers principally satisfied Nicholas I and the adjutants who constituted his circle; only select units participated, and there could be no practical value in those stylized field quadrilles. Alexander II perpetuated the tradition, but larger and more complex exercises that involved maneuvers by opposing forces gradually eclipsed the Tsarskoe Selo parade ground shuffle. Particularly in the Polish salient, annual maneuvers became a fixture of military district summer activity, and they were joined each year by the emperor. The "Emperor" maneuver itself, by the mid-1870s, no longer resembled Nicholas's bucolic picnic gatherings but instead encompassed thousands of acres of countryside south and west of Krasnoe Selo. All these changes arose from a vague combination of imposed regulation, local inspiration, and universal encouragement. By the 1890s, exercises could involve two army commanders (military district commanders) who tested their (and the Main Staff's) assumptions about the problems of mobilization, concentration, and first engagements in a European war. This sort of fieldwork was possible in the 1880s in the frontier districts.[63]

After the German success of 1870–1871, virtually all European armies adopted (to a greater or lesser degree) the Prussian system of training maneuvers. In Russia that transition began even earlier, after the Crimean War, because the Russians had not only the benefit of foreign thought on the matter but also the imperative of their own recent abysmal performance.[64] During the 1870s the Main Staff dramatically expanded the Krasnoe Selo maneuver area near St. Petersburg for the purpose of accommodating larger units (on the scale of corps versus corps) for annual maneuvers. Some general staff officers also sought to place handbooks or planning guides into the hands of unit commanders, to decentralize responsibility for troop combat readiness, and to introduce necessary local flavor into exercises. By the 1880s general staff officers had developed an interest in the technique of effective field training of forces, which elevated the quality of their increasingly sophisticated guidebooks.[65]

In 1882 a plan for annual infantry exercises came into effect.[66] The plan did nothing to ensure that low-level tactical training would be effective, but it demonstrated the Main Staff's insistence on at least minimal training requirements down to the company level. Through an accumulating series of unit exercises, from the level of company through battalion to regiment, the plan guaranteed every infantryman thirty-five days of marksmanship training per year, a week of range estimation practice (*glazomernyi opredelenie*), nineteen days of small-unit and battalion tactics (unopposed), and nine days of battalion and regimental tactics (two-sided, or opposed). The plan directed formal training in these and other skill for 52 days per year at company level, another 38 days at battalion level, and 13 in regimental groupings (a total of 103 days per year).[67] The authors emphasized not only the skills associated with attack and defense but also individual *glazomer*, range estimation, and exercises to develop unit cohesion, cooperation, and coordination.[68] The formal training requirement was merely preparation for additional, unregulated maneuvers and exercises for which the Main Staff issued a circular and a guidebook in 1884.[69] The plan's promise, however, rested on the willingness of commanders to prepare for the training and to see each stage of the plan through to completion.

Obruchev insisted also on the value of very large scale exercises that, realistically speaking, trained only staffs and commanders. Such maneuvers took place about every two years and involved forces from at least two military districts. In 1876 and again in 1882, Russia's summer maneuvers grew to include division-sized formations of cavalry and up to four corps-sized formations (with about forty thousand men in each corps). The Pereiaslavl maneuvers in 1882 began with six corps, a scale one German observer thought impractical in peacetime (because of interference with commerce, a concern that would hardly have bothered Obruchev). The purpose of large-scale maneuvers was not to train troops or junior officers but to provide brigade, division, and corps commanders (and, more important, their staff officers) a taste of the difficulty of handling mass armies in the field, or carrying out planned actions in the "fog of war."[70] Once higher staffs instituted a system of thorough reporting and evaluation of exercise results (which did not happen until the mid-1880s), the large-scale maneuver also provided important data on the reliability of a staff's planning assumptions.

In 1886, summer maneuvers took place in every military district except Irkutsk and Priamur, and for the first time in Turkestan and Omsk. Combined arms (infantry, cavalry, artillery) characterized the exercises throughout Europe and the Caucasus, and the maneuvers included large-scale cavalry formations (division or larger) at thirteen sites. A German observer noted that most of the exercise fields were in the vicinity of permanent caserns (of which forty-five existed in 1886). Only in Moscow and Kazan districts did forces operate away from their permanent camps, which exposed those units to unfamiliar terrain—and lots of marching.[71] The same observer estimated that three-quarters of all infantry and cavalry (including reserves) and four-fifths of Russia's artillery participated in the summer maneuvers.

These training and maneuver periods continued in 1888, with the largest gathering near Elizavetsgrad, where about 120,000 men and 450 guns from Odessa and Khar'kov districts exercised. In 1890, in Volhynia, forces under Generals Gurko and Dragomirov (commanders of the Warsaw and Kiev districts) met in relative secrecy to play out the Russian plan for a first engagement with Austria in the Kovel-Lutsk-Dubno area. The exercise's objective was the precise execution of a plan of concentration and engagement (as the ubiquitous German observer described it).[72] By 1891 troops from seventy-four caserns participated in exercises and maneuvers, and the majority spent at least part of their time in unfamiliar terrain instead of on home operating ground. About 80 percent of all Russian reserve battalions participated with their parent regiments. Overall levels of unit participation were reported by the same German observer. He also noted that, because of Russian budget shortfalls, the railroads would be used only for units at greatest distance from the exercise areas; other troops would arrive on foot (Table 4.2).

Although individual general staff officers understood the importance of small-unit tactical training, the focus of senior officers of the Main Staff was clearly on the large-scale maneuver, because only there could the plans hatched in St. Petersburg and on district staffs be tested. That pattern was established in the 1870s, long before the Main Staff had learned to craft a viable mobilization schedule. The experience of these activities offered Obruchev's planners refreshment of a sense of geographic dimension and space, and a refinement of their sense of time

Table 4.2. 1891 Field Maneuver Participation (by district)

District	Battalions (%)	Squadrons (%)	Batteries (%)
St. Petersburg	74	96	100
Vilna	95.1	100	100
Warsaw	100	98.7	100
Kiev	96.6	99.1	96
Odessa	86	97.8	76.5
Moscow	100	100	66

Source: W., "Die russischen Sommerübungen im laufenden Jahre," *Internationale Revue über die gesammten Armeen und Flotten,* 9, no. 4 (July–September, 1891): 1007–1016.

and movement within that space. Without those imaginative senses, the military experts with the Main Staff and key military district staffs could not have undertaken the abstract estimations involved in mobilization scheduling.

Form Follows Function: New Organs

It was fortunate for Russia that Main Staff officers developed in the 1870s new planning competency more rapidly than their organization responded structurally to those needs. When the staff arrived at mid-decade, its planning specialists had worked for a few years to Obruchev's strategic agenda. But the expertise that men like Colonels Georgii Bobrikov, Filadel'f Velichko, Pavel Lobko, and Fedor Fel'dman acquired came within essentially the same organization that Miliutin had formed ten years earlier. The tasks created as a result of Obruchev's work on the 1873 secret conference had accelerated the pace of change for staff officers. When rebellion disturbed the Balkans in 1875, the staff scrambled to put in place ad hoc groups devoted solely to mobilization preparations. Up to then, VUK had gradually streamlined the established bureaucratic structure and established interdisciplinary study groups of experts drawn from throughout the organization to address some of the narrowly technical questions. By the mid-1870s the permanent departmental offices served virtually as adjuncts to the various committees and commissions, where the real power lay in matters of planning and strategy. This method of organizational reform—periodic refinement of the structure by creation of specialized, ad hoc committees and commissions—persisted until the turn of the century.[73]

This system could not, of course, operate as efficiently or effectively as the Prussian-German staff system that it increasingly mirrored in responsibility but not in authority or structure. However, to assume that the Main Staff needed a "European-style . . . mandate, stature, and complement" (as one scholar put it) in order to be effective[74] places an inappropriate yardstick against the organization's performance. Probably more so than the German body, the Russian staff reacted to the vision and will of just a few senior staff officers; at least in the 1870s there was no consistent "staff culture" animating planners throughout the organization.

From its re-creation in late 1865 the Main Staff had two principal departments (I and II *Otdeleniia*) concerned with the forces and with planning; it retained both until 1900. There also were four departments involved in personnel, accounting, and records, which are of no interest to this account. Within the two principal departments, no division survived unmolested in the course of the following three decades of change. Until 1876, officers assigned to I Department ("for organization of forces") attended to a wide variety of chores: organization of the army, its combat readiness, composition and structure of unit staffs, inspection of units, equipment, unit histories, religious instruction. As part of the general reorganization of 1875–1877, those various tasks were categorized and divided among seven desks (*stoly*) in the new structure.

The II Department handled the "disposition, transportation, and training of forces." Its range of responsibilities encompassed almost the entire mobilization process. The II Department's divisions investigated and reported on military roads and deployment sites, charted staging areas and quarters, and handled correspondence on selected fortress locations. Those sections supported most of the special committees of the Main Staff that were (or soon would be) in existence—Committees on the Direction of Lines of Communications, on Tactics, on Transportation of Forces by Railroad and Military Highways, and, most important of all, for Mobilization of Forces. From 1867 the department had a four-section structure to oversee administrative support of forces (First Desk), issuance of orders and commands to forces (Second Desk), force movement by railroad (Third Desk), and transportation by waterway (Fourth Desk). In 1877 the third section surrendered its railroad transportation tasks to the fourth section and took on the pressing responsibility for all army tactical training. The fourth section became the Main Staff's principal office for mobilization and transportation of forces, a role it continued to fill for another decade. The matrix on which all these offices fed—military statistics—made them foremost consumers of *intelligence*, which brought them into conformity with supreme military staffs everywhere as they exist to this day. In this schema, it is no surprise that the Military-Scientific Committee, which governed the gamut of statistical (i.e., intelligence) work for the ministry, received virtually all its support from II Department.

VUK spawned the Committee for Preparation of Measures for Mobilization of Forces (or simply, the Mobilization Committee) on 23 June 1875. That body was one of the organizational innovations logically necessitated by the 1873 strategic conference; the reason it took two years to create is a mystery.[75] The mobilization committee drew personnel from VUK, the main directorates *(Glavnye upravlenie)*, and the war ministry. Its broad charter was to examine combat readiness and prepare measures for placing the army on a wartime footing.[76] Hardly had its deliberations begun on the questions raised in Obruchev's 1872 memoranda, than its energies shifted decisively southwestward: the Balkans.

5

The Main Staff Plans a War

The first trial of Russia's new and "modern" war planning system arose in 1876, when Obruchev's colonels considered the possibility of war in the Balkans. The general staff's performance during those months of planning accounts better than anything else for the latitude extended to its strategic planning apparatus during the following decades. The story of the staff's brilliant performance (to use the emperor's words) also bears signs of a war planning system run amok, a "loose cannon" on the deck of the Russian ship of state. Preparation for a war with Turkey, begun in late 1875 as little more than a staff exercise, had gathered sufficient momentum by mid-1876 to offer Russia's political leaders real military choices in their policy toward the Ottoman Empire. But as the staff ordered more and more regiments to "reinforced" strength that summer and fall, the momentum of Obruchev's war preparations outran the diplomatic conditions on which his plan explicitly rested. Without Austrian complicity, a rapid Russian offensive to Constantinople would be impossible, something on which the staff and foreign ministry agreed. The alternative—a revival of the Crimean system—had to be avoided at all cost. But war preparation had its own logic and schedule. Obruchev urged no delay in mobilization once the army's preparations could proceed no further, even in the absence of an Austrian agreement. Alexander's rejection in October 1876 of hastiness merely postponed the military solution until the next spring. The experience of 1876 subsequently opened a chasm between the Main Staff's purely military considerations and the state's political interests, an un-bridgeable abyss that widened after the treaties of San Stefano (1877) and Berlin (1878). Within two years of war's end the Main Staff turned its gaze back toward Prussia and applied there the tools of planning it had honed in the Balkan war, but not only without consideration of political concerns. It also consciously searched for ways to exclude auto-cratic intrusions from its planning.

The 1875 Balkan Crisis: Background

Insurrection against Ottoman rule in the Balkans dated to the begin-ning of the century, but Italy's risorgimento inspired a more threatening brand of unrest: the demand for autonomy or independence from Otto-man rule among educated nationalists in Bucharest, Sofia, and other urban centers. In the course of an unsuccessful Cretan uprising, the peninsular dominions of Turkey conspired and agitated from 1866 and 1868 for a general uprising against the Porte.[1] Serbian Prince Michael Obrenovic's territorial interests under those secret agreements became explicit in a military agreement with Greece in early 1868. They en-compassed annexation of Bosnia and Herzegovina and rendered Serbia as unsavory a neighbor to other south Slavs as local Turkish administra-tors had been. After 1868 Michael's successor, Milan, opposed the influential political forces in Serbia that embraced a visionary and mes-sianic Serbian mission in the Balkans, a mission that domestic revolu-tionaries and foreign agitators encouraged.

For Russia, a growing interest in Balkan politics grew naturally from its enduring engagement at the Porte. The tsar's minister to Constanti-nople, N. P. Ignat'ev (1864–1876), took an active (if not entirely per-ceptive) role in the Serb-Greek-Montenegrian negotiations in 1867, and he entreated tirelessly and successfully at the Porte for creation of a Bulgarian exarchate. At least since Catherine's time, St. Petersburg had found the appeal to confessional politics a useful tool in its policy to-ward Constantinople; confessionalism also played a central role first in the politics of the Slavophiles and then in the transnational philosophy of the Pan-Slavs. Yet for the government (the foreign ministry's Asiatic Desk notably excepted) the question of the Straits—not the liberation of southern Slavic nationalities—was the first interest of state. If the

Russians anticipated south Slav liberation, it was under the leadership of Russia, not on the initiative of those peoples themselves.[2]

The outbreak of insurrection in Bosnia and Herzegovina in 1875 was due less to Ignat'ev's machinations than to the policies of Austria's leaders; in this, the Dual Monarchy's impenetrable domestic politics were decisive. But above the interests of particular social groups, Austria's general staff remained a consistent advocate for annexations behind Dalmatia (i.e., Bosnia and Herzegovina), a strategic necessity if the Adriatic coastal strip were to be made defensible. Ultimately, the annexationists outweighed foreign minister Andrassy, whose intention (as a Magyar) was to incorporate no more Slavs into the monarchy's patchwork quilt. With encouragement from his military suite, Emperor Franz Joseph made a month-long journey along the Turkish border of his Dalmatian territory in early 1875 and inspired various, principally Catholic, delegations from surrounding areas to consider the monarchy their salvation. The uprising began in July, and (Serbo-Croat) Austrian officials in Dalmatia provided rebels and refugees both shelter and support.

Failure of mediation efforts by the consuls of all the European powers in Herzegovina, and the sultan's refusal to contemplate more than pro forma reforms (December 1875) led Andrassy to prepare a diplomatic note insisting on thoroughgoing reforms, to which all other powers subscribed. The Porte accepted it almost completely, but the insurgents rejected it because it did not include foreign guarantee of reform. Austria's and Russia's foreign policy establishments understood that resolution of the crisis was, at least for the time being, still theirs to guide. All powers apparently appreciated the importance of avoiding any *unilateral* intervention, annexations, or territorial changes. On the other hand, potential for a *negotiated* Austrian and Russian occupation of Bosnia-Herzegovina and Bessarabia, respectively—that is, a final resolution to the crisis and the whole Eastern Question—did not displease either Berlin or London.

By February 1876 Bismarck saw his disengagement challenged by the apparent failure of the Andrassy Note, and before any other statesman he took steps to head off a collision of Russian and Austrian interests, in spite of their fleeting intimacy over the problem. And if Bismarck feared that intimacy, as Langer put it, he doubly feared their falling out.[3] He understood that British engagement might forestall

Russian intervention and help moderate any French policy counter to Germany's interest. The plan he proposed to London was simply joint sponsorship of comprehensive reforms, and acquiescence to Russian and Austrian intervention if the Porte rejected those reforms. If England agreed to this solution, then Russia could also be convinced; Austria would consequently have no choice but to give its assent also. The proposal received full backing of the British ambassador in Berlin (Russell), the queen, the prime minister (Disraeli), but not the foreign minister (Derby), and there the plan foundered.

The uprising became terribly brutal in early spring of 1876. In Constantinople, reform elements gained strength, and the sultan was overthrown as a pawn of foreign powers (most notably, of Ignat'ev). Sentiment against gratuitous meddling of outsiders led to savage and unrestrained repression of a revolution in Bulgaria, the infamous "horrors." Foreign ministers of the three empires, meanwhile, met in Berlin in early May and produced a memorandum that elaborated Andrassy's earlier note, with calls for an immediate armistice (and veiled threats of "efficacious measures" should the armistice produce no compromise). Britain would have no truck with the memo, however, because it was so apparently in favor of the insurgents. Bismarck was exasperated but not entirely displeased; Gorchakov was enraged and threatened to stand aside to allow the uprisings to take their course—something that Disraeli, too, was content to do that summer (probably knowing it would break up the Russian-Austrian cooperative). The Serbs, after an unsuccessful proposal to the Porte for Serbian absorption of Bosnia to solve the crisis, declared war on Turkey at the end of June 1876.

The Historical Problem of 1876

Literature on Russia's drift toward war from mid-1876 to April 1877 falls generally under this paradigm: Russian diplomatic caution was overcome by public agitation that provoked a war for which the army had not prepared. Following a long summer of European discussions on the Eastern crisis, Alexander II declared partial mobilization of the Russian army on 1/13 November 1876.[4] Until that date (and thereafter as well), Russia's senior diplomats had believed that war with the Ottoman Empire could be avoided. Popular opinion, however, was not so sanguine. The collapse of Serbian forces defending the Djunis Heights at the end of October 1876 not only opened the way for Turkish occupation of Belgrade but also resulted in heavy losses among Russian army volunteers fighting with the Serbs. Serbian resistance collapsed. Russian patriotic fervor, in favor of intervention, had voices in the press and within the court and provided momentum to portions of Russia's diplomacy. Nevertheless, Gorchakov continued to parley with Western governments to shape a pacific solution. The highest policy-making circles mirrored these incongruous interests, from those in favor of war for reasons of honor and Slavdom, to those against because of the likely catastrophic economic and diplomatic consequences, with some torn by both perspectives.

Only in late September 1876, according to the best scholarship,[5] did the Russian army begin serious work on a plan of operations, in the event that diplomacy should fail. Soon after the Djunis debacle, the tsar put in motion the Main Staff's hastily crafted plan for army mobilization. In November 1876 the army made its preparations for the war, which finally came on 31 March/12 April 1877 after a final round of diplomacy failed to prevent war. The collapse in July 1877 of the army's offensive outside of Plevna [Pleven] merely reflected the shortcomings of the military establishment, as well as its ill-conceived and unrealistic expectation of a quick war.[6]

This paradigm, however, is thoroughly mistaken on at least its account of the Main Staff's war planning in 1876, and on the quality of the work. Previous misjudgment of the staff's activities masks its responsibility for making war possible in the first place, as well as its subsequent rise in stature, competence, and independence as a result of its experience. The Main Staff's sequestered activities provided the mechanism to turn policy into military action (a universally acknowledged possibility from the beginning of the crisis), as well as the knowledge to impart caution to foreign policy if it threatened to go beyond the state's means. The work of these men, although not quite ignored by earlier chroniclers of the war,[7] has hitherto been examined only as a technical adjunct of Russian policy rather than as an integral part of the crisis's dénouement. Diplomatic actors were aware of the imminence of war *throughout 1876*, although their activities probed for an escape. Every senior person in the government in 1876 had lived through the Crimean War a mere twenty years earlier. The danger of confrontation with a European coalition formed a living part of the entire government's memory, regardless of the belligerency or caution of its members individually. Thus, the conventional wisdom (according to one controversial formulation) that Pan-Slavic zealots in the emperor's entourage successfully pushed war deliberations toward crusading activism does not stand under closer examination.[8] From where, then, did the foreign ministry's confidence come, that allowed its representatives to demand the virtual surrender of Ottoman sovereignty without concession or concern for sensitivities of other European powers? Through what assurance did the government free itself from anxiety for the state's security (*tout le Monde contre nous*, as Germany's ambassador characterized the Russian government's spirit)? An illusion of security through military readiness and preparation is what the Main Staff's planners provided.

The Main Staff's assurance came much earlier than the summer or fall of 1876; in fact, it was available even in the spring of that year. War planning offered a compelling, rationalized agenda for diplomatic and political measures in the absence of a coherent war-avoidance policy. A crisis with foreseeable military consequences, such as Russia found itself in by 1876, demanded that policy at least have a dialogue with military "considerations." It was this dialogue, to which Obruchev and his staff officers contributed one voice, that allowed Russian foreign policy to find its logical outcome in 1877.

Dusting Off the Plans

The Main Staff's post-Crimean involvement in the Eastern Question did not begin with the crisis of 1876. A decade earlier, a young junior secretary of VUK had submitted a memorandum to the war minister on strategic and military considerations in the event of war with Turkey. Obruchev's September 1866 memo sketched out Russia's "closely interrelated political and strategic objectives," should war with the Ottoman empire come. Obruchev's assumption was that the seizure of the Straits (the only military objective imagined at the time) could best be assured by winning the trust of Balkan states along the Black Sea littoral. That might be achieved by setting as Russia's war aim the liberation of Balkan peoples from Turkish oppression. Subsequently if, "before the walls of Constantinople, the Russian army meets the vanguard of an Anglo-French force, then [our army] will not meet it alone, but shoulder to shoulder with all the liberated peoples."[9]

The limits of Obruchev's political perception are clear from his formulation of Russian interests and methods at the Straits. First, the implications of his suggestion that Russia could achieve military success through cooperation with "forces from below" had at least an echo of his activities earlier in the decade. But equally clearly, Russia would be playing with fire to countenance an alliance between tsarism and the *narod* (the people)—any *narod*—to achieve the state's objectives. In any event, Russia did not invite local contingents of Balkan nationalists to assist it in the fray until it was already thoroughly entangled on the wires around Plevna. The proposition also demonstrates at once Obruchev's understanding of the possible power of "popular will" when facing Britain yet also his low expectations of Russia's army to face successfully the task his memorandum had set it.

Strategically, his opinion was likewise of mixed complexion. On the one hand, he understood that the only way Russia could be sure of imposing its will on the Ottoman empire would be to threaten the capital. His appreciation of the political cost of a Balkan offensive was myopic at best (although certainly more clearly stated than the thoughts of any other officer of the general staff). The assumption that Britain would accept a Russian fait accompli at the Straits, whether or not it settled the interminable Eastern Question, is simply bizarre. British fleets in Besika Bay and the Skagerrak could effectively blockade Russia indefinitely, and there would be little the Russians could do about it. Unlike the Germans, Russian general staff officers *never* spoke of the possible commercial consequences of action in their proposals, although maritime commerce remained essential to the empire's development and modernization in the absence of thoroughgoing railroad network development. Obruchev's "purely military consideration" of objectives in a Balkan war was parochial and dangerous, given the well-known complexities of British commitment to Turkey's viability, and the perpetual fear of the Crimean coalition's revival. His conceit in discounting British concerns was matched only by his strategic pessimism and caution, an interesting combination. The 1866 memo also forecast Obruchev's southward gaze after the war, as he cast about for a way to break Russia's strategic containment.

In the 1860s Obruchev betrayed the widespread anxiety of a reconstituted Crimean coalition again confronting the empire, and implicitly admitted that Russia could not alone face such a coalition another time.

Fuller has asked whether Obruchev's revolutionary past, which in 1866 was of very recent vintage, might have informed the pessimism, even strategic despair, that characterized this officer's outlook throughout his career. "In the 1860s and 1870s the radicals with whom Obruchev had once associated believed that autocratic power in Russia was as fragile as an eggshell. One more serious reverse either at home or abroad might be enough to topple the tsarist empire."[10] Scientism's promise of military effectiveness, however, had carried Obruchev beyond such views, as it clouded his assessment of state interests. Obruchev did not fully appreciate that he needed to incorporate carefully balanced diplomatic and political considerations into Russia's next war plan if a war were to be prosecuted successfully.

General staff surveys of Russia's strategic landscape improved in quality and multiplied in number in the late 1860s. By the end of the decade, Main Staff officers had fleshed out Obruchev's earlier reflections on the next war with Turkey in Europe. In 1869 planners reached consensus on the probable political and military circumstances of a conflict and identified Austria-Hungary, rather than an Anglo-French alignment, as a source of military threat to any future Balkan campaign. Miliutin and General F. F. Berg, commander in chief of forces in the Warsaw area, agreed that Austria would be a threat *only* in the event of a Turkish war; they made no mention of other circumstances in which Austria might threaten war with Russia.[11] From those political considerations the Warsaw district staff gathered most of St. Petersburg's planning information through field surveys of expected assembly areas and march routes to the theater of war, and estimated forage capacities of the whole southwest region.[12] Long before other district staffs had begun this sort of work, the Warsaw staff was conducting annual staff field rides in "military-statistical preparation" of its operating area, all under the careful guidance of the Main Staff in St. Petersburg.[13]

Late in the autumn of 1875, perhaps as early as that October, Obruchev (now VUK's permanent secretary) established an ad hoc group to begin preparations for a war with Turkey, even before any serious governmental discussion of war had begun.[14] The recently created mobilization committee, one institutional product of the 1873 secret strategic conference, governed the study group. Although Obruchev established the mobilization committee during the Bosnian-

Herzegovinian uprisings, the new committee's chief purpose was for planning war with the Teutonic powers.

The committee gave its ad hoc group three tasks. First, the group would set up a system for gathering information about the *real military readiness* of the Russian army for such a war, essentially military-statistical preparation. Second, it would elaborate and direct "measures for the most efficacious allocation of resources and for replenishing shortages of material" before and during a war—logistical preparations. Finally, the committee would "compose the general mobilization plan."[15] The routine this small group established provided a modus operandi the Main Staff followed in its later work of war planning. The committee's labors for the first time defined a new Russian way of war fighting, in close conformity with the methods settled upon in Prussia precisely a decade earlier. These were the first stumbling steps of the rationalized general staff on its path to professional maturity.

A commission, formed in special session of the mobilization committee, attacked the first task of evaluating military readiness in the army. Under the chairmanship of the young director of the committee, Major General Velichko, the subgroup drafted new standards for calculating accurately the military preparedness of regular army units, then applied these statistical standards to the army's peacetime establishment. That work had begun by December 1875.[16] Although Velichko's methodology applied initially to the Balkan problem, it later answered the committee's broader concerns along the Polish frontier.

The committee worked out a draft concept of operations for a Balkan campaign. Much of the preparatory work was based on existing VUK and Main Staff records. However, important additional intelligence was gathered by general staff officers traveling incognito around the middle Balkan area between 1873 and late 1875. These officers included Obruchev himself, as well as Colonels Petr Parensov (soon to be provisional war minister of Bulgaria), Georgii Bobrikov (under the cover of the Russian Red Cross), I. K. Kinshasa's (a Bulgarian in Russian service since the last Russo-Turkish war and Miliutin's secret chargé in "Christian areas of northern Turkey"),[17] and Nikolai Artamonov. Their data on Turkish order of battle supplemented an engineering survey of potential Danubian crossing points conducted from December 1875 to January 1876 by three military engineers, Maziukevich, Bitner, and

Karpichev.[18] A steady flow of reports from military attachés (all general staff officers) in Balkan capitals on disposition of Turkish forces complemented these Main Staff reconnaissances.[19]

In the first week of 1876, at Obruchev's direction,[20] Artamonov prepared a series of lectures based on the mobilization committee's draft plan for presentation to officers of the St. Petersburg military district. Artamonov was a brilliant, thirty-five-year-old *genshtabist* with a strong background in geodesic and topographic sciences. His earlier service included stints with the general staff academy and in the topographic section of the Main Staff, in which capacity he had most recently examined the anticipated Balkan battlefields.

A Soviet historian has argued convincingly that Miliutin and Obruchev ordered the presentation of these lectures to test the accuracy of Main Staff calculations and assumptions.[21] Artamonov presented his public lecture cycle in April 1876 in the palace of Grand Duke Nikolai Nikolaevich, senior, under the title "Concerning the Strategically Most Advantageous Manner of Action against Turkey." The response must have been gratifying because in May Obruchev directed the mobilization committee to compile the lectures into a planning memorandum of the same title, which Miliutin presented to the tsar five months later.[22] This memorandum served as the principal guide for war preparations until early 1877.

Artamonov's (and Obruchev's) plan rested on a simple argument. Historically, all of Russia's military experiences against Turkey in the Balkans followed such a pattern that, if Russia were drawn into siege warfare around the Turks' Danubian defenses, it would lose the war. Artamonov argued that the enemy's capital had to be the main objective of the war, and that the more rapid and resolute the pursuit of that goal, the sooner Turkey would sue for peace. The evidence for this conclusion was straightforward: Saltykov and Rumiantsev's 1774 campaign (which resulted in the Peace of Kuchuk-Kainarji), compared with the limp 1853–1854 Paskevich-Gorchakov operation[23] in the Principalities and Bulgaria. The remainder of the memo dealt with obstacles to a Russian advance on Constantinople; selection of a march route that presented the fewest and least imposing obstacles; and the timely preparations necessary to overcome those obstacles.[24] In essence, success would depend on Russia's ability to *plan* properly rather than to *fight* especially well: the war had to be one of movement, not one of annihilation.

In terms of strategic daring, Artamonov's memorandum could have come from the Prussian General Staff (and, in fact, General Moltke's 1841 reflections on Balkan campaigning were frequently cited). Artamonov's plan all but ignored the political context of a war. With no mention of Great Britain's likely response to an invasion of Turkey, Artamonov makes passing mention of European acquiescence to a Russian solution to the Eastern Question. Perhaps he anticipated fait accompli coming to Russia's aid; in any case, no larger political context was presented in the document. Nor were military contingencies considered. The forces anticipated for the campaign, and subsequently mobilized, were the minimum numbers needed for Artamanov's lightning campaign, not for the brutal operation Russia in fact faced in northern Bulgaria in 1877.

Could Russia single-handedly solve the problem? he asked. In reply, "of course, not." Without pause, however, he continued, "Consequently a move across Asia Minor in this case has only secondary importance, and in the event of a [wider] European war has no importance at all. On the contrary, in that case *it will be most useful to transfer the superfluous part of the Caucasus army to the European war theater.* However, if we presume a *free hand [sloboda deistviia] for Russia* to arrange affairs in the East, then of course, the shortest route to Constantinople across the Balkan peninsula is preferable."[25] The delusion of "purely military considerations," about which Clausewitz warned politicians and generals, is clear throughout the thirty-page plan. The Main Staff's planners *knew* that Europe would be unlikely to accept unilateral Russian intervention in the Eastern Question, yet they implicitly dismissed those concerns as someone else's problem (presumably, the diplomats'). The conceit of experts had established itself in the emerging staff culture.

The tone of the document underlines a general staff ethos that also had emerged from German military philosophy by that time: for a war to be beneficial, it must "be fought in a way that achieves great profit at minimum cost," while decisively resolving the problems from which it arose.[26] In the finest Prussian tradition, the plan assumed rapid, offensive action: the memo gave little attention to defensive considerations other than rear security and "sanitary" blockades of bypassed Turkish positions. Artamonov's insistence that the Turkish "Quadrilateral" forts along the lower Danube (Rushchuk, Shumla, Silistria, and Varna) should be bypassed completely and the quickest routes through the trans-Balkan passes seized was the most daring of his propositions. Only in this way, he declared, could a *small* army descending on Constantinople force a peace on the Ottoman Empire.

The only contingency Artamonov placed on his proposition was the question of Austrian action. "From this it follows that, for a successful war with Turkey, above all it is necessary that we have *guarantee of the complete neutrality of Austria, or the strength to paralyze its action.*"[27] Aside from this caveat, this plan contains the earliest formulation of a solution to Russia's chronic inability to mobilize and concentrate its whole army. At least in a war with Turkey, mobilization of *limited* forces might speed concentration and the offensive; this, in turn, would provide the means both for a short war and for avoiding an entanglement with Austria. Such a military capability would also completely redraw the strategic balance in east-central Europe, although the Russian planners did not realize this at the time. Rapid and effective—two characteristics that had never been applied to Russia's ability to mobilize its army—were precisely the military qualities that Germany's strategic planners discounted.

In any event, the short war solution remained unattainable during the spring of 1876 for technical reasons. So, as the Eastern crisis unfolded in 1876, this plan imposed a diplomatic imperative on the foreign ministry: securing Austrian agreement for Russian military action. Chancellor Gorchakov took the first tentative steps within a month of Obruchev's approval of Artamonov's work, at the June meeting at Reichstadt with his Austrian counterpart, Andrassy.

Initially the committee had explored six different routes from the Danubian crossing to Constantinople, based on combinations of transportation and distance but all retaining a common objective, Constantinople. Artamonov then modified and narrowed the choices to two: first—Rushchuk, Osman-Bazar, Slivno, to Adrianople; and second—Sistova, Tyrnov, Kazanlyk, to Adrianople.[28] When, in early 1877, Grand Duke Nikolai's field staff began its planning work at Kishinev, however, neither of these routes was chosen. Rather, they pushed the main line of advance still farther westward. Although Artamonov had joined the

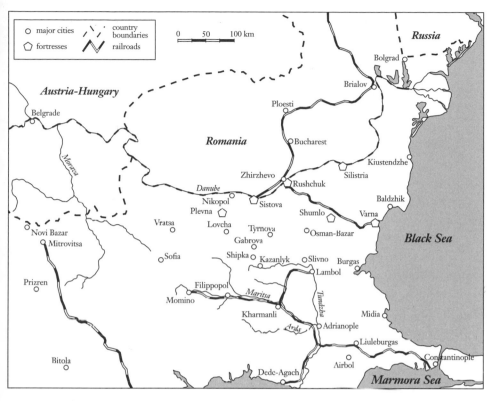

Map 2. Balkan theater of military operations, 1876–1878.

field staff by the end of 1876, his new colleagues appear not to have appreciated his planning work in St. Petersburg, and did not understand that the concept-of-operations memo was his work. Nevertheless, the key aspect of the committee's plan—of avoiding a route through the heavily fortified eastern part of Bulgaria—guided the field staff's planning (see Map 2).[29]

The Campaigning Season Begins

In May 1876 the necessity of taking concrete steps for force mobilization "unexpectedly" impinged on the hitherto simple task of gathering information and general planning. The urgency may have arisen from anticipation of the summer campaign assumed in the plan; the Reichstadt meeting, at which Gorchakov would present lengthy memoranda pressing for intervention, had already been arranged in May. And certainly the Bulgarian atrocities and the arrival of a British fleet at Besika Bay (outside the Dardanelles) exacerbated matters. The concept of operations, as it stood at that moment, became the document on which the committee and the Main Staff based an extensive series of orders, regulations, and directives to prepare the army for mobilization.[30] During the subsequent weeks and months, the planning groups worked frantically to satisfy the committee's two remaining assignments, as well as the specifics of Artamonov's plan. In general, those measures fell into two categories: the preparation of a reserve *(zapasnyi)* mobilization schedule and transportation timetables, and other temporary measures for bringing the army to its wartime footing.

The Main Staff had first begun preparing mobilization schedules in 1869–1870, updating twice yearly the timetables and rosters of enlisted reserve call-up.[31] The schedules, mere hints of the intricate plans that would be drafted starting in 1887, simply established blocks of call-ups and assured that there was rail- or water-borne transport to deliver the most distant troops to their units' mustering points. Schedule No. 6 had been in preparation since the spring of 1876; Chief of Main Staff Geiden and Obruchev ratified it in August 1876.[32] However, in addition to personnel callup, the new schedules included estimates of the requirements for cavalry remounts and forage, for which virtually no provision had been made earlier. The problem had been discussed at length in the war ministry in 1874 and 1875, as a result of the 1873 conference, and the ministry had drafted new statutes, but none had been approved or promulgated. At length the staff directed an inventory of remount stocks within thirty-three *gubernii* of western Russia; those surveys arrived in the capital in August 1876. Even though the war planning apparatus operated quickly and decisively, the chancellery organs of the war ministry remained lethargic: they did not distribute the law governing acquisition or maintenance of cavalry remounts until the end of September.[33]

Transportation of forces from all over European Russia was, technically, an even greater challenge; the decade of staff research on railroad resources injected further anxiety rather than complacency. Annenkov's Committee on Transportation of Forces directed the preparation of train schedules on all lines in European Russia for transportation of forces southward. The circular prescribed a standardized format and gave Annenkov the information planners needed to judge immediately and accurately the full capacity of rail transportation should war come. By June and July the responses of all southern railroad systems gave planners sufficient data to establish the timetables for troop train movements. The technical inspectorate of MPS's Directorate of Railroads advised planners on the surge capacity of individual spurs and links, as the staff tested the timetables in August and September. In addition to accounting for initial transportation of regiments and cargo, the plan had to gauge the appropriate distribution of locomotives and rolling stock throughout the system, as transport shifted from personnel to cargo—and casualties. Annenkov's committee submitted its report on 8 September.[34]

New statutes for the transition to a war footing continued to appear. In early August the committee urged the Main Intendancy Directorate to speed preparation of the army's logistics train for a possible imminent mobilization. Mobile divisional field hospitals multiplied "for the event of war" under new statutes.[35] The staffs of various military districts apparently comprehended the significance of the activity because, even when not directly involved, they made their own contribution. Warsaw district was concerned, for instance, with St. Petersburg's plans for the Junker schools should war come: Would they be closed? Would the officer-instructors be attached to the field army or district forces? Would the advanced students be mobilized? The Main Staff undoubtedly recognized the crippling shortage of junior officers that the field army faced, and in late May it considered the pathetic steps of replacing fencing instructors with civilians throughout the military schooling system.[36]

After the scare of early May and some discussion of partial mobilization (of two full army corps) in August upon completion of the schedules and transportation plans, the Main Staff (on the war minister's direction) issued orders on 21 September to "place on a war footing" all forces in the Odessa and Khar'kov Military Districts, and forces of the Caucasus front earmarked for military operations in that theater. Miliutin, in Livadia with the tsar, directed Obruchev to join the royal suite from St. Petersburg with the Main Staff's latest strategic thoughts on war. He also directed Geiden to undertake "the most energetic activity" in preparations for "offensive operations" that would "begin simultaneously on two fronts: from the Transcaucasus into Asiatic Turkey . . .

[and] from Bessarabia across the Principalities."[37] Miliutin clearly wished for war as his planners pressed into the final stage of their preparations.

On 25 September Miliutin transmitted the tsar's decision to extend mobilization to the Kiev Military District, and to move readied units toward the frontier, thus adding one or two corps to the field army. Units from Moscow district would immediately fill their places in Kiev, "even if still in peacetime condition";[38] movement began three weeks later when four divisions from around Moscow moved into Kiev district and joined the order of battle.[39] In Miliutin's premobilization directives, issued by enciphered telegraph from the Crimea between 21 and 27 September, the war minister (upon Alexander's direction) set in motion the mobilization of the Caucasus front. What precisely were "premobilization" measures? For field units they included virtually all preparation for combat except absorption of *zapasnye* contingents and the transportation and concentration of the army for combat. Those measures increased unit strength from a "normal" (peacetime) level to "reinforced" level at 75 percent of strength. Most important, a premobilization order authorized district and unit commanders to purchase vast numbers of horses, their forage, and supplies.[40] For the permanent local forces (fortress units, cadres, etc.), such measures placed those units on a wartime footing. Thus, for example, all sapper and rifle brigades in the Caucasus received mobilization orders, as did the Alexandropol fortress regiment and its artillery,[41] and the corps' wartime field command organization was set up.[42] Finally, the war minister ordered mobilization of artillery parks associated with the corps' four divisions on 28 September.[43]

To fulfill the central role of *intratheater* transportation which the Main Staff anticipated for railroads, the mobilization committee proposed on 14 October the purchase of fifteen steam engines for the Danubian army, at a cost of five thousand rubles each. Miliutin approved the purchase from Livadia a week later.[44] The staff in Tiflis had just received its final districtwide mobilization orders by secret Main Staff reply (*otzyv*) dated 9 October (No. 806), on the basis of which the district's chief of staff ordered the commanders of the Kuban and Terek oblasts to begin mobilization preparations on 22 October (No. 96 and No. 97).[45] The only remaining step to place this army into operational order was the call to colors of reserve forces, which the tsar issued on 1 November.

War Planning's Pas de Deux with Diplomacy

Even earlier than August, the tsar's circle of advisers had considered the consequences of a declaration of war against Turkey. Before Gorchakov and A. H. Jomini (son of the founder of the general staff academy and senior counselor in the foreign ministry) fashioned the Reichstadt understanding with Andrassy in late June, the mobilization committee had completed its preliminary campaign planning and prepared estimates of the military balance in the Balkans. The coincidence of the *timing* of that meeting and completion of the core of the war plan is remarkable; there is no more compelling explanation of the committee's shift from war plan *preparation* to *implementation* than the interventionist position Gorchakov took at Reichstadt.

Russo-Austrian discussions did not result in final agreement regarding the Balkan revolts, but they pointedly underscored the conferees' desire to "observe an absolute neutrality," and they reiterated "the recent propositions, of maintaining nonintervention in the states involved."[46] The secret portion of the discussions, regarding Austria's and Russia's prerogatives in the event of a Turkish victory, defeat, or collapse, went far beyond the public statements. Even apart from the vast discrepancies in the two ministers' records of the agreement,[47] the discussions resolved nothing, from Miliutin's or the mobilization committee's perspective. The problem of a *Russo*-Turkish war, and Austria's attitude in that case, was simply not addressed: the talks dealt with development of the existing crisis, not with its widening.[48] Gorchakov failed to get concrete assurances during the secret exchange, and neither Russia's political nor military interests found satisfaction in the protocol. That the Main Staff knew of the foreign ministry's diplomatic activities is clear; whether the foreign minister was ignorant of the shape and advanced progress of war planning, or simply held stubbornly to the conceit that a diplomatic solution could produce the same results as combat, is unclear. Gorchakov's failure to secure Austrian agreement to coordinated military action served neither the army's nor the Russian government's goals. The war minister assured Gorchakov, in response to an article of 29 June in *Novoe vremia*, that even Prussia needed time to mobilize, and Russia *would never be as ready to march as it was then!*[49]

The next day (four days after conclusion of the Reichstadt discussions), Miliutin wondered what had in fact been clarified (much less secured) for Russia by the Reichstadt exchange: "From the present state of affairs . . . naturally arises the question: whether it is possible that Europe, and especially Russia, is able to extend and firmly to maintain the principle of nonintervention especially in view of the obvious open sympathy for Turkey on the part of England and Hungary."[50]

Adding to the government's confusion were doubts at the highest levels of the foreign ministry. On 28 June, in passing, Baron Jomini had "tossed out some kind of queer phrase" about Russia's unpreparedness for war; perhaps the foreign ministry really did remain ignorant of the army's preparations. Miliutin had also heard such comments in public, although any anxiety over Obruchev's and the Main Staff's work on the war plan affected him less than the need to provide accurate advice to the tsar and grand duke regarding Russia's true military condition. On Wednesday, 30 June, armed with mobilization readiness estimates prepared by the mobilization committee, he explained to the emperor and the grand duke "the true situation and [eliminated], at least in them, those anxious thoughts that we were still not at all able to conduct a war. From the aforementioned work, it was clear to see that, in spite of many things still remaining defective in our military organization, never had our army been as *prepared* for war as now."[51]

Alexander's anxiety over the reaction of other powers to another Russo-Turkish war should have been assuaged by the empire's diplomatic efforts; it was not. If the foreign ministry's "dilettantism"[52] extended beyond Gorchakov's inability to secure more than some fuzzy understanding with Austria, that was not the problem here. Despite the foreign ministry's display of unified action and discipline, Russia's ambassadors in several key capitals pursued independent initiatives, which compounded imperial doubts. Ignat'ev's activities among Ottoman Christians and in the Porte were invariably undertaken without Gorchakov's or the tsar's approval. These initiatives were coordinated with neither the Main Staff's plans nor Russia's diplomatic objectives. He fanned simultaneously the ire of the foreign minister, the suspicions of the foreign diplomatic corps, the fears in Vienna, and the anger of other Russian diplomats at the Porte.

In London, since 29 May/10 June Shuvalov had been courting "most secret" overtures from Disraeli for a "direct understanding" between the two governments. Disraeli, still smarting from his foreign minister's lone spoiling of the Berlin agreement on Turkish reforms, opened the probe. The Russian ambassador immediately learned that Disraeli's policy resulted from his suspicion of Andrassy, which promised in the future to keep those two powers apart in their handling of Russia's designs in the Balkans (and which Gorchakov subsequently played upon in a *notice confidentielle* to Vienna).[53] The British, however, were not propelled by Shuvalov's warning that, in Sumner's words, "the imminent risk of conflict in the Balkans demanded urgent action." That urgency, coincidentally, arose at the same time as the "unexpected development" that had propelled the Main Staff into preparations for hostilities.

Russia's subsequent turn toward Austria at Reichstadt marked the failure of Disraeli's intervention on behalf of a mutually acceptable solution to the crisis, and thus was also a setback for Bismarck, who saw British engagement as his own salvation. After London rejected the Berlin memo on 16 May, the tsar "became more and more firmly entrenched in the belief that nothing but hostility to Russia could be expected from Disraeli and his government." Queen Victoria had warned the prime minister of this possibility. By the time Britain next entered the center of negotiations (in Constantinople in December), Russia's diplomatic goal was above all to tie Austria securely to the Russian solution, *not* to avoid war.[54]

Throughout the summer Gorchakov entertained the worst fears concerning Britain, despite Shuvalov's interesting discussions with the prime minister. Those fears animated the correspondence he sent from his German spas to Deputy Foreign Minister Giers, who was managing business in St. Petersburg. After Britain dashed the German-Austrian-Russian concord on Turkish reform (the Berlin Memo) in May and instead dispatched the fleet to Besika Bay, Gorchakov grew increasingly despondent. His weekly instructions to St. Petersburg dwelled on the worst possible outcome to the crisis: "the occupation of the Straits by England, and the arrangement of the rest [of Europe] in a most hostile

way toward Russia."[55] The Austrian "problem" occupied Russia's statesmen from Reichstadt onward, just as Artamonov's report had insisted it
must, before a war could begin. The diplomatic and military appara-
tuses were converging on the question of state policy in the Balkans,
even if slowly.

In mid-July, during an emotional interview with Miliutin, the emperor recalled the dark days of 1854 and 1855, and the situation that
engulfed his father. He ruminated soberly about the *Dreikaiserbund* and
the risk of an *offensive* war: "Besides, we must not forget that the secret
alliance I concluded with Germany and Austria is exclusively a defensive union; our allies bound themselves to take our side if we are attacked, but they have not bound themselves to support us if we initiate,
in the case of an offensive of our own undertaking, and in such a case, it
may turn out as was the case in the Crimean war: again all of Europe
capsizing on top of us!"[56]

The specter of 1853–1856 never released Russia's leaders from its
grip. But rather than producing paralysis, perhaps that sword of Damo-
cles clarified for the foreign ministry the course it would ultimately
pursue. The Main Staff's work on preparing the army for a war, rather
than Gorchakov's diplomatic notes, gave the government confidence to
act. As the tsar, Miliutin, and Gorchakov converged on Warsaw in
mid-August for summer maneuvers, their correspondence and diaries
hinted at a new perspective on Britain's isolation and their wavering
commitment to localize European involvement in the approaching Balkan confrontation. On 14/26 August Prince Milan's forces in Serbia
faced defeat, and he decided, "after a few days of hesitation," to "accept
the suggestion of the London Cabinet . . . for reestablishment of the
peace."[57] Five days later, however, the sultan was deposed. The ascen-
dance of nationalist Turkish reformers marked a hardening of the Ottoman position. The collapse of the British solution reopened the question: Which power would exercise its interests in solving the crisis?

The failure of Britain's armistice plan, the French ambassador in St.
Petersburg reported, was grave and perhaps a "turning point" *(le moment supreme).*[58] From London, Harcourt cabled the French premier
that, in the words of the Russian minister there, it was the "decisive
hour."[59] Jomini, writing from Warsaw, admitted that he could not share
Gorchakov's optimism *(puisse-je être mauvais prophète!)*, with "neither an
armistice, nor mediation, nor a conference" decided on. In any case,

the status quo could not promote Russia's interests: prolonged defense would weaken (if not destroy) the Serbs, and anything else would simply allow the Turks to reinforce their position.[60]

The mission of Field Marshall von Manteuffel on 22 August/3 September to Alexander in Warsaw may have been a diplomatic windfall for the foreign ministry, for it provided Gorchakov the hope that Austria might be brought to reason by its influential neighbor, Germany. To the war planners in St. Petersburg who had already discounted any German threat in the event of war, the note was irrelevant, or at best offered merely a theoretical possibility. Germany could help only to the extent that it would neutralize Austrian interference in a Russo-Turkish war; for the moment there was evidence that Germany wished to avoid *any* involvement in Russia's fight with Turkey, *even* if Austria intervened.[61] Bismarck was of the opinion that, "even if we must disagree with [Alexander's] solution [to the crisis], we will return the friendly disposition he showed us" in earlier years. "That we fight a war, as a favor for Russia, a war which does not serve our own interests, he would not demand, nor has he asked it of us. However, that we will remain in every instance a benevolent and neutral neighbor as he does wish of us, he should, in my opinion, be able to count."[62]

Hence, Miliutin may reasonably have assumed in August that, if Russia came to blows with Austria, Germany would hesitate as long as the clash remained localized and secondary to operations against Turkey. A week later, an entry in Miliutin's diary suggested that the diplomatic constellation was perhaps coming into clearer alignment. Although "the Sphinx" had not yet spoken, no longer could "Germanic" hostility be assumed toward a Russian solution to the Eastern Question.

> The mission of Field Marshall Manteuffel had no other meaning than to preserve the sense of gratitude toward our sovereign . . . Quietly living in Varzin, the German chancellor has not yet spoken . . . Like the Pythian, the indeterminate answer. England and France reluctantly continue proposing a conference . . . Austria itself cannot act openly, cannot sincerely go in concert with us. Gorchakov himself sees in the present state of affairs nothing rosy, and is already pronouncing the word, *isolement*, for which Russia must be ready; *à isolement*—very close to war.[63]

Bismarck had reasons for reticence. He had parried Gorchakov's proposal a few weeks earlier that Germany host a conference on the crisis; he did not wish to occupy the hot seat on an issue in which Germany had no stake. That role would fracture the Three Emperors' League by casting Germany's allies in two opposing camps. France would side with Russia, if only to put Germany in an awkward position, while Britain would align with Austria. As if this were not enough, there was the additional complication of a collision of personalities: Lord Beaconsfield and Prince Gorchakov, "two ministers of equally dangerous vanity."[64]

Not Whether but When: Livadia in October

Alexander scrutinized and approved the Main Staff's work in October at the imperial summer resort at Livadia in the Crimea. We have no evidence of foreign ministry involvement in (or substantial knowledge of) the staff's or committee's work up to the fall. The tsar, his family, and their retinue retired there after traveling in Europe and attending the maneuvers. The war minister and later his aide, Obruchev, were with the royal suite in the Tauris Mountains. The chancellor, Gorchakov, accompanied by the foreign ministry's senior counselor, Jomini, likewise traveled with the royal suite to the Crimea following three months in central Europe. The foreign ministry itself had continued operations in Gorchakov's extended absence under the administration of Giers, the deputy foreign minister.[65]

At the beginning of September 1876, Gorchakov telegraphed Oubril, his ambassador in Berlin, to get the kaiser's current views: the Russian army might be forced to march.[66] On 11/23 September, the foreign minister also telegraphed Novikov in Vienna and directed him to attempt negotiations with Andrassy for an agreement, in order to head off an anticipated Turkish counterproposal to a Russian plan for Bulgaria.[67] Two days later Gorchakov sweetened the offer with a proposal to the Austrians for concrete spheres in the Balkans.[68]

With the tsar now in Livadia, Bismarck had hurriedly recalled Schweinitz from summer vacation and sent him off to the Crimea. But Alexander remained interested in "extraordinary" personal communications with Wilhelm through the permanent Prussian adjutant to the Russian suite, Lieutenant General von Werder. On 13/25 September Alexander again[69] queried his uncle as to what precisely Germany's position would be in the event of a confrontation between Russia and Austria over the worsening Balkan problem. The timing of this communication clearly was not coincidental—it occurred at precisely the moment Miliutin was about to dispatch orders for the start of premobilization. But the storm the tsar's note produced in the German government (and Bismarck in particular)[70] remained hidden from those at Livadia. While Bismarck delayed his answer to the inquiry, an answer he knew would bring no comfort to the Russians, the final military conference for selecting a mobilization date began in the Crimea.

Svechin and others have mistakenly argued that the plan for war began to take shape only after mid-October 1876 (i.e., as a result of events at Livadia), which gave the Russians too little time to prepare for a campaign, the difficulty of which they misunderstood.[71] However, preparations had begun almost a year earlier. Furthermore, a pivotal document (dated 22 September 1876), which encapsulated the mature war plan, reflected the measures already taken and "encouraged" an immediate declaration of hostilities. When Obruchev arrived in Livadia a few days after Miliutin's summons, he carried his 22 September memorandum, bearing the title "Some Considerations in the Event of War with Turkey."[72]

Obruchev recognized the fundamentally different character that "the next war" with Turkey would have, not least as a result of the changes in the Russian army and the strategic situation. The nature of the new situation was measured against the circumstances of 1853–1856. "The general opinion of Europe is that, with the loss of the Black Sea fleet, our operations against Turkey will become exceedingly difficult . . . [However,] even without a fleet, we will be able to take a most resolute stand."[73] Based on his 22 September memorandum, and other earlier discussions of the course of a Balkan war, Obruchev constructed the so-called First Variation, which he passed to the war minister in a report dated 1 October, in Livadia. He subsequently presented this version of the plan (and Artamonov's report) to the tsar in reports on 3 and 4 October, in the presence of Miliutin, Gorchakov, and the *tsarevich*.[74]

The First Variation dealt principally with the Balkan theater of war.[75] The first paragraph concluded with a clear declaration of the central war aim: occupation of central Bulgaria, followed by a rapid thrust to Constantinople. "In all probability we will here meet England, and if they . . . persist in support of Turkey, we will be forced to fight England also." Like Shuvalov, he was unimpressed with Britain's ability to interfere militarily. He continued that, given its own foresight and preparation, the Russian government need not fear such a culmination in the march to war: "In any case we are not to avoid [such a] clash with England, and it is better to meet them in Constantinople than to fight them on our coastline. If luck is on our side, we will take Constantinople and be done with both Turkey and England at once. It would be a great mistake to fear unnecessarily taking Constantinople, and in advance plan to limit any developing success of the army."[76]

Obruchev no longer considered Austrian opposition an intractable problem; rather, England's obstinacy was of greater (but not serious) concern. Furthermore, he no longer considered military support of the "liberated peoples" of the Balkans necessary for success at Constantinople.

"It is very likely," he concluded his introduction, "that if we, taking Constantinople, recognize its international community, then *Europe* not only will not resist us, but will even be glad that the interminable, frightening Eastern Question is at last resolved [emphasis added]." Russian policy sought to seize the initiative in the Balkan problem by rapid military results and energetic diplomatic action. Obruchev was sure that a European concert would ratify the results. This, he hoped, would prevent a repeat of 1853–1854.

In the section "General Character of the Operation," Obruchev explained in detail the imperative for speed in the campaign. Only with "extraordinary speed" could Russia prevent the development of "a broad European coalition," forestall the army's decimation by disease, and complete the war before the nation's resources were exhausted. Two operational principles would guide the campaign as it unfolded. First, the Danube would be crossed "instantly" when hostilities began (although not necessarily upon declaration of war). Then the commanders, avoiding "disastrous siege warfare," would isolate and bypass surviving Turkish strong points that might threaten the rear and disorganize the advance. The plan's fundamental ethos was rapid movement southward. Unfortunately, the plan's objectives proved more easily expressed than attained, particularly when Miliutin intervened to recommend a pause in the advance after the army had crossed the Danube.

The route southward took account of an exposed left flank along the

Black Sea (and inhospitably barren coastal lands), as well as the disposition of Turkey's defensive belts (the Quadrilateral system). By an advance down the center of Romania, across the Danube, and into central Bulgaria, the Russian army would facilitate success in its operational and strategic objectives: (1) the army could (as necessary) offer assistance to native populations against the Turks; (2) that route closely coincided with existing railroad lines; (3) the army would start from the southernmost Danubian bend, taking advantage of a longer unopposed transit through Romania; and (4) an army could bypass Turkish defenses in eastern and western Bulgaria.[77]

Obruchev's plan offered a three- to four-month campaign from mobilization to arrival at the Bosporus.

mobilization	14 days
concentration at the border	7–10 days
movement to middle Danube (foot)	35 days
(Romanian rail)[78]	24 days [517 km]
Danube crossing	3 days
reorganization of rear; seizure of Rushchuk	7 days
Balkan crossing (cavalry detachments):	3 days
(infantry detachments)	7–10 days
movement to Adrianople[79]	8 days [300 km]
into Constantinople	14 days [200 km]

Obruchev also argued the case for an alternate route south of the Danube, which would take greatest advantage of existing railroads. That alternative committed the army to capture of Rushchuk, one of the Quadrilaterals, and would have given the advancing army rail support for all but 115 versts (122 kilometers) of the route.[80] However, he added that railroad lines would be usable only until November 8, at which time winter blizzards would probably close the tracks. The implications of this plan are obvious. The Main Staff anticipated an *immediate declaration of war*, for which it was willing to sacrifice the diplomatic guarantee of Austrian acquiescence (the sine qua non of earlier planning). If Russia could mobilize a small army to move quickly into an offensive across Bulgaria, it would win peace before Christmas and, presumably, before Britain and Austria could act.[81]

The plan closed with a special section entitled "Precautionary Measures against Austria." Obruchev anticipated "treachery" from Austria, arguing the possibility of its suddenly siding with Britain. An Austrian mobilization would threaten the entire right flank of Russia's advance and thus force immediate cancellation of the operation. That, more than the British fleet at the Bosporus, could derail the Russian offensive timetable. Nevertheless, the Austrian threat remained an afterthought; by October the mobilization committee was so set on war that it could not contemplate delay for political reasons. In view of the seasonal limitations, Obruchev argued that military considerations would have to take precedence. But the Main Staff was not to have its well-planned war just yet, and full mobilization would likewise wait. Political prudence—or, more accurately, ministerial politics—asserted itself when the timing of the First Variation (fall offensive) was postponed until the plan's original political consideration was satisfied: an agreement with Austria. So with the New Year the Main Staff injected itself into the negotiations with Vienna and helped conclude an agreement.[82]

Although the formality of October's Livadia conference may suggest a turning point in the decision for war,[83] the tsar had already approved many of the most important preparations months before the war counsel, propelled by his most trusted adviser, Miliutin. Coincidentally, Obruchev drafted a plan for the reorganization of a new Bulgarian national army that Russia would help establish, presumably *after* a war in the Balkans. Obruchev dated the plan 4 October, the day after he reported to the tsar.[84] If anything, Obruchev's presentation and the related discussions involving Reutern (finance minister), Ignat'ev (minister to Constantinople), and others constituted a step that finally brought them all into the already well-advanced preparations for war. From this period, for instance, expenditures for supplies and equipment increased rapidly (e.g., in the approval of railroad engine purchases). On 26 October the tsar's suite returned to the capital, where Miliutin was relieved he could at last work uninterruptedly on preparation for reserve mobilization.[85] Following last-minute delays, as Werder and other messengers carried dispatches from Alexander to the emperors of Germany and Austria, mobilization was announced on 1/13 November, after which the field armies' staffs began planning their campaigns (and interests outside the Main Staff adapted the Obruchev/Artamonov plan to their own needs, as Grand Duke Nikolai and even Miliutin played at grand strategy).

Bismarck's correspondence from early October reflects his absorption with the question of Russo-Austrian war, with only fleeting attention to the proposals then being floated by Britain and France for a Balkan cease-fire and concerted action. "The question of [Russian] war against Austria" occupied his agenda virtually daily.[86] Knowledge of the final outcome of Russia's war preparations could not have been known to the German government. But one finds a remarkable afterthought that Bismarck attached to a memo to the kaiser on 2/14 October (about a week after Obruchev's arrival in Livadia and the day after the start of the conference there). After discussing the Russian rejection of terms for a cease-fire in the Balkans, the chancellor ruminated briefly: "In conclusion, and without reflection on the preceding, I observe purely academically, that I found rash the Russian refusal regarding the six-month [cease-fire], like so many other recent Russian decisions. I suspect that the Russian policy has grounds for refusal, however I would have found the latter more skillfully broached [*geschickter angebracht*], if they had tied it to a secondary issue [*Nebenfrage*] or to certain stipulations raised by Russia. Besides, Russia is not prepared for war today."[87]

What Europeans could see was the progress of Russian mobilization. Within four days of the mobilization decree, ten of forty-four European *gubernii* had completed the call-up of *zapasnye* conscripts; by the end of the next day, the seventeen *gubernii* that had completed induction accounted for 75 percent of all men liable for recall. By the fifteenth day of mobilization, all *gubernii* reported full rosters, except areas of the Caucasus where the numbers were insignificant in any case. Obruchev considered mobilization completed within three weeks,[88] and Miliutin thought mobilization *and* concentration completed within six weeks.[89] Zaionchkovskii notes that the success of the 1876 call to colors depended heavily on reform measures taken in the 1860s and early 1870s. The stunning speed with which military districts carried out their orders, however, was more a result of a long year of prior planning and preparation.

Austria's Acquiescence and War

According to Obruchev's 1 October memo (and in contrast with his earlier assessments), an agreement with Austria was highly desirable, and an understanding with Romania essential. Obruchev himself played a substantial part in each diplomatic exchange,[90] but his part in the

Budapest agreement is both pivotal to later (postwar) developments and enigmatic. Obruchev arrived secretly in the Hungarian capital from St. Petersburg just before Christmas to join (or, as Sumner speculates, to stiffen the resolve of) the Russian ambassador in Vienna, E. P. Novikov, in negotiations with Andrassy.[91] Colonel Parensov (assigned to the operations section of the Field Army staff, under the buffoonish Lieutenant General K. V. Levitskii) likewise arrived for a two-week stay in Vienna to divine the Austrian army's intentions in the event of war. It appears that the field headquarters knew nothing of Obruchev's negotiations going on at the very same moment. Although inclusion of "military experts" like Obruchev in diplomatic negotiations of this sort was not unusual, an officer of Obruchev's stature on a diplomatic mission (particularly while the staff made feverish preparations for war) demonstrated the importance of those negotiations to war planners.[92]

Regardless of whether the negotiators worked on the basis of negative aims (the avoidance at all costs of collision between themselves) or positive ones (coordinated action to solve definitively the Eastern Question),[93] Obruchev's role was the same. Initially, he provided technical advice on proposals for limited use of Austrian railroads for hospital trains, and military measures to secure the neutrality of the Danube as quickly as possible after the start of war. St. Petersburg approved the draft on 15/27 December 1876, although Andrassy would not allow these technical commitments to take effect until conclusion of a political agreement. Among Obruchev's resources was a map, on which he had sketched out the various political boundaries to be observed during and after a war. The mystery of that map's fate would play an important role later because it included (according to Ignat'ev, in his highly suspect memoirs)[94] clear demarcation of a "big Bulgarian" entity, as the Russian's had proposed at the Constantinople meeting in December 1876. Andrassy's initials on and acceptance of the map, with demurral only regarding Montenegrin frontiers, would have justified the territorial extractions of the San Stefano treaty, from Obruchev's perspective. And if Russia had any moral grounds for complaint about Austrian duplicity following San Stefano in 1878, the existence (and loss) of that map provided it. Andrassy had the map (as he reported to the German ambassador in Vienna) but later would not produce it.

Russia's representative signed the military agreement with Austria on 15 January 1877, as the Treaty of Budapest.[95] Grand Duke Nikolai had made contact with the Romanians in November through the good offices of A. I. Nelidov (Ignat'ev's counselor of embassy in Constantinople) for the purpose of securing a purely technical, military agreement for passage of Russian forces. Nelidov, with the assistance of general staff Colonel Prince Mikhail Alekseevich Kantakuzin (Cantacuzene), had concluded with Prime Minister Bratianu the framework of a military agreement by early December. The points of the convention had been drafted by Obruchev for Kantakuzin. Gorchakov disdained any political or binding agreement, and he felt there was nothing Russia needed to offer to, or compensate Romania for, in the event of war: Romania *would* cede Bessarabia, whether or not there was a convention, and the Russian army *would* pass through its territory, likewise. Prince Charles of Romania was also in little hurry to conclude an agreement (although he knew one was necessary). When Gorchakov finally had his Austrian agreement and the commencement of hostilities was just days away, the parties ratified the agreement.[96]

The commander in chief of the Field Army, Grand Duke Nikolai, was an officer beloved by the troops, and not without military sense. But he had rejected war minister Miliutin's nomination of Obruchev as his chief of staff because he knew of Obruchev's radical past.[97] Near incompetents and toadies led the field staff from its heads, General N. N. Nepokoichitskii and Major General K. V. Levitskii down, even though many of the assigned junior staff officers—the colonels and lieutenant colonels—arrived from Obruchev's VUK staff. On the other hand, the campaign began promisingly. The advance through Romania, an unprecedented nighttime crossing of the Danube under fire, and daring initial cavalry forays toward the Balkan mountain range, promised a short, brilliant war. But the problem of leadership—from theater level down to tactical level—would compromise most of the advantage that the Main Staff's preparations had promised by the summer of 1877.[98] Furthermore, abandonment of the staff's plan left the army undermanned for the more cautious and systematic campaign that it would have to fight. In particular, the army's weak right (western) wing was too slow and irresolutely handled to shield the advance southward from the Danube. General Kridner, its commander, decided he needed to take Nikopol, just south of the river, thus allowing Osman Pasha's forces from western Bulgaria to stream into Plevna.

The arrival of the imperial suite in the Balkan theater of war sapped the army and corps commanders of what daring and initiative they otherwise might have displayed. Despite promises of noninterference, the tsar overrode his brother's bold (although perhaps reckless) plan to concentrate his forces beyond points of stubborn Turkish resistance (Rushchuk, Nikopol, Shumen, Plevna). Fear of imperial disagreement drained the energy of commanders, but there was also ample evidence that they lacked basic field command skills. The autocratic system simply did not allow someone other than an imperial family member to make wartime decisions; capable officers likewise showed little inclination, when in command positions, to act any more decisively or effectively than grand dukes or dynastic hangers-on.

Meanwhile, in the Caucasus theater of war, Grand Duke Mikhail (and his chief of staff, General Loris-Melikov) slumped back to their base line when their offensive foundered. After that abysmal summer of campaigning in the Caucasus, the tsar agreed to Miliutin's suggestion to assign Obruchev there to save that campaign, which he promptly did. And once starvation broke Turkish resistance in Plevna (in November), army columns under Skobelev, Gurko, Radetskii, and Kartsov completed the drive across the Balkans, recapturing some of the tactical genius that the war's beginnings had promised. Alexander II's military myopia and irrationality displayed themselves vividly when he dismissed his brother for not seizing Constantinople, even though the Russian army, lacking siege artillery, arrived at San Stefano as a disease-ridden shadow of its former self. In the intervening months between the brilliant mobilization and attack into Bulgaria, and the regaining of operational initiative in November, the Russian army lost tens of thousands dead and wounded. It was clearly less a question of material disparity or morale failure than simple military leadership by the imperial family and its servitors, what can be called the effects of "grand dukism."

Militarily, the Russian army got three things right in 1876–1877. First, it planned and executed a flawless nighttime crossing and seizure of Danubian bridgeheads without the benefit of a fleet and in the presence of Turkish riverine forces. Second, it successfully neutralized the Quadrilateral fortress system in eastern Bulgaria according to plan, and it prevented Turkish forces located there from joining the defenses to the west and south. Third, the army got troops as far as Plevna and invested it. But the field leadership had already departed from

Obruchev's bold plan and attempted to improvise the operation. The results were catastrophic human-wave assaults on the Plevna redoubts. Finally, the tsar called in another experienced technical specialist, General E. I. Totleben, an engineer who ended the spirited but futile attacks and (according to the original plan) starved out the Turkish force in the town. The Main Staff's plan, had it been used, would not have obviated the weakness of field leadership and the inability of commanding officers to improvise in difficult circumstances.

The performance of railroads under the direction of General Annenkov was remarkable in comparison with anything Russia had attempted before. In the principal theater of operations in the Balkans, the effective size of the field army increased rapidly after January 1877.[99] Particularly when collapse of offensive operations at Plevna forced the field staff to abandon its prepared timetables and plans, the army began to grow for a drawn-out war:

8 July:	8 divisions (in Bulgaria)
18 July:	12 divisions
30 August:	18 divisions
31 October:	31 divisions[100]

From July until November 1877, the system averaged between four and six troop and military freight trains daily into the theater of war, which delivered over fifty million kilograms of military cargo from July 1877 to February 1878[101] (See Table A-1 in the Supplemental Data section).

The Caucasus theater confirmed the value of careful planning and the cost of dilettantism. Grand Duke Mikhail, assisted by General-Adjutant M. T. Loris-Melikov as chief of staff, were to tie down the Turkish forces (about one hundred thousand troops) in that theater. The initial offensives had success against weak enemy detachments, but when it ran into the defenses of Kars, Loris-Melikov lost heart and withdrew to the Russian border. The campaign, in Menning's words, "then lapsed into operational torpor."[102] On Miliutin's recommendation, at the height of the first attempts on Plevna, the tsar ordered two fresh divisions to the Caucasus and agreed to assignment of another technical specialist, Obruchev, to take over planning in that theater.[103] In early October, Obruchev's coup d'oeil in company of rigorous planning led to a stunning envelopment of Turkish forces screening Kars. His plan employed rapid, covert night marches and tactical use of long-range telegraphic communications to coordinate the assault on the Turkish front and rear. The capture of Kars at the end of the month was an equally remarkable demonstration of field command and staff work; five days of feinting actions and careful preparation of the assault forces rewarded Obruchev with a successful night attack on the German-designed defensive system.[104] The campaign demonstrated the central role of combat initiative among junior officers to the success of operations, particularly during the final assault on Kars (although at great cost, particularly among junior officers). But the Caucasus also had a long history of innovative military professionalism, and effectiveness was an ingrained part of the military ethic in that theater far removed from the capital. In the absence of skilled leadership, the highly developed combat effectiveness of forces stationed in the theater could not succeed. Obruchev's daring but carefully considered plan gave back to the regiments the freedom to operate as they had for decades in Caucasus operations. Russia was rewarded with large territorial gains (six hundred thousand square kilometers under San Stefano) and, with the fall of Kars, the opening of the door into Ottoman Armenia.[105]

Conclusions

Miliutin's discussions of campaign timing with the tsar were accompanied by the advice to begin the campaign as soon as was practicable. Until the winter of 1876, Miliutin had argued more for decisiveness than caution in going to war with Turkey; finance minister Reutern's concern for exhaustion of the state's resources was not convincing to Miliutin, and, in the end, not to Alexander either.[106] Miliutin's interest in a war largely shielded Obruchev's preparations because it was based not on "whether war" but on "when war." The war minister merely delayed a premature declaration of mobilization until the Main Staff's work had advanced sufficiently to avoid a repeat of 1854. At Livadia Obruchev delivered assurance that militarily, all was ready and the financial burden of war was swallowed as the cost of an extraordinary political opportunity that war at that moment seemed to offer.[107] The tsar did not have to heed Miliutin's or the Main Staff's insistence on war, however, and diplomatic preparations continued until successfully concluded.

There is no question, based on Miliutin's memoirs, that Alexander's declaration of mobilization was made after much sober consideration of state interests.[108] There is no evidence of spontaneity or rashness in the final decision, much less in the myriad steps taken during the first half of 1876. Given the enormous cost of drawing up the field army and accumulating stockpiles, it would be untenable to argue that the war was a consequence of failed diplomacy. Neither the Constantinople conference (December 1876) nor the London protocol (March 1877) witnessed moderation of Russian demands, a softening of Turkish resolve, or the willingness of others to intervene decisively. In October the tsar's counselors were realistic: the Turks were neither willing nor able to compromise their sovereignty, and instead, were expecting Britain to be their champion and to deter Russia. Some knew war was likely in May 1876, when Britain rejected the plan drafted by Russia, Austria, and Germany; everyone knew it after October.

However, Obruchev, arguing military necessity, attempted in October 1876 to discount political reality as the year's final campaign season began, and cautious diplomacy had to intervene to avert a possible disaster. Obruchev repeatedly affirmed between 1866 and October 1876 that Russia could act unilaterally against Turkey. He continued to argue that, with greater sophistication, after 1878. That affirmation of freedom could have been the result of ignorance regarding British policy toward Turkey. (The view certainly coincided with a period of British military unpreparedness, especially in the Royal Navy, that materially restrained Disraeli's ability to back with force a unilateral policy toward Russia and the Straits.) The picture of Miliutin's alter ego—and the documents—does not support the proposition that he simply misunderstood Britain's position. Most probably it was his conviction that thorough planning in and of itself could satisfy Russia's political and strategic needs: the right plan *could* obviate political and diplomatic disadvantages, such as British intransigence at the Straits. Unaware of Bismarck's active role in German military success in 1870, he might also have aspired to see the Russian army reshape Russia's sphere of interest in the way Moltke's army had Prussia's sphere.

Curiously, the strategic perspective that underlay the mobilization committee's plan, as well as the San Stefano treaty,[109] assumed that Russia could exercise a military-strategic condominium, *à isolement*, over the disposition of states in the Balkans. The war fleetingly proved that assumption to be correct, even though Europe's reaction in 1878, and subsequent decades of Russian caution in European affairs, belie the fact. The linchpin in all these political-military developments was the illusory expert opinion of the Russian Main Staff, which, like the Prussian staff, was becoming a major silent participant in state policy formulation. When the Main Staff turned its attention back toward the Teutonic powers in 1879 and 1880, it had a wealth of practical experience on which to build the war plan that would be, it was hoped, Russia's strategic salvation.

II

Professionalism's Fruits

6

Experts versus Amateurs

The Russian Main Staff's ad hoc war planning began at the end of 1875 and lasted until Grand Duke Nikolai's field staff took over those activities in December 1876. General staff officers assigned to the field army's staff observed closely the incompetencies of many of the nonspecialists who held command and senior staff positions. The performance of grand dukes and senior officers like General-Adjutant Nepokoichitskii (Grand Duke Nikolai's chief of staff) or his operations assistant, Lieutenant General Levitskii, markedly distinguished them from planners in the capital.[1] Temporary groups under Obruchev had done their work well. Their thoroughness, upon which even the tsar commented favorably, produced two results that influenced the Main Staff's future activity: strategic and military autonomy, and an elevation of staff prestige to rival the Guards Corps.

The Main Staff's planning organs would come to exercise authority to direct Russia's war preparations and to define the empire's military-strategic goals. Those were realms into which other government departments (e.g., the ministries of interior and communication) had previously injected themselves, usually haphazardly, or which had received only passing attention, such as when crisis loomed. The business of war preparation changed so much and so rapidly after 1876 that Obruchev and his lieutenants effectively excluded outsiders from interference in the work. Specialization applied not only to the manning of Main Staff departments and committees but also to key staff billets on the western military district staffs. St. Petersburg had to be sure of the competence of its planners in Warsaw, Vilna, Kiev, Odessa, and Khar'kov.

Nothing could infringe on the privileges of Guards Corps officers, given their proximity to the throne and to constructed dynastic myth. Nevertheless, the Main Staff competed with that other powerful St. Petersburg military coterie simply by reason of the elevated importance of its work and, concomitantly, through the rising *professional* stature of officers designated to the general staff. Admittance into the General Staff Corps alone could not supplant Guards service as the sine qua non for high field or district command. However, the Guards' gold braid by itself was insufficient to assure ascent to the loftiest or most militarily influential positions. In this odd relationship lay an important paradox: simultaneous admission to both the most technically modern and the most archaically tradition-bound groups of the imperial Russian army officer corps became the route to career success. This conclusion is hardly surprising, given the widening cleavages that fractured all of elite society and accompanied the blurring of distinctions that previously defined "progressive" or "traditionalist" factions. Fragmentation of the state's upper crust was one result of ambivalence among the tsar's servitors toward "state thinking" (*gosudarstvennost'*) and its inherited narrative of autocratic authority.

It would be more than two decades before the Main Staff began publication of its monumental history of the 1877–1878 war.[2] During those intervening years Obruchev and his colonels studied intensively the staff problems exposed by the war. The most important of these was the dearth of rigorously trained general staff officers to fill all the headquarters, field staff, and unit staff positions during wartime, a shortfall that Obruchev could not resolve. On the other hand, he could further rationalize the system that made strategy (VUK) and put in place an organization subordinated to VUK that could provide hard strategic information and craft military options. In other words, he institutionalized the process of strategy formulation that he himself had spent most of the 1860s and 1870s learning. Leer's students and successors in the academy likewise had begun to explore the language and ideas that connected national resources and interests with military strategy. Military-statistical thinking had taught the academy's graduates that population base and transportation infrastructure mattered more than ever;

how those related to strategy formulation required new forms of expression and thinking.

Obruchev also sketched out in early 1880 a new strategic position for the empire that would steer the Main Staff's attention and labors until the eve of World War I. Obruchev's sense of strategic reality established the fundamental context of all mobilization work and thus cemented the staff's "monopoly of expertise" in strategic planning. With Alexander's approval of his "Basic Memorandum" *(Osnovnaia zapiska)* on mobilization in January 1880, Obruchev provided the Main Staff's planning basis and gave the state a strategic policy that had been debated by no one other than himself and the war minister. After 1881, with his elevation to Chief of Main Staff, Obruchev could control the mobilization planning work carried on by his colonels. Those subordinates had, without exception, field experience from the Turkish war. The group's efforts during the 1880s ultimately made credible Obruchev's courting of a French military understanding in the early 1890s, which was the reasonable consequence of the strategic course Obruchev charted in the 1860s and formalized in early 1880.

The nature of staff work carried with it little excitement. Those activities that constituted professionalized general staff work in the late nineteenth century were mundane: a tenacious if tedious accumulation of data, examination of solutions to small technical problems, preparation of intricate schedules and timetables. That was (and is) what a modern staff systems was about: the grasp of the *importance of the unexceptional* in relation to the cosmic in military planning questions having deep future and contingent significance. The accumulation and melding of fragmentary information was the heart of the war plan as well. Not grand strategic visions and sweeping war plans, but railroad loading capacities and rates, horse and fodder inventory, riverbed contours and frontier valley traverses were the meat of the Main Staff and its military district affiliates. Only by those small works could the staff anticipate an effective mobilization; when they occurred routinely and systematically within the framework of Obruchev's grand vision, then "professionalization" followed. The labors of railroad commissions and development of staff rides during the 1870s paid great dividends during the next decades.

With work specialization and a new strategic agenda came an acceleration of war preparation work on the Main Staff. The mobilization committee's reliance on intelligence and counterintelligence work rapidly increased; its attention to long-term planning of railroads and lines of communication through Poland intensified; and a progressive refinement of the western "contingency" war plan against Germany and Austria-Hungary brought Russia's military preparation to a high level of sophistication (if not effectiveness) by 1887. Concentration of these activities in Obruchev's organization also established the staff's technical monopoly in war planning, a practice that Obruchev's planners reinforced through secrecy. Nonexperts thus were excluded not only from the most important positions in the central and district planning apparatus but also from knowledge of precisely where Russia's security planning was going.[3] With time, those changes squeezed nonspecialist officers out of many of the more important district staff positions in the European theater. Similar changes had already occurred on Moltke's staff in Berlin. The staff method developed by the Great General Staff—a "stereotyped yet flexible procedure," in Michael Howard's words—necessarily characterized the work of much of Russia's Main Staff as well.

Moltke and the Russians

The story of Moltke's Prussian staff has been told from so many perspectives and in such detail that it hardly bears retelling here.[4] However, the story has never been juxtaposed against Russia's success in 1876–1877. Like European diplomacy during the 1876 Eastern crisis, the course that Moltke's strategic thinking took assumes important new dimensions in light of Russian mobilization success. The staff mechanism he developed to conduct mobilization planning (like Obruchev's Russian one) demonstrated the danger of strategic thought outdistancing state policy. More important, it also corroborated the indispensability to the state of political oversight, of intervention by a political actor to control the risks such disparity could produce. The events of 1876 to 1878 subsequently set up conditions that made the collapse of Russo-German relations in 1890 a much more straightforward matter. Through its military experts Russia had by 1890 committed itself to a strategy that labeled Germany the only threat and principal enemy, regardless of what the dynasty's leader thought of his German relations. The tsar's machine had gone precisely where he had allowed it to.

The Main Staff's performance in 1876 *by itself* changed the strategic balance in Europe, although the full effect of that change would not be felt for some years. Throughout the Eastern crisis Bismarck had realized that Germany, too, faced the danger posed by any Russo-Austrian war that might result from Gorchakov's incautious policies. It was only Bismarck's insistence on impartiality, when confronted with competing demands from Germany's two *Dreikaiserbund* partners, that prevented the Balkan war from widening in 1876, or the Russo-Turkish one from spreading in 1877 or 1878. The chancellor had concluded by the fall of 1876 that, if war were necessary with one or the other, Germany would side with Austria—if only for domestic political reasons.[5] And without committing himself to either, formally or informally, Bismarck remained of this opinion until he formulated the Dual Alliance with Vienna a year after the war (1879). The year 1876 proved that the Three Emperors' League could not, as Bismarck would continue to hope, "protect the 'flabby parts' of the three empires."

For Field Marshal von Moltke the lessons of 1876 and 1877 were technical and entirely military. He observed the Russian mobilization after November 1876 and calculated that, in a crisis, Russia could thenceforth have ready two hundred thousand men on the East Prussian frontier by the sixteenth or, at latest, the twentieth day of mobilization. He did not know, however, that Russian general staff officers had painstakingly labored for almost a year to prepare the 1876 mobilization. And although an army of two hundred thousand was a fraction of the force Prussia had mobilized in 1870, nevertheless it would allow Russia to unhinge any defensive mobilization Germany might make in its eastern provinces, if circumstances again were to necessitate war with France. A Russian advance into Prussia, like General Gurko's brilliant twelve-thousand-strong cavalry foray to Shipka Pass in June 1877, would then take at most an additional five to ten days.[6] In the future, Moltke believed, Germany's security would rest on the interval of those four weeks, between a Russian declaration of mobilization and when it was sufficiently strong to attack.

Moltke's study of the Russian problem hardly began in 1876 and 1877. Nor did his activity until then focus exclusively on the Rhine frontier region. In 1858, as the new Prussian chief of General Staff, he began a campaign for expansion of the railway network of the North German states (in which he had a financial stake, coincidentally), in cooperation with the Minister of Commerce August von der Heydt. The military impetus was Prussia's disastrous mobilization against Austria in 1850, which contributed substantively to the "Olmütz humiliation" at Austrian hands. Prussia had tried to mobilize 490,000 men by railroad; it took over two months because no one had ever planned such an operation before, and because the transportation system remained under civilian direction (and subject to commercial considerations) throughout the crisis. Even nine years later, Prussia's mobilization in support of armed mediation in the Franco-Austrian War revealed serious deficiencies in the mechanization of mobilization.

Although the commerce ministry's and general staff's goals and purposes diverged, they had sufficient ground for agreement on accelerated network expansion. Their cooperation on railroad construction resulted in a rapid increase in both line-mileage and dual-track construction on east-west lines (the latter being particularly important for the use of mobilization-related networks). Simultaneously, Prussian army units (some of corps size) improved their performance in mobilization exercises, and embarkation and transportation times decreased by 50 percent. In its 1866 war with Austria, Prussia mobilized *and* concentrated 280,000 troops in twenty days. Four years later Prussia could mobilize three times that number of troops on the French border in the same time. Politically, Austria and France were greater dangers than Russia. Nevertheless, all of Moltke's war plans from 1863 to 1870 depended on *negotiation* of Russian neutrality before hostilities began elsewhere, something that Bismarck's diplomacy consistently delivered his military establishment. Fortuitously, by the time Moltke perceived in Russia a credible military threat, railroad lines running from the east through Berlin to the Rhine already formed the system needed to rush German troops between the eastern and western frontiers, the cornerstone of Moltke's post-1871 plans.[7]

Not long after the 1871 armistice with France, Moltke elaborated in a *Denkschrift* the dangers facing Germany. Russia, he believed, would either center its attention on the Slavic populations of the Balkans, which would bring it into collision with Austria, or more likely would deploy its enormous standing army against its neighbors from the Polish salient. In either case, a Russian army could not quickly begin operations against Prussia given even the most propitious circumstances; Germany possessed the military trump card of dense rail network development. Instead, the next German war, if it were on two fronts, would begin where the danger lay—*am Rhein*.[8] The pace of events in late 1876 confounded Moltke's assumptions. It also confronted his staff with a multitude of new and potential dangers. The general staff's estimate of Russia's mobilized strength, together with emerging patterns of Russian troop movements in Poland, suggested to some German officers that the target was Austria as well as Turkey; Russia's operational army exceeded substantially the size necessary for a Balkan war, in their estimate.[9] At the same time Moltke himself was wrestling with the possibility of another, simultaneous war between Germany and a French-Austrian alliance. Those were the two countries, he reasoned, most likely to take immediate advantage of the eastern crisis to even scores with Germany. Russia was poised for a Balkan campaign and would thus be indisposed to counteract an Austrian mobilization, as it had in 1870.

But by the beginning of February 1877, Moltke had set aside his fear of a Franco-Austrian expedition after observing the Russian mobilization.[10] The Russian call-up proceeded like clockwork, with regiments throughout European Russia absorbing their reserves and moving relatively smoothly toward their concentration areas near Bessarabia. The German military attaché in Petersburg, Major Lignitz, was a more sober (if not skeptical) observer than either ambassador Schweinitz or the *Prusskii fligel'-ad"iutant* to the tsar, General Werder. He had considered the 1876–1877 concentration of Russia's army around Kishinev flawed, ipso facto of underdeveloped railroads. However, he did not think the same handicap affected Russia's ability to concentrate in the Vilna or Warsaw Military Districts.[11] On the other hand, neither Moltke nor Lignitz knew how extensively the Russians had prepared for the 1876 mobilization.

By springtime, Russia's move to the Bulgarian border awaited only the declaration of war against Turkey. By then Russian staff officers had ample reason for satisfaction with the running of the system.[12] This Russian army, by reason of its effective mobilization, was poised to carry out whichever war plan the supreme commander settled on. And, in principle, only railroad development would constrain Russian mobilization in another European crisis. Russia's mobilization planners knew their work made the army a more credible force than the one they (and Moltke) had assumed would march in the next European war.

From Moltke's perspective, if war were to break out between Germany and Russia, Russian occupation of the coastal provinces (with the ports of Königsberg and Danzig) would be not only "a worthwhile acquisition for Russia" but also a practical possibility. That agitated the field marshal's fears sufficiently to deepen his despair over Germany's prospects for future decisive military results.[13] Moltke considered Prussia's Upper-Silesian and Archducal Posen districts of no interest to Russia: either territory, if annexed, would be indefensible and could only exacerbate the problems Russia already faced with its own Polish subjects (a view that echoed Obruchev's own rhetoric fifteen years earlier).

Russia's Main Staff, like its Prussian counterpart, was prone to mistake a neighbor's capability for its intentions; that was and remains a weakness of any staff system dependent on "statistics" (intelligence) rather than politics for its direction. Statistics took the place of policy, and then in turn influenced policy. Given Russia's defensive and reactive strategy, however, the Main Staff's anxiety typically strengthened St. Petersburg's circumspection, rather than driving it to follow risky and aggressive policies. Although Bismarck and Moltke alarmed the Reichstag with warnings about Russian deployment and armed strength, they well knew that Germany, too, framed its plans on Russia's potential, not its intentions.[14]

That Russia might possess the capacity to mobilize a major force within a credible period had not figured in Prussian military planning before 1877. Now the Great General Staff had deadlines for war in *both east and west*, should mobilization be declared. The "two-front war" became the fatal, permanent characteristic of German war planning from February 1877 onward because Russia had demonstrated the *capability* to plan and mobilize its European forces effectively during a crisis. Moltke, never a student of the balance of power, could not articulate a political circumstance in which Russia would wish to pursue some design on East Prussia or Germany, nor German interest in any Russian territory. He wrote to agriculture minister Lucius von Ballhausen in April 1878, "The Russians are unpleasant neighbors; they have absolutely nothing which one would take for oneself from them after a victorious war. They have no gold, and we couldn't use the land."[15] Nor could Moltke find a military rationale for war with Russia—that is, reliable intelligence of Russian intentions or evidence of hostile plans—until the mid-1880s. By then Russian railway construction and frontier fortification made it clear to the German staff that its two-front strategy could not assure quick dispatch of Russia. The decay in Russo-German relations was already well advanced by then, and the hardening of political views on both sides provided Germany's general staff sufficient reason to plan for war against Russia, even as Russia's staff did likewise. In essence, the weapon created and perfected by Moltke was adopted by Obruchev and the Russians and then turned against him.[16]

Obruchev and the New Course

The German question perplexed Obruchev and his Main Staff planners (as well as the tsar and his ministers and representatives) continually after 1871. The 1873 secret strategic conference established terms for discussion of the problem. The unrealized promise of that policy-framing conference notwithstanding, Russo-German agreements such as the Three Emperors' League subordinated Russia's state interests to dynastic desires. Absenting political accord on national security, the strategic horizons that Obruchev sketched between 1868 and 1873 governed Russia's strategic planning: regardless of what the tsar, the foreign minister, or even the war minister did, the Main Staff followed its own reasoning. For instance, when Bismarck tentatively aligned Germany's interests with Austria's in March 1878, the emerging new constellation did not stand in the way of dynastic amity or Russo-German agreements. To Obruchev's staff, however, Bismarck merely continued the betrayal that had figured in their calculations from 1876 onward. At best, in Obruchev's view, Germany "thanked" Russia for its selfless support of German unification in 1870–1871 by betrayal in Berlin in 1878. Other officers saw Russia's "defeat" in Berlin as a product of conspiracy. "Supposedly Russian" diplomats (many with German names) did not challenge Bismarck's alignment with Austria and Britain, which "liberated" Russia of an independent "Big Bulgaria." Within two years Obruchev was acting independently on his distrust of Germany.[17]

Bismarck was eager to disrupt the resurrection of a Crimean coalition in 1879, as Britain and Russia squared off over Anglo unilateralism in interpretation of the Straits clauses of the Berlin treaty. In regard to Protocol 18 of the Berlin settlement, the British representative declared that Her Majesty's government recognized no binding authority at the

Straits except the *independent* policy of the Ottoman sultan (i.e., not the international treaties of 1841, 1856, or 1871, which regulated operation of the Straits in peace and war). This, at least, was the Russian diplomatic interpretation of British policy. In response, the Russian government began a search for "alternatives" to Britain's arrogance, in the form of a realistic plan to seize the Straits and solve the Eastern Question once and for all. Alexander II's memorandum to the minister of finance in 1879 produced merely the first disappointment: the military needed a minimum of two hundred million rubles to build naval and commercial vessels and equip an amphibious force for a successful descent on the Bosphorus—money Russia simply did not have.[18] The treasury would take years to recover from its recent one-billion-ruble extravagance in the Balkans.

Bismarck sought to introduce some small measure of stability to the Continental system and bound Austria-Hungary to Germany by a treaty the terms of which were transmitted officially to Russia only in May 1887. The Austro-German Alliance (Dual Alliance, September/October 1879) was intended not to support Vienna's ambitions in the Balkans but to "dig a trench between her and the western Powers," thus forestalling renewal of a "liberal alliance" of the Hapsburgs with Britain. St. Petersburg naturally had a copy of the secret parts of the agreement before the end of 1879, although apparently no one but the Russian chancellor and a few others seem to have known of this.[19]

On his own initiative Russia's ambassador in Athens, Count Saburov, proposed to Bismarck in September 1879 the three ingredients for mutual security in the form of an alliance: German neutrality in an Anglo-Russian war; Russian neutrality (and use of its influence to assure the neutrality of any other party) in a Franco-German war; and Russian respect of Austro-Hungarian integrity on the condition that Vienna limited its sphere of interest in the Balkans.[20] Bismarck's rejection of a bilateral agreement presented Miliutin the opportunity to promote the war ministry's strategic assessment of Russian interests.

Despite Germany's perpetual words of "happiness and friendship," Miliutin asked, could Russia really pretend not to be disturbed by the "sight of a colossal increment to the military strength of Prussia?" Would Russia really be expected to act differently than the rest of Germany's neighbors and forego attention to its own military readiness? And what, he asked, should Russia make of the Germans' reproach for a concentration of Russian "cavalry 'masses' along our long Prussian border?" The mass, Miliutin pointed out, consisted of only four divisions (sixteen regiments, of which four were Cossacks—hardly sufficient or appropriate formations for offensive action) along the "whole length of the Prussian border from the Neman estuary to the Oder." Russia, for its part, did not constantly reproach Germany for its intensive new strategic railroad construction through East Prussia to the Russian border, construction that would allow Germany to mobilize in half the time of Russia and concentrate its forces for the attack in a quarter the time it would take Russia. "The boundless ambition of the German Chancellor . . . [and] the apathetic and humble position of France . . . may raise in the near future such events which will not allow Russia to remain indifferent, witnessing them." In short, an alliance with German was to the war minister a boundless folly because Russia's and Germany's interests stood irrevocably opposed.[21] Miliutin's opinion did not influence the diplomats, and Saburov proposed resurrection of the Three Emperors' League instead of a bilateral alliance the following January. The proposal did not disturb Bismarck: it was merely intended, he ruminated to the prospective Russian ambassador, to protect the three empires' weak spots. Miliutin had already stated the military establishment's position, opposition that endured until the end of the empire.

Internal to the staff, the lessons of the 1876–1878 experience were straightforward and sobering: Russia's military organization was "insufficient" to the task of a war against a European coalition, and it was essential to "increase the size and improve the quality of most material and technical means necessary for the conduct of a European war."[22] The Main Staff understood those lessons strictly in terms of war readiness: the staff needed trained personnel in sufficient numbers if it was to respond quickly and appropriately to the "ballooning demands levied by [any new] emergency."[23] The Russian army and its general staff would, however, never have them. For over a year following the Congress of Berlin, general staff officers examined Russia's future in light of Germany's "unmitigated hostility." The officers around Obruchev shaped strategy and war preparation on the basis of unrelieved anxiety and suspicion of Germany. Obsession with the mobilization plan followed, as the only possible safeguard of the empire's position in Europe.

In late 1879 Obruchev's assistants prepared four studies collectively entitled "Considerations Concerning Plans for the Conduct of War."[24] The "Considerations" contemplated new circumstances, premised on the precipitation of Continental blocks hostile to Russian imperial security, in which war in Europe would erupt in the future. First, the studies authors' asked, what would be the potential strength of a European coalition comprising Germany and Austria-Hungary, with or without Romania? (This anticipated Romania's adherence to the Dual Alliance almost four years before it occurred, a remarkable political assumption for Russian war planners to make.) At an operational level, what assumptions could Russia make concerning the organization and concentration points of adversaries' forces along the western frontier? What were Russia's strength and means of action in the event of a general European war? And finally, what would be the approximate areas of concentration for a Russian army in such a war?[25] It is no surprise that these four studies mirrored the framework for military-statistical work completed during the previous two decades.

Obruchev digested the conclusions and drafted his Basic Memorandum, which, when confirmed by the tsar, represented a seminal shift in Russian strategic policy. Insofar as the Crimean War had not produced a strategic shift of comparable magnitude (merely a *social* revolution, with the emancipation of the serfs), the 1877 war was of farther reaching importance to Continental relations than Nicholas's war had been. The period from 1876 to 1878 had created for Miliutin, Obruchev, and their staff the opportunity to propose a clear restatement of the empire's strategic condition and priorities, which they presented in such a way as to forestall interministerial interference. The document, a mere five pages, exerted great influence on Main Staff activity; later planners alluded to it repeatedly as the fundamental reference point for their strategic deliberations, although other agencies of government knew nothing of its existence. In early January 1880 Obruchev submitted the memorandum to Miliutin, who briefed it to the tsar. After Alexander approved the memo's findings, Miliutin tersely annotated the paper, then returned it to the Main Staff on 29 January 1880. Miliutin's one-page ratification made the Basic Memorandum the basis for Main Staff activity and planning.[26] "It becomes clear to all that overwhelming success goes to him who mobilizes his army more quickly, and strikes his still unprepared opponent with mass," Obruchev reported.[27] Insofar as Russia would *never* be the quickest to mobilize, its strategy would be permanently defensive.

Disaster in Crimea, Obruchev argued, had induced the state to relieve the population of burdensome support of an army concentrated in the western provinces. The 1863 Polish uprising and Prussia's successes (1866–1870) had demolished the assumption that Russia could afford to spread its army from the Vistula to the Kama Rivers. Domestic and international threats to Russia's existence necessitated reconcentration of the army in Poland. This would be so, Obruchev concluded, at least until such time as Russia committed sufficient resources to build the strategic railroad network he had advocated for the past fifteen years. In the meantime, the army in Poland would remain behind the Vistula, avoiding any provocation to Germany; regardless of Moltke's protests, however, the survival of the empire depended on maintaining sufficient cavalry between the river and the border to screen a Russian mobilization in the event of German mobilization.

No scholar had remarked on Obruchev's Basic Memorandum before William C. Fuller, Jr.'s 1992 study.[28] However, no scholar has recognized the memorandum for what it was: a statement of strategic assumptions, the bedrock essential to formulation of a war plan. Given Continental realities, Russia would always enter a war with the Germanic powers in either a defensive or a "defensive-offensive" position, depending on circumstances. The former option called for strategic defensive operations across the entire front, and massive cavalry raids into East Prussian concentration areas to disrupt and delay a German offensive (an option Obruchev had long considered). The second option, the "defensive-offensive" plan, provided that in unexpectedly favorable circumstances the army could launch a reserve force into an offensive toward Austrian Galicia, the only portion of the entire European front that geographically offered even the least hope for success of offensive operations, as was repeatedly proved correct during 1914, 1915, and 1916.[29] Coincidentally, it was also an area of enduring political interest to Russian nationalists.

The memorandum had limited circulation in the staff's planning sections in January 1880, but it also went out to commanders of forces and their chiefs of staff in the key European military districts: Warsaw, Kiev, Vilna, Odessa. Perhaps surprising for such an important planning document, the war ministry did not pass it to the foreign ministry until 1883. The octogenarian adjutant-general P. E. Kotsebu (Kotzebue), supreme commander *(komanduiushchii)* of Warsaw district forces (and governor-general), reported that, if anything, Obruchev's estimates were optimistic. Kotsebu characterized the Warsaw salient as "the empire's greatest strategic weak point." He insisted that Russia's principal enemies, Austria and Germany, must always be assumed to operate in tandem, and that the war plans of the Central Powers reflected this. His immediate concern was the district's fortress system: it was the *only* part of Russia's defense that could possibly be made ready for a sudden onslaught, because Russian mobilization and concentration would take far longer than Germany's (as "Germany and Austria obviously knew"). Thus, the fortress system had to be brought up to and maintained at an advanced state of readiness; there would be no time in a crisis to do that.[30] But before the districts could know what to do, St. Petersburg had to have an agenda for itself.

The Main Staff derived four responsibilities from the 1880 strategic survey. First, planners had to arrange a new force disposition in European Russia that would minimize the danger to Poland in the event of war with Germany. That deployment would have to secure Poland for an unforeseeable number of years, until railway network development, as well as army mobilization plans, could create new, dynamic strategic options for defense. Those options simply did not exist in 1880. Second, the cornerstone of static deployment, the fortress system, had to be strengthened and brought to a high level of readiness. Third, the Mobilization Committee had to bring the standing army's deployment into alignment with its slow mobilization apparatus in order to optimize conveyance of mobilized units from all over the empire to a handful of locations. The plans would have to reorganize both field force disposition and the planned concentration areas to allow choice (perhaps relatively late in a crisis) of either the defensive or defensive-offensive plan, an almost impossible task given the arrangement of railway networks in the western salient. Finally, the St. Petersburg staff had to know their enemy better than he knew them: intelligence would be a pivotal equalizer as a crisis drifted toward war. The Main Staff did not hesitate to share its new burden; planning assignments and fieldwork flowed to key district staffs as they never had before. From early 1880 onward the western military district staff served essentially as extensions of Obruchev's mobilization planning offices in St. Petersburg, and the colonels who Obruchev selected for those forward posts took to Kiev, Warsaw, Vilna, and Khar'kov the same intense engagement with information and system as occupied their counterparts in the capital.

District staffs found they could influence strategic railroad development only indirectly, by the proposals they submitted to St. Petersburg for army mobilization and concentration. They conducted this work under the rubric of "theater preparation." It included examination of routes between concentration points and the frontier; preparation of depots and forage stores; and, most important, evaluation of options that would allow district forces to defend their sectors while also shielding the reservists' assembly and concentration areas.[31] The railroad arteries into tsarist Poland were the concern of Main Staff planners, but district staffs drove work on the secondary network of lines that would carry troops to forward areas for concentration. From the perspective of the plan, this division of responsibility was rational; the outcome, however, was wasted resources and the ire of other agencies of government, as secondary rail lines were laid, then abandoned, because of changes in the minutiae of the schedule. Economy and efficiency were possibly the concerns that least interested Main Staff planners or their district subordinates, although it was precisely those concerns that animated the finance ministry and cost the army resources for its key railroads.[32]

Strategic Flanks, Fronts, and Fortresses

The first deployment plan to emerge from Obruchev's new organization, the so-called 1880 Plan, was a stopgap draft at best and merely refined existing deployment patterns. The permanent dispersals it anticipated in Warsaw, Vilna, and Kiev districts could not, by themselves, assure the security of the state. Obruchev agreed with Kotsebu on this matter: delay of an invasion depended on the fortress system in conjunction with cavalry raids to disrupt German mobilization in East Prussia. The window of vulnerability remained open for most of the remainder of the decade, as the war ministry struggled for resources to satisfy the *minimum* transportation objectives which the tsar's strategic conference had identified in 1873 and the war ministry had repeatedly confirmed since.[33] As the rail network slowly grew after 1873, the complexity of the mobilization plan also increased. But in 1880 the empire's security still rested on static forces spread thinly over twelve hundred miles of western frontier.

For twelve years Obruchev had argued that the *very existence* of the empire depended on successful defense of Poland. The Main Staff's 1880 concept of defense left the weight of forces in the Warsaw district and designated those units the Western Army. Two weaker armies anchored the flanks: on the right, the Neman Army (in Lithuania, the Baltic districts, and the St. Petersburg approaches), and on the left, the Volhynia Army (Volhynia, Podolia, southern Russia). The center rested on a monstrous reserve in eastern Poland, appropriately designated the Main Army (Grodno to Pinsk, west of the Pripet marshes). The field army consisted of 764 battalions, 483 squadrons, and 2,400 guns; Table A-2 in the Supplemental Data section elaborates the deployments between 1880 and 1883. Obruchev's comments implied that security of Poland depended on maintenance of the *whole army* at a high state of readiness. The Warsaw district and St. Petersburg staffs, however, had a more reasonable objective. They hoped to maintain the fortress-citadels, the anchors of the strategic front, in a permanent state of premobilization readiness.

Did Obruchev believe that a German attack was an *imminent* danger or simply a long-term possibility? Each conviction posed a quite different military problem. Undoubtedly, he hoped to repeat the army's 1876 premobilization success, with preparations spread over some months, if relations with Germany deteriorated: a quiet period of preparation before declaration of mobilization was essential. He therefore either ignored his real apprehensions or did not fear an unprovoked attack.[34]

By late 1882 the distribution, designation, and strength of the forces had changed substantially, although plans for their operational employment remained the same.[35] Deployment of the Western Army formed a semicircle around Warsaw, with reserves near Sedlets (Siedlec). The Belostok Army had quarters around Brest-Litovsk in peacetime, and the Northern Army waited between Kovno and Grodno, with its reserves near Vilna. The Southern Army screened the Ukrainian flank, with reserves near Zhitomir. Two general reserve armies occupied billets near Minsk and in the vicinity of Moscow. The deployed forces numbered over 1,100 battalions, 650 squadrons and *sotnias* of cavalry, and 1,840 guns under this new army field organization; Map 3 illustrates these displacements by 1885.

The formations that constituted the front line were anchored at the northern and southern termini, called in this plan the Left and Right Flanks. Large stretches of the Baltic coastline and almost the entire

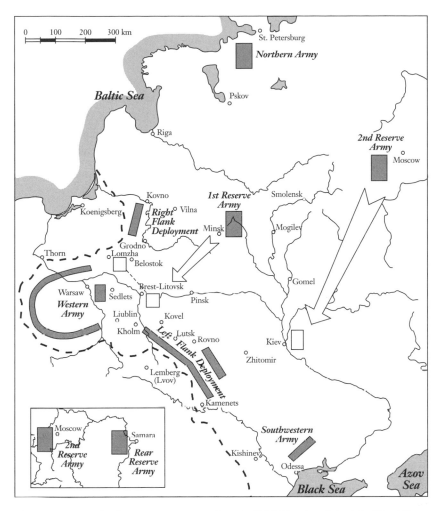

Map 3. Strategic deployment in western Russia (Mobilization Schedule No. 11), 1885.

Romanian frontier remained open. The late-1882 plan also established a modest "deep reserve" in the empire's interior (between Moscow and Samara), the military value of which remains unclear. Inclusion of these three new congregations brought the mobilized field army to well over 1,300 battalions, 700 squadrons, and 2,000 guns. The Main Staff planned to proportion strength away from the center of Poland, toward the Vilna and Kiev wings, and to create a second large reserve army standing deep in the interior, around Moscow. The new disposition anticipated concentration of the First Reserve Army in the vicinity of

Brest-Litovsk, ready to move into the gap between the Western and Northern Armies (to the area around Belostok). The Second Reserve Army, earmarked for transfer to the Kiev area, would be ideally situated to exploit an open right flank of any Austrian advance toward Warsaw, or to back the Southwestern Army if the Main Staff chose the defensive-offensive plan. Implicitly, the plan of disposition recognized that western Poland was indefensible, at least by mobile field forces, but also remained alert to the potential for parrying an Austro-German offensive by crushing the wings of any thrust into Poland. Obruchev's 1880 prescription for concentrated defense of the western border remained intact.[36]

After the organizational adaptations of 1876, the Main Staff's structure changed only in relation to the specialization of its work. In early 1885 the staff acquired a new department (IV *Otdelenie*) that combined diverse administrative support functions and the Main Staff Section for Transportation of Forces and Freight.[37] Aside from some further minor adjustments in 1886 and 1887, the Main Staff had by 1885 assumed most of the responsibilities that it retained until the Russo-Japanese War. The effect of these shifts was to relieve the staff's main operations department (II Department) of most nonmilitary responsibilities such as payments to railroad companies for troop transportation. As the staff learned more about war planning, it found itself burdened with ever more responsibilities, and it perpetually spawned committees and commissions, as well as other more specialized groups to deal with those.[38]

Yet even as "modernization" transformed the work of the staff, the organization was slow to catch up. Like the Main Staff's military-statistical work two decades earlier, the staff itself in the early 1880s operated essentially ad hoc; "special" work groups rather than permanent offices did mobilization planning, a category of work that Russia would not formalize in its general staff organization until, as war minister, Kuropatkin established the two General-Quartermaster sections in 1904. In the meantime, a deepening division and redivision of the work that made up mobilization preparation merely mirrored the complexity of war planning in the age of railways.

In 1882 Obruchev established a "Temporary Commission for Planning the Reinforcement of Warsaw, Novo-Georgevsk, and Veprzh (the three great Polish citadels), which he headed. Soon afterward, the commission became the longer-term Temporary Commission on Defensive

Construction in the Western Front, which functioned until 1894. The group broke work down into manageable tasks: construction of fortifications and "fortified places" along the western frontier strip (Vilna, Warsaw, Kiev Military Districts); construction of forts in Finland; and construction of fortifications in the Caucasus and Crimea.[39] Likewise, the older Committee for Preparation of Measures for Mobilization of Forces took on a new shape and title as the Main Staff Committee for Mobilization of Forces (in which form it continued until 1903). In addition to evaluation of army combat readiness and examination of the means for bringing the army to war footing, the committee became home to all preparation of Russia's contingency plans for a war in Europe—that is, for its most important war planning. Organizationally, all of these study circles operated under the supervision of VUK and the II Department, and they shared personnel among themselves and with the department.

Not every effort of Main Staff officers focused on war with Germany and Austria, of course. The perpetual Bulgarian and Balkan difficulties of the early 1880s offered planners ample opportunity to explore alternatives to meeting Britain at the Straits. One such study, prepared in 1882, remains of interest less for its contribution to Russian strategic history than as an illustration of deepening understanding of Central Asian campaigning. The report, "Considerations in the Event of War with England in the Central Asian Theater of War," included appendixes on the greatest range of concerns: systems for extracting three thousand liters of water per hour in the desert; a study of the medical difficulties encountered during Britain's 1881 Egyptian campaign; and plans for taking Herat through nighttime assaults. The diary of Lieutenant Colonel Iurii Dmitrievich Mel'nitskii, written during a covert 1881 reconnaissance of the route between Ashkhabad and Mashhad, supplemented the other studies, and all were solidly within the traditions of military-statistical work.[40] Men who were at the center of Main Staff planning work (such as Mel'nitskii) had developed broad knowledge and specialized skill through military-statistical practice, and their activities were indistinguishable from military intelligence.

Russia's strategic impotence—it had not caught up with German mobilization performance, and would not—haunted Obruchev after the Turkish war. If even by a victorious (and costly) war Russia remained unable to assert its interests at the peace table, what hope did it have to secure its interests against the undefeated Germans in central Europe? Although his staff remained completely attached to the problem of defensive mobilization against Germany and Austria, a strategic alternative proposed itself to Obruchev shortly after the end of the war. He came to believe that Russia's real interests required orchestration of diplomacy and military policy to repeat, in essence, the Russo-Turkish partnership that led to the treaty of Unkiar Skelessi (1833). The geographic boldness of Obruchev's scheme, and its removal from the realm of reality, were stunning. Only two areas justified the sacrifice of Russian blood: Subcarpathian Rus' and the Bosphorus Strait. A month after approving the Basic Memorandum, and within days of his assassination, Alexander II directed the war ministry to begin preparation of forces for an amphibious move against the Straits. Early in 1882 colonel Vasilii Ustinovich Sollugub submitted background papers for a plan of attack,[41] but the new emperor's attention to the counsel of his finance ministry derailed construction of a new fleet of battleships and transports on the Black Sea.

By 1885 Obruchev had worked out his strategic reorientation, which he shared not with his superior, Vannovskii, but with his mentor, retired war minister Miliutin. Russian diplomacy and military pressure would shift the strategic center of gravity south from the Polish salient into the Balkan peninsula. In essence, Russia would encourage Vienna (at great expense to the Dual Monarchy's domestic, fiscal, and international standing) to pursue its foolish interests in the western Balkans. The pressure on Turkey would drive Constantinople into Russian arms. In return for "defending" Turkey, Russia would receive a "sliver" of territory on the Bosphorus, and thus control of that Strait. With Russian armies already massed in Poland, Austria's army stretched out across Bosnia, Herzegovina, and even Albania, and new Russian strategic railroads toward the Hungarian border in operation, the Austrian rear would be compromised and Austria would lose Transcarpathian Rus'. In essence, the German Empire's southern flank would be turned, and Russia's security won.

Obruchev's vision was without rival into the new century. Echoes of it are found in strident planning of southerly offensives against Austrian Carpathia from the 1880s onward, and even in Brusilov's 1916 offensive. It resounds in Russian diplomacy during the 1908 Balkan crisis and in Russia's policy toward the Straits during the Great War.[42] But political will was not the real issue: as with strategic railroads construction and artillery modernization, the fisc failed Russia's and Obruchev's ambitions. Obruchev lamented in 1885 that, even if the war and naval ministries were to receive the required funds immediately, equipping the landing force would take at least another two years, and he had no reason to believe that the state would be any more able to underwrite that commitment in 1887 than it had been since 1879.

Obruchev's breathtaking idea certainly outpaced Russia's economic capacity, but not the passivity of the other great powers. Wildly ambitious tactical considerations aside, Britain was by no means bound to its 1878 policy at the Straits, nor Bismarck to his line of separation between Russian and Austrian interests on the peninsula ("from Salonika to Mitrovits"). Yet, consciously, Obruchev had traversed a great distance since 1868 or even 1876. He had abandoned south Slavic "forces from below" to achieve Russia's interests, and clearly distanced himself from Pan-Slavic posturing. He was no friend of oppressed south and west Slavs. Indeed, his bleak assessment of Russia's gain from the preceding nine decades of war "for their independence" cast him as a most pessimistic, and strangely realistic, judge of war's benefit to Russia's progress.

Cooperation and Conflict between St. Petersburg and the Provinces

Although Obruchev's Basic Memorandum lay behind shifts in the Main Staff's development in the early 1880s, the origins of the empire's strategic dilemma dated to the unification of Germany. The political and military repercussions of 1870 resonated in the secret strategic conferences the tsar convened to establish the direction of Russia's European security. Although effectively crippled by interministerial bickering and obstruction (the result of autocracy's unique, disunified political system), the conference's strategic "Conclusions" were not overturned for thirty-five years and continued to guide war ministry thinking even when the state's financial managers refused to fund their programs. Satisfaction of the military objectives devolved to the war ministry, where the Main Staff and VUK disaggregated each problem and prepared ad hoc solutions that were sometimes woefully inadequate and inappropriate. The Main Staff delegated segments of the work to the military district staffs on the western frontier, where a multitude of statistical responsibilities fell after 1873. Some years passed, however, before district staffs learned how to conduct the sorts of work being assigned by St. Petersburg.

The death in 1874 of General-Adjutant Berg, commander of Warsaw Military District, interrupted the work of the district's staff on an evaluation of northwest Poland's preparedness for an invasion. The 1877–1878 war also diverted attention and manpower away from this work. By 1878 Berg's successor, Kotsebu, was finally in a position to report on the preparation of a strategic front from Warsaw to Grodno between the Bug and Narew Rivers, a task formally assigned in August 1876.[43] Then, as a result of Obruchev's 1880 memo, Kotsebu also submitted some blunt remarks on the danger his district anticipated from Germany. According to his staff's "best intelligence," Germany had in place an army ready for operations against Russia's Polish possessions: "Germany will throw a portion of its strength on the lower and middle Neman [Niemen], a second [group] of two or three corps across the Beborz [Bobr] River and middle Narev in the encirclement of our forces situated in Tsarist Poland, and Austria will advance its main force between the Vistula and Bug Rivers, screened by a special detachment from the direction of Volhynia and Podolia."[44]

The great citadel-fortresses of Novogeorgevsk, Ivangorod, and Warsaw would be vital to derailing such an offensive. Novogeorgevsk, located just north of Warsaw at the confluence of the Vistula, Bug, and Narev Rivers, faced the right flank of any German advance out of East Prussia across the Narev. The size and mobility of that garrison's field force was the key to the fort's usefulness. Citadel Warsaw obstructed the axis along which the two enemies would advance in order to link up; it was also the principal rail junction in central Poland, and connected the major lines to Thorn and Krakov. Ivangorod, at the meeting of the Vistula and Veprzh Rivers, sat on the left flank of any Austrian advance toward Warsaw up the Vistula valley; like Novogeorgevsk, the size of its field forces would prescribe its capacity to interfere with an Austrian offensive.[45] Not surprisingly, this possibility had been considered during the 1873 strategic conference, but up until 1880 the threat had produced little apparent corrective activity.[46]

The Vilna Military District staff also faced difficulties, but largely of its own making. Vilna reported to Obruchev their initial deployments and intentions in the event of war with Germany. Their draft was mechanical, unimaginative, and shallow, demonstrably a pro forma response to the mobilization committee in its lack of serious consideration. Within three weeks Obruchev and his new assistant, Major-General A. N. Kuropatkin, had dissected the plan and shot back ten pointed questions that required "further elaboration." St. Petersburg's criticisms went a long way toward demonstration of the sort of plan the district staff *should* have submitted in the first place. Intolerance of rigid formalism—but one unhappy characteristic of Vilna's original deployments—emerged from the committee's critique, and Obruchev wished to have other district staffs benefit didactically from Vilna's disagreeable experience.[47] Thereafter, each European district had to submit draft plans of how their forces would screen army mobilization locally from German interdiction and protect the concentration of mobilized formations.

Kuropatkin had taken charge of the activities of the mobilization committee in early 1883 after a brief period as head of the staff's Asiatic Section (*Aziaticheskoe chast*).[48] He made an immediate imprint on the empire's strategic planning system. Despite two tours of duty in Central Asia, serving with some of the empire's most flamboyant generals, he came to the Main Staff with a reputation among contemporaries (and confirmed by later observers) as a poor combat leader—but perfect staff officer (*shtabist*). That impression was reinforced by his performance during the Russo-Japanese War. General Skobelev's sister later related to Count Witte that her dashing brother thought Kuropatkin was "a very good executive assistant [*ispolnitel'*] and an extraordinarily brave officer, but that he (Kuropatkin) as a combat commander appears completely incompetent in wartime, that he could execute orders but not give them; he did not have the appropriate military fiber or character for that. He was brave in the sense that death did not scare him, but cowardly in the sense that he will never be able to assume responsibility." Witte, that greatest of gossips of late imperial Russia, also recorded A. A. Abaza's impression. Abaza, then a senior statesman and old ally of Miliutin, described Kuropatkin as "a sensible and brave general, and he will have a remarkable career, he will become war minister. And he will rise much higher even than war minister. But do you know how it will all end? . . . In the end everyone will be disappointed in him . . . because the clever and brave general has the soul of a staff clerk."[49]

Even solidly Marxist historians describe Kuropatkin as "not a bad staff officer, but a man unable to take independent decisions."[50] Emblematic of autocracy's disastrous role in government was the dynasty's role in advancement of Kuropatkin to the ministryship in 1897, rather than to the office of Chief of Main Staff. The brilliance of his staff work between 1883 and 1890 propelled Russian war planning rapidly down the road of systematization, and showed him to be a precise analogue of his contemporary Alfred von Schlieffen (exemplar of the *Fachidiotie*, and Moltke's successor). These were the "demigods" of the general staff system (in Bismarck's words), men lacking the preceding generation's reverence for war's inscrutable complexity and danger, and without interest in the forces of statecraft or national psychology that bore so heavily on grand strategy. Indeed, for these new technicians the perfectible war plan superseded any "grand strategy" that might draw together the threads of diplomacy, economy, national aspiration, and military force.[51] Above all, Kuropatkin and Schlieffen reveled in the promise of a technically perfectible war plan and found affirmation of their faith in the era's scientifically inspired positivism as the true route to effectiveness.

Responding to Kuropatkin's terse criticism of his work, Vilna district's chief of staff submitted a "corrected" concept of operations, which for the first time included reference to German corps deployment facing his sector, and the concentration points and probable operational objectives of those opposing forces (obviously all relevant concerns to any contingency plan).[52] The proposed deployment also incorporated new flexibility, more like a fluid zone defense than a positional one, all of which suggested an elevated appreciation of the uncertainties the district's forces would face in a European war.

For the next two and a half years, the mobilization committee worked closely with Major General Vasilii Aleksandrovich Bunakov and his staff to improve Vilna's preparations. Bunakov, with combat experience in 1877 and a previous posting as chief of staff to an army corps, was Kuropatkin's senior; he would occupy the chief of staff's billet in Vilna for almost a decade. But in October 1885 Kuropatkin raised some basic questions about the practicability of Bunakov's efforts when he questioned the district's assessment of carrying capacity of the main roads along which reinforcements were destined to move during mobilization.[53] Bunakov's staff could not resolve the discrepancies nor assuage Kuropatkin's doubts; in fact, it was not until 1890 that St. Petersburg and Vilna finally negotiated a solution to the troop transportation problem.

Warsaw's reply to Kuropatkin's inquiry reflected the far greater consideration that Kotsebu, his chief of staff Naglovskii, and others there had already given the problem of war with Germany.[54] Naglovskii's report reiterated the mobilization disadvantages Russia still faced, and which were well known to St. Petersburg. He argued that, in order to bring mobilized forces quickly to their designated operating areas, the district's assembly and dispatch centers had to be placed as near as possible to the frontier. However, that was where those vulnerable facilties would face the greatest threat, particularly from German cavalry raids. The one solution was (as before) the maintenance of fortresses on a virtual war footing, continually. To balance the district's responsibilities to defend central Poland and harass eastern Prussia would be particularly difficult, "since in this relation we are in an especially thankless situation in comparison with Germany's cavalry which, as already mentioned above, will surpass ours along the border from the fourth or fifth day of mobilization."[55]

With St. Petersburg's approval, Naglovskii's delayed submission of the draft plan Kuropatkin had requested, and in September 1883 the district staff sent in a proposal for safeguarding force mobilization, district railroads, and assembly and dispatch points. The mobilization committee annotated and approved the plan in October.[56]

At its disposal each district staff had various sources of intelligence that also fed St. Petersburg's needs. Similarly, the Main Staff collected information directly from its own agent and attachés throughout Europe. Although the system by which information passed in and out of the war ministry's various offices was primitive, the volume and value of military intelligence gathered by VUK were extraordinary. The breadth of Russian intelligence success may be gauged from the *routine* intercept of all foreign diplomatic telegraph traffic within the empire (recall Bismarck's railings during Werder's Livadia mission in 1876), the sustenance of spies at the highest levels of Austria's General Staff, and even by the purloining of the French ambassador's aide-mémoire of his most secret talk with Bismarck in November 1879.[57]

Whether intelligence information would be made available in the offices where it was needed, however, was another matter. The Main

Staff might deny a district's request for information relating to some planning project then under way, or sanitize and synopsize sensitive information before forwarding it to staff planners. For instance, during the fall of 1884 the Warsaw staff asked the Main Staff Chancery for intelligence on the carrying capacity of German and Austrian railroads in wartime. Obruchev's successor as permanent secretary of the VUK, Major General Fel'dman (also late attaché of the embassy in Vienna, and Miliutin's son-in-law), replied that the committee had materials in the form of tables attached to the main Mobilization and Concentration Plan, but that the chief of the Main Staff would not approve the district staff's independent use of the information.[58]

Instead, at two conferences (6 December 1884 and 25 January 1885), members of VUK decided to establish a program for the acquisition of intelligence by the Warsaw district staff, both inside and *outside* of Russia's borders. The committee wanted Warsaw to arrange to gather information in six categories:

- Relating to the enemy's border zone (collected by small parties of officers)

- Relating to any enemy movements toward Russian forces on the Narev, and elaboration of the routes for such approaches

- Relating to allocation between fortress and field units of the forces earmarked for the first engagement with the enemy, and the designated positions for those encounters

- Relating to the planned seizure and fortification on the first day of war of the confluence of the San and Vistula Rivers

- Relating to the deployment of the district's newly assigned reserve battalions for Warsaw

- Relating to the defensive arrangements for Putulsk and in general the sector between the Vistula and the Mlava-Novo-Georgevsk railroad line[59]

Three of these intelligence goals involved espionage work in East Prussia by Russian general staff officers. All of the information satisfied new requirements established by VUK and Kuropatkin's mobilization committee. Finally, none of the information could be acquired by attachés, either by bribe or by personal reconnaissance. Russia had a general staff that not only consumed military intelligence information but also gathered it, often by the most dangerous of covert means. Obruchev and Kuropatkin themselves had conducted such activity in the late 1870s, in connection with plans for a seizure of the Straits; not surprisingly, they expected their subordinates to continue the practice.

Kuropatkin's New Program

General Kuropatkin's criticism of the efforts of western district staffs on the general war plan grew in pointedness after he took over the operations of the mobilization committee in early 1883. His appointment to that post, on Obruchev's recommendation, was undoubtedly the most important Main Staff appointment of the 1880s. If he thought the direction of district preparations was rudderless, their activity during his first year in St. Petersburg[60] did little to dispel that impression. As a result of wide variations in quality and content of district work, Kuropatkin drafted for Obruchev's approval the first of the Main Staff's annual schedules: "The Program of Work in Preparation for War to be Followed in the Main Staff in 1884–1885."[61] The document in itself is unimposing: it listed a dozen questions that needed resolution during the coming work season (which ran through the winter months) and contained assignments for every office in the Main Staff and the directorates. If over the two previous years the Main Staff had tinkered with a workable deployment of the army, now it turned its attention to the thornier problem of the "organization . . . of the intendancy, artillery, engineering and military-sanitation services, both in the army's deployment areas and in the rear areas" of those forces.[62]

Kuropatkin admitted that the committee's staff officers made the greatest contribution to the program.[63] General Staff colonels V. U. Sollogub[64] and Iu. D. Mel'nitskii,[65] as well as lieutenant colonel Dmitrii Petrovich Zuev,[66] prepared the comprehensive program, with the aid of specialists from the main directorates; Kuropatkin then detailed them to oversee the work. The sorts of things that interested the Main Staff in the mid-1880s, and the distance the Russian army had yet to go to prepare adequately for war with the Dual Alliance, were implicit in the goals of Kuropatkin's first program. The first three tasks fell to Zuev. Under his guidance the Main Staff first completed estimates for rail transportation requirements for all reserve divisions of the First Call-

Up *(ochered)*, and for all Cossack regiments of the Second Call-Up, under war plans A and B (i.e., the defensive and defensive-offensive options). Preliminary estimates of "rail transport for all [artillery and engineer] parks" fell to this study section also. Second, Zuev examined all of the studies submitted by Warsaw, Kiev, Vilna, and Odessa district staffs in 1884. He verified whether the "staffs had *done the work properly*" and in an orderly way (in the way ordered by the Main Staff), and whether the other three district staffs had yet reached Warsaw's level of preparation and quality. Then, "on the basis of the work delivered from these four districts [the Main Staff] will draw up directions for further assignments on the questions of screening mobilization ([i.e.,] the preparation and means of our cavalry); on screening and demolition [*prikrytie i razrushenie*] of railroads; on moving detachments forward for the first engagement and on other [issues]."[67] Zuev's final charge was monitoring work on the reinforcement of rear areas, which included the development of lines of communications (transportation, staging routes, and *withdrawal routes*), and preparation of staging areas for artillery, engineers, hospitals, intendancy, and so forth.

Mel'nitskii oversaw all correction to the military-statistical compilations completed in 1883–1884; the changes would be based on studies and sketches done by general staff officers during the summer maneuvers and staff rides. His responsibility extended to virtually all Main Staff statistical and topographic holdings that related to the western frontier area. Further, he had to retrieve from each of the four western district staffs copies of any materials relating to the frontier not already in the Main Staff's library and draft a guide to future collection. His section undertook a "statistical elaboration" of new and probable lines of advance into East Prussia, Austria, and Romania from the four western military districts. Cartographic updates rounded out Mel'nitskii's responsibilities: "new, minutely detailed maps of the arrangement of German and Austrian forces on the frontier," an update of VUK's 1876 maps of East Prussia, and of other such cartographic materials of Galicia prepared by the Kiev district staff.[68]

The remaining tasks fell to the concerned main directorates:

Artillery: accumulation of information on its preparation of the
   "main theater of war" (i.e., the western front), to be broken down
   into the categories of First Line (frontier strip), Second Line (in-

terior provinces), fortresses, and siege parks. Kuropatkin also wanted appendixes on the peacetime and wartime equipment order of battle, and on estimated reserves of obsolete rifles and ammunition *for a people's war* [*narodnaia voina*].

Engineers: complete information on war preparedness of the frontier fortress system, on the speed of completion of preparatory work once war is declared, and the general condition of all equipment and training of reserve engineering units (telegraph, pontoon, sapper, railroad battalions).

Intendancy: preparation of estimates of the total consumption needs for all forces from a declaration of mobilization to completion of concentration. For this, Kuropatkin pointed the directorate toward the districts' data.

In an apparent afterthought Kuropatkin suggested that the commander in chief of the Caucasus submit some thoughts on the next wars with Turkey and Persia. He also directed the concerned districts to prepare estimates for "action" against Bukhara, then Afghanistan, and finally India (by way of Afghanistan: Turkestan to Herat and then across to Bamian and on to Kabul). An invasion of China likewise intrigued Kuropatkin.[69]

There is no need to judge the thoroughness of this list of tasks; it is clear that St. Petersburg's interests were eclectic and tended toward some of the minutest details. The Main Staff at the same time left the work up to the districts, which had real practical and pedagogic value for provincial staffs. By collection of increasingly specific military intelligence, and preparation of more specialized plans, each district staff not only satisfied St. Petersburg's (and Kuropatkin's) thirst for thoroughness but also developed new staff work skills and closer engagement with local conditions. And as long as the Main Staff levied progressively more exacting demands on district staffs, they might continue to improve in performance of their duties.

Kuropatkin's system of setting schedules of work, evaluating completed work, and addressing new goals for both center and districts developed a momentum of its own. In the spring of 1885 Kuropatkin signed out orders for further work on provisioning of forces[70] and the medical establishment[71] in the western border districts. The main directorate of the war ministry cooperated in all matters involving re-

serves, sanitation, the intendancy organization, preparations of handbooks and regulations, the gathering of data and materials, and so
forth.[72] Eighteen months after beginning the project, Kuropatkin could
write that "all the principal studies concerning the organization [of the
army] in the event of war . . . were concluded." His plan—to subdivide
into manageable segments for study the nearly impossible task of drafting a unified European war plan—had worked. Between March and
May 1885, the mobilization committee's members finalized their reports on the problems of preparation for a war. Obruchev approved
these seven reports, which then became the cornerstones for a multifac-
eted "General Plan for War" which Kuropatkin's colonels began preparing in mid-1885.[73]

Of course Kuropatkin and others at the heart of the Main Staff organization occasionally had concerns besides their correspondence with
Warsaw, Vilna, and Kiev. The 1885 war scare was one such instance,
although the limited attention that "crisis" received from the mobilization committee certainly diminished the stature of events. The reason
that Russia's relations with Bulgaria deteriorated steadily after Alexander II's assassination need not detain this account.[74] The St. Petersburg
planners, however, must have found most of the activity that sur-
rounded the Philippopolis rebellion (which led to unification of Bulgaria and Roumelia) distracting. The mobilization committee had put
the finishing touches on Mobilization Schedule No. 11 in October
1884, and it insisted that no activity should be undertaken to upset
that plan. A partial mobilization of forces in the Transcaspian area and
Turkestan (a total of thirty-seven battalions, forty-four *sotnias* of Cossacks, and eighty-six guns) would satisfy that injunction by incorporat-
ing the fourth (*zapasnye*) battalion in each regiment. All other measures
would be defensive: fortresses on the exposed coastlines (Black Sea,
Baltic Sea and Finland, *and* the Pacific Ocean) would be strengthened
and forces in Central Asia alerted, all within ten to forty-five days. If the
Caucasus had to be mobilized, that would be accomplished in conformance with Schedule No. 11 (four to six weeks, for the seven divisions
stationed there).[75]

What followed was a confused sequence of partial mobilization
measures. On 5 April war minister Vannovskii sent a "notification of
intent" to the commanders of Petersburg, Kiev, Odessa, Khar'kov,
Kazan, and Caucasus districts, to prepare for partial mobilization.[76]

This was extended to Vilna, Finland, and Moscow districts on 12 April; the same day, a draft war plan, extracted from Schedule No. 11, went to all affected district chiefs of staff,[77] which allowed district staffs to begin preliminary work from existing schedules. The next day the imperial *Ukaz* that directed the limited mobilization for which districts had already prepared, went out.[78] The exercise continued for a couple more weeks; Petersburg worked out the small problems in the mobilization plan that the drill uncovered (for instance, units not on the correct rosters, or sent to the wrong district), before the partial mobilization was abruptly ended. Given the limited range of measures ordered—even as a partial mobilization—it is difficult not to consider it the mobilization committee's chance to practice what it was planning. The process left no apparent mark on serious mobilization work, which continued uninterrupted in April and May. Kuropatkin made no mention of the committee's efforts when he composed his historical summary less than two years later. In many regards, the 1885 war scare was, from the Main Staff's perspective, merely an expansion of the 1882 war-with-England frolic.

When, in late 1887, this cycle of the Eastern Question reached its apogee, it was the Prusso-German and Austrian general staffs that planned "prophylactic" offensives against Russia. They assumed that Russia was itself preparing for war against Bulgaria (and Austria) early in 1888. Moltke, Waldersee, and their Austrian counterparts intended to launch a winter campaign against Russia, which Bismarck promptly blocked.[79] Apparently Obruchev's staff remained oblivious to those preparations: neither defensive nor offensive contingency plans occupied its members. It fell to Kuropatkin, the kingpin of Russian mobilization planning, to respond to belligerent press reports emanating from Vienna that warned of Russian preparations for war.[80]

The Elements of Schedule Preparation

By 1884 or 1885 Kuropatkin's group had settled into a process for planning that served their limited needs reasonably well. Those needs were simple because Russia was still without a mature reserve system, and thus many of the scheduling difficulties that confronted German planners still lay in the future. Furthermore, the means of mobilization, as was well known, simply did not support *too* sophisticated a mobilization plan: the lack of railroads, particularly sufficient lines into the Polish salient, rendered any plan that relied on rapid transportation largely chimerical. Although all that would change within a few years, at middecade the Main Staff's system for mobilization scheduling was linear, unhurried, and more an exercise that developed skills than one that produced a viable plan. An examination of the "stereotyped yet flexible" procedure offers a glimpse of the enormous range of expertise and interests that characterized general staff work in Russia, as elsewhere.

After Obruchev and VUK chose an outline for a new mobilization plan (e.g., the new disposition of forces in Poland, the areas of concentration after a call-up, the character of the first engagements), the mobilization committee took over the elaboration process. (Figure 7.1 depicts the sequence of activity.) The mobilization committee carried on a dialogue with each main directorate and frontier district staff, some of which have already peppered this account. Communications with the former were, at least until 1887, on the basis of primus inter pares so coordination on questions that involved the intendancy, military-medical service, artillery, and engineering directorates could resist satisfaction. Not until Kuropatkin established "mobilization sections" in each directorate, responsible to his Main Staff mobilization commission rather than the directorate,[81] could the committee readily utilize other specialists in the war ministry.

Consistently, the activities of Warsaw, Vilna, and Kiev districts dominated the attention of the committee. Communications between St. Petersburg and the district headquarters resembled a negotiation over how to satisfy VUK's larger strategic scheme. Assignment of specific units to a corps within one or another district was left to the mobilization committee. That decision, of course, depended on often elusive or inscrutable military-statistical knowledge: From where, in what strength, and on what schedule would an enemy attack come? Obruchev and Kuropatkin often were unwilling to share that most basic (and sensitive) intelligence with district staffs.[82]

Logically, the committee would prefer to assign units that mobilized most lethargically (for instance, from the interior of Russia) to "quiet" fronts. Corps formations of the Vilna district facing East Prussia consistently contained regiments that could be rapidly mobilized. Likewise, the indigenous structural peculiarities that weakened this corps or that division in a frontier sector also affected the committee's freedom to change operational plans for the district as a whole. Finally, the character of one army's assembly rate could pose an unacceptable restriction on where additional (or alternative) regiments might be deployed. Consider the Neman army, located on the northern flank of Warsaw salient, (Table 6.1).

Vilna district staff's report of the mobilization advantage enjoyed by the Army of the Neman placed that army's corps among the faster mobilizing formations on the western front. With most of its units at full strength by M + 14, that army would have roughly two cavalry-heavy corps ready for operations against East Prussia two weeks after mobilization began. With good reason, only regiments with comparatively rapid assembly rates would be added to the Neman army; that, in

Table 6.1. Mobilization Increments of the Army of the Neman

	Field Forces				Reserves	
Day M +	Battalions	Squadrons	Sotnias	Guns	Battalions	Guns
3				6		
4		12				
5				12		
6		6	6			
7	12	12				
8	16	6		48		
9	4			12		
10					5	
11					5	
12	8				10	
13	20			48	5	
14	12			48	10	32
15				48	5	
16	12			48		32
Total:	84	36	12	264	40	64

By M + 26: another 16 battalions and 60 sotnias added

Source: RGVIA, F. 402, op. II, d. 60, l. 4, dated November 1884.

fact, was the case as the right flank grew in weight—and retained its relative mobilization advantage (compared with armies farther south, in the Kiev Military District) into the 1890s. Table A-3 in the Supplemental Data section compares the mobilization rates of the different army groups by early 1891.

Invariably, the difficulty at middecade for both the mobilization committee and the district staffs was selection of which preparations, from among so many necessary, should occupy their time. Kuropatkin wrote his old friend Naglovskii (chief of staff, Warsaw): "In St. Petersburg we have begun the winter work season. The events on the Balkan Peninsula [Bulgarian crisis] are reported in some feverish shades. It all demands a reckoning: what to prepare, and what not. My boss [Obruchev] is anxious for news of your work in the frontier district. He wants you to dispatch the work of last September."[83]

More than likely the work about which Obruchev fretted most was the summer's horse inventories, for if the army would not be moving by train, then it would certainly move by horsepower. During the summer of 1876 the army had rushed to prepare for war as it inspected and inventoried enough mounts to carry a campaign to the Straits. A war against Germany and Austria would demand more horses in a much shorter time. Mobilization plans demanded that everything—including the precise allocation and availability of remounts—be planned and coordinated with the transportation schedule in peacetime. The fact that, at middecade, no agency of the Main Staff had even reliably *imagined* (much less tabulated) such figures (upward of a million horses) was reflected in the absence of data in the pertinent fields of finalized, printed mobilization schedules. The data finally appeared in *printed* form only in 1890 and 1891, and then it did not spring, like Minerva from the head of Jove, complete and perfect. The figures from 1890 (see Tables A-4 and A-5 in the Supplemental Data section) were of sufficient accuracy to justify committing to print, although they probably echoed in scale the earlier estimates. Also of interest here is the precise classification of horse stocks based on development of a system of livestock inspection and categorization. The Main Staff anticipated the shape of that system and its operation in the hurried steps it had taken in 1876. Also noteworthy is the added complication of the plan that balanced each district's livestock against its own and neighboring districts' needs. And, of course, the added complexity implied yet greater transportation demands that had to be staffed by the central organs. The mind-numbing thought of shunting tens of thousands of horses and tons of their fodder back and forth across European Russia on the eve of a future Continental war must have been bracing to mobilization committee planners.

The assignment of regiments and divisions to the new plan completed the mobilization committee's three-month labor on the draft schedule. Kuropatkin's committee passed the transportation requirements to the Railroad Section of the Committee for Transportation of Forces. That section scrutinized the mobilization and concentration objectives for what was practicable, and informed Kuropatkin of what was not. Those primitive plans included *only* transportation one way— from interior to assembly points and on to deployment areas at the front (for men, their horses, and their supplies). If the section's work concluded successfully, it would have in hand the rail movement plans for every district of European Russia within four and a half months. The army's requirements then went to the Railroad Directorate of MPS, where plans for mobilization of the railroad system were hatched, and a contingency mobilization railroad schedule took shape.

The transportation committee's railroad section was probably the office that first discovered the time differential that distinguished mobilization under the "defensive" and "defensive-offensive" options.[84] The schedule of concentration of forces by rail under the latter strategy had a four-day advantage over the more conservative defensive plan. The demographics and peacetime deployment pattern of the army favored southern Russia; it offered the greatest source of fodder for horses, and was home to the greatest number of *zapasnye* (reserve) troops. Thus the more southerly army concentration favored for defensive-offensive action (against Austria-Hungary) benefited the efficiency of that mobilization plan. Two decades later a nameless staff historian gave no hint that, as a result of the discovery of this advantage, one strategy became preferable to Obruchev or war minister Vannovskii. And aside from foreshortened mobilization, Obruchev and Kuropatkin understood that, if a war with the Central Powers were to be accompanied by renewal of Franco-German hostility, then a strong, successful blow against Germany's ally would be at least as valuable, strategically, as a weaker, less predictable encounter with Germany. Geography assured Germany that it could parry a Russian thrust toward Austria as easily as it could from across the Neman River.

The procedure Kuropatkin and his assistants developed from 1883 to 1886 was only a stepping-stone, because important changes in the complexity of mobilization preparation and planning quickly overtook them. Yet like many other things the Main Staff undertook after 1871, its development and *standardization* of a procedure for this work had inestimable value in the training of the staff's next generation of planners. And if systematic planning robbed staff work of some of its excitement as extemporaneous practices gave way to routine and procedure, it also prepared staff officers for an intensification of work that set in before the end of 1887.

Russia's First Modern War Plan

In one bold and ambitious step Kuropatkin tried to place wartime direction of the empire's armies, traditionally in the hands of grand dukes and their favorites, into the hands of the St. Petersburg Main Staff and its adjuncts, the frontier districts' staffs. His reasoning in this effort not only struck at established dynastic prerogatives and practice but also pushed Russian military philosophy into a realm that even the Prussians refused to enter. Kuropatkin built on a proven and still maturing staff apparatus to establish in peacetime the conditions that would propel Russia's armies into their first, pivotal battles if war with Germany came—all beyond the control of the tsar's uncles, brothers, and cousins. The mechanism for the coup was a new war ministry organ that would seize control of virtually all decisions of strategy and preparation well before outsiders could aspire to such authority during a crisis. The philosophy that underpinned Kuropatkin's move rested on assumptions concerning both the reliability and the indispensability of staff planning, and implicitly on the deplorable skills of Russia's combat leaders at all levels: the less any of them could interfere in strategy during the transition to war, the better would be Russia's chance of survival.

Kuropatkin buried his idea deep in the second and third sections of his "Program" for work during 1886–1887. The program's main premise stood unaltered (if more refined) from Obruchev's Basic Memorandum and, in fact, from the conclusions of the 1873 secret strategic conference as well. The war readiness of Russia's neighbors was so great that as early as two weeks from a declaration of war the enemy would concentrate a massive combined-arms force on Poland's border, and within the first month a collision of "decisive character" would occur in the western theaters.

In our previous wars, between forming the army and its direction into combat, there passed many months. During these months a plan for war was drafted and organizations were elucidated, all to the satisfaction of the army's various views. For the structure of the latter individuals were appointed within the various field authorities, who conducted studies and assembled various data from the area of concentration of the army . . . Composition of the [war] plan and its bases was subjected to examination by the responsible higher organs of the war ministry, approved by the commanders in chief, and finally put into action.[85]

In the next war, he continued, that way of operating would not be possible. No matter how rapidly the supreme field authority and its staff were assembled, they would not even arrive in the army's assembly areas until *after* military operations had begun. Kuropatkin assumed that, "in the event of war with Austria and Germany, Russia must send forward no less than three operational armies." To be able to do that—and Kuropatkin implied no expectation of victory—the army had to have in place a two-phase plan that had already established all the preconditions for a transition to war. The first phase would be called the "General Plan for War" and the second, a "Plan for Mobilization and Concentration of Forces."[86] Once these plans were in place, they would be guaranteed against change, "guarantee even in peacetime by the war minister's approval." The complexity in particular of the railroad transportation elements warranted this treatment, since interference in the schedules would impose "severe penalties on the time taken to assemble forces."[87] Germany's war planning practices would not arrive at this stage of rigidity for another two decades.

With Kuropatkin's new program the staff organized its planning activities around a new, presumably better-integrated, framework. Instead of thinking in terms of two separate strategies (the defensive and offensive-defensive options), a single umbrella plan guided the specifics of mobilization. Within their structures the general and mobilization plans would perpetuate the bifurcation of Russia's strategic options. In fact, by 1886 the "offensive-defensive" strategy had begun to fall from favor in the face of growing German strength in East Prussia; if Russia were to hope to survive war with the Dual Alliance, it would have no choice but massing its strength on the Vistula rather than facing the Carpathians. Obruchev and Kuropatkin nevertheless maintained plans for some offensive operations against Austria, and Russia's deployments reflected those elusive ambitions.[88]

Kuropatkin proposed and war minister Vannovskii approved two simple measures that changed the way Russia would approach its next European war. First, the commander in chief of forces (*komanduiushchie voiskami*—CinC) in each western military district received authority to adopt *any measure* he deemed necessary to screen his mobilization, the concentration of his armies, and to secure his district and its reception of reinforcements. Kuropatkin also carefully divided between each CinC and his district chief of staff the responsibilities (and *authority*) for preparations. By middecade every district chief of staff was a designated General Staff officer (*zachislen v General'nyi Shtab*); the most important among them had already held important mobilization-related positions on the Main Staff or its key committees. The same would not be true of the district CinCs for another decade or more.[89]

The division of responsibility Kuropatkin envisioned was unambiguous: the district CinC was to collect all the implementation telegrams and war credit approvals that arrived from the capital. His chief of staff, on the other hand, monitored the combat readiness of troops and the availability and allocation of cavalry remounts, and controlled all details of unit deployment; he also controlled the intelligence collection activity, elaborated operational plans for the first engagement with the enemy, and coordinated the absorption of reserve and fill-out (*zapasnyi*) troops as they arrived in the district. The chief of staff also handled all matters concerning readiness of magazines, engineering and artillery parks, depots, lines of communication (rail, telegraph, waterway, and roads), transportation resources, and military hospitals. Kuropatkin invested the chiefs of staff with the greatest authority for ensuring precise implementation of the Main Staff's war plan. The burden of responsibility mirrored Prussian practice, in which a general staff officer could nullify decisions made by field commanders if those might interfere with sucessful implementation of the mobilization plan. Fuller dates this development to publication of the 1890 Regulation; although the document appeared three years after Kuropatkin's proposal, and five years after a special commission had begun review of wartime field authority regulations, the chief of Main Staff had already approved Kuropatkin's plan in 1887.[90]

Second, the chief of Main Staff (acting for the war minister) retained *sole authority* for preparation and activation of the war plan. During the period of transition to belligerency, the CinCs and their district chiefs of staff could activate each section of the plan only upon receipt of "confirmation from the cognizant organs of the war ministry," that is, upon declaration of mobilization of the army and transfer of field authority to the districts. The decisive question this arrangement did not answer was whether Kuropatkin and Obruchev envisioned the commencement of hostilities more closely to resemble the languorous pace of events in 1876–1877, or events as they occurred in July 1914. Although experience and Obruchev's strategic vision adumbrated the former expectation, language in the new regulation accurately anticipated a grim compression of time if a crisis exploded into war with the Central Powers.

At the heart of the military bureaucracy Kuropatkin created the mobilization commission, which succeeded the committee he had headed for two years. The new organization solidified the primacy of mobilization planning in two ways. First, it consolidated the most important planning activities, previously situated in different offices or departments of the Main Staff, into a semipermanent organization, replacing the ad hoc committee in existence since 1875. Of more importance, the commission acquired the war minister's authorization to proceed with its work directly under the chief of Main Staff's oversight. Insofar as responsibility for all military preparation fell to the minister alone, and that responsibility was explicitly codified in the "Regulation on Field Authority for Forces in Wartime," the mobilization commission became the implement for Obruchev's *operational control* of the army in both wartime and peacetime,[91] or so Kuropatkin hoped. War minister Vannovskii effectively turned over responsibility for strategy and operational planning to Obruchev, the "assistant war minister," and did not interfere with the direction in which Obruchev or his protégés moved the staff, the army, the ministry, or the realm.

Nineteen years later, with Kuropatkin as occupant of the war minister's office, Russia mobilized its army largely through the means he had put in place in the late 1880s. But the Russo-Japanese War was not the conflict that the Main Staff had wanted or anticipated. And Kuropatkin's and Obruchev's staff system could not assure it a successful conclusion. Subsequently, the field command apparatus installed in the 1880s, which isolated the war plan from the interference of nonspecialists, ultimately fell victim again to "grand dukism" (and, unfortunately, to the least competent militarily of all Russia's "grand dukes," Nicholas II) in imperial Russia's final war. More accurately, however, "grand-dukism" was only a fraction of a much larger problem that would face the Russian army until its final disintegration.

Conclusions and Judgments

At every level of field command the Russian army had been crippled by incompetence, dilatoriness, and amateurishness in the 1877 campaign. Field leadership was simply unprofessional by even the most modest standards of the late nineteenth century. By Prusso-German standards it was a threat to the empire's existence.[92] With grand dukes in command of the two armies operating in the European theater, and their toadies or nephews in charge of all but one of the combat detachments, modern analysts may perhaps be excused for giving Russian officers in the line the benefit of a doubt. The incompetence did, however, spread downward to the lowest officer levels of the army, Guards included. Nothing else could account for the carnage, a result of mindless and ineffective battlefield tactics, which contributed to the hundreds of thousands of Russian casualties (fifty-six thousand dead) in less than seven months of campaigning.[93] Between 1880 and 1887 Kuropatkin removed the grand-ducal factor from the military equation, he thought, and thus checked the least reliable link in the wartime chain of leadership. Absence of grand dukes from field command in 1904 deprived Russia's general staff, however, of this excuse for military failure.[94]

German mobilization and war planning rested implicitly on a culture of effectiveness that permeated Prusso-German military practices from top to bottom. Those practices depended essentially on the army's peacetime training under the guidance of career noncommissioned officers (NCOs). Initiative and tactical freedom were expected of NCOs from the rank of corporal upward and command latitude in operational missions complemented the General Staff's intense planning and preparations during peacetime. Germany's military philosophy seemed the best accommodation to Clausewitz's evocative nightmare of warfare as inconceivable friction and confusion, gamble, and chance ("the very last thing that war lacks"). The German General Staff had to see itself as "a swimming teacher who makes his pupils practice motions on land that are meant to be performed in water."[95] Alloyed to a sophisticated mobilization infrastructure (i.e., a central staff and railroads), the "German method" allowed the Chief of General Staff to unleash the German army at the border with some assurance that chance was the *only* force that could still derail his work. That expectation could not comfort Russia's general staff officers, as the experience of 1877 reminded them. Russia simply could not produce the quality of combat leader that the "German method" demanded.[96] In 1877 the Main Staff had seen its work overturned in favor of dash and, alternately, paralysis on the battlefield. Now, lacking combat leaders, having a poorly developed cadre of career NCOs, and with a barely competitive mobilization infrastructure, Kuropatkin attempted to ameliorate the handicap by setting in place an authority superior to the field command—a mobilization plan.

The Main Staff also built on a relationship with the western military districts that dated to the very beginning of Miliutin's ministry. After the great success of the 1876 mobilization, the districts seemed to carp far less about the volume of "paperwork" demanded of them by St. Petersburg. Production of military-statistical studies was the blood of the Obruchev-Kuropatkin mobilization system. Information that flowed to the center from Poland animated the whole Main Staff bureaucracy and overshadowed lingering doubt about the importance of the "chancellerists." It is hardly surprising that Kuropatkin, whom Skobelev predicted would never make a combat commander but would be a great staff officer, thrived as Russia's mobilization guru. By the late 1880s Obruchev and Kuropatkin had provided Russia with a professional *and* competent staff. They also maneuvered to control the variables that could upset their careful planning. The year 1887 began with the placement of the final touches on their (and Russia's) first modern, practicable mobilization plan. The completion of that plan represents the full evolution of a Prussian system of war planning in Russia, despite the absence of similar structures. But Russia lacked— and would continue to lack, even after conclusion of the French "project"—real combat effectiveness. That, as Russia's enemies knew, was the ingredient of military success that could be neither planned nor taken for granted.

7

Progress and Stalemate

The extraordinary labors of Obruchev, Kuropatkin, Naglovskii, Sollogub, Zuev, and a dozen others between 1880 and 1887 allowed members of the Main Staff the comfort of two unaffordable delusions. First, they believed that the growing sophistication of their mobilization plan somehow also ushered in a fundamental change in the way the autocratic regime's first family would fight its next European war. They went so far as to write that expectation (or misperception) into drafts of a new field regulation and to develop mobilization schedules on the principle of independent staff command authority. The second delusion was that Russian combat effectiveness was sufficiently guaranteed by the simple, sacrificial spirit of the peasant-soldier. Yet initiative and leadership in combat throughout the officer corps were abysmal, as proved in 1877–1878 and before, with only the rarest exceptions. The scientific minds of the Main Staff seemed to believe they could plan away that crippling shortcoming, or simply ignore it. These two contradictions, between the "plan" and policy, and between the "plan" and reality, rise to prominence in the thought of senior planners and in the concerns of a new generation of *genshtabisty*, junior officers entering the planning system.

If given a well enough scripted start to the next European war, the leadership of the field army and staff could be isolated from elements that might jeopardize pivotal opening battles, and the critical initial collision would be carried by masses of hearty troops. The first delusion was an impetus to important changes in Russia's mobilization schedules from 1887 onward, and axiomatic to any military "project" between France and Russia. The second illusion—that bad combat leadership would somehow take care of itself—aroused little apparent concern within the staff. That, however, did not prevent younger general staff officers, mainly military historians and theorists, from advancing proposals to develop commanders' initiative and independence in the field.

In more than just a metaphoric sense, Obruchev was planning for war between his Main Staff and Moltke's Great General Staff, not between Russia and Germany. In the golden age of general staffs, it was both the capabilities and the war plans of an opponent that animated each staff, not the muddy (and somehow disreputable) concerns of diplomacy and politics. Thus, the plan Obruchev hatched had to beat the Germans' plan. Obruchev's inclination to plan against *capability* rather than against intent (as he displayed it particularly before the 1873 secret strategic conference) arose from Germany's *ability* to threaten Russia rather than from evidence of the Reich's hostile intentions.[1] Narrow professional opinion (the "purely military considerations" in Clausewitz's formulation) allowed Obruchev ultimately to outweigh foreign minister Giers between 1892 and 1893 when discussion around the throne turned on the question of a military compact and alliance with France. From Obruchev's perspective, the French agreement finally closed the "wide-open frontiers" about which he had worried since 1880, and completed the preparation of a sort of hermetic defense plan: neither diplomatic isolation, nor grand dukes, nor incompetent generalship could henceforth endanger the empire's security.

Although the French connection had, in Fuller's measured view, "rescued the entire process of Russian war planning by granting it a foothold in the world of the feasible,"[2] it also allowed the Russian army's strategists and planners to continue to ignore the army's woeful combat effectiveness.[3] When more junior *genshtabisty* turned their attention to the leadership question, their proposals enjoyed wide hearing, particularly in the capital, but prompted little innovation until after the East Asian disasters. The concerns those officers raised are interesting because of implied criticism of a system of war preparation that uniformly ignored their tocsin, and because some of those men later rose to high field commands in the Great War (and, in at least four cases, ultimately to professorial rank in the Red Army's first general staff academy).[4]

The development of Russia's war planning apparatus—that is, its central and district staff organizations and the mobilization plans they produced—reached its apogee around the time of the French discussions (about 1891). The way the Main Staff's mobilization committee comprehended the international situation and then addressed shortfalls in the empire's security attests to the chronic myopia afflicting even the brightest general staff officers when their concern turned to matters involving politics. Obruchev's tendentious presentation of the Franco-German problem demonstrably influenced the Main Staff's planning for war, even as his mobilization plans moved onto an impressive level of precision and sophistication. Concern about Russia's real combat readiness barely disturbed the confidence of general staff officers familiar with the mobilization work. That disturbance would, however, fuel later "Young Turk" calls for military reform from below.

Mobilization Schedule No. 12

Even as his colonels put the final touches in place on a new mobilization schedule (No. 12) in 1886, Chief of Main Staff Obruchev invested the organization that produced it with new authority and autonomy. During most of that decade the Main Staff's II Department acted as the principal support element of Obruchev's Committee for Force Mobilization, and it worked through the committee's subordinate component, Kuropatkin's Special Mobilization Commission. Kuropatkin was undoubtedly the most important appointee to the Main Staff in the 1880s, the model technician of schedules and planning. His imprint on Russia's general staff outlasted even his service, eventually as war minister. By 1886 the II Department had acquired responsibility for all operational matters, as well as cognizance over correspondence of a political nature that crossed the war minister's desk. It also planned the army's annual maneuvers. In this breadth of authority it resembled the Great General Staff's Mobilization and Railroad Sections, *combined*, and the organization became even more centralized, authoritative, and specialized.

Miliutin (with Obruchev's help) had first organized the department into four desks, each under a desk officer (*stolonachal'nik*), in 1866. That

organization's Third Desk oversaw force movements by rail, and the
Fourth Desk oversaw troop and cargo transportation by waterways. As
a result of the 1877 Russo-Turkish War, all transportation *and* mobilization planning moved to the Fourth Desk. The final reorganization of
the mobilization infrastructure under Obruchev came in December
1886 when he (acting on Kuropatkin's initiative) dismantled the Fourth
Desk entirely, after creating two new coordinating organs directly under the chief of Main Staff (and reporting through Kuropatkin's commission).[5] Obruchev also changed the name of Kuropatkin's "special"
(i.e., temporary) commission to Commission for Preparation of Measures in the Event of War. Henceforth it became Kuropatkin's sole
charge, as the Main Staff's most rapidly rising star secured organizational autonomy and added a layer of insulation from minister Vannovskii's oversight. Coincidentally, the 1886 structural shuffle echoed
on recent (1883) unburdening of Germany's war planning organization
from the oversight of anyone but the General Staff's chief, Moltke.[6]

Mobilization Schedule No. 12 marked something of a watershed in
Russian war planning, for it was the first Main Staff plan predicated on
final fruition of Miliutin's 1874 reform. During the schedule's effective
period, the Russian army would for the first time reach its full theoretical active and reserve (*zapasnyi*) strength. Men conscripted in 1874 had
completed their six years of active duty by 1879; they would finish their
fifteenth and final year of service (nine years in the reserves) in January
1889, and would pass into the lowest mobilization category (militia—
opolchenie). From Schedule No. 12 onward, general staff planners took
Russia's *full* mobilization strength as a basis for mobilization schedule
planning. The increase in that schedule's complexity reflected consideration of the mature reserve system and the enormous pool of trained
manpower from which planners could draw.

The first obstacle Kuropatkin faced as he began to prepare massive
mobilization timetables to support Schedule No. 12 was abstract and
intellectual: simply to conceptualize the dimensions of a new plan and
the course by which it might be written. The plan's preparation had to
grow from "extensive and highly complex considerations and estimates
for a war" involving a mature reserve system.[7] Kuropatkin's colonels
sketched out the flow of the planning process, with milestones, target
dates, and organizational responsibilities. Because the planning sequence would guide not only commission work but also the coordina-

tion of plan segments with the preparations of other offices, its arrangement had to incorporate a decade of lessons on plan preparation. Since about 1880 the planning system had operated unilinearly: the mobilization committee first prepared its statement of purpose (so-called general considerations, from month 1 through month 3 of the cycle). It passed those to the railroad section of the Main Staff, and a few months later (month 6), after completion of schedules for reserve movement from mustering depots to unit assembly points, the section passed its addition to the plan to military district staffs. The districts considered local concentration plans and carried out route reconnaissances to complete the army's portion of the schedule. MPS's railroad directorate would then prepare local timetables for intradistrict movement.[8]

Two serious shortcomings characterized this system: inefficiency and tediousness. Although the men who acted on a particular phase of the plan might contribute to another section, the linear sequencing of work militated against full-time effort by all staff planners: when the mobilization committee's work was done after three months, its members dispersed to other staff activities until the next schedule cycle began. (Recall, for instance, that a significant number of Main Staff officers had adjunct positions at the academy.) Similarly, because one phase of planning followed another, the entire cycle took an extraordinarily long time to run. Only a new structure to the planning cycle could compress it sufficiently to fit into a more rational and better-coordinated annual scheme—that is, into closer conformance with budgetary and conscription cycles (Figures 7.1 and 7.2).

That new scheme came into effect in mid-1887. It incorporated complex divisions of labor into the process's phasing and intensified the work in the planning bureaus. From 1887 onward the planning process followed its new "stereotypical yet flexible" scheme, a standardized ten- to thirteen-month cycle that in effect reinforced the authority of the mobilization committee, the mobilization commission, and their support staffs.

In contrast to the earlier system, the mobilization committee worked virtually perpetually under the new system. The mobilization schedule bifurcated, reflecting the two sorts of field formations for which mobilization plans were needed, and the committee's work on the general plan stretched out beyond six months. After two months of preparing draft mobilization directives to cover existing field formations (so-called Category I units), the committee turned to the more complex task of mobilization for the hundreds of independent reserve formations (Category II). The Railroad Section received Part I of the schedule from the committee for elaboration of a general rail transportation plan and a concentration plan, between Month 2 and Month 6 of the cycle, and took over preparations of the transportation plan for Part II of the schedule as soon as it finished work on Part I.[9]

On military district staffs, work on the schedule's two parts was also staggered: district staffs had between six and eight weeks to work on Part I (from Month 4 to 6), then a six-week hiatus before they received Part II for preparation. Their planning responsibilities included both conveyance scheduling and unit march routes (rail or foot) from the assembly points to concentration areas near the border. In the latter phase the district staffs were to cooperate closely with the railroad section of the Main Staff, which was scheduling the rail transportation plan for army concentration. Finally, district chiefs of staff farmed out parts of the plan to corps and divisional staffs for field reconnaissance of routes. They needed to know locations of potential bivouac sites, forage capacity of each frontal sector (to support the vast numbers of horses), sources of water, centers of potential hostile (Polish or German) populations, and the like. That fieldwork, in which all general staff officers were thoroughly tutored at the academy and in service, then fed St. Petersburg for the next planning cycle. Some problems uncovered in field surveys could be addressed only by planners at the center, which reinforced the real authority of Kuropatkin's commission (retaining day-to-day control of the process) and its adjunct working sections.

The commission had worked throughout the summer and fall of 1886 on various aspects of reserve mobilization and took reports and opinions from not only the concerned Main Directorates within the war ministry but also the Warsaw and Moscow Military District staffs. The reserve mobilization problem was twofold: first, how would men of each regiment's fourth reserve *(zapasnyi)* infantry battalion be brought together with the unit's officer and noncommissioned officer cadre? The difficulty arose from changes that had taken place in the mechanics of Russian mobilization: after the early 1880s, unit assembly points (where reserve battalions joined their regiments) were displaced from the regimental deployment site in all frontier military districts. This added one more phase of movement to each regiment's positioning for

Month

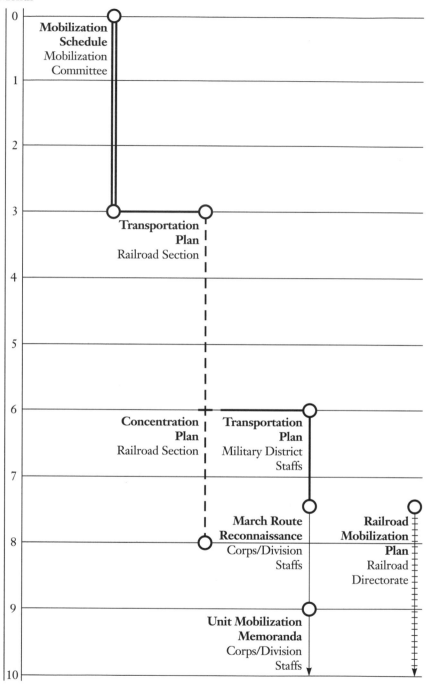

0

Mobilization Schedule
Mobilization Committee

1

2

3

Transportation Plan
Railroad Section

4

5

6

Concentration Plan
Railroad Section

Transportation Plan
Military District Staffs

7

March Route Reconnaissance
Corps/Division Staffs

Railroad Mobilization Plan
Railroad Directorate

8

9

Unit Mobilization Memoranda
Corps/Division Staffs

10

Figure 7.1. "Schematic: Current procedures for composition of a mobilization
schedule," pre-1887. (*RGVIA*, F. 401, op. 4, d. 56–187, l. 61ob)

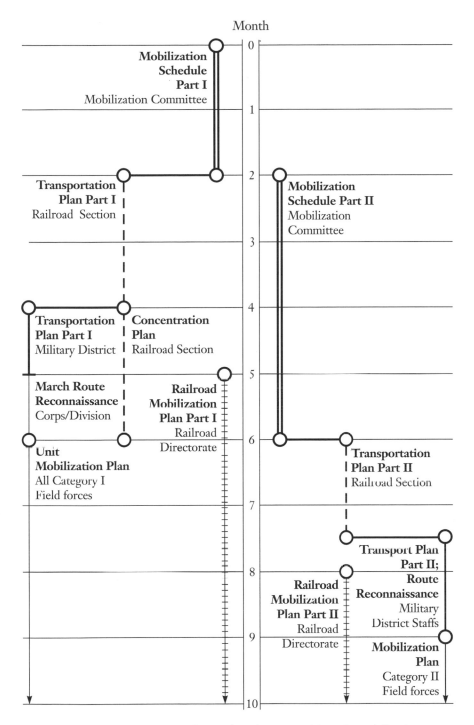

Month

0 — **Mobilization Schedule Part I** Mobilization Committee

Transportation Plan Part I Railroad Section

2 — **Mobilization Schedule Part II** Mobilization Committee

Transportation Plan Part I Military District — **Concentration Plan** Railroad Section

March Route Reconnaissance Corps/Division — **Railroad Mobilization Plan Part I** Railroad Directorate

Unit Mobilization Plan All Category I Field forces

Transportation Plan Part II Railroad Section

Transport Plan Part II; Route Reconnaissance Military District Staffs

Railroad Mobilization Plan Part II Railroad Directorate

Mobilization Plan Category II Field forces

Figure 7.2. "Schematic: Proposed procedure for composition of a mobilization schedule," 1887. (*RGVIA*, F. 401, op. 4, d. 56–187, l. 62)

combat. The reserve battalions assembled, drew weapons and horses, and then would be transported intact to their frontline positions. Thus, the question became principally one of intendancy and district railroad scheduling, once the higher plan was set in place. This led to the second problem: Where should reserve battalions (particularly reserve artillery battalions, with their cumbersome equipment and train) assemble? Correspondence between the mobilization committee and military district staffs continued until the end of 1886, when St. Petersburg approved technical district-level solutions.[10]

Kuropatkin's commission also tackled the chronic problem of tallying, inspecting, procuring, and transporting huge numbers of horses. Earlier attempts to systematize the remount plan had failed, even as other portions of the mobilization plan moved forward. In both Schedule No. 10 (July 1883) and Schedule No. 11 (March 1885), remount figures had appeared in manuscript on the final printed plans,[11] figures that doubtless never left the general staff building on Palace Square. The operational army's demands for horses grew rapidly in the 1880s and by decade's end had reached almost 450,000—less than 10 percent of which were for cavalry regiments. In the early 1890s the figures grew again, as the Cavalry Inspectorate raised the numbers of remounts in each reserve cavalry section by 100 percent and more.[12]

These changes—in manpower, reserve organization, horse stock allocation—fundamentally changed the depth and sophistication of Schedule No. 12, and Russian mobilization planning in general. In early 1887, under the committee's direction, Kuropatkin's commission set about composing the army's first contingency plan for large-scale force movement by railroad.[13] Under the title "General Mobilization Schedule," the commission drafted ten appendixes for railroad scheduling, a massive compilation of timetables, routing directions, and rolling stock assignments. Mountains of supporting studies and district reports buoyed the kernel of the schedule. Schedule No. 12 was quite unlike anything previously attempted on the Main Staff. The details of this work are of practically no lasting interest, but for their scope and reliance on modern transportation technology, yet the schedule may appropriately be called Russia's first "modern" war plan.[14] Its displacement from an articulated, responsible, political reality, however, was potentially as injurious to Russia's interests as the Schlieffen plan would be to Germany's two decades later.

The 1887 Main Staff Conference

War minister Vannovskii, as well as his Main Staff chief Obruchev, described completion of Mobilization Schedule No. 12 (1 April 1887) and its adjunct document, the draft of the army's new wartime Field Regulation, as "a key turning point" in the history of the Main Staff.[15] The two documents together empowered the Main Staff to conduct war planning through a uniform system of troop allocation and deployment. That planning uniformity, they believed, would allow the army to respond with *either* of the so-called options—for "defensive" and "offensive-defensive" action—in the course of an unfolding international crisis.[16] Although the imposition of planning standardization did not overtly change the subordination of strategy to political judgment and diplomatic circumstances in "any unfolding political situation," the contrary predisposition of the war ministry was clear. In Vannovskii's report to the tsar (which, of course, Obruchev prepared) the war minister casually observed that the second option (entitled "active defense" in this formulation) had been "fully supported by Aleksandr Nikolaevich [Alexander II]." This revelation, if veritable, would date precisely the tilt toward offensives against Austria to Obruchev's Basic Memorandum, which the tsar approved in January 1880. That was the first and probably only time the war minister requested Alexander II's approval of Russia's new bifurcated strategy.[17]

Obruchev's invocation of Alexander III's late father worked in his favor in a number of ways. Alexander II may actually have placed his war planners in the role of strategic "magicians" (in Fuller's words) in 1880, by "fully supporting" the least feasible defensive posture. Or perhaps Obruchev in 1887 simply prepossessed Alexander III toward a course to which Russia was unequal, to justify and perpetuate the preceding seven years of work. Most likely, however, Obruchev was creating a plausible *prehistory* for the Main Staff's preferred war plan—a plan that was unworkable, unless France forced Germany into a two-front war. Obruchev clearly knew that neither Russia's resources nor its general staff plans could possibly render the offensive-defensive plan feasible, and in the political circumstance he described, even Poland was indefensible. As he had written to foreign minister Giers in 1883, the Teutonic powers had placed Russia's frontier districts "in a state of unconditional siege . . . There is no doubt that Germany and Austria-

Hungary are incomparably stronger than we and can mobilize and concentrate their armies on the frontier much more rapidly than we. Our
borders are completely open."[18]

In early 1887 Obruchev convened a Main Staff conference on the
new Mobilization Schedule and Field Regulation. Coincidentally, Russia faced its gravest period of international tension since 1878. The war
scare of 1887 capped almost two years of crises. A partial mobilization
of the Russian army in 1885 during the Afghan confrontation almost
brought Russia to war with Britain, and mutual threats of war between
Austria and Russia over Bulgaria's future were a continuous motif of the
period. Pan-Slavic nationalists lamented that Russia's only real gains
from its last Turkish war—its unabashed satrapy in Bulgaria—were rapidly slipping away, to Austria's advantage. Parallel tensions agitated
Germany and France (thanks principally to the bellicose French war
minister, Boulanger). Most of Europe, thus, anticipated general war,
although Russian military intelligence already recognized that none of
Russia's western neighbors wished to fight. Only Russia's military attaché in Vienna, Lieutenant-Colonel D. P. Zuev,[19] was flooding the
tsar's (and Obruchev's) desk with reports of feverish Austrian war preparations.[20]

In those late spring days of 1887 the chief of Main Staff called together the frontier military districts' chiefs of staff, Main Staff planners, and academy theoreticians to discuss Russia's strategic future.[21]
Vannovskii summarized the results for Alexander III shortly after the
meeting,[22] a report that stands as an outstanding yardstick of just how
far the war ministry had come since 1880—and how great its perceived
military inferiority still was. Although the report encompassed the full
range of military concerns for Russia's security within the European
system, much of that merely echoed the anxieties of 1873 and 1880.
Beyond the myriad details of the report's description of army development, deployment, and preparation for war, only two aspects stand out:
the reported changes in Russia's railroad capacity, and Obruchev's appreciation of political reality in Europe.

Rapidity of mobilization and concentration was, in Obruchev's view
throughout the 1870s and 1880s, the sine qua non of military preparedness. Hence, railroad network development invariably occupied first
place in any consideration of Russia's strategic situation. Compared
with Germany's fourteen strategic railway lines to the frontier and Aus-

tria's six, Russia had seven, with a total capacity of over 180 trains daily (Table 7.1).

During the 1880s the government double-tracked most remaining single-track lines from Russia to the principal marshaling points in Poland; those lines included Vilna-Belostok-Warsaw, Orel-Briansk-Gomel-Brest, Kursk-Kiev-Rovno-Kovno-Kovel, and Odessa-Rovno (refer to Maps 1 and 3). By 1887 Russia's maximum (surge) rail capacity was somewhat better than Prussia-Germany's had been in 1870, but during the preceding fifteen years Germany's rail carrying capacity had almost doubled.[23] The meeting's participants considered all factors of army size, frontier distance, and concentration of mass and concluded that *still* Russia could not possibly concentrate its field army for the first battles in less than thirty-nine or forty days.[24] This situation did not surprise even MPS, which itself later concluded that "among the half dozen projects undertaken during the reign of Alexander III the most important (from a technical point of view) were related to waterway regulation and exploitation. And all of them had commercial or economic, rather than strategic, rationales."[25]

The deployment plan, the report continued, had been enumerated down to divisional level, and it detailed the concentration sites for each unit according to the two strategic options. Over half of the divisions

Table 7.1. Railroad Surge Capacity, Western Region, 1887

Line	Trains Per Day		
	Passenger	Military	Surge
St. Petersburg–Warsaw	3	12	11
Moscow–Brest	3	24	20
Gomel–Brest	1	13	8
Kiev–Brest	2	12	11
Odessa–Volochinsk	1	12	11
Riga–Mozh.–Kashedary (Auxiliary)	2	9	7
Vilna–Baranovichi–Belostok (Auxiliary)	1	13	8
Total:	**13** +	**95** +	**76 = 184 trains per day**

Source: RGVIA, F. 402, op. II, d. 76, l. 20ob., "Imperial Memorandum of the War Minister," signed by Vannovskii, countersigned by Obruchev, dated 12 June 1887.

remained at the same location under both plans. As an afterthought Obruchev and Vannovskii mentioned a third option, in addition to Plans A ("defensive") and B ("defensive-offensive"), for an offensive against Germany and defense facing Austria: Plan V. It varied from Plan B only in that "four corps (10 divisions) including the Grenadiers are to be transferred from the Southwestern Army to the Vistula Army."[26] They elaborated no further than that, more or less relegating the idea to a much later era when, in fact, Plan G (1912) would turn the preponderance of Russian strength against Germany.[27]

Fuller argues strongly that if Obruchev harbored any thought of choosing, in a crisis, between Plans A and B, it was nothing less than strategic fantasy: the confusion that would accompany any European crisis could only complicate for Russia's leaders the selection of the "correct" plan for those circumstances, and the danger of miscalculation would be calamitous.[28] Obruchev would have added that dynastic indecision in such circumstances would destroy the empire. The risk of paralysis, pace Fuller, did not render Russia's contingency planning "ridiculous" or "unrealistic." By comparison, Germany's strategic problem was considerably more complex than Russia's, its two potential war theaters being on opposite sides of the country. Yet even the great Moltke insisted on preparation of numerous contingency plans throughout the 1870s and 1880s, each one elaborated in finest detail. The Vannovskii/Obruchev report demonstrated that the military options which their conferees discussed did not hinge on a switch *in midstream* from one plan to the other, or that they might *ever* contemplate such a shift, or that it might be politically advantageous. In fact, the 1887 draft *Polozhenie* (Regulation) structurally inhibited such an eventuality—explicitly for the very reasons Fuller himself notes.[29]

The war ministry's work may be criticized for the *political* circumstances it imagined might exist in some contingent future. Germany could complete mobilization of the field army in six to seven days, but even then all would depend on Austria and France. Although the war minister went no further than questioning "the standing of the Austrian-German alliance," to have even posed that question in the late 1880s displayed shallow political perception (particularly while Obruchev's military attaché in Vienna, Colonel Zuev, was vigorously reporting to the contrary). The war minister's (and his chief of Main Staff's) views on France in mid-1887 are even more disturbing. *If*

France's relations with Germany were unsettled, they argued, then three-quarters of the German army would go westward. *If*, on the other hand, the French did not threaten war, then the Dual Alliance would be free to throw sixteen corps, seven cavalry divisions, and nine *Landwehr* (reserve) divisions against Russia.[30] If Obruchev harbored any fears about the disorder and confusion that might attend a decision among *Russia's* mobilization plans during a crisis, he certainly anticipated no similar disruption that might characterize Germany's infinitely more complicated strategic problem—all the while assuming those two radically different and politically naive alternatives existed for Germany. Of course, the Russians might have believed that the great Moltke could actually carry off such a remarkable feat, at the very time the field marshal was despairing of ever solving the Reich's strategic dilemma.

In the considered view of Russia's strategic thinkers, the Dual Alliance would face one of two military possibilities. Either Germany would be preoccupied with France, or it would operate together with Austria against Russia. Vannovskii briefly posited the outcome in the first case: Austria would launch an attack on Poland and, "cheered by any initial Austrian success, Romania and perhaps even Turkey and England might join" in. The second case—a passive, neutral France— clearly agitated the tsar's reporters much more. "If war occurs during a long period of peace between Germany and France, then the Alliance will descend on Poland, pushing Russia back to the Vistula."[31] Russia's strategic plans henceforth were based on this simplistic and most unlikely international political constellation.

How could such a set of circumstances be proposed, and in fact deemed the most probable one for Russia's future, by the officers of the Main Staff? The only circumstances under which France might remain neutral in a Russo-German war would be through reconstitution of the Crimean system—but with England acting as a brake on France (which after 1870 was a most unlikely possibility). Obruchev and his assistants allowed "military necessity" to cloud their appreciation of political reality, as they had in 1876. Behind their appreciation of the Continent's political constellation lurked both bureaucratic intentions (in support of defense budgets, railway construction, and rearmament) and the simple, cold logic of Russian military isolation. But there was more: Obruchev had been in close private contact with his French counterpart, Boisdeffre, for years[32] so it is untenable to think he could have simply *mistaken* French military (or political) intentions, particularly at the height of the 1887 crisis. Vannovskii's and Obruchev's strategic evaluation was disingenuous or naive—or both. And it almost certainly presaged the binding military relationship with France that Obruchev had hoped for, and that foreign minister Giers rightly resisted. The contradiction between Russian military expertise and planning, and its state policy and diplomacy, had never been clearer than on the eve of the Franco-Russian negotiations.

The conference went on to discuss three ways its chosen scenario could play out, without apparently hesitating for a moment on the great improbability of the script. Assuming French passivity, the conference examined the Central Powers' three offensive options. In the first operational scenario, German forces might descend from Posen and Silesia onto the central Vistula area to invest the Warsaw-Ivangorod complex while Austrian forces moved out of Galicia toward Brest. German cavalry would sweep down toward Belostok, Grodno, and Vilna from East Prussia, and the Austrian right wing might attack through Lutsk, Dubno, and Rovno toward Kiev (a scenario which the commanders of Kiev and Warsaw Military Districts played out in huge summer maneuvers three years later). According to the second possibility, the German army's entire weight would strike out from East Prussia toward Warsaw-Ivangorod to seize the Vistula's left bank and then turn toward Belostok. Austria would attack through Liublin (Lublin) and Kholm (Chelm) and northward toward Sedlets (Siedlec) and Brest. The third alternative was most grim: if Russia were distracted elsewhere (in Asia, or on the Baltic and Black Sea coasts), then the enemy could operate freely behind Warsaw after a descent on Libau or Riga, and then move on St. Petersburg or Moscow. The Austrians would attack directly toward Kiev.[33]

The Main Staff's planners had very reliable intelligence on German and Austrian army deployment, information that supported any of the operational scenarios Obruchev offered. Before 1890 the Main Staff had accumulated data on Austrian order of battle, mobilization plans, concentration schedules and locations, and both the capacity and condition of Austria's six strategic rail lines. Since the early 1880s corps and district staff officers had fed detailed information to St. Petersburg on German force disposition along the frontier, and general staff topographers thought they could predict which routes German units would favor to cut St. Petersburg's communications with the Polish districts. Russian intelligence about Germany's overall mobilization schedule did not match the secrets retrieved about Austria's until the late 1890s, but voluminous details sketchily profiled Berlin's plans.[34] German and Austrian army deployments convinced Obruchev that he could describe the strategies that the Central Powers would be *capable* of pursuing. But in the absence of careful consideration of the international political terrain, he could not anticipate the new direction that German strategic planning took—for a precariously timed two-front war.

Refining the Schedule: 1888 and Beyond

The sophistication of Main Staff planning could not make up for the continued lethargy of railroad development in Poland; the military railway network showed little improvement in 1888. Some work continued on dual tracking of the principal trunk lines into Poland, but few new branches and interline connections were put into operation. A short section of track (20 versts/21 kilometers) entered service on the Ivangorod-Dombrovsk line, work that in May 1877 district commander in chief Kotsebu had told St. Petersburg was of the highest strategic importance (even as he struggled with mobilization for Russia's war in the Balkans).[35] A section (116 versts/123 kilometers) also became operational on the Riga-Viazma line. The balance of the 1,270 versts (1,346 kilometers) total put into operation that year was laid in Central Asia, the Urals, the Caucasus, and northern Russia.[36]

Even after approval of Schedule No. 12, mobilization committee refinement of the railroad plans did not pause. Until the rail network possessed complete interconnectivity of main lines in European Russia, the army's timetables for each trunk were in jeopardy, should a blockage occur at one of the numerous system bottlenecks: Brest, Gomel, Rovno, Grodno, Kovel, Sedlets, Belostok, Vilna. The mobilization committee's intention was to reorganize the transportation timetables so that each plan could function independent of the others, without regard to the relative strategic importance of any.[37]

The committee consulted railroad experts from outside the ministry to have each separate railroad plan subjected to criticism and examination in a commission composed of railroad specialists. This testing of the committee's work would have revealed oversights or errors, undoubtedly to the benefit of the plan's rigor and practicability. Clearly, however, the refinement of timetables could only ameliorate *systemic* infrastructural weakness to a point; the larger problem remained that western Russia simply needed more kilometers of rail to support the plans general staff officers envisioned.

Workup of materials for the new schedule (No. 13, approved 1 April 1889) included various new studies: how would the assembly points, concentration areas, and forward rail lines be screened or protected? How quickly could civil rolling stock be converted for military use? How would the growing number of telegraph lines be protected, both physically and from tapping by enemy agents? The solution to many of these problems depended on intelligence of the enemy's intentions, particularly of how quickly and by what mechanisms the enemy would mobilize and concentrate. In the spring of 1888 a memo regarding "Plan B" (the defensive-offensive option) of the last mobilization schedule compared Russia's assembly and concentration capability with the committee's best information on Germany's and Austria's (Table 7.2).

Table 7.2. German, Austrian, and Russian (Plan B) Mobilization and Concentration Capacities, 1888

Day (M +)	German Army			Austrian Army			Russian Army		
	Battalions	Squadrons	Guns	Battalions	Squadrons	Guns	Battalions	Squadrons	Guns
5	—	48	12	—	148	72	14	236	6(
10	127	296	378	75	178	204	196	302	31?
15	311	296	1224	219	213	548	443	374	1,01?
20	405	296	1728[a]	334	241	1,060	567	416	1,412
25		—		433	266	1,308	673	437	1,74?
30		—		502	302	1,416[a]	793	474	2,14?
35		—			—		854	539	2,37?
40		—			—		904	657	2,54?
45		—			—		960	719	2,75?
50		—			—		992	727	2,84?
55		—			—		992	763	2,90?
60		—			—		992	811	2,91?

Source: RGVIA, F. 402, op. 2, d. 115, ll. 3–4ob: "Memorandum to the work on Plan B, Schedule No. 12, April 1888.

Notes: [a]Mobilization completed.
[b]Russian Operational Army concentrated for operations.
[c]Approximate force equivalence.

Table 7.3. Field Army Mobilization Capacity, 1884/1888

Day (M +)	1884 Plan			1888 Plan		
	Battalions	Squadrons	Guns	Battalions	Squadrons	Guns
10	142	270	300	192	302	318
30	694	456	1790	793	474	2114

Source: RGVIA, F. 402, op. I, d. 115, l. 5.

The data convinced Obruchev that the Russian army (thanks to St. Petersburg's labors) had markedly improved its mobilization capacity during the intervening four years. Compared with 1884, the army would be able to mobilize more than twelve additional infantry regiments and five cavalry regiments during the first ten days of a general mobilization (Table 7.3).

Whatever else Obruchev and his assistants believed about Russia's mobilization capacity, there can be no doubt that by the late 1880s the empire could assemble, transport, and concentrate an army on its western frontier sufficient to guard the integrity of tsarist Poland—at least on paper. By M + 10 (ten days after declaration of mobilization), the strength of the opponent roughly equaled Russia's effective force; under no circumstances could the Central Powers muster a force of sufficient preponderance to confidently undertake a strategic offensive. Russia's interior lines of communication in Poland would have rendered German local superiority of transient benefit because every Russian unit in Poland could march virtually the breadth of the theater in ten days. No one on the Main Staff, of course, said such a thing (i.e., no record exists of it being said), probably because German economic preeminence and military might intimidated all who viewed it.

The committee's and commission's occupations ranged over many technical questions concerning the schedule, but the comparative pace of Russian and Austrian-German concentration remained the staff's preoccupation. Kuropatkin's commission dissected the mechanics of the Central Powers' systems in a search for weaknesses, bottlenecks, and strengths. Its interest in the speed of German mobilization increased after completion of Schedule No. 12, after awakening to the importance of increments of days or even hours to the first engagement's outcome. Austria posed less of a threat to Russia than did Germany. In 1888, with a relatively complete and usable plan at last in place, the next update to the schedule would necessarily depend on the reliability and refinement of Russia's intelligence from Germany (and Austria). Estimates of the German mobilization timetables was the information of highest importance to Kuropatkin's planners. By the summer of 1888 general staff officers who worked on this problem presented studies that answered a few questions about the mechanics of German mobilization and pointed to ways those mechanisms' weaknesses might be exploited. Lieutenant-Colonel A. M. Butakov (military attaché in Berlin since 1884) produced two particularly interesting reports, which came to Obruchev and VUK for preliminary consideration.

Butakov based his first study ("In How Many Days Can the German Army (Standing) Mobilize Its Infantry, Cavalry, and Artillery?")[38] on close observation and analysis of German regimental mobilizations during the July 1888 summer maneuvers and "various published materials." From the general data he then derived timetables of mobilization for all infantry, cavalry, and artillery units, in regimental size and larger in East Prussia. Germany had a system of "premobilization" measures (partial mobilization, the equivalent of Russia's "reinforced peacetime" condition, which the Main Staff had ordered in mid-1876) by which it could place many cavalry units on the border in less than a week. The force, however, would be "feeble" until all units were filled out with their reserve contingents. On the other hand, if Germany declared full mobilization from the first day, instead of incrementally (i.e., as a crisis unfolded), its army would be ready to concentrate for military operations between eight and thirteen days for infantry, from six to twelve days for cavalry, and about eight to nine days for artillery. Only two factors seemed to affect the pace of mobilization of any regiment: the relative local concentration of the unit before declaration of mobilization (i.e., single or multiple garrison points) and the local development of the railroad network in each regiment's area. The gravest danger this system posed to Russia was the threat of a cavalry raid en masse out of East Prussia to cut the rail lines in Russia, especially the St. Petersburg–Warsaw line between Grodno and Belostok.[39]

"From which day of mobilization of the standing German army does the mobilization of reserve battalions (1st category of *Landwehr*) and *Landwehr* battalions (2nd category) begin, and how long will that take to complete?" Butakov asked in the second study.[40] Given the conclusions of the first study, Butakov argued that the key to Russian "success" would lie in accurate knowledge of German reserve mobilization. If Germany faced delays in straightening out orders for reserves, the entire German mobilization and concentration would be delayed. Butakov's study of reserve mobilization timing revealed that many "irregular factors," such as the quality of reserve noncommissioned officers and junior officers, would have a great impact on whether the German General Staff's plans could be carried out. An indication that this was a potentially important Achilles' heal, he said, was that reserve and *Landwehr* mobilization did not begin until two to four days after activation of regular forces, so that reserve "disorder" could not dislocate active forces' mobilization. The Germans purposefully staggered the process even though it would cost them a half week for completion of a call-up.[41] How St. Petersburg could use Butakov's studies, unquestionably of value to mobilization schedulers, was problematic: How could knowledge of an opponent's weakness, and conceptualization of a stratagem to exploit it, be of use in the face of Russia's own material, infrastructural, and operational handicaps?

By the late 1880s the weight of statistical data supporting military-scientific studies bore heavily not only on the Main Staff in St. Petersburg but also on the district staffs, which actually gathered much, if not most, of the hard intelligence.[42] Grasping the potential for pointless or duplicative district staff work, in mid-1888 St. Petersburg prepared an outline of information essential for war planning. The index helped guide district staffs as they planned their own local collection activities and brought some convergence between local requirements and information that St. Petersburg needed (the outline may be found in Table A-6).[43] The Main Staff's categories were sufficiently broad to allow almost infinite subdivision (in conformance with increasingly complex mobilization plans). But they also provided the districts little guidance on what the Main Staff really needed.

Studies like Butakov's heralded the sort of new work that animated subsequent schedules, beginning with No. 13, which came into effect during the spring of 1889. At the very start of that year, Kuropatkin issued a directive to the Main Staff that set out the statistical requirements and studies he needed for preparation of the next schedule.[44] He demanded new transportation timetables that reflected the modest improvements in the network, as well as studies that reflected the new sophistication of Russian mobilization planning and, interestingly, a deeper level of intellectual abstraction. Implicitly, Kuropatkin's questions pointed to the advances he assumed had already been made in the staff's capacity for deductive thought and deep future–oriented planning.

To what extent, he asked, would troop movements overstress Russia's railroads? He asked for estimates (deduced from data on the Russo-Turkish and the Franco-Prussian Wars) for the initial four to six months of war, of: consumption of ammunition; casualties in dead and wounded; requirements for new recruits and horses; requirements for new small arms and artillery; and requirements for new personal equipment (such as uniforms) and medical supplies. He wanted estimates of the provisioning stocks necessary to support concentrated forces, broken out by respective rail line. The staff had to provide estimates of all rail movements they anticipated would follow completion of mobilization and concentration of the operational army. Finally, Kuropatkin wanted to know the logistical requirements for the lowest categories of reserve forces, the first- and second-category militiamen (*ratniki opolcheniia*). That data he wanted, based on the loss of *all existing equipment*, and transportation of replacement materials to the militia assembly points.[45]

Completion of Schedule No. 12 freed Kuropatkin to consider for the first time some of the implications of modern European warfare and its impact on a conscript army and state, in human and material terms—but only from a planner's point of view. The gradual precipitation of a new, trained (if somewhat elderly) manpower pool, never before considered in serious military terms, also prodded the Main Staff to ask finally whether Russia's next war *might* necessitate recall of those *staristy* to the colors. Most of his questions concerned the support expected of railroads following commencement of hostilities. The staff knew that the rail network was not up to the task of transporting the whole operational army into its western Russian positions early in a crisis, and little about that condition would change for another decade. However, the officers who bore responsibility for planning tsarist Poland's defense did not seem to let that impede their preparation for war with "Germany-Austria" (as they sometimes referred to the Central Powers). The momentum of "deep future–oriented thinking" itself carried forward their labor; staff officers compounded the complexity of each year's plan as they prepared the next version. They continued to plan around (or ignore) intractable obstacles that interfered with matching Germany militarily. For instance, they adapted their plan to a weak rail system by stationing as much of the army in the western districts as the land would support, and thus relieved the railroad of some of its burden.[46] But the solution of each technical problem served merely as a reminder of the great difficulties the staff still labored under.

The Gulf between Plan and Combat Effectiveness

In March and April 1888 Baron Korf of the Cavalry Inspectorate visited three cavalry regiments in southern Russia and the southwestern *gubernii* to audit their training and preparation for mobilization. The results of the inspections were uniformly distressing, at least from the perspective of any war planner. The 19th Dragoon Regiment ("Novo-georgevsk"), for instance, stationed in Kherson *guberniia*, lacked information on the most recent mobilization plans for the unit, its staff officer had not seen the plan for squadron action in the event of mobilization, and the regiment's basic mobilization memorandum had not been confirmed by the divisional commander.[47] Although none of the regiments Korf visited that spring were frontier units, all were slated for the massive right wing of the Southwestern Army group (in Volhynia), the force most likely to begin offensive operations in a general war.

Although only episodic, the results of those inspections probably were not isolated but instead typified the persistent gulf between activities (and assumptions) of Main Staff planners in St. Petersburg and the readiness of regiments in the field. In contrast with the preparedness of Germany's line regiments, Russia's lacked a military culture of low-level initiative-taking that would have obviated many simple, peacetime administrative shortcomings.[48] Routine waste of resources was (and remains) characteristic of any large military economy. In Russia's case those same inefficiencies, coupled with the lack of initiative, directly impeded the most fundamental preparations for mobilization and war. Furthermore, waste did not accompany superior performance in tactical and operational arts, as it could in other military systems.

The case of the 19th Dragoons is instructive. Were a general mobilization to be called—without the benefit of an extended crisis and time to gear up first to "Reinforced Peacetime" strength as in 1876—the regiment would not know in which corps it would operate;[49] where its mounts and remounts would come from; on which day of mobilization it was scheduled to board trains for transportation westward; how it would get to its assembly area (or even where that area was); or where it would concentrate for the first engagement. In fact, the regimental commander was not even sure that the division commanding officer knew the regiment belonged to him. In the sort of crisis for which every Main Staff energy had been expended, this level of unit disorder and lethargy would be a virtual guarantee of mobilization disaster. What it might mean, once the battle was joined, frightened a number of junior general staff officers.

The crisis of unit commander initiative, in peacetime or in combat, had bothered Miliutin for the duration of his tenure as war minister. He reported his thoughts on the problem to his tsar in 1862. The disgraceful state of the central military administration, he had said, where overcentralization choked off all initiative and accountability, had resulted from the practices of the army's leadership. Those same practices had resulted in "a shortage of initiative particularly among unit commanders, and especially in war time, [which] became apparent more than once and brought them grievous results."[50] Miliutin and Obruchev were subsequently successful in unfettering the minds involved in war planning; they neither attempted nor achieved similar results in the rest of the officer corps. The war ministry's centenary monument later observed: "Eventually history will clarify what prevented General-Adjutant Miliutin from putting into practice the intention of improving in sufficient measure the command structure of our army. In any case, there is no doubt that even in improving on his ideas, our General Staff could not compensate for the deficiencies and weaknesses on the part of the command structure."[51]

Begun in the 1870s, Obruchev's aggressive program of staff rides for both general staff and line officers provided a climate for individual initiative in the Prussian *Stabreise* tradition. Obruchev's participation did not outlast the 1870s; absenting his direct influence, the officers who participated were unlikely either to develop sophisticated tactical coup d'oeil (*glazomer*) or to get encouragement for their initiative. The war game cycle that was in full force by the 1880s likewise did not nurture an environment to test or develop junior officer tactical sense or initiative. German observers noted that exercises were not set up as strategic problems so much as for "the correct execution of a fixed exercise schedule" by the opposing commanders and their staffs.[52] Commanders in chief, like Generals Gurko (of the Warsaw district) and Dragomirov (of Kiev), wanted to test their portions of the mobilization schedule in 1890, from reserve assembly through a hypothetical first engagement with the enemy. The development of company and battalion commanders' tactical skills were not their concern. Apart from staff rides and *Kriegspiele*, a late-nineteenth-century army had no other means for developing junior officer leadership qualities; the Russian army gradually allowed both techniques to atrophy. Arguably, the very preoccupation that heralded the staff's resurgence in the 1880s— the viable mobilization plan—also obscured the extent of paralysis of tactical leadership from St. Petersburg's line of sight.

There was at least one young enemy of doctrinaire strategic prejudices in operational planning or military science, and of uninspired execution of orders in battle. That was Captain A. M. Zaionchkovskii, who had thoroughly examined the problem of combat leadership by the mid-1890s. His service on the staff of the Guards and St. Petersburg Military District gave him access to the most important military forum in the empire (the same one in which Artamonov had aired his plan for war with Turkey in early 1876). In 1893 he wrote a brilliant critical analysis of Skobelev's celebrated tactical actions during the 1877 campaign.[53] That work on offensive battle led immediately to two studies on the relationship of command flexibility to combat success; he believed that in modern war increased elasticity (*elastichnost'*, i.e., freedom of action) in orders sent to units at least down to brigade level would allow commanders to exploit local circumstances to the advantage of the entire force.[54] Skobelev aside, Zaionchkovskii nevertheless argued that development of unit initiative reached its full and final fruition in the 1870–1871 campaign, particularly the operations around Vert, Mars-de-Tour, Travelot, and the Sedan operation. Zaionchkovskii believed that forging a mass army into "a single will and a single mind" in the theater of war—while not robbing its parts of their independence and initiative—was the most difficult problem facing military theory in the modern era.

Given the Russian army's feebleness in "offensive battles," the likes of which Zaionchkovskii and the French knew would characterize the

next major European war,[55] why did the French respond so vigorously—insistently—to Obruchev's proposal for a military alliance? To
what degree did French chief of staff Boisdeffre's personal relationship
with his Russian counterpart underpin the military convention they
drafted in mid-1892? And what perceived strategic imperatives propelled French and Russian policy? From a strategic perspective, the two
powers shared similar choices in the early 1890s: economic and possibly
political subordination to imperial Germany, at least under a German
droit de regard; standing alone in uneven competition with Germany;
or a war with Germany in alliance with another power.[56] It remained
entirely unclear that Russian general staff officers (especially Obruchev)
seriously believed Germany could defeat them, despite their arguments
to the tsar to the contrary, as even their own figures showed. Thus,
their cautiousness militated firmly in favor of an "insurance" plan: the
French project. Russian officers were not convinced that war with Germany was "inevitable"; such a proposition is not supported by Main
Staff planning documents. Without question, however, Obruchev's apprehension over the prospect of keeping a local (i.e., Russo-Austrian)
war, in fact, "localized" dated to 1878 or earlier, and *that* was a consistent motif of the chief of Main Staff's strategic planning.[57] Obruchev
understood *from the early 1870s* Russia's need for a military alliance
against Germany to guarantee its long-term independence.

By the late 1880s Russia could produce a plan for mobilization and
war that was credible, and more important which *German* experts, on
the basis of observation of Russian deployments and railroad development, also found credible. The Germans held no such high opinion of
France's military capability. Whether the Russian army could execute
the plans its general staff drafted mattered less than the competence of
Russian staff work, that is, the ability of the staff to support Russian
policy in contracting and then sustaining military strategy and alliance
obligations. Russian statesmen, and their tsar, were sufficiently ambivalent about the German threat not to be panicked into alliance with
France. Obruchev and many general staff officers held a contrary view.
Objectively, only their defensive plan was feasible in the absence of a
guarantee of French belligerency, but that plan was not their preferred
option. Those same staff officers probably had little faith that the Russian "steamroller" could outweigh the technical excellence of Germany's economic and military system. The middle ground, the compro-

mise between offensive and defensive, lay in the so-called defensive-of-fensive plan, and it depended on the French alliance. Obruchev and Kuropatkin paved the way to the French alliance in 1887 by drafting a mobilization plan that *could not* answer the perceived political problem it purportedly addressed, a problem that clearly did not reflect existing or foreseeable circumstances. Obruchev's and Kuropatkin's mobilization plan thus presented the emperor a military imperative for alliance where no clear imperative existed.

Obruchev was not about to let his "Project of a Military Convention"[58] bind Russia's strategic direction to France's political needs, even though that same short document did just that to Russia's diplomatic freedom of action, at least as far as Germany was concerned. When French *État-Major* delegates arrived in Russia in 1892 to evaluate their new ally's military condition, they concluded that, from a general staff perspective, the only persistent requirement was for Russia to improve continually its means of mobilization and concentration, that is, to refine perpetually its mobilization schedule and transportation system. The French persisted in their attempt to direct Russian strategic planning over the next two decades, making for an unbridgeable chasm between the two. Not until 1912 did Russia's Main Staff institute Plan G for a massive offensive against Germany—the strategy that supported French interests, but not Russian. On the other hand, the perpetual problem of combat effectiveness—and here the French were as myopic as the Russians—could never compete for the attention of general staff officers, next to the mission of war and mobilization planning. Right up to 1914 the plan, not combat effectiveness, was the central theme of French alliance discussions with Russian general staff officers.[59] During the final decades of peace, the tsar's colonels lost sight of the competence and many of the habits they had learned under Miliutin, Obruchev, and Kuropatkin. In effect, they would "deprofessionalize" themselves as staff officers, as the Russian empire and its officer corps struggled from one crisis of autocracy to the next.

8
Conclusion

Obruchev, in his mid-sixties, had every reason to believe he would be the emperor's choice to lead the war ministry when the ailing Vannovskii passed from the scene. Russia's general staff was, in more than a figurative sense, *his* general staff: he had virtually created the staff's culture and provided it, for three decades, with a clear and largely unchallenged strategic program. He had nurtured and guided it through one war and two very serious international crises, and finally given it the diplomatic instrument that would allow its labors to bear fruit. He was mentally alert, physically vigorous, and without question the empire's preeminent strategic thinker and leader. Young Nicholas II instead chose Obruchev's protégé, Kuropatkin, to replace Vannovskii in 1898. Obruchev, left with no honorable choice but resignation, departed with Nicholas's approval that March. Obruchev left St. Petersburg and settled at his small château in the Dordogne, taking his personal papers with him and abandoning Russia for the rest of his life.[1]

With Obruchev's departure the Russian general staff became complacent, its "deep future–oriented" vision telescoped into preoccupation with administrative details, plan revisions, and, eventually, interminable struggles between progressives and reactionaries. However serious Obruchev's strategic predispositions and prejudices may have been, his vision of proper Main Staff operation had kept Russia's war planning mechanism focused on the German threat, without interruption, since the late 1860s. Organizational refinements had always served Obruchev's planning program; in his absence they came to serve political and nonstrategic purposes. In the area of manning, Obruchev had ensured that only technically qualified and experienced officers occupied the planning structure, and hoped that they would eventually also come to dominate key field command position. After his departure, Kuropatkin failed to insist on similar rigorous selection processes. By the time Nicholas fired Kuropatkin five years later, the era of military experts' domination of strategy was approaching its end. Kuropatkin's staff wizardry and organizational experience led him, on the eve of the East Asian war, to undertake wide-ranging reorganizations that finally transformed the maze of committees and commissions that had done war planning since the 1870s into formal staff bureaucratic organs. Resembling the powerful quartermaster generalships that characterized Germany's general staff, Kuropatkin's new staff reached the high point of rationalization. Yet at the same time St. Petersburg paid little attention to staff assignments in key western military districts, and after Kuropatkin's fall a bevy of officers with little or no exposure to staff culture (as Obruchev had molded it) rose to the highest positions in the new staff organization.

The Main Staff first lost its ad hoc planning organs in Kuropatkin's introduction of general quartermaster offices in 1902–1903, building on an initiative that dated to Obruchev's last years, to increase the power and centralization of the war planning apparatus. Just as Vannovskii had brushed aside Obruchev's recommendation that the army's chief operational planner (himself, at the time) should report directly to the emperor, so too did Kuropatkin when the new chief of Main Staff, Sakharov, resurrected the project and likewise pressed for planning autonomy. Kuropatkin and his successors refought the civil-military relations battle of 1858–1861 and 1873, between proponents of general staff subordination to ministerial control and those urging dynastic oversight, but now on the basis of rationalization of planning and the exigencies of modern warfare. The East Asian debacle (and Kuropatkin's departure) opened the way for concentration of the army's war planning talent in the resurrected GUGSh[2] and liberation of that organ from both war ministry *and* Main Staff control. The choice of individuals to lead GUGSh, in tandem with revived Romanov interference in military affairs, abbreviated any potential improvement in planning for which the new organization's proponents may have hoped. Instead, behaving much as its German counterpart did, GUGSh jealously sequestered its activities from the observation of war minister and the chief of Main Staff, duplicated the work of those other organizations, and competed for ever-scarce resources with them, while diluting the army's influence in the highest circles of government. At heart a product of structural deficiency, this organizational failure had its source in flagging institutional culture: the men who oversaw the reorganized general staff after Kuropatkin's departure did not share common work experience or culture, or even sympathetic views of Russia's strategic interests. Even the academy's traditions of strategic theorizing were undergoing severe testing after 1905. In the face of centrifugal forces acting on the planning staff and disintegration of its corporate ethos, the impetuous and dynastically conscious emperor asserted his prerogatives in military matters in ways that few of his three predecessors had dared to.

General F. F. Palitsyn had spent almost thirty-five years in St. Petersburg assigned to Guards cavalry regiments (never on the Main Staff or with military district staffs on the western front) before Nicholas designated him chief of GUGSh, a position he held throughout its period of independence from the war ministry (1905–1908). General V. A. Sukhomlinov, a Guards cavalry officer with some field staff experience but no service on the Main Staff, was assigned successively as chief of staff and then commander of the Kiev Military District. After a brief assignment as head of GUGSh during the Bosnian crisis (1908), he then led the war ministry into the Great War. His legacy was a strong anti-intellectual prejudice and preoccupation with East Asia as Russia's most important strategic priority.[3] Even the respected military theorist and writer N. P. Mikhnevich had never had an assignment in strategic planning on the Main Staff or on a western military district staff before he took over as chief of Main Staff in 1911. His years at the academy did not prepare him well for the bureaucratic infighting or equip him to resurrect the Main Staff from its subordinate position as a support organization. On the other hand, Generals Rediger, Zhilinskii, and Ianushkevich[4] had spent most of their professional lives within Obruchev's system; their exposure to his influence and strategic priorities brought them into conflict with men whose competence in matters of planning was suspect.

In some measure the issue of staff competence, a reflection of acculturation and common strategic outlook, accounts better than other explanations for the remarkable swings in Russian army deployment and strategy shortly before the Great War.[5] The 1910 western disposition, for instance, unimaginatively mirrored the deployment worked out by Obruchev and Kuropatkin between 1883 and 1885. In the absense of new solutions to Russia's now acute security problems, planners fell back on what was cheap and worked. The unity and organizational independence that Obruchev and his colonels had asserted from the 1870s through the 1890s subsequently proved not only pervious to dynastic interference but also frangible in the absence of unifying experience, such as military-statistical work or pursuit of a workable mobilization plan.

Nicholas II confronted the military professionals less directly than he did his ministers, but with equally destructive effect on state interests and competent administration. Like his predecessors, Nicholas did not engage the challenge of planning and preparation for war in the European state system. At the same time, he was unable either to relinquish to experts the authority to lead the army in war and peace or to invest sufficient time and interest in their problems to exercise responsibly his sovereign role. Indecision crippled him, as much as it did his field commander Kuropatkin during the Russo-Japanese War, and in turn led to fragmentation of field command authority in East Asia as the army went from defeat to defeat. Nicholas's intervention in a debate raging among general staff officers in 1912 over combat doctrine encapsulated his peevish, petulant assertion of dynastic prerogative and his irritation with fundamental professional and theoretical questions. He terminated further constructive criticism of tactics and operational philosophy by declaring, "Military doctrine consists of doing everything which I order."[6] And when Nicholas accepted without comment General Sukhomlinov's 1910 mobilization schedule and its accompanying redeployment plan, he registered no consciousness of having overthrown almost a quarter century of strategic consensus on the German military threat, fashioned originally by Obruchev.[7] Nicholas took the dynasty's congenital dilettantism in military matters to new heights in the late 1890s by his unwitting ignorance of his own crippling limitations in virtually every sphere of military life. Even military technicians of Obruchev's and Kuropatkin's caliber could not save the empire from

an autocrat who actually thought himself invulnerable to human failure
and wished to assert his sovereign authority without limitations. The
"crisis of autocracy" that began in the 1880s with Obruchev's and
Kuropatkin's efforts to isolate the empire's defenses from dynastic interference continued into the Duma era, when an autocrat finally lost
confidence (doverie) in the technicians' solutions.

For their part, the technicians' conceit could hardly prepare them for
their sovereign's impulsiveness, even as it blinded them to the political
realities of the European alignment. As in the 1870s, the post-1905
period found the general staff developing its strategic agenda independently of diplomatic considerations, and at times consciously in
conflict with Russia's minimal obligations under the French alliance. In
particular, Palitsyn's immoderate fear of Japan's ambitious designs on
Russia's Asian territories and interests was as myopic as Nicholas's and
Bezobrazov's brashness had been just a few years earlier. Yet like an
earlier generation of staff planners, Palitsyn did not shy away from
excluding state or dynastic authority from decisions of war (in his case,
devising mechanisms that initiated automatic mobilization in the Caucasus against Turkey in certain militarily defined circumstances, and
without reference to the Council of State Defense under the tsar's
second cousin).[8]

The crisis of autocracy caused havoc in imperial Russia's attempt to
devise a workable national security policy. Aside from the particular
weaknesses of individuals—Nicholas, Kuropatkin, Palitsyn, Sukhomlinov, and the rest—Russia was a leading participant in the European
political system before the Great War and had no choice in that matter.
Obruchev had understood this as an imperative to achieve an efficacious result in the event of war, which led to French project. Meanwhile
the solution to his problem—getting ready for a war with the dual
Alliance—tied the hands of the other Russian state institution involved
in Russia's security: the foreign ministry. Giers and his successors comprehended that Russia could benefit more from continuing to assert its
freedom of action diplomatically (as did Obruchev, given his disinclina-
tion to give up the defensive-offensive option aimed against Austria). If
Obruchev and Kuropatkin tied the foreign ministry's hands, then that
was merely the cost of bureaucratic success in autocratic Russia. Finally,
Germany itself, with sizeable appetites for territory to the east, was
unable to emerge from Moltke's shadow: the Great General Staff pro-

ceeded down a path of progressively narrowing alternatives that abetted the ambitions of expansionist elements in the court, foreign ministry, and society.

THE ORIGINS OF general staff professionalization lay in new forms of statistical and topographic mensuration developed in the staff before the mid–nineteenth century. To see, to describe, and to know the Russian empire were preeminent missions for the general staff, and its recruitment of very bright, philosophically "progressive" young men accounted both for the staff's unusual passage through seditious ferment and its yet unmeasured contribution to the self-definition of Russia as a state and nation. For general staffs everywhere, harnessing the revolution in information technology meant that they gained an edge over less perspicacious opponents, and sometimes they developed an appreciation of information as the basis of all modern infrastructure development. It also marked the convergence of information and infrastructure, epitomized vividly in the railroad revolution. With the tools of their scientific background in hand, general staff officers confronted the crippling backwardness that hobbled Russia's ability to defend itself, much less assert its interests in the European system of states. They developed new habits—aggressive intelligence collection, annual staff rides, well-supported strategic studies, field exercises of growing proportions, and, most important, systematic mobilization planning—to lead the army onto a road of modernization and strategic competitiveness. The cost was not insignificant: ferocious German antagonism following Berlin's recognition of St. Petersburg's progress; perpetual struggle for the seemingly endless resources necessary to launch a viable strategy; and the technicians' departure from dynasty-based myth that their sovereign still clung to. The dynastic regime accrued all these costs through its professional staff officers' recognition of the state's security dilemma and their conclusions about the solution. At first, the abstract and complex character of their undertakings—statistical accumulation, geographic and cartographic imaging, railroad and mobilization scheduling—protected them from intrusions.

New competences, deep future–oriented thinking, and a broadly based appreciation of comparative development drove the planning work at the center of the general staff organization. In the brief time after 1870, those new competences placed Russia in a position to assert its strength in support of its declared interests, without fear of being ill prepared (if still unable to *fight*). The result was an impressive mobilization in 1876, even by Prussian standards. Those new competences also led to the invention and application of a modern war planning process that functioned *solely* to solve the state's gravest strategic dilemma: defense against German aggression. Gradually, it also offered hope of securing by war Russian ambitions in Galicia. The process worked by means of improved information technology. The search for the ultimate plan coincided with maturation of the technician-dominated general staff, free of midcentury philosophical baggage. The search turned into an obsession, propelled in part by conceit, and reached fruition with the plan on which the Main Staff finally alighted in 1887. The staff was then locked into the search for an ally to make it practicable. And even in that realm the planners had a hand.

Obruchev paved the way to the Franco-Russian alliance not to enable Russia to wage aggressive war against Germany but simply to save the western borderlands, including tsarist Poland. In the late 1880s (as in 1876), Obruchev forwarded politically unsound judgments in support of his proposals for strategic or military action. His thinking seemed simultaneously to placate general staff officers of the Suvorov inclination (in ascendancy after Dragomirov's elevation to head the general staff academy in 1881) and to attend to the worries of the "realists" who knew that only a defensive strategy had any hope of success in a war with the Teutonic powers. By almost any measure, Obruchev's Main Staff fulfilled the ambitions Miliutin had harbored for it from the early 1860s. By the late 1880s, however, the failure of Russian diplomacy and the autocrat's political leadership either to constrain Obruchev's search for allies or to create the conditions for favorable alliance terms obstructed the final satisfaction of Russia's security needs.

Obruchev's right hand, Kuropatkin—the man who more than anyone fashioned the 1887 mobilization plan—and his circle of staff officers capped the Main Staff's evolution with his rise to the ministryship. From then onward, the Main Staff rapidly slipped into the background as a center for strategic planning. After repeated efforts by Obruchev to restructure completely the Main Staff around the war planning system, Kuropatkin managed just that. Even the titles of Kuropatkin's new department heads (general quartermasters) resonated of the Prusso-German system that Russian staff officers had followed in practice for years, even while locked in a structure essentially of French inspiration. Organizational genius did not eclipse Kuropatkin's larger conceits, however. By carrying off to the ministry chancellery those activities he had previously dominated—strategic planning in particular—Kuropatkin laid the groundwork for a bureaucratic (and political) tussle that stood unresolved when Nicholas's empire disintegrated. The most prized objective over which ambitious individuals struggled in the political and military realm was not doctrine, or theory of war, or even organization of forces, but the control of mobilization planning and its apparatus.

The paradox in all this was the unflinching loyalty and consistent conservatism of general staff officers, values that had accommodated the technician's mentality by the 1880s. Flickers of general staff officer radicalism, effervescent from the 1850s, were completely extinguished during the course of the 1860s. The attitudes of technicians like Kuropatkin who came to dominate the war planning mechanism after 1880 can be viewed as neither progressive nor traditionalist. Dispassionately systematic, rather than scientific, is the sense one has of their political and social views, which is borne out after the revolution by apologetic recollections in emigration of the general staff's righteous "apolitical" disengagement from the concerns of policy.[9] But what was "political" in autocratic Russia? Bureaucratic limitation on dynastic alternatives and prerogatives was charged with political significance. Exercise by experts—professionals—of authority beyond their right (or, often, capability) began the dismantlement of Russia's political myths of rulership long before the challenges of 1905 or 1917.

A high degree of technical competence influenced promotion and dominated appointments to critical staff positions from the late 1870s onward. The key assignments in the most important military districts of the European theater went to men with *proven* staff competence— and almost always extensive prior work in the central planning organs. Those key positions included the chiefs of staff (and assistant chiefs of staff) in Warsaw, Vilna, Odessa, and Kiev Military Districts and other staff officers on those staffs; the senior and junior secretaries in the chancelleries of VUK, the ministry, and the mobilization committee; the heads of the I and II Departments of the Main Staff, and desk officers in those departments; and certain positions in the Military-Topographic Department. In general, academy service was not advantageous to later assignment, especially to operational staff and field commands. Almost without exception the men who filled the critical planning positions began their commissioned service in Guards regiments; many never returned to the Guards. Progressivist, scientifically oriented meritocracy within a traditional conservative privileged elite is one of the quandaries this study's discussion of professionalization has explained.

The half century up to Kuropatkin's 1900–1903 reorganization had witnessed de facto changes in strategic centers of authority four times. Nicholas I, supreme commander and effective army chief of staff, was succeeded by a war minister of unequaled talent and prescience, to whom Nicholas's son Alexander readily deferred. Miliutin delegated to his protégé on the staff, Obruchev, the business of strategic (and thus political) planning beginning in the late 1860s and reaching a turning point with the 1873 strategic conference. Unleashed by Miliutin's departure in 1881, Obruchev then directed without interference Russia's higher military staff system for seventeen years, nominally under a most pliable war minister, Vannovskii. Their near-simultaneous departures in 1897–1898 opened the way for Kuropatkin's ascent. The quintessential technician took over the system and returned strategic control to the war minister's office. It is difficult to imagine Russia's strategic authority being embedded in a more flexible structure. A modern military organization, so reliant on the competence of extraordinary individuals, demanded institutional adaptability, given the political system under which it (and Russia) labored. Yet it was Obruchev's failure, in the final analysis, to solidify and fully regularize that organization that contributed to its subsequent tumultuous decline.

By the mid-1890s the memoirs of general staff officers assigned in St. Petersburg speak of growing lethargy, inactivity, preoccupation with appearance, even boredom. Work, of course, continued on the plan for mobilization against the Central Powers, but staff officers seemed, in their own minds, to believe the alliance had relieved them of their principal burden. Colonel E. A. Nikol'skii, a Main Staff planner at the turn of the century, later recollected an "unhurried, unpressured existence" and relaxed work hours within the organ that had just a decade earlier burned the lamp oil late into the night.[10] Obruchev had solved the strategic problem, and with his departure, staff officers no longer felt the sting of St. Petersburg to impel their work on solutions to planning problems. The cornerstone district staff on the western front, in Warsaw, likewise languished. Major General F. K. Gershel'man, another of Obruchev's protégés, after a visit to the district staff in 1902, found that "in matters of the defense of the Western frontier, nothing had been settled, nothing was finished. We wasted our time on a mass of often contradictory assumptions, [aimlessly] touching on everything and fixing on nothing, arriving at total distrust of our own decisions which changed constantly."[11]

From the mid-1890s Obruchev's alliance locked the tsar into a strategy that would survive until the collapse of the Provisional Government in 1917, by way of the staff's experience with improvisational war (1904–1905) and potential two-front war (1906–1914). The habit of strategic planning became in fact an *imperative* contrary to the real interests of state but also contrary to strategic interests. The Russian tsar and the German kaiser were not the charismatic warlords of dynastic myth but instead were rationalized *objects* of modernized, professionalized systems of state. Furthermore, the general staff system Miliutin and Obruchev devised later turned into a mechanism more concerned with turf and appearances than with Russia's security.

Russia's privileged, educated strata laid the path to state modernization and in the process wandered onto the hitherto uncharted consequences that no state servant either intended or anticipated. The general staff's place near the very center of both dynastic myth and state power has rendered it an extraordinary example of this. The full consequences would be overshadowed before 1914 by struggles among the general staff, the post-1906 Duma, and reactionary traditionalist elements around Nicholas II, struggles that hobbled continued military modernization and paralyzed any effective return to an autocratic narrative of legitimacy. After the civil war, it would be up to the nascent Red Army fully to rationalize general staff work and the staff's role in the state.

There are three paradoxes in the final denouement of this evolution. First, the episodic evidence of decline in professional attitudes among Main Staff officers that began some time in the 1890s, approximately coincident with Obruchev's departure, points to a mere patina of professional culture. How thin and fragile was the "professionalization" that had transformed Russia's general staff work from the 1860s onward? Was it merely the expression of the will of individuals—

Obruchev, Velichko, Lobko, Kuropatkin? This phenomenon of declining professionalism, if not calling into question the depth of cultural penetration such forms of "modernization" can reach, certainly demonstrates the fleeting effect *nauka* and scientism have on bureaucratic processes. As argued in the introduction to this study, professionalism may be quickly lost if *processes* of work misplace the imperative of progress; thus, professionalism and a sense of technical positivism are inseparable. In the Main Staff's case, that displacement might tentatively be dated to the French alliance. Nevertheless, the influence of men like Obruchev is of inescapable significance.

Other dilemmas are briefly stated but quite inexplicable. How was it that the Main Staff's success in one area—war and mobilization planning—blinded it to problems in many other areas and locked the system into a political straitjacket? The question raises doubts about the realism of *any* of Russia's military and strategic thought, and military men's dedication to certain assumptions beyond their expertise—what I have called professional conceit. Did Obruchev merely respond to his own understanding of strategic relations, and did political reality outrun his vision after the ascension of Nicholas II? Germany's military and cultural malevolence was real and growing after 1871, but did Obruchev's Francophilia obscure from his consideration a better exit from isolation for Russia?

Finally, the greatest paradox is this: How could the apotheosis of professional military staff development be achieved amid the rot of a system that prized the capabilities of grand dukes over professionals? Within the answer to this question lies the key to the demise of autocracy and tsarism.

Supplemental Data

Table A-1. Railroad support of Balkan operations, July 1877 to February 1878

	Trains			Daily Average
	Troop	Freight	Total	
July 1877	148	19	167	5.4
August	154	21	175	5.7
September	137	18	155	5.1
October	80	45	125	4.1
November	27	37	64	2.1
December	14	30	44	1.5
January 1878	11	44	55	1.8
February	21	27	48	1.7

Freight transportation, July 1877–February 1878

Artillery freight:	20,534,380 kg	(40.91%)
Intendancy freight:	17,941,258 kg	(35.74%)
Engineering freight:	4,984,979 kg	(9.94%)
Troop-related:	3,332,321 kg	(6.64%)
Red Cross:	1,292,098 kg	(2.57%)
Medical:	966,617 kg	(1.93%)
Naval:	585,457 kg	(1.16%)
Postal-telegraph:	483,694 kg	(0.96%)
Imperial headquarters:	72,056 kg	(0.15%)
Total:	**50,192,861 kg**	

(*Opisanie Russko-Turetskoi voiny*, IX/2, 305–310)

Table A-2. Organization and Deployment of Forces in the West, 1880–1882/1883

Field Army Deployment, 1880.

Western	Neman (or Northern)	Volynian (or Southern)	Main Army
232 battalions	140 battalions	148 battalions	244 battalions
128 squadrons	90 squadrons	108 squadrons	157 squadrons
678 guns	432 guns	468 guns	798 guns

(*RGVIA*, F. 400, op. 4, d. 445, ll. 68–71)

Field Army Deployment, 1882/1883.

Western (or Vistula)	Belostok Detachment	Northern
227 battalions	0 units from the	153 battalions
135 squadrons	1st Reserve Army	144 squadrons
618 guns		274 guns

Southwestern (or Volynian)	First Reserve	Second Reserve
331 battalions	268 battalions	132 battalions
132 squadrons	156 squadrons	78 squadrons
78 guns	596 guns	274 guns

(map in: *RGVIA*, F. 402, op. 2, d. 60, l. 32)

Field Army Deep Reserves, 1882/1883.

Right Flank (Petersburg)	Left Flank (Odessa)	Rear (Samara)
144 battalions	36 battalions	32 battalions
12 squadrons	12 squadrons	12 squadrons
64 guns	64 guns	64 guns

(map in: *RGVIA*, F. 402, op. 2, d. 60, l. 32)

Table A-3. Army group mobilization estimates, 1891 (Vsepoddanneishchyi doklad Voennogo ministerstva, 24 May 1891.)

Facing East Prussia and Germany:

Day M +	Battalions	Squadrons and Sotniias	Guns
Neman Army:			
10	32	62	72
14	76	62	216
Assembly of line units complete by:			
30	180	84	464
Belostok Group:			
10	28	26	28
14	52	26	156
Concentration completed by:			
23	68	53	216
Vistula Army:			
10	84	154	194
14	152	172	366
Concentration completed by:			
24	176	184	494
Total (M+14):	280	260	738

Facing Austria-Hungary:

Day M +	Battalions	Squadrons and Sotniias	Guns
Bug Group:			
10	28	28	60
14	60	28	156
Assembly completed by:			
Infantry—21	112	32	348
Cavalry—37	112	81	372
Southwestern Army:			
10	56	132	84
14	112	168	216
Assembly completed by:			
Infantry—26	276	236	878
Cavalry—41	276	326	952
Belsk/Brest Reserves:			
14	16	53	78
Assembly completed by:			
26	100	53	318
General Reserves (Minsk/Kiev):			
24–48	88	84	172
Total (M + 14):	188	249	450

(*RGVIA*, F. 402, op. II, d. 207a, ll. 1–2)

Table A-4. Data on District Remount Inventories and Assignments, 1891–1892, Remount stock requirements per Mobilization Schedule No. 14 (December 1890)

District	Troops (1000s)	Cavalry	Artillery	Cartage		Pack	
				I razriad	II razriad	I razriad	II razriad
St. Petersburg	161.2	5,348	7,868	21,653	682	—	—
Finland	25.7	71	1,506	2,089	88	—	—
Vilna	245.1	2,692	15,649	32,966	17,293	—	—
Warsaw	204.6	3,660	17,914	28,608	5,196	—	—
Kiev	225.9	5898	19,663	35,038	9,189	—	—
Odessa	137.1	3,518	12,950	17,195	8,537	—	—
Moscow	263.5	12,570	33,832	44,710	1,152	—	—
Kazan	156.2	2,546	13,880	25,409	792	—	—
Caucasus	134.8	3,430	7,540	18,999	2,256	1,410	378
Fleet	11.3	na	na	na	na	—	—
Reserves	na	2,047	109	869	996	—	—
Subtotal:	1,565.4	41,780	130,911	227,536	46,181	1,410	378

Total Remount Requirements: 448,196

Additional horses drawn from "In-Reserve" populations of Vilna, Warsaw, and Kiev Military Districts:

cavalry	2,047
artillery	109
cartage (I)	689
(II)	886
Total:	4,021

Notes: The determinations of I or II Category (*Razriad*) of livestock are unclear. The categorization probably indicated a military veterinary judgment of quality and thus the strength or size of the animal. (*RGVIA*, F. 401, op. I, d. 454, ll. 388, 412)

Table A-5. Remount inventory, assignments, and sources per Mobilization Schedule No. 15 (May 1892)

Origin	Total	Destination Military District								
		St. Petersburg	Vilna	Warsaw	Kiev	Odessa	Moscow	Kazan	Caucasus	Don
St. Petersburg	40,326	35,048					5,242			
Finland	2,812*									
Vilna	78,493	3,102	68,137		5,889		1,365			
Warsaw	59,717			59,717						
Kiev	77,641				77,641					
Odessa	45,250					45,250				
Moscow	106,862				525	2,236	100,586	3,515		
Kazan	36,581						654	35,927		
Caucasus	36,966								36,966	
Don	5,417									5,417
Other	4,522		1,004	2,265	748	505				
Subtotals:	40,998		69,141	61,982	84,803	47,991	107,847	39,442	36,966	5,417
Total Remount Transfers: 494,587										

Notes: Finland neither provided horses for nor received horses from other districts.
(*RGVIA*, F. 401, op. I, d. 505, l. 9)

Table A-6. Questionaire of Intelligence and Data Requirements for the Four Frontier Military District Staffs, June 1888

  I. Register of the establishment of the army
     [list of all army units]

 II. Full composition [*ukomplektovanie*] of the army in peacetime
    A. Map of formation areas
    B. Schedule of new [annual] recruits
    C. Plan for transportation of recruits
    D. Plan for transportation of Cossacks

III. Basis for organization of the army in wartime
    A. Calculation of enlisted reserves
    B. [Enlisted reserve] allocation by [military] district
    C. Requirements for reserve transportation from district to district
    D. Requirements of the army for horses
    E. Conscription Schedule No. 13 [the document that preceded its corresponding Mobilization Schedule]
    F. Mobilization requirements for officers
    G. Register of mobilization expenditures

IV. Basis for concentration of the army
    A. Estimate of concentrations of neighboring armies in Germany and Austria-Hungary
    B. General plan for the concentration of our Army
      1. Plan A: In the event of war with Austria with some participation by Germany
      2. Plan B: In the event of war simultaneously with Germany and Austria
    C. Plan for transportation of forces per Plans A and B

  V. Particular tasks relating to the Mobilization and Concentration of the Army
    A. Mobilization of the railroads
    B. Preparation for war of the Warsaw, Vilna, Kiev, and Odessa Military Districts
      1. For screening mobilization [from German cavalry forays]
      2. For preparation of army provisions
      3. For preparation of artillery
      4. For preparation of army sanitary units
      5. For organization of halting stations [*etapy*]

(*RGVIA*, F. 402, op. II, d. 25, ll. 53 + ob)

Notes

Introduction

1. Arden Bucholz, *Moltke, Schlieffen and Prussian War Planning* (New York: Berg/St. Martin's, 1991), 15.

2. William C. Fuller, Jr., *Civil-Military Conflict in Imperial Russia, 1881–1914* (Princeton, N.J.: Princeton University Press, 1985), for the impact of penury and ministerial bickering on Russia's strategic condition.

3. "Expert element": *The Authority of Experts: Studies in History and Theory*, ed. Thomas L. Haskell (Bloomington: Indiana University Press, 1984), introduction.

4. Preoccupation with the *plan* led two eminent scholars (Petr Zaionchkovskii and William Fuller) to misclassify a brief but important 1880 memo (the so-called Basic Memorandum) as a war plan. Fuller calls the 1880 document a "fully articulated mobilization and deployment plan" (*Strategy and Power in Russia 1600–1914* [New York: Free Press, 1992], 341). Although the Main Staff had assembled "mobilization schedules" since the 1860s, its own judgment of those by the mid-1890s was unforgiving: none until No. 12 (1887) was of any military value. None approached the detail of the 1876 work for the Russo-Turkish War. Taking archival volume as a yardstick of significance (assuming some *minimum* amount of elaboration and thus paper volume), then no plan before No. 11 (1884), occupying thirteen archival *dela*, qualifies as more than a sketch of an operational concept. Number 10 (1883), in contrast, fills only one *delo*. Fuller and Zaionchkovskii blurred the distinction further by discussing Mobilization Schedules No. 12 and No. 19 in precisely the same terms as the "1873 war plan" (i.e., the "Conclusions" from the secret strategic conference of February 1873). No such 1873 plan existed—at least not in a form comparable to the 1880's schedules. Fuller has done an insuperable job on the *importance* of the 1880 "document," but on its medium he is silent.

5. David MacLaren McDonald, *United Government and Foreign Policy in Russia, 1900–1914* (Cambridge, Mass.: Harvard University Press, 1992), 5–6, citing

"Pis'ma S. Iu. Vitte k D. S. Sipiaginu," *Krasnyi Arkhiv* 18, 31–32. McDonald's examination of this formulation of the autocratic operation is without equal because it explains precisely the paradoxes that also concern this study.

6. Bucholz, *Prussian War Planning*, 12–16. On academic-staff interaction: John W. Steinberg, "The Education and Training of the Russian General Staff: A History of the Imperial Nicholas Military Academy" (Ph.D. diss., Ohio State University, 1990), introduction. For French exceptionalism: Allan Mitchell, *Victors and Vanquished: The German Influence on Army and Church in France after 1870* (Chapel Hill: University of North Carolina Press, 1984), chap. 4.

7. W. Bruce Lincoln, *In the Vanguard of Reform: Russia's Enlightened Bureaucrats, 1825–1861* (DeKalb: Northern Illinois University Press, 1982), chap. 1 (but compare pp. 41–43).

8. J. L. H. Keep, *Soldiers of the Tsar* (Oxford: Oxford University Press, 1985), 258–260.

9. The literature is vast on German modernization. A useful start: Richard J. Bazillion, "State Bureaucracy and the Modernization Process in the Kingdom of Saxony, 1830–1861," *German History*, 13 (1995): 305–325. Bazillion cited Dieter Langewiesche, that even "political modernization could be used to defend traditional positions of power" after the failed so-called liberal revolutions; this produced freedom by the state, not *from* the state: L. Krieger, *The German Idea of Freedom* (Chicago: University of Chicago Press, 1972), chap. 1.

10. Alfred J. Rieber, *Merchants and Entrepreneurs in Imperial Russia* (Chapel Hill, N.C.: University of North Carolina Press, 1982), 416.

11. Lincoln, *In the Vanguard of Reform*, 41–43, 49–51, 67–76, chap. 6, and passim. Departure of N. A. Miliutin, P. D. Kiselev, L. A. Perovskii, and A. P. Zablotskii by the 1860s, according to Lincoln, marked the eclipse of social reformist elements. The generation of rising "young men"—general staff or MVD— also had little connection with the ideology and philosophy that had carried its predecessors.

12. Isaiah Berlin, "The Sense of Reality," in *The Sense of Reality: Studies in Ideas and Their History* (New York: Farrar, Straus and Giroux, 1996), 1–39. A stimulating discussion of positivism in nineteenth-century Russia is Richard Pipes, *Struve: Liberal on the Left, 1870–1905* (Cambridge, Mass.: Harvard University Press, 1970), 30 ff., 52–54.

13. The naval staff crisis of 1909 dramatically illustrated the twin shoals on which reform floundered: Francis William Wcislo, *Reforming Rural Russia: State, Local Society, and National Politics 1855–1914* (Princeton, N.J.: Princeton University Press, 1990), 274–276.

14. McDonald, *United Government*, conclusion.

15. Memoirs of each emperor's family—sons, nephews, uncles, and even the distaff members—reinforce the observations of other members of the elite close to the court: family identity orbited closely around the circle of officers in the Guards' regiments: N. A. Epanchin, *Na sluzhbe trekh Imperatorov* (Moscow: Nashe nasledie 1996), pt. 3.

16. The designation *General'nogo shtaba* indicated membership in a particular body of officers, the General Staff Corps. Other specialized groups had their own designations (e.g., "of the Engineering Corps"). Use of "general staff" throughout this study, however, refers more loosely to offices that did war planning in St.

Petersburg—disparate committees, departments, and desks, most (but not all) of which fell under the chief of Main Staff *(Glavnyi shtab)*. This usage may offend some specialists, but it serves as a convenient shorthand for an otherwise cumbersome designation.

17. P. A. Zaionchkovskii, *Voennye reformy 1860–1870 godov v Rossii* (Moscow: Moscow State University, 1952), and *Samoderzhavie i russkaia armiia na rubezhe XIX–XX stoletiia* (Moscow: Mysl', 1973), placed military concerns in the center of the struggle between reformers and traditional conservative elements in Russian government. Alfred Rieber's study of the tsar's correspondence on the eve of Emancipation affirms the importance of military concerns: *The Politics of Autocracy: Letters of Alexander II to Prince A. I. Bariatinskii, 1857–1864* (Paris: Mouton, 1966). Although Zaionchkovskii wove together domestic politics, economic underdevelopment, foreign concerns, and strategic history, his concern was the struggle between reform and reaction between 1856 and the end of the century.

18. Theoretical writings stand in great favor among historians who analyze Russia's military development. As testament to the general staff academy's fervent prejudice in favor of "systems" it is indispensable. But theory of war is not philosophy, and to attribute the general staff's strategic worldview to its academic military theory would seem to put the cart before the horse. John Erickson, *The Russian Imperial/Soviet General Staff*, College Station Paper No. 3 (College Station, Tex.: College Station Papers, 1981), emphasizes cerebral activities in the general staff academy rather than Russian planning work or the empire's international relations. Peter Von Wahlde, "Military Thought in Imperial Russia" (Ph.D. diss., Indiana University, 1966), and Carl Van Dyke, *Russian Imperial Military Doctrine and Education, 1832–1914* (New York: Greenwood Press, 1990), analyzed the main camps among the academy's military thinkers, but neither study associated those with strategic developments. G. P. Meshcheriakov, *Russkaia voennaia mysl' v XIX v.* (Moscow: Nauka, 1973), and L. P. Beskrovnyi, *Russkoe voennoe iskusstvo XIX v.* (Moscow: Nauka, 1974), found material elements of greater importance than theoretical battles in their surveys of the imperial army. Clausewitz is the prism through which one historian investigated military theory, but with no reference to Russia's strategic dilemmas: Olaf Rose, *Carl von Clausewitz: Wirkungsgeschichte seines Werkes in Russland und der Sowjetunion 1836–1991* (Munich: Oldenbourg, 1995). Walter Pintner, "Russian Military Thought: The Western Model and the Shadow of Suvorov," in *Makers of Modern Strategy from Machiavelli to the Nuclear Age*, ed. Peter Paret (Princeton, N.J.: Princeton University Press, 1986), 354–375, is generally unilluminating on the significance of the military academic debates, not least the place of critics such as Jan Bloch in military-theoretical development. A few contemporaries noted the discontinuity between theory and application; see A. V. Gerua, *Posle voiny: O nashe armii* (St. Petersburg, 1908), 6–9, for his criticism of the theoreticians' shortcomings after a later military disaster.

19. Eliot Freidson, *Professional Powers: A Study in the Institutionalization of Formal Knowledge* (Chicago: University of Chicago Press, 1986), xi.

20. Bruce Menning's work is a splendid analysis of the operations and doctrine that shaped the Russian view of war, but it does not tackle in depth the abyss that separated war planning from combat effectiveness: *Bayonets before Bullets: The Imperial Russian Army, 1861–1914* (Bloomington: Indiana University Press, 1992).

21. Cultural bases of this history were ignored by Soviet historians. See, e.g.,

S. A. Tuishkevich, "Razvitie voenno-istoricheskoi nauki v Rossii vo vtoroi polovine XIX—nachale XX vv.," in *Filosofiia i voennaia istoriia*, ed. E. I. Rybkin et al. (Moscow: Nauka, 1979); or the selection of essays in *Russkaia voenno-teoreticheskaia mysl' XIX i nachala XX vv.*, ed. L. G. Beskrovnyi (Moscow: Mysl', 1960). The most useful soviet work on this era is in the otherwise tendentious series *Revoliutsionnaia situatsiia* (cited in chapter 2).

1. Expert Knowledge and the Problem of Higher Military Staffs

1. For the argument against "development-through-accumulation" approaches to scientific progress, see Thomas S. Kuhn, *The Structure of Scientific Revolutions* (Chicago: Univeristy of Chicago Press, 1969), introduction.

2. Richard Stites, *Revolutionary Dreams: Utopian Vision and Experimental Life in the Russian Revolution* (Oxford: Oxford University Press, 1989), 19–24. For the importance of bureaucratic aspects of strategy making, see MacGregor Knox, "Conclusion: Continuity and Revolution in the Making of Strategy," in *The Making of Strategy: Rulers, States, and War*, ed. Williamson Murray et al. (New York: Cambridge University Press, 1994), 615–621. B. Croce, *Storia d'Europa nel secolo decimono*, 250, cited in Roberto Vivarelli, "1870 in European History and Historiography," *Journal of Modern History*, 53 no. 2 (June 1981): 188.

3. Charles E. McClelland, *The German Experience of Professionalization: Modern Learned Professions and Their Organizations from the Early Nineteenth Century to the Hitler Era* (Cambridge: Cambridge University Press, 1991), 9; emphasis added.

4. The officer corps' conservative character is examined in P. [A.] Zaionchkovskii, "Russkii ofitserskii korpus na rubezhe dvukh stoletii," *Voprosy istorii*, 4 (1981): 21–29; Peter Kenez, "A Profile of the Prerevolutionary Officer Corps," *California Slavic Studies*, 7 (1973): 121–158; Matitiahu Mayzel, "The Formation of the Russian General Staff 1880–1917: A Social Study," *Cahiers du Monde russe et soviétique*, 16, nos. 3–4 (1975): 297–321; John Bushnell, "The Tsarist Officer Corps, 1881–1914: Customs, Duties, Inefficiency," *American Historical Review*, 86 no. 4 (1981): 753–780; and Hans-Peter Stein, "Der Offizier des russischen Heeres im Zeitabschnitt zwischen Reform und Revolution (1861–1905)," *Forschungen zur Osteuropäischen Geschichte* [Berlin], 13 (1967): 346–504. Only Mayzel's study focuses exclusively on the General Staff Corps; the others conclude with some uncertainty that, despite the privileges that separated general staff officers from line or even Guards officers, *culturally* they were all indistinguishable. By the 1880s the academy's course included a supplemental third year; the breakout of students at each stage in the 1882/1883 academic year shows their service background:

	Junior Class	Senior Class	Suppl. Class
Guards	39	26	39
Line Cavalry	7	5	3
Infantry	21	9	4
Artillery	38	22	16
Class totals	106	62	62

Adapted from N. P. Glinoetskii, *Istoricheskii ocherk Nikolaevskoi akademii General'nogo shtaba*, (St. Petersburg, 1882). Appendix 7, 378–385.)

Even taking into consideration varying class sizes, the Guards contingent and the artillerists suffered the lowest academic attrition. See Mayzel, "Formation," and Steinberg, "Education and Training," for discussion of the academy's rigors and the students' performance.

5. For an explanation of this common phenomenon, see C. Moksos, "The Emergent Military," *Pacific Sociology Review*, 16 (1973): 255–279.

6. A rigorous definition might also answer the question Why was Russia's so-called *intelligentsiia* singularly ineffective in moving the state toward a more effective political form after 1825? And why are some militaries, so thoroughly "professional" in their own eyes, also so lacking in thoroughgoing military effectiveness?

7. MacGregor Knox, "The 'Prussian Idea of Freedom' and the Career Open to Talent: Battlefield Initiative and Social Ascent from Prussian Reform to Nazi Revolution, 1807–1944," in Knox, *Foreign Policy and War in Fasist Italy and Nazi Germany* (Cambridge: Cambridge University Press, forthcoming).

8. Max Weber, *Economy and Society*, 2 vols., ed. Gunther Roth and Claus Wittich (Berkeley: University of California Press, 1978), chap. 8, § 4, and chap. 11, § 2, substitutes rationalization, and legalistic and economic considerations for formal knowledge and practical skill as definitions of "vocation" *(Beruf)*. Weber makes no use of the term "profession." His "rationalism" (approximating the use of "scientism" here) describes the methodical *means* (but not knowledge) for a job.

9. Methodological treatment in essays constituting Part I of: *Between Tsar and People: Educated Society and the Quest for Public Identity in Late Imperial Russia*, ed. Edith W. Clowes et al. (Princeton, N.J.: Princeton University Press, 1991).

10. Harley Balzer, "The Problem of Professions in Imperial Russia," in *Between Tsar and People*, 184.

11. These patterns describe precisely the education of P. P. Semenov-Tian-Shanskii, the great geographer, explorer, and statistician, and D. A. Miliutin, the war minister who oversaw reform of the army, respectively. They were, incidentally, close friends from early adulthood and were related by marriage.

12. McClelland, *German Experience of Professionalization*, 8–9. Cf. the classical definition proposed by M. R. Haug: (1) a monopoly on expert knowledge; (2) an altruistic public image; and (3) self-definition of standards of performance. A combination of these characteristics appears in almost every historian's attempt to frame a definition.

13. Balzer, "Problem of Professions," 195–198. Balzer admits that professionals themselves came to see the "proper performance of their professional activity" (i.e., how they did their work) ultimately governing their social and political behavior. "Freedom from state tutelage" was an *outcome* of professionalization, not an ingredient of it.

14. Eliot Freidson, "The Changing Nature of Professional Control," *Annual Review of Sociology*, 10 (1984): 1–20; Freidson, "The Theory of Professions: State of the Art," in *Sociology of the Professions: Lawyers, Doctors and Others*, ed. R. Dingwell and P. Lewis (London: St. Martin's, 1983).

15. For the "outsider's perspective," see Balzer, "Problem of Professions"; and Fuller, *Civil-Military Conflict*, chap. 1. A departure from the "characteristics" method is G. Teitler, *The Genesis of the Professional Officers' Corps* (Beverly Hills, Calif.: Sage Publications, 1977); although focused on *processes* of social transforma-

tion, Teitler (like his subjects) assumes the unfortunate equation of change with progress—bourgeoisification was, he argues, the unavoidable and essential transformation en route to professionalism.

16. See McClelland, *German Experience of Professionalization;* also Cornelis W. R. Gispen, *New Profession, Old Order: Engineers and German Society, 1815–1914* (Cambridge: Cambridge University Press, 1989); and Geoffrey Cocks and Konrad Jarausch, eds., *German Professions, 1800–1950* (Oxford: Oxford University Press, 1990).

17. Samuel D. Kassow, James L. West, and Edith W. Clowes, "Introduction: The Problem of the Middle in Late Imperial Russian Society," in *Between Tsar and People,* 2–6.

18. S. Stewman, "Organizational Demography," in *Annual Review of Sociology,* 14 (1988): 173–202; B. Levitt and J. G. March, "Organizational Learning," *Annual Review of Sociology,* 14 (1988): 319–340. Levitt and March see the learning process as routine-based, history- and experience-dependent, and performance-oriented.

19. The metaphysical term "architectonics" *(arkhitektonika)*, first used at the beginning of the nineteenth century and frequently after 1840, encapsulates this systematization of knowledge. See the *Oxford English Dictionary,* 2nd ed., and the reissue of Vladimir Dal', *Tolkovyi slovar' v chetyrekh tomakh* (Moscow, 1989), vol. 1:25. On the better-known influence of architectonics on Bogdanov (in his coining of "techtology") and other silver age thinkers and artists: James Billington, *The Icon and the Axe* (New York: Vintage, 1966), 489–492.

20. Freidson, *Professional Powers,* 4–5, 158–166.

21. Jacques Ellul, *The Technology Society* (New York: Vintage Books, 1964), 21; emphasis added. Ellul concludes, however, that the primary aim of technique is not problem solving but "efficient ordering" of information, and (as Foucault also argued) thus marks the "perimeter" of democratic society. Also, Maurice Pearton, *Diplomacy, War and Technology since 1830* (Lawrence, Kan.: University of Kansas Press, 1984) 64–68, 95–105.

22. John Kenneth Galbraith, *The New Industrial State* (Boston: Houghton Mifflin, 1971), 31.

23. Fuller, *Civil-Military Conflict,* chap. 1.

2. Science and Military Statistics in Nicholas's Army

1. This pattern is observed for other fields in Richard S. Wortman, *The Development of Russian Legal Consciousness* (Chicago: University of Chicago Press, 1976); John R. Gillis, *The Prussian Bureaucracy in Crisis, 1840–1860: The Origins of an Administrative Ethos* (Palo Alto, Calif.: Stanford University Press, 1971); and in the literature by McClelland and Pearson cited previously.

2. Civil administration proved less capable of attracting competent servants; in addition to the host of caricatures in Gogol's novels, see S. Frederick Starr, *Decentralization and Self-Government in Russia, 1830–1870* (Princeton, N.J.: Princeton University Press, 1972), 3–10. For comment on institutional origins of *deloproizvodstvo*—rationalized administrative procedures—see Daniel T. Orlovsky, *The Limits of Reform: The Ministry of Internal Affairs in Imperial Russia, 1802–1881* (Cambridge, Mass.: Harvard University Press, 1981), 25, 48. George L. Yaney, *The Sys-*

tematization of Russian Government: Social Evolution in the Domestic Administration of Imperial Russia, 1711–1905 (Urbana: University of Illinois Press, 1973), 4–6, skirts a key aspect of systematization and rationalization of government: for it to occur, each ministry had to introduce reforms that eliminated administrative *proizvol* (ad hoc work patterns, as well as broader bureaucratic caprice). Mere rationalization of *regulations and personnel policy* was not enough. Fundamentally, work habits and attitudes had to be regularized and bureaucrats inculcated with a new work ethic, precisely as Lincoln described in *Vanguard of Reform*, chap. 2. On Nicholaevan military administrative reforms and the rising profile of the military desk officer, see Frederich W. Kagan, "Reform for Survival: Russian Military Policy and Conservative Reform in the Reign of Nicholas I, 1825–1836" (PhD diss., Yale University, 1995), chap. 7 (esp. 280–282, et seq.). The *deloproizvoditel'* should not be confused with the *stolonachal'nik*, literally "desk chief," who occupied a place between the desk action officer and the *nachal'nik otdeleniia*, the department head. The action officer was usually a lieutenant colonel; the desk chief, a senior lieutenant colonel or junior colonel; and the department head, a colonel or higher.

3. Acknowledged by Peter Morris, "The Russian in Central Asia, 1870–1887," *Slavonic and East European Review*, 53 no. 5 (October 1975): 521–538. Scientific origins of the penetration of Central Asia are eclipsed in Morris's account by questions of a lingering political insubordination behind Russia's advance. The empire's creative elements, no less than its imperialists, conjured exotic visions from Russian penetration of the vast Eurasian steppe, the sort of seductive, imagined cultures that central European reality simply could not support.

4. Likewise for the British case: Thomas Richards, *The Imperial Archive: Knowledge and Fantasy of Empire* (London: Verso, 1993), 1–9, on much later manifestation of the imperial fetish for knowledge.

5. Discussion of the "era" is found in Harald Westergaard, *Contributions to the History of Statistics* (London, 1932), chap. 5; Silvana Patriarca, *Numbers and Nationhood: Writing Statistics in Nineteenth-Century Italy* (Cambridge: Cambridge University Press, 1996), 1–9, 13–21. Patriarca, like Benedict Anderson and other cultural historians, is interested in statistics as a tool of Foucaldian "governmentalization," an implement of power through the taxonomic process of naming. In this quirky (and ahistorical) view, "representation" and nation building, rather than state building, is the nineteenth-century statistical project. Strategic imperatives do not appear in the discussions, although in many cases the military stood squarely behind the impulse "to know"—and not just in Russia.

6. Patriarca, *Numbers and Nationhood*, 15, citing M.-N. Bourguet, *Déchiffrer la France*, 49–50, where she describes *Staatenkunde* as the "morphology of the state," a formulation applicable in breadth and intent to Russia's military statistics.

7. Theodore M. Porter, *The Rise of Statistical Thinking, 1820–1900* (Princeton, N.J.: Princeton University Press, 1986), 5–6. Parliament had earlier drawn on enumeration to guide its deliberations. In the early nineteenth century, development of error theory (a precursor to midcentury statistical practice) also had a powerful impact on geodesy, one of the Russian general staff's principal scientific interests, in view of its role in applied physics, ballistics, and artillery training. Also: *Encyclopaedia Britannica*, 11th ed., s.v. "Statistic"; *La Grande Encyclopédie*, notes the distinct form (but not branch) of statistics called "geographic statistics," which closely ap-

proximated the balance of Russian nineteenth-century practice in the form of cartographic and surveying descriptions.

8. Orlovsky, *Limits of Reform*, 38–40. Despite its early start, MVD did not then adopt a workable *deloproizvodstvo* (work management process) even by the mid-1860s. This restrained its effective use of information. I. V. Kozlov, *Petr Petrovich Semenov-Tian-Shanskii* (Moscow: Prosveshchenie, 1983), 43–44.

9. Cf. "scientistic movement" of the period: J. Ben-David, *The Scientist's Role in Society* (Englewood Cliffs, N.J.: Prentice-Hall, 1971), chap. 6.

10. The long roster of sanctified army, Guards, and general staff officers involved in radical activity at midcentury may be found in V. A. D'iakov, *Deiateli russkogo i pol'skogo osvoboditel'nogo dvizheniia v tsarskoi armii 1856–1865. (Biobibliograficheskii slovar)* (Moscow: Nauka, 1967). Venturi says that the general staff academy "seemed to be extensively won over" by secret societies within its walls: Franco Venturi, *Roots of Revolution: A History of the Populist and Socialist Movements in Nineteenth-Century Russia*, trans. Francis Haskell (Chicago: University of Chicago Press, 1983), 269.

11. Neither historians of radicalism nor those of the military seem to have appreciated Obruchev's dissonant course. Venturi, for instance, was apparently unaware that Obruchev was a general staff officer, or that one organ he contributed to, *Velikoruss*, was produced on general staff presses!

12. Useful information on Guards service (which composed part of the background of 80 percent of Alexander II's ministers) may be found in W. Bruce Lincoln, "The Ministers of Alexander II: A Survey of Their Background and Service," *Cahiers du Monde russe et soviétique*, 17 (1976): 470–471, although Lincoln considers military background an *aberration* in Alexander's selection of ministers.

13. D'iakov, *Deiateli*, s.v. "Lavrov, Petr Lavrovich," particularly the citations.

14. The file on Obruchev's dismissal, his appeal to the director of the academy, and subsequent reinstatement in September 1857: RGVIA, F. 544, d. 454, 7–25 September 1857 (incomplete file).

15. E. Willis Brooks, "The Improbable Connection: D. A. Miliutin and N. G. Chernyshevskii," *Jahrbücher für Geschichte Osteuropas* 37 no. 1 (1989): 34–38.

16. Obruchev's colleague both as coeditor and at the academy as professor of military administration (a field closely related to military statistics), Anichkov appears not to have been admitted to the General Staff Corps after graduation from the academy because his name is not in the General Staff list of 1874. He was killed in 1877 during the Russo-Turkish War. D'iakov, *Deiateli*, 20; *Spisok General'nogo shtaba, Po 1 Fev. 1874 g.* (St. Petersburg, 1874), s.v. "Anichkov"; Brooks, "Miliutin and Chernyshevskii," 35 n. 46. Also, the useful discussion in Keep, *Soldiers of the Tsar,* 357–362, with comment on the wider radical circle at the academy.

17. Few studies tap French sources on Obruchev. See Peter Jakobs, *Das Werden des französch-russischen Zweibundes 1890–1893* (Wiesbaden: Harrassowitz, 1968), 29–33, using military archival materials from Chateau Vincennes. Regrettably, Jakobs makes only passing note of Obruchev's career up to the mid-1880s, but he establishes the long duration of the general's French connections.

18. RGVIA, F. 544, d. 494, on Obruchev's trip; N. N. Obruchev and N. P. Ogarev, *Chto nado delat' voisku* (London, 1861, 1862). In pamphlet form the work is rare, but the text appeared in *Kolokol* (8 November 1861), and is found in most editions of Ogarev's collected works.

19. Compiled as a book, Obruchev's articles appeared under the title *Nashe finansovoe polozhenie* (St. Petersburg, 1866).

20. *RGVIA*, F. 544, d. 494, l. 21, dated 10 May 1860.

21. O. R. Airapetov, "Pol'skoe vosstanie 1863 goda i N. N. Obruchev," *Rossiia i Reformy. Sbornik statei*, vol. 2 (Moscow: Medved, 1993), 34–39, argues that Obruchev did not refuse orders but had in fact been ordered by the new war minister, Miliutin, to join the consultative committee and another "editing commission" working on army reform. The "myth" of Obruchev's insubordination was, as Airapetov points out, promoted most vigorously and publicly by the emperor's brother, Nikolai Nikolaevich senior. The documents he cites, however, do not contradict the traditional view as elaborated here, that Obruchev refused to go and was subsequently protected by Miliutin, who assigned him to key committees along with Obruchev's recent colleague, Anichkov. Airapetov's observation that 1863 was a turning point among officers of so-called liberal inclination is well taken. Miliutin's deep fear that the uprising would derail military reform, just as it began, was well-placed and probably shared by the young officers around him—even those who might have sympathized with the Poles.

22. *RGVIA*, F. 544, d. 615. On his mission: ll. 4–6ob; Obruchev's report (6 October 1864): ll. 16–23ob. He had been raised to the General Staff Corps only a few months earlier, so Miliutin's hand may be discerned in the foreign sequestration. His refusal to join his division would have conformed with vague promises he, Sleptsov, and other "Land and Liberty" general staffers had given Polish revolutionaries in November 1862, to act so as to "prevent the tsarist government from sending fresh troops to Poland" in an uprising; cited in Keep, *Soldiers of the Tsar*, 362. On the *écoles d'application*: John Hubbel Weiss, *The Making of Technological Man: The Origins of French Engineering Education* (Cambridge, Mass.: MIT Press, 1982), 13–16.

23. Ulam speculated at one other extreme, citing Obruchev as a revolutionary of Herzen's stature, conviction, and commitment, and like-minded in every way. Menning observed in mild disbelief that Obruchev had "improbably become involved" in the first *Land and Liberty*, the protopopulist movement of the early 1860s, as one of its founders. George Kennan, in his sympathetic sketch of the officer, thought that Obruchev "made the mistake" of enlisting the services of Chernyshevskii for the editorship of *Voennyi sbornik*, although Obruchev, in fact, worked for the radical publicist rather than the other way around. Even if Obruchev were able to resume successfully his military career, as Kennan argues, thanks to Miliutin's protection (which seems to be at odds with the facts), that does not explain how Obruchev became involved in open *political* criticism of the military from 1858 at the latest, onward. Willis Brooks, in his remarkable synthesis of the principal *cultural* and intellectual intersections between modernizers inside and outside of state service, tackles the paradox: reformist circles made no distinction between the civil and military spheres, and neither did individuals. For provocative (although overdrawn) presentations of the Obruchev paradox, see Adam B. Ulam, *In the Name of the People: Prophets and Conspirators in Prerevolutionary Russia* (New York: Viking, 1977), 61, 71–72, 91–94. Among the incredulous: Menning, *Bayonets before Bullets*, 17–18; and George F. Kennan, *Fateful Alliance: France, Russia, and the Coming of the First World War* (New York: Pantheon, 1984), 14. Outstanding on these relationships is: Brooks, Miliutin and Chernyshevskii," 21–43. One sketch of

Obruchev, of limited use on this question, is from archival material: A. Barbasov, "Russkii voennyi deiatel' N. N. Obruchev," *Voenno-istoricheskii zhurnal*, 15, no. 8 (1973): 100–105. Mementos of Obruchev's life include: "N. N. Obruchev," *Russkaia starina*, no. 10 (October 1908): 55–62; A. Bil'derling, "Nikolai Nikolaevich Obruchev," *Voennyi sbornik*, no. 1 (1911): 1–20. Kennan believed Obruchev's personnel papers not extant; on the mystery of their fate, see Oleg Rudolfovich Airapetov, "K sud'be arkhiva N. N. Obrucheva," *Vestnik Moskovskogo universiteta*, ser. 8 "Istoriia," no. 2 (1993): 80. Airepetov's *dissertatsiia*, "Nikolai Nikolaevich Obruchev: Zhizn i Deiatel'nost'" (Moscow State University, 1994) covers the years 1830–1881; his supporting publications include "Pozitsiia Voennogo ministerstva pered Russko-turetskoi voinoi 1877–1878 za osvobozhdenie Bolgarii," *Rossiia i reformy: Sbornik statei*, vol. 1 (Moscow: MGU, 1991); and "O planirovanii Osvoboditel'noi voiny 1877–1878," *Rossiia i reformy: Sbornik statei* vol. 3 (Moscow, 1995). Until Airapetov's study becomes generally available, scholars must rely on the brief and underdocumented subsidiary essays Airapetov has published. One immediate difficulty Airapetov presents is his persistent categorization of Obruchev as "liberal," hardly justified by the officer's activity or service.

24. *RGVIA*, F. 410, op. 1, d. 184, ll. 1–69 ("Stat'ia chastnaia ofitserov v osvoboditel'nom dvizhenii XIX v. [Avtor ne ukazan. XIX v.]," approx. 1862); F. 38, *Departement General'nogo shtaba*, also includes references to numerous general staff officers involved in the revolutionary movement in Poland, including such figures as Z. Serakovskii, Ia. Dombrovskii [Dabrowski], L. Zverzhdovskii [Zwiezdowski], and I. Savitskii. Eventually, some thirty officers were executed and over one hundred exiled. Official Soviet hagiography, although emphasizing the progressive Russocentric character of the movements, nevertheless illuminates these individuals most helpfully: D'iakov, *Deiateli*; V. A. D'iakov, "Zametki Vladislava Kossovskogo o peterburgskom podpol'e i pol'skoi emigratsii nakanune vosstaniia 1863 g.," in *Revoliutsionnaia Rossiia i revoliutsionnaia Pol'sha (vtoraia polovina XIX v.)*, ed. V. A. D'iakov et al. (Moscow: Nauka, 1967), 391–420; and T. F. Fedosova, "Pol'skii komitet v Moskve i revoliutsionnoe podpol'e 1863–1866 gg.," *Revoliutsionnaia Rossiia*.

25. G. P. Meshcheriakov, *Russkaia voennaia mysl' v XIX v.* (Moscow: Nauka, 1973), 85–88, documents examples of Belinskii's and Herzen's direct influence.

26. Deeper currents connecting scientific empiricism and positivism to politics dated *at least* to the 1840s: Ilmari Susiluoto, *The Origins and Development of Systems Thinking in the Soviet Union: Political and Philosophical Controversies from Bogdanov and Bukharin to Present-Day Re-Evaluations* (Helsinki: Suomalainen tiedakademia, 1982), 20–27.

27. See, inter alia, Martin A. Miller, *Kropotkin* (Chicago: University of Chicago Press, 1976), 63; and the dismissive view in: Aileen Kelly, *Mikhail Bakunin: A Study in the Psychology and Politics of Utopianism* (Oxford: Oxford University Press, 1982), 146–148.

28. Venturi, *Roots*, 448–449. Thus: "Natural sciences, as they are understood in our society, cannot be used as a guiding rein in the labyrinth of human relations." Also: Samuel H. Baron, *Plekhanov: Father of Russian Marxism* (Stanford, Calif.: Stanford University Press, 1963), 62.

29. Their graduates dominated French foreign policy before World War I:

M. B. Hayne, *The French Foreign Office and the Origins of the First World War 1898–1914* (Oxford: Oxford University Press, 1993), 27–28. On Sciences Po's origins: Gerard Vincent, *Sciences Po: Historié d'un reussite* (Paris: O. Orban, 1987), chap. 1. The Russian and French institutions did not intend to create *savans par elles-mêmes* (academic scientists), but technological men who could apply scientific theory and general learning to practical problems—a product of *culture générale technique:* Weiss, *Technological Man*, chap. 8.

30. Richard Pipes's formulation, "liberal conservatism," as a category among constitutionalist elements, has no parallel in the French idea. His discussion of civil elements springing from the positivist, scientifist environment merits close consideration, however: *Struve: Liberal on the Left*, 286–292.

31. D. A. Miliutin, "Voennye reformy imperatora Aleskandra II," *Vestnik Evropy* (1882), reveals no hint of such an intent; he had, however, intended the work to be multipart but apparently wrote no more upon learning of imperial disapproval when the first part appeared.

32. *RGVIA*, F. 544, d. 1, for reports on the subversive activities among students in the general staff academy from 1832 to 1872; MVD continued its investigation of the activities of "secret circles" at the academy until March 1872. F. 544, d. 606, on the ejection of professor of geodesy Captain Galenzovskii from the General Staff list for abetting the Polish uprising and then going into hiding. See also the "Special Appendix," *Spisok ofitserov . . . 1832–1882 gg.*, in Glinoetskii, *Istoricheskii ocherk*, 32–204, for names of those dismissed from the academy or General Staff Corps "for cause." See also V. A. D'iakov and I. S. Miller, *Revoliutsionnoe dvizhenie v russkoi Armii i vosstanie 1863 g.* (Moscow: Nauka, 1964); and D'iakov, *Deiateli*. On Obruchev in particular: E. S. Vilenskaia, "Novye arkhivnye materialy o deiatel'nosti «Zemli i voli» (1862 g.)," *Revoliutsionnaia situatsiia v Rossii v 1859–1861 gg.*, vol. 5, ed. M. V. Nechkina (Moscow: Nauka, 1965), 33–51.

33. The Miliutin brothers, as members of a generation of reform-minded officials, are discussed extensively in Lincoln, *Vanguard of Reform*. Miliutin's early auto biography and related sources: D. A. Miliutin, *Vospominaniia*, ed. with introduction by W. Bruce Lincoln (Newtonsville, Mass.: Oriental Research, 1979); also, A. K. Baiov, *Graf Dmitrii Alekseevich Miliutin* (St. Petersburg, 1912), and an obituary in *Razvedchik*, no. 1110 (February 1912): 87–90. In English: Forrestt A. Miller, *Dmitrii Miliutin and the Reform Era in Russia* (Nashville, Tenn.: Vanderbilt University Press, 1968); and E. W. Brooks, "D. A. Miliutin: Life and Activity to 1856" (Ph.D. diss., Stanford University, 1970), which was superseded in part by republication of the first volume (Tomsk, 1917) of Miliutin's *Vospominaniia*. Also Brooks's "Miliutin and Chernyshevskii," carefully elaborates the convergences noted here.

34. [Miliutin,] *Vospominaniia*, 50–69; Brooks, "D. A. Miliutin: Life and Activity," 24–39.

35. Perevoshchikov contributed to "The Contemporary" *(Sovremennik)* and "Notes of the Fatherland" *(Otechestvennye zapiski)*. On Miliutin's path: [Miliutin,] *Vospominaniia*, 133–167; also, Brooks, "D. A. Miliutin: Life and Activity," 40 et seq. Lincoln, "Ministers of Alexander II," 469–470, Appendix 1 (483), for importance of rigorous education to career success.

36. [Miliutin,] *Vospominaniia*, 313–415, for his 1840–1841 travel; Brooks, "D. A. Miliutin: Life and Activity," 89–90; and other communications.

37. [Miliutin,] *Vospominaniia*, 313–321.

38. D. A. Miliutin, *Rukovodstvo k s"emke planov s primeneniem matematiki* (Moscow, 1831).

39. A. Gololobov, "Nasha akademiia general'nogo shtaba," *Voennyi sbornik*, 79, no. 5 (1871): 5: 61–135; also, Steinberg, "Education and Training," 45–55. [Miliutin,] *Vospominaniia*, 308.

40. The texts he wrote for the course were *Kriticheskoe issledovanie znacheniia voennoi geografii i voennoi statistiki* (St. Petersburg, 1846), and *Pervye opyty voennoi statistiki*, 2 vols. (St. Petersburg, 1847–1848). Semenov, *Istoriia poluvekovoi deiatel'nosti IRGO*, 2 vols. (St. Petersburg, 1895–1896), vol. 1:44; M. V. Ptukha, *Ocherki po istorii statistiki v SSSR*, 2 vols. (Moscow, 1959), vol. 1:204–205. In mid-1845 Miliutin became head of the third instructional department (III *Vospitatel'noe otdelenie*), which offered him greater independence in revising curriculum, and thus marks the point at which he began to shape the character of the academy: *RGVIA*, F. 544, d. 275, concerns his 1845 assignment.

41. Zaionchkovskii, "D. A. Miliutin," 11–12; emphasis in original. Brooks's work in the *Vospominaniia* materials is crucial for the period between 1841 and 1856: Brooks, "D. A. Miliutin: Life and Activity," 112–136; Ptukha, *Ocherki po istorii statistiki*, vol. 1:234, credits Miliutin with creation of military statistics as a distinct field of study and training.

42. Zaionchkovskii, "D. A. Miliutin," 14.

43. Van Dyke, *Russian Military Doctrine*, 21.

44. V. Sukhomlinov, *Vospominaniia* (Berlin, 1924), chap. 1, for his academy years.

45. Van Dyke, *Russian Military Doctrine*, 68–69. On Comte in Russia, see Andrzej Walicki, *A History of Russian Thought: From the Enlightenment to Marxism* (Stanford, Calif.: Stanford University Press, 1979), 242–244, 273. Comte's circle in Paris was also the focus for the earliest known attempts to apply modern statistical methods to social groups under the rubric *sociologie*.

46. Bucholz, *Prussian War Planning*, 185–187.

47. Ibid., 188.

48. Arden Bucholz, *Hans Delbrück and the German Military Establishment* (Iowa City: University of Iowa Press, 1985), chap. 1. Prussia's problem with Clausewitz resulted from selective reading and poor scholarship (compounded by an adulterated edition of the key source): Jehuda L. Wallach, *The Dogma of the Battle of Annihilation: The Theories of Clausewitz and Schlieffen and Their Impact on the German Conduct of Two World Wars* (Westport, Conn.: Greenwood Press, 1986), 9–82.

49. G. A. Leer, *Metod voennykh nauk (strategii, taktiki i voennoi istorii)* (St. Petersburg, 1894), 189.

50. *Polnoe Sobranie Zakonov Rossisskoi Imperii*, 45 vols. (St. Petersburg, 1830), ser. 1: 32 §224–971.

51. See, inter alia, Kenez, "Prerevolutionary Officer Corps," 121–158, for the tensions between general staff officers and their regimental counterparts.

52. *RGVIA*, F. 544, d. 668, ll. 2–3 (request and justification, December 1868), l.4 (approval, May 1869).

53. *RGVIA*, F. 544, d. 469 (materials on his study abroad); Menning, *Bayonets before Bullets*, 38–39.

54. *RGVIA*, F. 544, d. 670: "General examination list of officers of the Practical

Course [second year]," which contains an interesting tabulation of the grades of all 1868 graduates in each subject.

55. Late-twentieth-century practice places function—purpose—at the helm of information (intelligence) collection; the result is greater efficiency in collection but larger lacunae in the structured knowledge.

56. David A. Rich, "Imperialism, Reform and Strategy: Russian Military Statistics, 1840–1880," *Slavonic and East European Review,* 74 no. 4 (1996): 621–639.

57. *Zapiski Imperatorskogo Russkogo geograficheskogo obshchestva,* vol. 4 (St. Petersburg, 1850), 1–47.

58. L. S. Berg, *Istoriia russkikh geograficheskikh otkrytii* (Moscow: Nauka, 1962), 144–152. The poet Taras Shevchenko, better known for his Ukrainian national sensibility and exile, accompanied the team to make sketches of the Aral Sea coastline. Fort Shevchenko, on the sea's east coast, was named for him. A. Lur'e, "Taras Shevchenko i Aleksei Butakov," *Krasnyi flot,* 1946: 57.

59. [Lieutenant General] A. I. Maksheev, *Puteshestvie po Kirgizskim stepiam i Turkestanskomu kraiu* (St. Petersburg, 1896).

60. *RGVIA,* F. 544, d. 321: 1849 memo from war ministry Chancellery on the new languages (staffed by civilians), and establishment of a Rb. 1,000 annual prize for the best manuscript written by a graduate in Persian; ibid., d. 377, for initial activities of new language sections, mid-1850s.

61. Topography, in particular, is concerned not with identity differences but with definition of the "other." The role of Russian military topographers in this activity fascinated viewers of Kurosawa's *Deszu Usala,* which deals with the tension between cultural understanding and distinguishing otherness—"ours" and "theirs."

62. Contemporary recollections of junior *genshtabisty* offer no insight into reorganization; articles appearing in *Voennyi sbornik* illuminated only the outcome, not the course, of reorganization.

63. The Treaty of Aigun defined a frontier along the Amur as far eastward as its juncture with the Ussuri. Negotiations for territory downriver from that juncture—an area de facto already in Russian possession—fell to another general staff adventurer, General-Adjutant Count N. P. Ignat'ev, who secured it by the Treaty of Peking in 1860. A. L. Narochnitskii, *Kolonial'naia politika kapitalisticheskikh derzhav na Dal'nem Vostoke 1860–1895 gg.* (Moscow: Nauka, 1956), chap. 1; Dietrich Geyer, *Russian Imperialism: The Interaction of Domestic and Foreign Policy, 1860–1914,* trans. Bruce Little (New York: St. Martin's Berg, 1987), 86–88.

64. W. Bruce Lincoln, *Petr Petrovich Semenov-Tian-Shanskii* (Newtonsville, Mass.: ORP, 1980), 26–32; J. N. L. Baker, *A History of Geographical Discovery and Exploration* (New York: Cooper Square Publishers 1967), 234–239.

65. *Departamenta general'nogo shtaba, Voenno-statisticheskoi obozrenie Rossiiskoi imperii,* 17 vols. (St. Petersburg, 1848–58). On the war ministry's decision to publish: *RGVIA,* F. 401, op. 5, d. 417, l. 83: "Preface to the Report on Military-Statistical Work," n.d. [late 1864/early 1865]. On organization of the compilation: ibid., ll. 83+ob. The series continued in another twenty-five volumes into the late 1860s under a different title, *Materialy dlia geografii i statistiki Rossii.*

66. I. F. Babkov, *Vospominaniia o moi sluzhbe v Zapadnoi Sibiri 1859–1875 gg.* (St. Petersburg, 1912). Cf. *Spisok General'nogo shtaba* (St. Petersburg, 1874/1889), s.v. "Babkov" for career.

67. Of particular interest to the business of mapping the empire, see his "O

khod topograficheskikh issledovanii ozera Balkhash i ego priberezhii," and on the process of imperial colonialization: "Obshchii vzgliad na ustroistvo russkikh poselenii severo-vostochnoi chasti Kirgizskoi stepi." Their appearance under IRGO auspices in the 1860s testifies to the close relationship between geographic arts and imperial expansion in Russian scientific and government circles.

68. Babkov's work was responsible for nothing less than cracking the Russian *inner periphery* (borrowing LeDonne's analytic framework), for subsequent incorporation of the Zhungarian passes. See John LeDonne, *The Russian Empire and the World 1700–1918: The Geopolitics of Expansion and Containment* (New York: Oxford University Press, 1997), 187–188 and his Map 7 for the geographic arrangement of these strategic points.

3. Main Staff Reform between Sevastopol and Sedan

1. The modern formulation of this view of Nicholas originated with A. E. Presniakov, *Apogei samoderzhaviia: Nikolai I* (Leningrad, 1925). More recently Nicholaevan militaria have received comment from Nicholas Riasanovsky, *Nicholas I and Official Nationality in Russia 1825–1855* (Berkeley: University of California Press, 1955), chap. 1; and W. Bruce Lincoln, *Nicholas I: Emperor and Autocrat of All the Russias* (DeKalb: Northern Illinois University Press, 1978), 24–26. See, however, the more nuanced view in Fuller, *Strategy and Power,* 250–252, for an appreciation of Nicholas as strategist and war maker. Richard Wortman, *Scenarios of Power: Myth and Ceremony in Russian Monarchy,* vol. 1 (Princeton, N.J.: Princeton University Press, 1995), chaps. 11–13, moves the discussion onto a new and entirely more satisfying plane. He examines the myths and symbolism of Nicholas's regime, in particular the intersection of domestic and military ideals in Nicholaevan Russia.

2. A. M. Zaionchkovskii, *Vostochnaia voina 1853–1856 gg. Prilozheniia,* 2 vols., 3 suppl. (St. Petersburg, 1908–1913): *Prilozhenie No. 150* (Nicholas's personal letter to Supreme Commander Warsaw, 17/29 May 1853, directing the operation of an army in the Principalities, and Prince Gorchakov's command of forces); and *RGVIA,* F. 1, op. 1–7, dd. 20389–20406, for *Uchebnye* materials containing Nicholas' premobilization orders to IV and V Corps, dated December 1852. His assistants provided lists of ready units; they did not prepare comprehensive plans for mobilization. The same use of premobilization measures occurred in 1876; those orders, however, were preceded by months of staff preparation, to which the mobilization's success attested.

3. Zaionchkovskii, *Vostochnaia voina,* 188: *Prilozhenie No. 30.* Gorchakov apparently had only the thinnest intelligence on Turkish forces beyond the Danube; Nicholas's diplomatic faux pas predated the Menshikov mission, before which he anticipated the outcome—war. See *Prilozhenie No. 98,* Nicholas's note on the Eastern Question.

4. For instance, Zaionchkovskii, *Vostochnaia voina,* 470, 472 (*Prilozhenie No. 164, No. 166,* on the standardized allocation of horses for the mobilized army; the General Headquarters did not anticipate *remount* requirements, nor units' current

stocks, nor uneven local availability of horses or fodder). The latest word on the origins of Russia's Crimean imbroglio (both diplomatic and military) is David M. Goldfrank, *The Origins of the Crimean War* (London: Longman, 1993); Goldfrank placed the above archival information and his copy of Zaionchkovskii at my disposal. On Nicholas's army: John Shelton Curtiss, *The Army of Nicholas I, 1825–1855* (Durham, N.C.: Duke University Press, 1965); and, more recently, the "bottom-up" view of the regimental economy, Elsie Kimerling Wirtschafter, *From Serf to Russian Soldier* (Princeton, N.J.: Princeton University Press, 1990); previously cited works by Keep, Bushnell, and Stein also pertain. Historiography on the Nicholaevan army, government, and society is extensive and will not be cited further.

5. These developments are well described in existing historiography; Zaionchkovskii, *Voennye reformy*, is still the cornerstone work, although it is not the strongest work on reform of the general staff academy; Miller, *Dmitrii Miliutin* is a satisfactory complement to Zaionchkovskii's work and particularly useful for its bibliography. On Prince Bariatinskii, Miliutin's principal opponent and onetime commander, who led the "Prussianists" in the reform camp, see also: Rieber, *Politics of Autocracy*; and Zaionchkovskii, *Samoderzhavie i russkaia armiia*, chap. 1. The Prussian-French split also extended into the field of strategy and theory of tactics: David R. Jones, *The Advanced Guard and Mobility in Russian and Soviet Military Thought and Practice*, SAFRA Papers No. 1 (Gulf Breeze, Fla.: Academic International, 1985), 59–62.

6. E. Willis Brooks, "Reform in the Russian Army, 1856–1861," *Slavic Review*, 43 no. 1 (1984), 63–82.

7. *Stoletie voennogo ministerstva 1802–1902 gg.*, 13 vols. (St. Petersburg, 1902–1914), vol. 1, Appendix, 19–51. See also: Miller, *Dmitrii Miliutin*, 21–24.

8. Joseph Bradley, *Guns for the Tsar: American Technology and the Small Arms Industry in Nineteenth-Century Russia* (DeKalb: Northern Illinois University Press, 1990), introduction, chap. 5.

9. In addition to the aforementioned works on Miliutin's reforms by Zaionchkovskii *(Voennye reformy)* and Miller *(Dmitrii Miliutin)*, see also Robert F. Baumann, "The Debates on Universal Military Service in Russia, 1870–1874" (Ph.D. diss., Yale University, 1982), which remains valuable. John Bushnell posed the question of reform failure (in terms of combat effectiveness) in his paper "Miliutin and the Balkan War: Military Reform vs. Military Performance," in *Russia's Great Reforms, 1855–1818*, ed. Ben Eklof, John Bushnell, and Larissa Zakharova (Bloomington: Indiana University Press, 1994), 139–158. One general staff veteran of the 1877–1878 war also noted this failure of the reforms: P. A. Skalon, *Moi vospominaniia 1877–1878 gg.*, 2 vols. (St. Petersburg, 1913), vol. 1:10–11.

10. *Stoletie voennogo ministerstva*, vol. 1:453–454; [*RGVIA*], *Putevoditel'*, vol. 1 (Moscow: GUA, 1979), 86–87.

11. "Kratkii obzor deiatel'nosti voennogo ministerstva v 1863 g.," *Voennyi sbornik*, no. 7, 1864, 40. Each issue of *Voennyi sbornik* included a section, "*Russkoe voennoe obozrenie,*" which is a gold mine of information on structural changes in the war ministry. A. Kavtaradze, "Iz istorii russkogo general'nogo shtaba," *Voenno-istoricheskii zhurnal*, 13 no. 12 (1971): 76–77. Quote from: D. A. Miliutin, *Proekt zapiski o preobrazovanii General'nogo shtaba* (n.p., n.d.)., cited in Kavtaradze, "Iz istorii," 76.

12. The best brief summary: Kavtaradze, "Iz istorii," 75–80. For the war ministry's resolutions and decrees, consult its annual *Svod voennykh postanovlenii* (St.

Petersburg), a multivolume digest structured in parallel with the military establishment's organization. The most important decree on reorganization is found in *PSZ* ser. II: 53 § 58773 (1869).

13. Military topography developed as a special section of the military administration after 1816; materials on its expansion and independent status are found in: *RGVIA*, F. 40 [*Voenno-topograficheskoe delo*].

14. Zaionchkovskii, *Voennye reformy*, 106.

15. Including the ten Main Directorates and the Cavalry and Sharpshooter Inspectorates; quoted in Fuller, *Civil-Military Conflict*, 8.

16. Zaionchkovskii, *Voennye reformy*, 106–134. Miller, *Dmitrii Miliutin*, 82–85, emphasizes the war minister's wish to avoid development of a segregated and narrowly specialized technical culture among *genshtabisty;* the specialization of staff work, however, was well advanced even in 1862: *Vsepoddanneishii doklad voennogo ministra 15 Ian., 1862*, reprinted with the imperial marginalia in *Prilozhenie k opisanomu ocherku razvitiia voennogo upravleniia . . ., Stoletie voennogo ministerstva*, vol. 1:87–173. Temporarily, the supreme staff bypassed ministerial office, as following the Russo-Japanese war and during the Second World War. In early 1995 deputies in the Russian Duma, opponents of defense minister Grachev, argued for the transfer of the general staff to the president's office, an unexpected revisitation of the battle Miliutin had fought 130 years earlier.

17. Allan Mitchell, "'A Situation of Inferiority': French Military Reorganization after the Defeat of 1870," *American Historical Review*, 86 no. 1 (1981): 59.

18. Zaionchkovskii, *Samoderzhavie i russkaia armiia*, 61–62; cf. Vitte *Vospominaniia: detstvo, tsarstvovaniia Aleksandra II i Aleksandra III (1849–1894)* (Berlin, 1923), 274–275, for a different version of this self-appraisal.

19. Fuller, *Civil-Military Relations*, 66; V. G. Chernukha, *Vnutrenniaia politika tsarizma s serediny 50-kh do nachala 80-kh godov XIX veka* (Leningrad: Nanka, 1978), chap. 4.

20. Vannovskii profoundly misjudged Obruchev's direction in modernization when he declared that he could keep the chief of Main Staff's *liberalism* under satisfactory control—as if that were where the danger to dynastic prerogative lay by the 1880s! Vitte, *Vospominaniia: Detstvo*, 274–275.

21. *RGVIA*, F. 401, op. 5, d. 417, ll. 83–86: Appendix to "Report of GUGSh, III Otdelenie, 24 August 1864," on activity in 1857.

22. On Lieven's and Major A. I. Lavrent'ev's work on the *Statisticheskoe opisanie* and *Voenno-statisticheskoe obozrenie: RGVIA*, F. 401, op. 5, d. 417, ll. 3+ob: "On the execution of military-statistical work of the general staff up to the present time," 20 December 1863 by Lieutenant General Prince N. S. Golitsyn. Thirty-seven year old Golitsyn worked on VUK and was head of the central statistical office of the war ministry. Lavrent'ev joined VUK in the mid-1860s and succeeded Chernyshevskii as editor of *Voennyi sbornik* (as well as *Russkii invalid*).

23. *RGVIA*, F. 401, op. 5, d. 417, ll. 4ob–5.

24. Quoted from *Doklad Ministra Vnutrennykh Del 1830g.*, in, M. Raeff, *Michael Speransky: Statesman of Imperial Russia 1772–1839* (The Hague: Martinus Nijhoff, 1957), 53.

25. *RGVIA*, F.401, op. 5, d. 417, l. 1ob.

26. *RGVIA*, F. 401, op. 5, d. 417, l. 74: "Opinion of Colonel Maksheev on the military-statistical work undertaken by the general staff, introduced for considera-

tion by the Consultative committee," 25 January 1864. Maksheev was professor of statistics at the academy, and he later joined VUK.

27. *RGVIA*, F. 401, op. 5, d. 417, l. 6ob.

28. *RGVIA*, F. 401, op. 5, d. 417, ll. 75–76. The staff had sought information on the "theory of military statistics" in other countries for two decades by the time Maksheev wrote this memo.

29. *RGVIA*, F. 401, op. 5, d. 417, ll. 77ob–81ob.

30. *RGVIA*, F. 401, op. 5, d. 417, ll. 16ob–17.

31. *RGVIA*, F. 401, op. 5, d. 417, ll. 87+ob: Memo from *Zhurnal zasedaniia Soveshchatel'nogo komiteta General'nogo shtaba*, dated 24 April, 1865, no. 8, §3; on collection formats: ibid., ll. 103–104ob; guidelines for collection: ibid., ll. 105–107ob, war ministry resolution (19 December 1868) on authority of general staff officers in preparation of the *Voenno-statisticheskoe obozrenie*.

32. *RGVIA*, F.401, op. 5, d. 417, ll. 132–137: "Program for the Military Survey of the Southwestern Theater of Military Operations," undated [1886 or 1887].

33. *RGVIA*, F. 401, op. 5, d. 417, ll. 138–144ob: Lieutenant General Fedor Aleksandrovich Fel'dman to Chief of Main Staff Obruchev, January 1889 (emphasis added). Among other general staff postings, Fel'dman served a pivotal half decade as attaché in Vienna (1876–1881).

34. On map depots: *Arkhiv vneshnei politiki Rossii* (AVPR), F. 138, op. 467, d. 14, ll. 201–206 (Lessons of 1870); *RGVIA*, F. 400, op. 3, d. 371, ll. 1–9ff, "Concerning the Correction of Military Maps, 1874–1875," cited in Fuller, *Strategy and Power*, 277.

35. Fuller, *Strategy and Power*, 276–278; Geyer, *Russian Imperialism*, 33–42; and the well-known works of Gerschenkron and Von Laue. Economic underdevelopment and its infrastructural manifestations are the staples of Soviet historiography of the reform period, e.g., A. M. Solov'eva, *Zheleznodorozhnyi transport Rossii vo vtoroi polovine XIX v.* (Moscow: Transport, 1975), 116–120, passim.

36. Obruchev made this point in early 1864: *Set' russkikh zheleznykh dorog. Uchastie v nei zemstva i voiska* (St. Petersburg, 1864), 1–5; *Russkii invalid*, 1864: 22, 23, 24, serialized the pamphlet. Young Obruchev was far more interested in the economic goals of construction in 1863 and argued that those objectives and strategic interests were by no means incompatible, as western European experience had already demonstrated. He apparently discovered the real incompatibilities as he became more closely engaged with the question after 1865.

37. Vitte, *Vospominaniia: Tsarstvovanie Nikolaia II*, 2 vols. (Berlin, 1922–1923), vol. 1:449–451.

38. The new lines were Moscow-Kursk-Khar'kov-Rostov; Moscow-Kozlov-Voronezh; Orel-Riga; Moscow-Nizhnii Novgorod; and St. Petersburg-Warsaw: *Istoricheskii ocherk razvitiia zheleznykh dorog v Rossii s ikh osnovaniia po 1897g. vkliuchitel'no*, 2 vols. (St. Petersburg, 1898), vol. 2, Table 1. 1861—1492 versty, 1865—3590 versty, 1871—10090 versty, 1875—17770 versty. On the period 1865–1875: S. D. Kareisha, "Kratkii istoricheskii ocherk vozniknoveniia i razvitiia zheleznodorozhnoi seti na zemnom share," *Trudy nauchno-tekhnicheskogo komiteta narodnogo komissariata putei soobshcheniia*, No. 20 "Stoletie zheleznykh dorog" (Moscow, 1925), 20. There is no study of the commercial-strategic problem in Russian railroad development policy, despite the obvious importance of the question to any rigorous examination of Russian economic development.

39. See A. Kvist, *Zheleznye dorogi v voennom otnoshenii* (St. Petersburg, 1868), and, for a historical perspective, A. I. Maksheev's book of the same title (St. Petersburg, 1890). Also, G. N. Karaev, *Vozniknovenie sluzhby voennykh soobshchenii na zheleznykh dorogakh Rossii (1851–1878)* (Moscow, 1949), 11–21.

40. *RGVIA*, F. 400, op. 3, d. 35, ll. 1–4ob: letter from Major General L. P. Batiushkov, Chief of II Department, to Director, Nicholas Academy of the General Staff, 24 February 1864. Batiushkov and Major General M. I. Ivanin (Chief, I Department) led an exploratory committee that became the core of the Special Commission. Representatives included GUGSh, MPS, General-Adjutant Krabbe's Maritime Ministry, and agents of the Nicholaev and Main Societies of Railroads (and numerous military engineers and sappers).

41. See the comments of a finance ministry observer: M. von Reutern, *Die finanzielle Sanierung Russlands nach der Katastrophe des Krimkrieges 1862–1878 unter dem Finanzminister von Reutern* (Berlin, 1914), 186–187. The two commissions worked through the 3rd Desk *(Stol)* of the Main Staff's II Department. *RGVIA*, F. 400, op. 3, d. 35, ll. 37–40: letter to Miliutin from Main Staff proposing a new railroad regulation for transfrontier movement and commission focus on strategic *offensive and defensive* roles of railroads in wartime.

42. The First Commission's activities (November 1866 to December 1867): *RGVIA*, F. 400, op. 3, d. 35, ll. 228–248ob: report from the Commission to the chief of Main Staff, 30 December 1867, signed Batiushkov. Mandate and planning scenarios: ll. 229–232.

43. *RGVIA*, F. 400, op. 3, d. 35, ll. 233–234. Other lessons of the Prussian example: the need for organic army railroad units within each corps; construction of double-track, rather than single-track, strategic lines; and development of high-level institutional commitment to military railroad planning. Ivanin endorsed all of the commission's conclusions; its final report was deposited with VUK, and the commission disbanded: ibid., ll. 253–254, 271+ob. Lieutenant General Batiushkov, a member of VUK, later headed the committee that oversaw the use of railroads for army mobilization.

44. Materials on the Second Commission (February 1866–September 1868) are in: *RGVIA*, F. 400, op. 3, d. 35. It was responsible for proposing network construction that would be of greatest strategic value to Russia (ll. 37–40ob: letter from General-Adjutant Zeugen to war minister Miliutin, 8 October 1866). Also, *RGVIA*, F. 400, op. 3, d. 3458, ll. 5–17ob: Annenkov's plan for the committee and forces; ll.75–76: note on military district staff assignments of railroad coordinators.

45. *RGVIA*, F. 400, op. 3, d. 175, ll. 19–58: "Memo from Commander in Chief of Forces in Odessa M.D., General-Adjutant Kotsebu, to the war minister . . .," 3 March 1869.

46. *RGVIA*, F. 401, op. 5, d. 419, ll. 23ob–24: "Concerning the measures necessary to prepare the District and Forces for War," 28 October/9 November 1869, signed Kotsebu. His second priority was provision of steam-powered mills and bakeries in Brest-Litovsk and Mogilev!

47. *RGVIA*, 400, op. 3, d. 3456, ll. 3–7: "Information on newly constructed railroads," 3rd Desk/II Department.

48. E. Willis Brooks: "The Military and Industrialization in Reform Russia: The Railroad Connection" (manuscript, 1987), 8–10, explains the interministerial debate about (and Miliutin's frustration with) the direction and progress of railroad

development. The paradox of military officers representing different ministries (e.g., Major General Mel'nikov, head of MPS), and then blocking and sabotaging each other's construction proposals, remains unilluminated; knowledge of strategic railroad policy is a glaring void in the literature on Russian industrial development. The problem in the 1860s may have been absence of strategic consensus within the general staff, much less the government, a handicap 1870/1871 began to cure.

49. *RGVIA*, F. 400, op. 3. d. 35, ll. 120–126, 135–137ob, 146–150ob: reports of the committee to the Main Staff, May–June 1867. Exercises exposed material and technical deficiencies with the system, such as insufficiently sturdy wagons for the artillery and unsuitability of standard freight carriages for horse transportation. The safe movement of cavalry mounts was a significant engineering challenge for some years. The staff turned to Prussia for technical solutions, and even lifted its new transportation regulation from Berlin, adopting *Bestimmungen über Militär-Transport auf Eisenbahnen* (Berlin, 1867) on Ivanin's recommendation (ibid., d. 35, ll. 208+ob.).

50. *RGVIA*, F. 400, op. 3, d. 3465, for the reports on the exercise and recommendations on technical changes to rolling stock. There is no indication of the exercise's success, perhaps indicating discouraging performance of the system.

51. *RGVIA*, F. 400, op. 3, d. 3482, memo dated 22 December 1869.

52. Although unsigned in the military-historical archival file, the document also is found among Miliutin's papers in *Otdel rukopisei* of the Russian State Library in Moscow (F. 169). It is inventoried as a draft report by Obruchev, according to Brooks: "The Military and Industrialization in Reform Russia," 12 n. Obruchev's report encapsulated expert thinking on the intersection of strategy, international relations, and railroad development. *RGVIA*, F. 401, op. 2–926 (1872), d. 19, ll. 300–319: "On the military necessity of railroads," 1868. On Miliutin's subsequent use of the memo see chapter 4.

53. *RGVIA*, F. 401, op. 2–926 (1872), d. 19, ll. 300–301.

54. *RGVIA*, F. 400, op. 3, d. 3464, ll. 13–30ob.: "On establishment of a military railroad command" (September 1868), had envisioned general staff officers as the principal decision makers at the guberniia level and above. Ibid., d. 3494, ll. 1–5 (16 May 1870), by Major M. N. Annenkov. In general, however, the 3rd Desk was preoccupied until 1869 with tariff rates, transfrontier connections, etc.; during the first few months of 1869 the office shifted its focus entirely to purely *military* aspects of railroad transportation. Solov'eva, *Zheleznodorozhnyi transport*, 80–92.

55. See biographical sketches of many railroad engineers and *uchenye* in N. A. Zenzinov and S. A. Ryzhak, *Vydaiushchiesia inzhenery i uchënyi zheleznodorozhnogo transporta* (Moscow: Transport, 1990). A satisfactory history of Russia's midcentury railroad development policy is not available; in addition to Solov'eva, see: J. N. Westwood, *A History of Russian Railways* (London: Allen and Unwin, 1964), and Richard Mowbray Haywood, *The Beginnings of Railway Development in Russia in the Reign of Nicholas I, 1835–1842* (Durham, N.C.: Duke University Press, 1969), especially for its useful bibliography. Information on MPS activity: Kareisha, "Kratkii istoricheskii ocherk zheleznodorozhnoi seti," 7–28; and S. N. Kul'zhinskii, "Evoliutsiia zheleznodorozhnoi eksploatatsii," *Trudy nauchno-tekhnicheskogo komiteta narodnogo komissariata putei soobshcheniia*, No. 20 *"Stoletie zheleznykh dorog"* (Moscow, 1925), 59–70.

56. Vitte, *Vospominaniia: Detstvo*, 75–76. Witte began his government service

on the Odessa railroad in 1870. Bobrinskii's views contrasted vividly with those of his successor, K. N. Pos'et, a man infected with the spirit of Saint-Simonism and the philosophy of great engineering works: Steven G. Marks, *Road to Power: The Trans-Siberian Railroad and the Colonization of Asian Russia 1850–1917*, (Ithaca, N.Y.: Cornell University Press, 1991) 70.

57. *RGVIA*, F. 400, op. 3, d. 35, ll. 127+ob., report of the Committee to the Main Staff, 30 May 1867.

58. A. P. Skugarevskii, "M. N. Annenkov," *Razvedchik*, 1204 (1913): 726–728.

59. "O primenenii zheleznykh dorog k voennomu delu," *Voennyi sbornik*, 1866/12.

60. *RGVIA*, F. 400, op. 3, d. 35, ll. 128–129, report of the Committee to the Main Staff, 30 May 1867.

61. Solov'eva, *Zheleznodorozhnyi transport*, 150–158; Vitte, *Vospominaniia: Detstvo*, 102, 110–112. Witte's criticism of his colleague Annenkov—a know-nothing, "a typical general staff officer, a great chatterbox"—is as immoderate as his own self-appraisal is arrogant.

62. *Stoletie Voennogo ministerstva*, vol. 3, pt. 4: 580.

4. Mortal Danger as Strategic Rebirth

1. AVPR, F. 133 op. 470 ("Kantseliariia"), ed. khr. 117–1870, ll. 373–374.

2. The only power remotely interested in Russia's actions in Khiva was Britain; from January 1874 no other state communicated with its St. Petersburg embassy on the subject: *AVPR*, F. 133, op. 470, d. 49–1874 *(Dossier special)*, for all deciphered diplomatic traffic. On Russian expansion, Seton-Watson, *The Russian Empire*, 441–444, but with corrective: Morris, "Russians in Central Asia," 524–525.

3. The French lesson: Mitchell, *Victors and Vanquished*, pt. 1; or, Mitchell, "'A Situation of Inferiority,'" 21–48. Warsaw's input: *RGVIA*, F. 401, op. 5, d. 419, 27–29ob: "Mobilization and Concentration of the German Armies on the Rhine in 1870," submitted by Warsaw Military District staff to the war minister, 19/31 December 1873. Prussian performance in 1848: Bucholz, *Prussian War Planning*, 38.

4. Treatments of Russia's reaction to German unification emphasize either continuity or break. Among the former are the works of Zaionchkovskii and his school (Soviet and American); among the latter, the works on material and economic determinants by, inter alia, Beskrovnyi and other Soviet military historians. Russian diplomacy and rising nationalism underscore changes that followed Sedan; even the Germans understood unification as fundamentally changing their historical relationship with Russia. Besides Bismarck's own ruminations (*Gedanken und Erinnerungen* 3 vols. [Stuttgart, 1898], vol. 1: chap. 23), see Hajo Holborn, *Bismarcks europäische Politik zu Beginn der siebziger Jahre und die Mission Radowitz* (Berlin, 1925), 7–9. See George F. Kennan, *The Decline of Bismarck's European Order: Franco-Russian Relations 1875–1890* (Princeton, N.J.: Princeton University Press, 1979), 44–46, for thoughts on the importance of 1870.

5. Fuller, *Strategy and Power*, 292.

6. Ibid., 288–292; Geyer, *Russian Imperialism*, chap. 4; post-Stalinist Soviet historiography on the 1860s ascribed Central Asian imperialism either to autocratic cooperation with bourgeois interests, an overstatement of the influence of extra-governmental groups on policy (as Fuller notes, a misjudgment that also extends to

Geyer's argument), or to collision with British imperialist interests in the region. On the former: N. A. Khalfin, *Prisoedinenie Srednei Azii k Rossii (60–90e gody XIX veka*, (Moscow: Nauka, 1965); and *Politika Rossii v Srednei Azii 1857–1868 godov* (Moscow: Nauka, 1960), translated and abridged by H. Evans, *Russia's Policy in Central Asia 1857–1868* (London/Oxford: Central Asian Research Centre, 1964). A statement of the latter interpretation: N. S. Kiniapina, *Vneshniaia politika Rossii vtoroi poloviny XIX v.* (Moscow: Nauka, 1974), and N. S. Kiniapina et al., *Kavkaz i Sredniaia Aziia vo vneshnei politike Rossii: vtoraia polovina XVII–80-e gody XIX v.*, pt. 3 (Moscow: MGU, 1984). On Gorchakov's famous circular to European capitals in December 1863/January, 1864 see treatment in David Mackenzie, *The Lion of Tashkent: The Career of General M. G. Cherniaev* (Athens: Georgia University Press, 1974), 32–55. Morris, "Russians in Central Asia," 521–538, frames the debate somewhat differently. The complexities of just how well St. Petersburg controlled its representatives interests him, much as it preoccupied contemporaries.

7. A. J. P. Taylor, *The Struggle for Mastery in Europe, 1848–1918* (Oxford: Oxford University Press, 1954), 193–200.

8. *RGVIA*, F. 401, op. 2, d. 90–1870, ll. 1 et seq.; first orders for *komandirovky* were issued 7 July 1870, a few days after Obruchev returned from consultations with the district staff in Warsaw (ibid., d. 82/70, 29 June). Taylor, *Struggle for Mastery*, 206–210. But for Alexander's pro-Prussian neutrality, which Taylor overlooks, see: Nicholas Der Bagdasarian, *The Austro-German Rapprochement, 1870–1879* (London: Associated University Press, 1976), 41–44. Prince Reuss reported to Bismarck from St. Petersburg that Alexander's pro-German sympathies after Sedan had quite isolated the tsar: Eberhard Kolb, *Der Weg aus dem Krieg: Bismarcks Politik im Krieg und die Friedensanbahnung* (Munich· Oldenbourg, 1990), 212.

9. For instance, P. Parensov, "Iz proshlogo: V Bolgarii. Vospominaniia ofitsera general'nogo shtaba," *Russkaia starina*, 39 (May 1908): 273: "Count Dm. Aleks. Miliutin . . . was a member (or "head") of the anti-German party (in Russia). . . ." Kennan, *Decline of Bismarck's European Order*, 44–59.

10. L. M. Shneerson, *Franko-Prusskaia voina i Rossiia* (Minsk: BGU, 1976), 252–256.

11. Vitte, *Vospominaniia. Detstvo*, 74.

12. L. L. Zeddeler, "Dvadtsat' piat' let tomu nazad. (Otryvok iz dnevnika)," *Istoricheskii vestnik*, 64, no. 4 (1896): 114–129; no. 5: 480–508.

13. G. A. Leer, *Publichnye lektsii o voine 1870–1871 gg.* (St. Petersburg, 1873), from *Voennyi sbornik*, nos. 1–12, 1873 (here, chap. 1). He also commented on the contemporary relevance of fortresses (which he praised highly) and irregular units (of very low value). The question of fortifications remained very difficult for all of Germany's neighbors, although Moltke had jettisoned interest in the strategic importance of fortified points by 1860: Bucholz, *Prussian War Planning*, 41–42.

14. The same could not be said for the critical-historical method, which came under withering attack in the 1880s. However, Leer's study on the Franco-Prussian War still found defenders two decades later: N. P. Mikhnevich, *Znachenie germano-frantsuzskoi voiny 1870–1871 gg. v istorii voennogo iskusstva. Kritiko-istoricheskoe issledovanie* (St. Petersburg, 1892).

15. *RGVIA*, F. 401, op. 2, dd. 98–1873 through 100–1873, almost five hundred pages of working papers and maps are unaccounted for either as originals or on microfilm. Related materials are available in, ibid., d. 296 (cited as *RGVIA*, F. 410,

op. 1, d. 175 ["Materials concerning the Russian Empire"]). Important archival materials on the agenda and summarizing the conclusion, but of uncertain provenance and without citation, are available from East View Publications: "Zakliuchenie sekretnogo soveshchaniia," including a printed agenda (14 "questions," hereafter *Voprosy*), the manuscripted "Conclusions" *(Zakliucheniie)*, and the Main Staff's own summary, by "question," of decisions that affected the war ministry *(GS-Zakliucheniie)*.

16. "D. A. Miliutin. Biograficheskii ocherk," *Dnevnik D. A. Miliutina*, 4 vols., ed. P. A. Zaionchkovskii (Moscow: Lenin State Library, 1947–1950), vol. 1:40–43; and Zaionchkovskii, *Voennye reformy*, 280–304. Zaionchkovskii may have been the last scholar to use the missing materials. In English see the latest addition to the literature: Fuller, *Strategy and Power*, 292–303, which with its accustomed precision places the conference's impact in a strategic, rather than Zaionchkovskii's domestic political, perspective. Also, Miller, *Dmitrii Miliutin*, 213–215. These last two works rely exclusively on Zaionchkovskii's account.

17. Obruchev recalled the underlying purpose of the conference in a lettter to Miliutin in 1885, entitled "Osnovnye istoricheskie voprosy Rossii i nasha gotovnost' k ikh resheniiu," *AVPR* F. 133, op. 470, d. 54–1900. ll. 89–113, and which appeared under the title "Pervaia nasha zabota—Stoiat' tverdo v Evrope," *Istochnik*, 6 (1994): 5–19 (hereafter "Osnovnye istoricheskie voprosy").

18. A. M. Zaionchkovskii, *Podgotovka Rossii k imperialisticheskoi voine. Ocherk voennoi podgotovki i pervonachal'nykh planov* (Moscow: GosVoenIzdat, 1926), 31.

19. Zaionchkovskii, *Voennye reformy*, 260–276. The memos were: "Concerning the Development of Our Armed Forces" and "Concerning the Principal Bases of Individual Military Obligation."

20. *"Soobrazheniia ob oborone Rossii."* No recent scholar has found the memos in *RGVIA*, although a copy probably exists in: Manuscript Division, [Lenin] Moscow State Library, *Arkhiv D. A. Miliutina* (F. 169), *Vospominaniia* materials, *karton* 27 item 4, or *karton* 37 items 4–6. However, Zaionchkovskii, *Voennye reformy*, 280–287, presents a careful summary of the twenty-five-page original. Fuller did not use the original but places its arguments (ex Zaionchkovskii) exceptionally well.

21. A. M. Zaionchkovskii, *Podgotovka Rossii*, 30–32, was the first published *Soviet* general staff study to perpetuate this corporate memory; the author was an 1890 graduate of the imperial general staff academy.

22. Zaionchkovskii, *Voennye reformy*, 280–282.

23. Ibid., 283. The lines supporting the German front: Petersburg-Warsaw, Moscow-Warsaw, Kursk-Vilna, Odessa-Belostok, Riga-Kovno.

24. Ibid.

25. *RGVIA*, F. 401, op. 4, d. 416, l. 30: Obruchev, "Concerning the Railroads Essential for Military Use," dated 12 November 1868, for VUK.

26. Miller, *Dmitrii Miliutin*, 194–195; P. A. Zaionchkovskii, "Podgotovka voennoi reformy 1874 g.," *Istoricheskie zapiski*, 27 (1948): 173–175.

27. Mitchell, *Victors and Vanquished*, chap. 2.

28. Zaionchkovskii, *Voennye reformy*, 285.

29. Ibid., 286.

30. Kotsebu appealed to Miliutin in early 1871 for intervention with Reutern concerning nonreceipt of funds allocated two years earlier (Rb. 800,000, of Rb. 10 million already approved for the project) for construction to connect the Peters-

burg-Warsaw and the Warsaw-Terepol lines, across the Vistula: *RGVIA*, F. 401, op. 2, d. 23, ll. 37–38.

31. *RGVIA*, F. 401, op. 2–926 [1872], d. 19, ll. 226–227ob. In view of those facts, Reutern proposed significantly paring Polish construction down from the planned 1,180 versts.

32. Zaionchkovskii, *Voennye reformy*, 286; see also the section "The Main Staff and Railroads" (chap. 3) for rail construction rates.

33. A. D. Bilimovich, *Tovarnoe dvizhenie na russkikh zheleznykh dorogakh* (Kiev, 1902), chaps. 2–3; T. M. Kitanina, *Khlebnaia torgovlia Rossii v 1875–1914 gg.* (Leningrad: Nauka, 1978), 53–60, on dynamics of grain transportation and commerce.

34. Fuller, *Strategy and Power*, 298–300.

35. *RGVIA*, F. 410, d. 175 (1872), chap. 1 ("Materials of the Secret Conference ... part IV (11 March–22 March 1873," m.f.).

36. *AVPR*, F. 133, op. 470, ed. khr. 53–1873 ("Guerre"), letter from Miliutin to Gorchakov, "Most Secret," ll. 1–2. This extraordinary precaution underlines the sensitivity of Obruchev's study and partially explains its rarity in archival holdings.

37. East View documents, *Zakliucheniie*, ll. 1ob. et seq.

38. *AVPR*, F. 133, op. 470, ed.khr.53–1873 ("Guerre"), all Miliutin to Gorchakov: [Special Commission report] 29 Jan. (ll. 3–4); [Caucasus report] 15 Feb. (ll. 7+ob.); [budgets] 24 Feb. [marked "Jan."] (9+ob.); [Austrian threat] 22 & 24 Feb. (ll. 10 & 11).

39. Dietrich Beyrau, *Militär und Gesellschaft im vorrevolutionären Russland* (Cologne: Bohlau, 1984), 302–304.

40. Fuller, *Strategy and Power*, 300; Zaionchkovskii, *Voennye reformy*, 294–296.

41. On the course of legislative considerations between March and July 1873: Baumann, "Universal Military Service," chap. 3 et seq. Menning, *Bayonets before Bullets*, 21–29, for a balanced summary of the tactical aspect of the question.

42. Fuller, *Strategy and Power*, 303–308. A more helpful way to frame the question might be: Did those same officers who had faith in the martial spirit *also* insist on adoption of technology, or did they always brush aside innovation in favor of unadulterated esprit?

43. Von Wahlde, "Military Thought in Imperial Russia."

44. The 6 May ratification in St. Petersburg led to Austrian subscription to a more general *political* agreement (Schönbrunn, June 1873) that Berlin also endorsed in October, creating the Three Emperors League. William L. Langer, *European Alliances and Alignments 1871–1890* (New York: Knopf, 1950), 23–25. Fuller, *Strategy and Power*, 293–295, is too eager to attribute the agreement to "chiefly fright," particularly as its origins lay in Berg's unilateral negotiations with Moltke, much as would Obruchev's with the French, two decades later. Berg was a confederate of the "Prussianist" Prince Bariatinskii, and known for his intimate friendship with the emperor, another Prussophile.

45. On Russia's tactical and operational intelligence system, and its severe flaws: William C. Fuller, Jr., "The Russian Empire" in *Knowing One's Enemies: Intelligence Assessment before the Two World Wars*, ed. Earnest R. May (Princeton, N.J.: Princeton University Press, 1984), 98–126.

46. *AVPR*'s annual files on war ministry topics *("Guerre")* demonstrate these routine communications. If the war ministry had alternate means of communications with its attaché in a mission they were for extraordinary circumstances. Note,

however, that military district staffs (especially Warsaw and Kiev) conducted independent liaison with attachés across the border, often cutting St. Petersburg out of the information circuit: Fuller, "The Russian Empire," 110–113.

47. *"Dossier special"* holding in *AVPR:* F. 133, op. 470 *(Kantseliariia ministra),* F. 151, op. 482 *(Politika),* and F. 138, op. 467 *(Sekretnyi arkhiv ministra).* These will be cited for specific examples but not otherwise. The ministry's Cryptologic Section *(Shifroval'nyi otdel)* also generated records (F. 141, "1731–1917," in three *opisi)* of diplomatic ciphers, keys, and all encrypted Russian diplomatic correspondence. All diplomatic communications were in French, with the exception of Germany's and some of Britain's, which code breakers rendered in the original language. The German language cipher experts were undoubtedly Russian subjects of German ethnic background, judging from the distinctive, genuinely illegible *fraktur* in which they did their work. In addition to the cable decryptions, copies of both routine and sensitive confidential correspondence between minister Schweinitz and Bismarck may be found in *AVPR,* F. 133, p. 470, ed. khr. 2–1875 *(Allemegne—Ambassadé).*

48. *AVPR,* F. 133 op. 470, ed. khr. 122–1873, all Loftus to Granville: ll. 137+ob (27 Oct.), l. 144 (20 Nov.); ibid., d. 49–1874 *(Dossier special)* materials also.

49. This aspect of staff education has often been overlooked. For instance, Menning, *Bayonets before Bullets,* 35, offers a few words; Steinberg, "Education and Training," does not examine the purpose of rides.

50. The first Main Staff field rides occurred in 1873; no archival or published evidence predates that year: *RGVIA,* F. 401, op. 5, d. 424, ll. 1–32ob: "Strategic Sketch of the Border Area Made during Field Rides in 1873 by Parties of Warsaw M. D. under the Leadership of Major-General Frirot," 18 October 1873; ibid., d. 424, ll. 32–44ob [five brief reports]: "Notes on reconnaissance of the Brest-Litovsk area, 23–24 September 1873." The printed report: *Polevye poezdki ofitserov General'nogo shtaba v 1873 g.* (St. Petersburg, 1874).

51. On Moltke's use of rides: Bucholz, *Prussian War Planning,* 30–31, 89–90.

52. Erickson, *Russian Imperial/Soviet General Staff,* 15; Menning, *Bayonets before Bullets,* 35–36.

53. *RGVIA,* F. 401, op. 3, d. 58–1875, ll. 1–23: "Execution of the Strategic Reconnaissance *[rekognostsirovka]* led by Lt.-Gen. Obruchev of the Defensive Right Flank of Tsarist Poland," dated May to late July 1875; details of all the 1875 rides may be found in: *Polevye poezdki v 1875 g.* (St. Petersburg, 1876).

54. *Polevye poezdki v 1875 g.,* 19–26, 37–38. *Arkhiv vneshnei politiki Rossii* (AVPR), op. 467 *Sekretnyi arkhiv,* d. 14, ll. 201–206 (1873), indicate that the lack of maps in Warsaw, Vilna, Kiev, and St. Petersburg districts was an important concern as early as 1871. That difficulty would certainly have affected the early staff rides in those areas.

55. *Polevye poezdki v 1875,* 9–11. Horsemanship thus had an important *practical* (rather than merely decorative) function in the general staff syllabus.

56. Ibid., 4–6.

57. Ibid., 41–93, for the exercises carried out during July and August in St. Petersburg, Moscow, Vilna, Khar'kov, and Kiev Military Districts.

58. *RGVIA,* F. 401, op. 3, d. 36–1876, ll. 1–67.

59. *Polevye poezdki v 1878–1879 gg.* (St. Petersburg, 1880), 2–3.

60. Ibid., 4–9. Evaluation by General-Adjutant Count Ignat'ev, the leader of one ride.

61. The Russian army did not use coup d'oeil in the tradition of Napoleon or the Prussians (i.e., taking in the strategic landscape from horseback in one glance). *Glazomer* (the Russian equivalent) suggested a measured appreciation of a situation, perception borne by full consideration of all factors and information—a professional evaluation.

62. Menning, *Bayonets before Bullets*, 48–50, attempts a brief sketch of army maneuvers and distinguishes only the "Great" maneuvers (at Krasnoe Selo) from "other" smaller-scale activities. His focus, General Dragomirov (author of the infantry tactics regulation), serves to distinguish the spirit of tactical excellence from the "wooden" performance of units that practiced his regulation in the field.

63. Find a useful official summary of the framework for field exercises between 1881 and 1894 in: *Obzor deiatel'nosti Voennogo ministerstva v tsarstvovanie Imperatora Aleksandra III, 1881–1894* (St. Petersburg, 1903), 80–85.

64. Note by Aleksandr Kazimirovich Puzyrevskii, trans. and ed., in: Boguslavskii [A. von Boguslawsky], *Voiskovye manevry. Ikh podgotovka, vedenie i ispolnenie*, from German (St. Petersburg, 1884), 38 n. Puzyrevskii began a rapid rise through the staff about this time; he was a full colonel less than five years after entering the General Staff Corps.

65. P. Kazanskii, *Rukovodstvo k voennoi igre* (St. Petersburg, 1873); [N. I.] Mau, *Posobie k resheniiu takticheskikh zadach* (Vilna, 1878); M. Kaigorodov and Ia. Prezhentsov, *Sbornik takticheskikh zadach k planam zapadnogo pogranichnogo prostranstva* (St. Petersburg, 1884); and K. Voide, *Mirnye manevry i ikh znachenie* (St. Petersburg, 1894), are of representative complexity. All four authors were distinguished graduates of the academy; Mau had accompanied Obruchev on the 1875 strategic reconnaissance and then served on the staff of Vilna Military District.

66. *Plan raspredeleniia godovykh zaniatii i instruktsiia dlia vedeniia zaniatii v pekhote* (St. Petersburg, 1882). The plan was drafted by members of the Committee on the Structure and Training of Forces, under General-Adjutant Chertkov.

67. Ibid., 19–23.

68. Ibid., 33–35, 55–56, 78.

69. *Sbornik takticheskikh zadach k planam zapadnogo pogranichnogo prostranstva. (Odobreny Tsirkulara Glavnogo shtaba 1884 g. No. 204). So spravochnym svedeniiami i primernymi resheniiami*, ed. M. Kaigorodov and Ia. Prezhentsov (St. Petersburg, 1884). The information on small-unit reconnaissance is especially thorough and detailed, and the author's concern with seeking the most advantageous conditions for engagement was demonstrated in his strong encouragement of nighttime reconnaissance patrols.

70. Boguslavskii, *Voiskovye manevry*, 79. Boguslavskii's book, published in Russian a year after its German introduction, received high praise in professional journals at the time. Russian general staff officers translated other German guides to troop maneuvers, such as: *Deiatel'nost' voisk v pole i na manevrakh* (St. Petersburg, 1872).

71. "Russische Korrespondenz," *Internationale Revue über die gesammten Armeen und Flotten*, 4, no. 4 (1886): 101–112. The *Internationale Revue's* usual Russian correspondents were D. Ivanov and S. Voronin.

72. "Die russische Herbstmanöver des Jahres 1890 in Wolhynien," *Internationale Revue über die gesammten Armeen und Flotten*, 9, no. 1 (1890): 543–558.

73. For the following discussion: *Stoletie Voennogo ministerstva*, vol. 1:646–650; ibid., vol. 4, pt. 2, book 2, sect. 1: 391; L. G. Beskrovnyi, *Russkaia armiia i flot v XIX*

veke (Moscow: Nauka, 1973), 204–206, a somewhat sketchy account of organizational development; introductory essays in *Opis 2 (I Otdelenie [po ustroistvu voisk])* and *Opis 3 (II Otdelenie)*, Fond 400 *(Glavnyi shtab)* (Moscow: *RGVIA*, 1968).

74. Menning, *Bayonets before Bullets*, 97.

75. The committee had a permanent staff, and budgetary approval for the new organization's additional personnel took at least a year to pass the Council of Ministers.

76. Permanent members were the chief of Main Staff, the assistant chief of Main Staff, the assistant chief of the War Ministry Chancellery, the chief of the Main Directorate of the war ministry, and a member of the Military Hospitals Committee. As Obruchev's creation, however, its agenda was set by VUK.

5. The Main Staff Plans a War

1. The literature on the "Eastern Question" (of which the Balkan problem was the most persistently intractable part, from the perspective of European chanceries) is vast, although much of it is over a half century old. See, inter alia, *Russia and the Balkans*, in breadth and depth the single greatest source on the eastern crisis. Consider also Langer, *European Alliances and Alignments*, chaps. 3–4; Mihailo D. Stojanovic, *The Great Powers and the Balkans, 1875–1878* (Cambridge: Cambridge University Press, 1939), chaps. 1–2; David Harris, *The Diplomatic History of the Balkan Crisis of 1875–1878: The First Year* (Stanford, Calif.: Stanford University Press, 1936), chaps. 1–2; and R. W. Seton-Watson, *Disraeli, Gladstone and the Eastern Question: A Study in Diplomacy and Party Politics* (London: MacMillan, 1935), chap. 2. More recently: Barbara Jelavich, *History of the Balkans*, vol. 1, *Eighteenth and Nineteenth Century* (Cambridge: Cambridge University Press, 1983), pt. 2. The following summary of the mid-1870s crisis follows Langer's concise description, principally.

2. [N. P. Ignat'ev,] "Zapiski Grafa N. P. Ignat'eva," *Istoricheskii vestnik*, 135 (January 1914): 442–445.

3. Langer, *European Alliances and Alignments*, 80.

4. To keep all dates "internationalized," in what follows each event is annotated with both its Julian and its Gregorian date, respectively, of Russia and everyone else, reflecting Russia's twelve-day lag behind other states' calendars.

5. Sumner, *Russia and the Balkans*, dates war preparation in St. Petersburg from "the beginning of October" (i.e., mid-September). Only Fuller noted the importance of early 1876 preparations: Fuller, *Strategy and Power*, 311–314.

6. Much of this is argued explicitly by Geyer, *Russian Imperialism*, 68–85. The assumption that the autocrat could and did participate *routinely* in decisions of state policy betrays Geyer's acceptance of the autocratic myth, a weakness he shares with the Pan-Slavs he discusses. In fact, as this chapter will demonstrate, experts had already begun to take crucial decisions out of the emperor's hands due to "expert" considerations, and even in times of crisis. On military effectiveness, L. G. Beskrovnyi believes material considerations—railroads, telegraphs, and large-scale force maneuvers—were of greatest importance in the 1877 experience: *Russkoe voennoe iskusstvo XIX v.* 313–315, 352–354; on motivations of honor, Richard G. Weeks, Jr., "Russia's Decision for War with Turkey, May 1876–April 1877," *East European Quarterly*, 24 no. 3 (1990): 307–333.

7. Sumner, *Russia and the Balkans*, chaps. 6–8 and Appendix 3. Karel Durman, *The Time of the Thunderer: Mikhail Katkov, Russian Nationalist Extremism and the Failure of the Bismarckian System, 1871–1887* (Boulder, Colo.: East European Monographs, 1988), 192–195, lists all the published sources but uses them so unsystematically as to miss the import of Obruchev's (and the Main Staff's) role. Soviet scholarship includes: A. P. Barbasov, "Novye fakty o planirovanii Russko-turetskoi voiny 1877–1878 gg," *Voenno-istoricheskii zhurnal*, 2 (1976): 98–104, an unanalytical summary of war planning, but it incorporates good archival references; and cursory outlines in other standard works: *Russko-turetskaia voina 1877–1878 gg.*, ed. I. I. Rostunov (Moscow: Voenizdat, 1977), 53–62; V. I. Vinogradov, *Russko-turetskaia voina 1877–1878 gg. i osvobozhdenie Bolgarii* (Moscow: Mysl' 1978), 96–98; and myriad centenary Romanian histories (see bibliography).

8. The "weight of public opinion" undergirds Geyer's impressionistic (and nonarchival) retelling of diplomacy and decision making. Geyer, *Russian Imperialism*, 70–75.

9. *RGVIA*, F. 485, d. 590, ll. 3ob.–4; *Russko-turetskaia voina*, ed. V. I. Vinogradov, 95–96.

10. Fuller, *Strategy and Power*, 317.

11. *RGVIA*, F. 401, op. 5, d. 419, ll. 1–10ob. and 13–14, for their correspondence in June and July 1869 on the defense of Volhynia in the event of hostilities with Austria-Hungary *as a result* of war with Turkey.

12. *RGVIA*, F. 401, op. 5, d. 417, ll. 130–137, for the survey schedule of the southwestern theater of military operations, undated (probably January 1869).

13. *RGVIA*, F. 401, op. 5, d.424, ll. 1–44ob.

14. The earliest document concerning the activities of the committee is dated 30 October 1875, but the files are not complete for the minutes of its meetings: *RGVIA*, F. 402, op. I, d. 17, ll. 106–1 ob. *Opisanie Russko-turetskoi voiny 1877–1878 gg. na Balkanskom poluostrove*, vol. 1: *"Obstanovka pered voinoi"* (St. Petersburg, 1901), 251.

15. *Opisanie Russko-turetskoi voiny*, vol. 1, 251.

16. *RGVIA*, F. 402, op. I, d. 17, ll. 105+ob.: "Minutes" of the commission, 11 December 1875.

17. *Dnevnik D. A. Miliutina*, vol. 2:41.

18. Nicolae Ciachir, *Razboiul pentru independenta Romaniei in contextul European (1875–1878)* (Bucharest: Ed. Stiintifica si enciclopedica, 1977), 20.

19. Some of the attaché reports are reproduced in *Osoboe Pribavlenie*, vol. 5, pt. I.

20. *Russko-turetskaia voina*, ed. Rostunov, 57.

21. Beliaev, *Russko-turetskaia voina*, 68. Beliaev believes that another individual who preferred to "remain in the shadows" authored Artamonov's lectures and dismisses the sketch as the *collective* product of the staff.

22. The text of the memo may be found in: *Sbornik materialov po Russko-turetskoi voine 1877–1878 gg. na Balkanskom poluostrove*, vol. 10, *"Soobrazheniia, kasaiushchiiasia plana voiny"* (St. Petersburg, 1898), 39–68. It is also located in the rare *Osoboe pribavlenie k Opisaniiu Russko-turetskoi voiny 1877–1878 gg. na Balkanskom polusotrove*, vol. 4, *"Soobrazheniia, kasaiushchiiasia plana voiny"* (St. Petersburg, 1901), 40–69. The following quotes are from the latter source. Also: Vinogradov, *Russko-turetskaia voina*, 96.

23. By coincidence, *Russkaia starina*, 87 (December, 1875) and 88 (January, February, and March 1876), contained detailed reminiscences of the Paskevich/Gorchakov Danubian campaign.

24. *Osoboe pribavlenie*, vol. 4:43–44.

25. Ibid., vol. 4:52; emphasis in original.

26. On the general staff "bias" see: Jack Snyder, *The Ideology of the Offensive: Military Decision Making and the Disasters of 1914* (Ithaca, N.Y.: Cornell University Press, 1984), 122–123.

27. *Osoboe pribavlenie*, vol. 4:55; emphasis in original; see also discussion on pp. 43, 69.

28. *Osoboe pribavlenie*, vol. 4:53–56.

29. Ibid., vol. 4:40 n. 1. For an illuminating discussion of the Field Staff, see "Kishinevskoe siden'e (Iz dnevnika D. S. Naglovskogo)," *Russkaia starina*, 112: 243–264.

30. Planning was interrupted "as a result of the necessity to get down to *urgent preparation for imminent partial mobilization* (which could not be foreseen earlier)." *Opisanie Russko-turetskoi voiny*, vol. 1:251; emphasis added.

31. Ibid., vol. 1:250.

32. Ibid., vol. 1:259.

33. "Russkoe voennoe obozrenie. O razvitii nashikh voennykh sil v posleduiu turetskuiu voinu (1876–1878 gg.)," *Voennyi sbornik*, 125 no. 1 (January 1879): 141. For a most useful recollection of the reception of this statute in the field and the way a typical (i.e., nonguards, noncavalry) unit might put it into effect, see, M. D., "Vospominanie voennogo priemshchika loshadei pri mobilizatsii armii v 1876 godu," *Voennyi sbornik*, 243, no. 9 (September 1898): 208–230.

34. *RGVIA*, F. 485, op. 1, d. 586, ll. 171ob (Annenkov's circular to railroads and railroad inspectorates, 8 April), ll. 22–35 (responses from Odessa, Azov, Kursk, and other railroad companies), ll. 40–42 (memo from MPS on increasing volume of the Orlovsko-Griazskii line by lengthening trains to eighteen carriages and wagons), ll. 43–44ob (Annenkov's report on the Kursk, Moscow-Nizhegorod, Shuisko-Ivanovsk, and Moscow-Brest lines and schedules, signed by Colonel N. M. Golovin).

35. *RGVIA*, F. 400, op. 2, d. 3190, ll. 1–2ob. (9 August 1876); ll. 18–19 (22–28 September 1876).

36. Junker school closure: *RGVIA*, F. 400, op. 2, d. 3171, l. 24; fencing instructors: *RGVIA*, F. 400, op. 2, d. 3171, ll. 1–2ob., ff. (27 April 1876).

37. *RGVIA*, F. 485, op. 1, d. 589, l. 2, and reprinted in *Osoboe pribavlenie*, vol. 4:7 ("Memo of Gen.-Adj. Miliutin of 21 Sept 1876 from Livadia"). See also Barbasov, "Novye fakty," 100; A. Karaivanov, "Planove na voiovashchite stepani," in *Russko-turetskata osvoboditelna voina 1877–1878: Sbornik statin po niakoi problem na voinata* (Sophia, 1977), 28–29; and I. I. Rostunov, "Boevye deistviia russkoi armii na Balkanakh v 1877–1878 gg.," in *Russko-turetskaia voina 1877–1878 gg. i Balkany* (Moscow: Nauka, 1978).

38. *Osoboe pribavlenie*, vol. 4:9 ("Memorandum to Gen.-Adj. Geiden from Miliutin, 25 Sept 1876"). Beliaev misdates all these measures by a full two weeks, placing them after the strategic conference at Livadia: *Russko-turetskaia voina*, 68–70. "Peacetime strength" was 55 percent of manning.

39. That is, on 12 October 1876. *Opisanie Russko-turetskoi voiny*, vol. 1:250.

40. *RGVIA*, F. 402, op. 1, d. 59, l. 1 (telegram from Livadia to Tiflis, 21 September 1876).

41. *RGVIA*, F. 402, op. 1, d. 59, l. 5 (telegram from Livadia to Tiflis, 22 September 1876).

42. *RGVIA*, F. 402, op. 1, d. 59, l. 9 (telegram from Livadia to Tiflis, 25 September 1876).

43. *RGVIA*, F. 402, op. 1, d. 59, ll. 12–13 (telegrams between Tiflis and Livadia, 27 and 28 September 1876).

44. *RGVIA*, F. 400, op. 3, d. 448, ll. 43–46 ("Journal of the Committee for Mobilization . . ."). Subsequently, five of the engines were assigned to the Caucasus and ten to the Balkan theater. The field railroad system the army used in 1877 may have been the same one demonstrated to the Russian general staff by a British entrepreneur, John B. Fell, in 1873–1874: *RGVIA*, F. 401, op. 5. d. 416, ll. 153–154ob.

45. *RGVIA*, F. 485, op. 1, d. 730, l. 4ob: "Description of Russian Measures in Preparation for War: Mobilization of 1876."

46. *Documents Diplomatiques Francais (1871–1914)*, Premier Serie (1871–1900) [hereafter *DDF*], vol. 2 (1 July 1875–31 December 1879), no. 72 (Vogüe to Decazes, 7 July 1876), and no. 73 (Decazes to Gontaut-Biron, 10 July 1876). For similar reactions in other European ministries, see also *Die grosse Politik der europaischen Kabinette 1871–1914* [hereafter *GP*], vol. 2, nos. 231, 233.

47. G. Rupp, "The Reichstadt Agreement," *American Historical Review*, 30 (1925): 503–510, compares the two records. See also the discussion in Langer, *European Alliances and Alignments*, 92–94. Text of the agreement is found in A. F. Pribram, *Secret Treaties of Austria-Hungary*, ed. A. C. Coolidge (Cambridge, Mass.: Harvard University Press, 1921), vol. 2:188–190, and reproduced in Sumner, *Russia and the Balkans*, Appendix 2 (in French).

48. Langer, *European Alliances and Alignments*, 93.

49. AVPR, F. 133, op. 470 (1876), d. 37, ll. 12–13ob.

50. *Dnevnik D. A. Miliutina*, vol. 2:52 ("30 June, Wednesday St. Petersburg").

51. Emphasis added; *Dnevnik D. A. Miliutina*, vol. 2:52 ("30 June, Wednesday St. Petersburg").

52. Geyer, *Russian Imperialism*, 73.

53. R. W. Seton-Watson, "Russo-British Relations during the Eastern Crisis," in *Slavonic Review*, vols. 3–6 [nos. 8–12, 14, 17] (1924–1928), 3: 669–682; Sumner, *Russia and the Balkans*, 166–167. See also Seton-Watson, *Disraeli, Gladstone and the Eastern Question*, 40–43. Cf. the skeptical view in: Harris, *Diplomatic History of the Balkan Crisis*, 359–360.

54. Sumner, *Russia and the Balkans*, 165. In essence, the British refused to set sail with any "Russian" policy, even if they agreed with it in principle.

55. Jelavich, *Russia and the East*, 17 ("Jugenheim, 12/24 June 1876"). See also entries for 7/19 June and 17/29 June. British military and naval preparations, although unimpressive to Shuvalov, at least suggested that the policy of nonintervention could find its limit of endurance. The French ambassador in Berlin saw the situation even more grimly; if "the five" failed to act together in the matter, would it not be "an open door for England" to solve the crisis? *DDF*, vol. 2:62 (Gontaut-Biron to Decazes, Ems, 6 June 1876). Gorchakov's ministry had broken the diplomatic code and could read the traffic of *every* embassy in St. Petersburg, with the occasional exception of Austria's and Sweden's. See the French-language transcription in the *Dossier special* for 1876 in: *AVPR*, F. 133, op. 470.

56. *Dnevnik D. A. Miliutina*, vol. 2:58–59 ("15 July, Thursday").

57. *DDF*, vol. 2, No. 79 (Decazes to Ambassadors in London, Vienna, St. Petersburg, Berlin, 26 August 1876).

58. *DDF*, vol. 2, no. 80 (Le Flo to Decazes, St. Petersburg, 28 August 1876).

59. *DDF*, vol. 2, no. 81 (D'Harcourt to Decazes, London, 29 August 1876).

60. Jelavich, *Russia and the East*, 20 ("Warsaw, 21 August [2 September] 1876").

61. Bismarck was hardly adverse to seeing Russia carve up Turkey, as a means of removing a major impediment to harmonious relations between the other two emperors. Germany under Bismarck was and remained an entirely disinterested participant in the perpetual eastern crises. Taylor, *Struggle for Mastery in Europe*, 239 n.

62. *GP*, vol. 2, 35 ("Varzin, 30 August 1876").

63. *Dnevnik D. A. Miliutina*, vol. 2: 74–75 (31 August, Tuesday, Livadia). See also the entry for 12 August, Thursday: vol. 2: 68.

64. O. von Bismarck, *Werke in Auswahl*, 8 vols. (Stuttgart: W. Kohlhammer, 1962–); vol. 5, pt. 1: 713 ("Varzin, 14 August 1876"). The chancellor's close following of Russian activity continued to cause him anguish; he noted on 30 August that the perception was growing in St. Petersburg "that Russia was handled coolly by ourselves. The notion is certainly incorrect; if however the tsar personally feels that this is so, then it would be painful to the intimate relations of the monarchs." *GP*, vol. 2: 34–35 (30 August 1876).

65. Jelavich, *Russia in the East*, ix–xi, 19–20.

66. *AVPR*, F. 138, op. 467, d. 19, l. 5, dated 1/13 September 1876 from Livadia.

67. Ibid., d. 19, ll. 15–17ob, dated 11/23 September 1876, from Livadia.

68. Ibid., d. 19, ll. 24–26, dated 14/26 September 1876, from Livadia; Russia would occupy Bulgaria, and Austria would get most of Bosnia-Herzegovina.

69. "Almost daily" inquiry, in Werder's words, referring back to his telegram from Livadia, *GP*, vol. 2, 52 (13/25 September 1876).

70. *GP*, vol. 2, 52–60. In reaction to Werder's telegrams *en clair*, Bismarck's marginal notes and memoranda "bristled" with anger: "It is really worse than gauche of Werder to offer himself as a tool of Russia, to help blackmail us for an embarrassing and untimely declaration"; ". . . a political calamity."

71. A. A. Svechin, *Evoliutsiia voennogo iskusstva*, 2 vols. (Moscow/Leningrad, 1928), vol. 1:361–362.

72. Obruchev also brought with him Artamonov's May report. See Barbasov, "Novye fakty," 99 n. 1. Most studies since 1976, insofar as they even deal with the question of war planning, have relied extensively on Barbasov's article for the plan's genesis. Karaivanov's "Prinost" na general N. N. Obruchev za podgotovkata i vodeneta na rysko-turskata osvoboditelna voina 1877–1878 g.," *Voenno-istoricheski sbornik*, 41, no. 3 (1972), pulls together information only from well-known published collections. He makes no mention of Obruchev's 22 September memo; nor did Svechin (*Evoliutsiia*, vol. 1: 361), nor Beskrovnyi (*Russkoe voennoe iskusstvo XIX v.*, 303–304). Nevertheless, Barbasov's comments on the military aspects of the final plan are reliable. The 22 September Obruchev memorandum is reproduced *only* in *Comisiunea istorica a Marelui Stat Major Rus, Razboiul ruso-turc din 1877–1878 in Peninsula Balcanica*, 2 vols., ed. Col. I. Gardescu (Bucharest: Tip. "L'Indépendance Roumaine," 1902), no copies of which are available in the United States.

73. *RGVIA*, F. 485, d. 590, l. 1 (also consulted by Barbasov); see also Karaivanov, "Planove," 28–29.

74. Ignat'ev was present for the first of these reports but not the second; his recollections make no mention of Obruchev's presentations. [Ignat'ev] "Zapiski," 432–434. Sumner's reconstruction from published sources is indispensable here: Sumner, *Russia and the Balkans*, Appendix 3, 602–604.

75. M. Gazenkampf, *Moi dnevnik* (St. Petersburg, 1908), Appendix 1: "Signed Report of Lieutenant General Obruchev of 1 October 1876."

76. Ibid., App. 1, 1.

77. App. 1, 3.

78. By rail from Bender through Galati, and Bucharest to Sistova on the middle Danube.

79. From Sistova, across the Balkans to Kazanlyk, down the Dag River to Adrianople.

80. Gazenkampf, *Moi dnevnik*, App. 1, 3–4.

81. A small army was a fast army: five infantry divisions, two cavalry divisions, ten Cossack regiments, a sapper brigade, and a siege artillery park were the forces his plan called for. He initially expected one division mobilized in the Kiev military district to guarantee Austrian neutrality.

82. Fuller, *Strategy and Power*, 308–317, examines the *final* war plan, agreed upon in April 1877 shortly before commencement of hostilities. There is little to be added to that account. Fuller notes the precedent of Artamonov's paper, but he believes that most war planning work took place during the fall of 1876, rather than that spring and summer.

83. Sumner, *Russia and the Balkans*, 215–216.

84. "Basis for Organization of Bulgarian Forces"; A. Barbasov, "Russkii voennyi deiatel' N. N. Obruchev" *Voenno-Istoricheskii Zhurnal*, 8 (1973): 102.

85. *Dnevnik D. A. Miliutina*, vol. 2:106 (29 October, Friday).

86. *GP*, vol. 2: 62 ("Varzin, 9 October, 1876").

87. *GP*, vol. 2: 65 ("Varzin, 14 October, 1876").

88. Zaionchkovskii, *Voennye reformy*, 338–339; Obruchev, "Osnovnye istoricheskie voprosy," 16. The summer's work on cataloging cavalry remounts paid handsome dividends: the army acquired most of its horses by M + 11 and reached its goal of sixty-three thousand by M + 16.

89. Analysis of mobilization: Airapetov, "O planirovanii Osvoboditel'noi voiny," 61–63. A second mobilization began in January 1877 to supplement the clearly insufficient forces mustered for the sort of operation that Grand Duke Nikolai Nikolaevich intended to pursue.

90. Barbasov, "N. N. Obruchev," 102, credits only Obruchev's work on the Romanian convention.

91. Letter from Gorchakov to Novikov, dated 15/27 December 1876, reprinted in Sumner, *Russia and the Balkans*, Appendix 2, 589–590.

92. Sumner, *Russia and the Balkans*, 282 n. 1; [P. D. Parensov], "Perepiska P. D. Parensova s K. V. Levitskim pered nachalam voennykh deistvii s Turtsii," *Russkaia starina*, 124 (1905): 605–613; [Naglovskii], "Kishinevskoe siden'ie," on Parensov's covert reconnaissance through Vienna to Rushchuk, Varna, and Shumla before moving on to Rogula and Novoselskii to get information from talkative sailors; Parensov had three thousand gold rubles for his mission.

93. Sumner, *Russia and the Balkans*, 276.

94. [N. P. Ignat'ev], *San-Stefano: Zapiski grafa N. P. Ignat'eva*, ed. A. A. Bash-

makov and K. A. Gubastov, (Petrograd, 1916), 266 n. 3; 340 n. 1; and the careful evaluation in Sumner, *Russia and the Balkans*, 283–284.

95. For the Budapest text: *AVPR*, F. 138, op. 467, d. 22, dated 3/15 January 1877. Also in: Pribram, *Secret Treaties*, vol. 2: 190–203; and *Key Treaties for the Great Powers 1814–1915*, 2 vols., ed. M. Hurst (New York: St. Martin's Press, 1972), vol. 2:511–515. The Budapest agreement clearly confirmed Reichstadt: *"l'établissement d'un grand état compact slave ou autre est exclu."* *AVPR*, F. 138, op. 467, d. 22–1877 and d. 32–1877/78 contains the foreign ministry's papers on the agreement, with edited texts. Only an *Aide-memoire confidentiel*, in ibid., d. 32–1877/78, ll. 42–46, mentions maps (of Bosnia-Herzegovina and of Serbia-Montenegro). Obruchev is mentioned nowhere in these dela.

96. On Obruchev's role: Barbasov, "N. N. Obruchev," 102, citing *RGVIA* documents; a discussion of the terms of agreement: Sumner, *Russia and the Balkans*, 290–298. Find the text in: *Key Treaties*, vol. 2: 515–523.

97. The tsarevich, Aleksandr Aleskandrovich, however, offered to take Obruchev as his chief of staff on the Rushchuk detachment.

98. Menning, *Bayonets before Bullets*, chap. 2, is the best concise, analytic narrative of the 1877–1878 war in any language. Menning's interests and sources, however, do not expose Russian combat or command leadership during the war to the devestating criticism they deserve.

99. Of the 711,000 men moved to the theater by February 1877, over 400,000 were in combat forces, 145,000 were assigned for observation of the coastline and the Austrian border, and about 150,000 supported the rear of the army (logistics, rear security, medical, communications, etc.): *RGVIA*, F. 485, d. 606, ll. 5ob–6 (Miliutin to Alexander, 7 February 1878).

100. G. A. Leer, *Strategicheskie etiudy* (St. Petersburg, 1885), 317–318.

101. *Opisanie Russko-turetskoi voiny*, vol. 9, pt. 2 (St. Petersburg, 1913), 305–310.

102. Menning, *Bayonets before Bullets*, 78. *Russko-turetskaia voina*, ed. Rostunov, 220, argues that the problems began with serious underestimation of Turkish strength. Yet even with the arrival of two additional divisions for the second Russian offensive (September), the manpower ratio was only 3:2 in Russia's favor. The problems of April to July lay elsewhere. Unlike the Balkan theater, it appears that Grand Duke Mikhail and Loris-Melikov neglected the "military-statistical preparation" (i.e., intelligence) of the theater.

103. The 1st Grenadier Division (Moscow) had to travel one thousand four hundred miles by rail to Vladikavkaz, then march two hundred miles to the front; the 40th Infantry Division (Saratov) traveled one thousand river and rail miles with the same march. Both formations were in place at Alexandropol within twelve weeks. Frances V. Greene, *Report on the Russian Army and Its Campaign in Turkey in 1877–1878* (New York, 1879), 387. Greene, the United States's first accredited military attaché, was attached to the imperial headquarters and knew of Caucasus operations through dispatch traffic that went to Kishinev. He apparently knew nothing of Obruchev's role in turning the other campaign around.

104. *Russko-turetskaia voina*, ed. Rostunov, 221–230. Rostunov's authorial collective glossed over the reasons for Obruchev's dispatch to the Caucasus, and the daring offensive he planned.

105. *Russko-turetskaia voina*, ed. Rostunov, 243; Greene, *Report on the Russian Army*, 416–419.

106. Miliutin, *Dnevnik*, vol. 2:93–4 (4 October, Monday). Reutern's memoirs assert an even earlier report to the tsar on the issue of cost of mobilization: when summoned in early September he reported on state finances with reference to the cost of mobilization. Reutern, *Die finanzielle Sanierung Russlands*, 119. Also: Airapetov, "Problema Russko-Turetskoi voiny," 52–55.

107. Sumner, *Russia and the Balkans*, 216 and 304, mistakenly believes that the war that Miliutin supported in October 1876 was the same one that began the next spring. However, the military establishment anticipated an *autumn* campaign at the time of the Livadian discussions. And his contention that Miliutin "apparently succumbed to the militant atmosphere at Livadia" at this crucial meeting ignores Miliutin's own keen interest in war, Obruchev's presentation, and the staff's confidence in success.

108. Geyer describes Miliutin as the tsar's most intimate and respected adviser; *Russian Imperialism*, 73–74, but his tendency to identify a structural link between Russian foreign policy and domestic agitation (as Fischer had demonstrated in Germany's case) is not convincing.

109. Airapetov, "Problema Russko-Turetskoi voiny," 50, on Obruchev's anticipation of the San Stefano settlement—eighteen months before the treaty's signature.

6. Experts versus Amateurs

1. Miliutin had nominated Obruchev and Major General Vasilii Nikolaevich Lavrov to the operational army staff; Grand Duke Nikolai Nikolaevich turned down both and instead chose Nepokoichitskii and Levitskii, two well-known toadies. Colorful judgment of field command incompetence came from young general staff officers from VUK, seconded to the operational army staff: [Naglovskii], "Kishinevskoe siden'e," 245–246. Lavrov instead commanded a Guards regiment and was killed during the course of the war.

2. V. A. Zolotarev, "Deiatel'nost voenno-istoricheskoi komissii Glavnogo shtaba russkoi armii po obobshchenii opyta Russko-turetskoi voiny 1877–1878 gg.," in *Vestnik Arkhivov Armenii*, no. 3, (1975): 115–117. The work of the historical commission (created as a temporary body by imperial rescript in March 1879) grew to four series:

Sbornik materialov po Russko-turetskoi voiny 1877–1878 gg. na Balkanskom poluostrove, 97 vols. (St. Petersburg, 1900–1910).

Sbornik materialov po grazhdanskomu upravleniiu i okupatsii v Bolgarii, 3 vols. (St. Petersburg, 1907).

Opisanie Russko-turetskoi voiny 1877–1878 gg. na Balkanskom poluostrove, 9 vols. (St. Petersburg, 1901–1909).

Osoboe pribavlenie k opisaniiu Russko-turetskoi voiny 1877–1878 gg. na Balkanskom poluostrove, 6 vols. (St. Petersburg, 1899–1911).

See also Stefan Shanov, "*Sbornik materialov po Russko-turetskoi voiny 1877–1878 gg. na Balkanskom poluostrove*—Nai-krupniia nositel na informatsiia za osvobozhdenieto," *Izvestiia na d"rzhavnite arkhivi* [Sofia], 56 (1988): 3–23; and Shanov, "Ruskata istoricheska nauka za Rusko-turskata voina 1877–1878 g. i za Osvobozhdenieto na B"lgariia," *Izvestiia: Voenno-istorichesko nauchno druzhestvo* [*Institut za voenna istoriia*, Sofia], 25 (1978): 146–179.

3. The widening of VUK's mandate, by expansion of the range of its foreign interests, occurred in 1885: *PSZ*, ser. III vol. 5: §2729.

4. A small sample of the most important sources: Peter Rassow, *Der Plan Moltkes für den Zweifrontenkrieg (1871–1890)* (Breslauer historische Forschungen, 1) (Breslau, 1938); *Die deutschen Aufmarschpläne 1871–1890* (Forschungen und Darstellungen aus dem Reichsarchiv, 7), ed. F. von Schmerfeld (Berlin, 1929); W. Kloster, *Der deutsche Generalstab und der Präventivkriegsgedanke* (Stuttgart, 1932). See discussion in Dennis E. Showalter, *Railroads and Rifles: Soldiers, Technology and the Unification of Germany* (Hamden, Conn.: Archon, 1975); Bucholz, *Prussian War Planning*, chap. 2 (although silent on all post-1876 strategic developments). Least explicable in its omissions: Dennis E. Showalter, "The Eastern Front and German Military Planning, 1871–1914: Some Observations," *East European Quarterly*, 15 (1981): 163–180, which notes none of what follows here.

5. Comment of Bismarck to Prince Chlodwig von Hohenlowe (Ambassador to Paris) on 29 September 1876, cited in Bagdesarian, *Austro-German Rapprochement*, 198–199.

6. Rassow, *Der Plan Moltkes*, 7–8.

7. Showalter, *Railroads and Rifles*, 39–48, 58–62; Bucholz, *Prussian War Planning*, 36–37, 46–54.

8. Rassow, *Der Plan Moltkes*, 3–4. The 27 April 1871 *Denkschrift*: "Aufmarsch gegen Frankreich-Russland" is reproduced in *Die Deutschen Aufmarschpläne*, 4–14.

9. C. A. Busch, "Die Botschafterkonferenz in Konstantinopel und der russisch-türkische Krieg," *Deutsche Rundschau* 35 no. 3 (November 1909): 207–209; Bagdesarian, *Austro-German Rapprochement*, 209, argues that Bismarck did not share the General Staff's fears.

10. *Die deutschen Aufmarschpläne*, 65–67: *Denkschrift*, "Zweifrontenkrieg gegen Frankreich-Russland," 3 February 1877.

11. Citing German foreign ministry documents: Bruce Waller, *Bismarck at the Crossroads: The Reorientation of German Foreign Policy after the Congress of Berlin 1878–1880* (London: Athlone Press, 1974), 135, 231–243. Waller ably traces the Germans' uses of data on Russian army deployments in Poland to pursue political objectives domestically and internationally.

12. [Naglovskii], "Kishinevskoe siden'e," 243–245. D. A. Skalon, *Moi vospominaniia 1877–1878*, 2 vols. (St. Petersburg, 1913), vol. 1: 7–19. Naglovskii was a young colonel assigned to the operations section of the field staff under Levitskii. After the war he rose to high rank as chief of staff of the most important military district, Warsaw. Skalon, later chief editor of *Stoletie Voennogo ministerstva*, served as aide to Grand Duke Nikolai Nikolaevich during the war and had a reputation for toadyism.

13. *Die deutschen Aufmarschpläne*, 65; with his army essentially split in two, "it must be left up to diplomacy to see if a peace settlement can be achieved," he wrote. Moltke's pessimism deepened throughout the 1880s, leading him to warn the Reichstag upon his retirement in 1890, "Woe to him that sets Europe on fire." Cited in Holger Herwig, "Strategic Uncertainties of a Nation-State: Prussia-Germany, 1870–1918," in Murray et al., *Making of Strategy*, 250–251.

14. Waller, *Bismarck at the Crossroads*, 234. Moltke told Bismarck in late 1879 that Russian strength in Poland had not changed appreciably since 1875. In early 1880 a German captain published (undoubtedly with general staff approval) a de-

ployment map of European Russia that attuned the German public to the eastern threat. That map greatly exercised war minister Miliutin: it was a near-perfect representation of deployment of every regiment, battery, and brigade (or higher) unit or headquarters west of Moscow (as well as the entire rail network). *RGVIA*, F. 400, op. 3, d. 658, "Concerning the Foreign Publication of the Deployment Map of the Russian Army," 15 March 1880; Ernest von Troltsch, *Dislokations-Karte der russischen Armee*, Entworfen nach den neuesten und besten Quellen (Stuttgart, 1880); counterespionage measures in Poland and relevent Vannovskii-Tolstoi (MVD) correspondence: *RGVIA*, F. 401, op. 5, d. 442 ("settlers" of German and Austrian origin around Brest-Litovsk and the Novogeorgevsk citadel). In the later 1880s Russian military counterintelligence followed the movements of Major Bernard Reichel as he brazenly scouted Russian positions along the border. Only the approval of Alexander III, however, finally led to ejection of Reichel and another German, Heinrich Keizat, from Poland! Ibid., d. 442, ll. 178–188 on cases. In Obruchev's and Vannovskii's view, anyone of German origin working on the railroad or postal-telegraphic system was suspect as well; they formed a temporary committee (1883–1885) to look into the question: materials in *RGVIA*, F. 401, op. 4, d. 51–1883.

15. *Die deutschen Aufmarschpläne*, 80 n. 1.

16. On origins of the mutual fear, see especially Andreas Hilgruber, "Die deutsch-russischen politischen Beziehungen (1881–1917)," in *Deutschland und Russland im Zeitalter des Kapitalismus 1861–1914* (Wiesbaden: Franz Steiner, 1977), 207–220; F. T. Epstein, "Der Komplex '*Die russische Gefahr*' und sein Einfluss auf die deutsch-russischen Beziehungen im 19. Jahrhundert," in *Deutschland in der Weltpolitik des 19. und 20. Jahrhunderts*, ed. I. Geiss and B.-J. Wendt (Düsseldorf: Bertelsmann Universitätverlag, 1973), 143–159. Aggressive Russophobia in its modern manifestation is found not merely among Prussian Junkers and officers but also among the liberal opposition after 1848; it was a fixture of German liberal and middle-class worldviews.

17. Waller, *Bismarck at the Crossroads*, 216, 241, reports that Werder knew of feelers from Obruchev toward the French for a military agreement sometime before the September 1879 meeting of the two emperors at Aleksandrovo. P. A. Saburov, Russian minister in Berlin and a vigorous proponent of alliance with Germany, recounts Bismarck's distressing account of the "Obruchev incident": *The Saburov Memoirs or Bismarck and Russia*, ed. J. Y. Simpson (New York, 1929), 106–109. H. L. von Schweinitz, German ambassador in St. Petersburg, carried on his own correspondence with Saburov: *Briefwechsel des Botschafters General von Schweinitz* (Berlin: R. Hobbing, 1928), 153–155. Obruchev made the approach first to W. H. Waddington, French foreign minister, after a rebuff from "French military men" (General Galliffet and Colonel Gaillard), at the summer maneuvers. Other accounts of the contact are summarized in: Kennan, *Decline of Bismarck's European Order*, 46–48. On German "thanks": Obruchev, "Osnovnye istoricheskie voprosy," 6. On "supposedly Russian" diplomats: Epanchin, *Na sluzhbe trekh Imperatorov*, 84. See further discussion in chap. 7, n. 32.

18. Obruchev, "Osnovnye istoricheskie voprosy," 17.

19. *AVPR*, F. 138, op. 467, ed.khr. 39, for the Austro-German alliance; Russian dismay concerning Bismarck's betrayal: *Saburov's Memoirs*, 288–290. Taylor, *Struggle for Mastery in Europe*, 260–266, argues that Bismarck's (unfulfilled) intent was

to strong-arm Vienna into grudging compromise with Russia concerning Balkan spheres of interest.

20. Saburov's interest was Russian policy toward Turkey, to which he thought Bismarck held the key. *AVPR* F. 138, op. 467, ed.khr. 39: 43–1879, for the memoranda and reports from Saburov, Giers, Orlov, Lamsdorf, Miliutin, and Zhomini regarding negotiations with Germany (21 September/2 October through 24 December 1879). Saburov discusses this in his memoirs, *Saburov's Memoirs*, 78–96. Also, Kennan, *Decline of Bismarck's European Order,* 74–75; Taylor, *Struggle for Mastery,* 266–267.

21. *AVPR* F. 133, op. 467, ed. lchr. 39: 43–1879, ll. 129–134, memorandum from Miliutin, Livadia, November 1879. The question of Russian cavalry bothered Russo-German relations repeatedly in 1879 and 1880 (and later). Bismarck, Kaiser Wilhelm I, and Ambassador Radowitz brought the problem to the attention of their opposite numbers, although Moltke appears to have been the force behind German concern: *Saburov Memoirs,* 98–106.

22. *Vsepoddanneishchii doklad Voennogo ministra 1880 g.* (St. Petersburg, 1881), 1–2. See also *RGVIA,* F. 1, op. 2, d. 31–1881, l. 1, marked "secret."

23. *RGVIA,* F. 402, op. I, d. 69, ll. 132+ob: "Sketch of mobilization committee activity 1880; Materials." Prussia's first modern war—1864—had proved exactly the same thing: Bucholz, *Prussian War Planning,* 45.

24. A. M. Zaionchkovskii, *Podgotovka Rossii,* 31–32.

25. *RGVIA,* F. 402, op. II, d. 25, ll. 23+ob: "Concerning the Course of Work in the Main Staff Preparatory to War in 1886 and 1887." As late as 1914 none of the official histories of the war ministry or its organs mentioned these studies (or, as noted, the 1873 strategic conference either); see, e.g., *Stoletie Voennogo ministerstva,* vol. 4, pt. 2, bk. 2, sect. 1: *Istoricheskii ocherk vozniknoveniia i razvitiia v Rossii General'nogo shtaba v 1802–1902 gg.,* chaps. 8 and 9.

26. *RGVIA,* F. 402, op. 2, d. 3, l. 1: "List No. 1 of works on the preparation for war, executed in the Main Staff in 1880. Basic Works"; *RGVIA,* F. 401, op. 5, d. 419, ll. 45+ob: "Copy of war minister's resolutions, 25 January 1880." As late as 1929, a new generation of Russian strategic planners still recognized the legend of the Basic Memorandum: S. K. Dobrorol'skii, *Mobilizatsiia Russkoi armii v 1914 godu. Podgotovka i vypolnenie* (Moscow, 1929), 21. Dobrorol'skii was the general staff's operations officer—successor in responsibility to Kuropatkin—when the Great War began.

27. *AVPR,* F. 138, op. 467, d. 76–1883, l. 7 (hereafter AVPR "Basic Memorandum").

28. Fuller, *Strategy and Power,* 338–350. Fuller cited the AVPR copy of the memo (p. 299 n. 85) but considered it a "war plan" based on a different two-part document: *RGVIA,* F. 400, op. 4, d. 445, ll. 68–78ob: "Historical sketch of the development of the question of Russian force strategic deployment on the western frontier," undated. (All materials in the *delo* date from 1901 to 1905.) There is no copy of the Basic Memorandum in *RGVIA,* where it should have been preserved. A. M. Zaionchkovskii alluded to changes in the war plan in 1880 but made no comment on their origins: A.M. *Podgotovka Rossii,* 33.

29. AVPR, "Basic Memorandum," ll. 8–9. Contextualizing the memo's argument: *RGVIA,* F. 402, op. 2, d. 25, ll. 23–24: "Concerning Continuation of Work in 1886 and 1887 in the Main Staff in Preparation for War. Sect. A: On Work Com-

pleted from 1880 to the Present." Authored by Kuropatkin, this document is a record of *how* the Main Staff functioned as an agency for war planning. It is the single richest archival source on development of Russia's first modern war plan (1887), and on the internal operation of the Main Staff. See also Fuller, *Strategy and Power,* 348–349; A. M. Zaionchkovskii, *Podgotovka Rossii,* 32.

30. *RGVIA,* F. 402, op. 1, d. 126, l. 282+ob: "Report from Commander in Chief of Forces, Warsaw M.D. January 1880." Cf. *RGVIA,* F. 401, op. 5, d. 419, ll. 46–49, for Kotsebu's report on the details of engineering preparations, 19 January 1880.

31. See, e.g., *RGVIA,* F. 402, op. II, d. 14, ll. 1–3: "Anticipated Allocation of Forces in Vilna M.D. . . . ."; district forces' only mission upon declaration of mobilization was screening of forces assembling and concentrating in the interior of the district.

32. Vitte, *Vospominanie. Nikolai,* vol. 1:449–450. The war ministry's economic and fiscal problems, to which such changing requirements contributed, were legion; see Fuller, *Civil-Military Conflict,* chap. 2.

33. *RGVIA,* F. 402, op. 2, d. 2, ll. 4–7 [*aide-mémoire,* signed General-Adjutant Miliutin, 26 Feb. 1887]. Also: Fuller, *Strategy and Power,* 303–308. Note that a fortress-centered strategy was nothing more than an indispensable, temporary defensive palliative.

34. A. M. Zaionchkovskii, *Podgotovka Rossii,* 31–33; Fuller, *Strategy and Power,* 339–341. See Table A-2 for the composition of the western armies in 1880.

35. *RGVIA,* F. 402, op. 2, d. 60, l. 32; F. 402, op. II, d. 25, l. 24, for the deployment in the second, "Offensive-Defensive" contingency.

36. *RGVIA,* F. 400, op. 4, d. 445, l. 68: "Historical Sketch of Development of the Question of Deployment of Russian Forces on the Western Frontier," early twentieth century. Table A-2 tallies the composition of the western and reserve forces in late 1882.

37. *RGVIA,* F. 400, op. 3, d. 664, "Order on Reorganization of Main Staff," 1 January 1885, signed by Obruchev. The permanent staff positions were authorized a year later; the staff gained slots for two general officers, five colonels/lieutenant colonels, and twenty-eight salaried staff members.

38. Main Staff evolution is sketched in introductory essays to the *opisi* in *RGVIA:* F. 400, op. 2: "I *Otdelenie (po ustroistvu voisk)*"; F. 400, op. 4: "*Glavnyi Shtab: Gen. Kvartirmeistr chast'*"; F. 402, op. I–II: "*Kom. dlia podgotovki dannykh k mobilizatsykh voisk*"; and F. 401, op. 6: "*Vremennye kom., obrazovannye pri Voenno-Uchënom komitete Glav. Shtaba.*" See also *Stoletie Voennogo ministerstva,* vol. 4, pt. 2, bk. 2, sect. 1, chaps. 8–9.

39. The commission's records are in *RGVIA,* F. 401, op. 6, dd. 1–51, "Temporary Commission on Defensive Construction on the Western Front (1882–1894)"; note the implied geographic spread of the "Western Front."

40. *RGVIA,* F. 402, op. 2, d. 35, ll. 9–11ob, 17–18, 55–66, 80–91.

41. *RGVIA,* F. 400, op. 4, d. 618, ll. 146–147. Dela 618 to 622 contain relevant materials. Apparently Obruchev made a personal, covert reconnaissance of potential landing sites at the Bosporus in 1873 or 1874, which dates his long engagement with this objective.

42. Obruchev, "Osnovnye istoricheskie voprosy," 15–19. 1908: McDonald, *United Government,* chap. 6. For Russia's Straits' policy and mission there: V. Shere-

met, *Bosfor: Rossiia i Turtsiia v epokhu pervoi mirivoi voiny* (Moscow: Tekhnologicheskaia shkola biznesa, 1995).

43. *RGVIA*, F. 401, op. 5, d. 419, ll. 31–44: "Report from CinC Warsaw Forces [Kotsebu] to Miliutin, 28 Feb 1878"; "Report on Preparation of the Novogeorgevsk-Grodno Strategic Front. From Kotsebu to Obruchev, 7 Mar 1878"; "Remarks on the Preparation of a Strategic Front from Novogeorgevsk to Grodno," by the Warsaw District Staff, signed chief of staff Lieutenant General D. S. Naglovskii. [n.d.]

44. *RGVIA*, F. 402, op. I, d. 126, l. 282.

45. Ibid., d. 126, ll. 284–285.

46. *RGVIA*, F. 402, op. II, d. 2, ll. 7+ob: "Report, signed by General-Adjutant Miliutin, 26 February 1887."

47. *RGVIA*, F. 402, op. 2, d. 14, ll. 1–3: "Anticipated allocation of forces in Vilna Military District . . .," 15 February 1883, signed Major General Bunakov, chief of staff; Obruchev's answer: ibid., ll. 4–5ob [signed Obruchev] 7 March 1883, annotated: copies to the chiefs of staff, Kiev and Odessa Military Districts.

48. Among his subordinates in the Asiatic Section was the "imperialists' imperialist," Przhevalskii, who entertained the most extreme visions of Russian expansion into Asia. Fifteen years after Obruchev had swung the staff's focus westward, military geographers and explorers of Przhevalskii's ilk continued to operate without mandate or limitation within the Main Staff.

49. Vitte, *Vospominaniia*, vol. 1:138–142.

50. K. F. Shatsillo, *Rossiia pered pervoi mirivoi voinoi. (Vooruzhenye sily tsarizma v 1905–1914 gg.)* (Moscow: Nauka, 1974), 7. Shatsillo's judgment resonated closely with General Skobelev's a century earlier. One of Obruchev's colonels also recorded an interesting rendezvous with Kuropatkin during the war: [Naglovskii], "Kishinevskoe siden'e."

51. Herwig, "Strategic Uncertainties," 250; and especially Detlef Bald, "Zum Kriegsbild der militärischen Führung im Kaiserreich," in *Bereit zum Krieg: Kriegsmentalität im wilhelminischen Deutschland 1890–1914*, ed. J. Dülffer and K. Holl (Göttingen: Vandenhoeck and Ruprecht, 1986), 150–153. One might argue that a consequence of Miliutin's political victories against Bariatinskii and the "Prussianists" in the 1860s was that the ministryship remained the supreme position to which any military officer could aspire (unlike the case in Germany). Hence Kuropatkin's later ascent *removed* him from the arena in which he could have contributed the most (the Main Staff), turned over staff responsibilities to men of inferior capability to himself, and ultimately cast him in a role for which he was clearly unsuited—field command during the 1904–1905 Russo-Japanese War.

52. *RGVIA*, F. 402, op. 2, d. 14, ll. 6–10ob, 20 April 1883.

53. Ibid., d. 14, ll. 46+ob. The roads in question were Lomzha to Grodno, Grodno to Kovno, and Suvalki to Grodno.

54. Ibid., d. 15, ll. 3–21, 28 March 1883.

55. Ibid., d. 15, ll. 4–5.

56. Ibid., d. 15, ll. 34–43: "Remarks of Maj.-Gen. Kuropatkin on work of the Warsaw Military District," 12 October 1883.

57. A preliminary study is Fuller, "The Russian Empire," 98–126. For correspondence between VUK and the foreign ministry regarding instructions to military attachés in Brussels, Bern, and Constantinople: *RGVIA*, F. 401, op. 4, d. 50,

ll. 1–9, 13–14, 29–30, 33–35ob., 102 + ob., 115 + ob. (November 1884–August 1886). See particularly the *"Spravka,"* l. 13ob. Russian successes in espionage multiplied during the following decades. The Main Staff had German and Austrian mobilization plans by 1895, and access to all encrypted diplomatic telegraph traffic (including Italy's) well into the First World War. W. W. Gottlieb, *Studies in Secret Diplomacy during the First World War* (London: Allen Unwin, 1957), made useful note of the last.

58. *RGVIA*, F. 402, op. 2, d. 15, ll. 60–61ob., including the request (26 September 1884) and reply (5 October 1884).

59. Ibid., d. 15, ll. 110ob + 111.

60. Major General Kuropatkin had returned from campaigning with Skobelev in Turkestan at the end of 1882.

61. Ibid., d. 25, ll. 10–16ob., 6 October 1884.

62. Ibid., d. 25, l. 24ob: "On the Continuation in the Main Staff in 1886 and 1887 of Work Preparatory to War" (ll. 23–37), written by Kuropatkin, undated.

63. Ibid., d. 25, l. 24ob.

64. When Sollogub was thirty-six, his principal job was section chief of the Main Staff's *II Otdelenie*. From 1881 to 1884 he was junior secretary of the Military-Scientific Committee's chancery and then a temporary attaché in Egypt. By 1905 Count Witte considered Sollogub to be "preeminent among our generals in the knowledge of military science," a "decent well-balanced man" and "one of the most intelligent, best-educated, and upright men to come from our General Staff." He thought him firm and decisive during the revolutionary upheavals of that year, but free of the "urge toward senseless brutality against peasant rioters," unlike other high officials. Vitte, *Vospominaniia. Nikolai*, vol. 2:137–138, 346–347.

65. Just thirty-one years old, Mel'nitskii had already held battalion command after seeing combat in the empire's campaigns in 1877–1878 and 1880–1881. His future lay in the VUK chancery apparatus.

66. Not yet thirty, Zuev had participated in transborder travels "for scientific purposes" and served as an adjunct professor at the academy. At the time of his work for Kuropatkin, he was a junior action officer in VUK's chancery.

67. *RGVIA*, F. 402, op. II, d. 25, ll. 10+ob.

68. Ibid., d. 25, ll. 11+ob.

69. Ibid., d. 25, ll. 12–14. An east-central Asian campaign would begin from Fergana Oblast, across the Terek Pass and Tungub River; or from Semirechensk Oblast across the Bedel and Terek Rivers to the Turdion and Koligar districts; or through Kuldja (China) and Khali or Iulduz, to Kurli and Karasha (Qara Shahr), that is, along the ancient Silk Routes into eastern Sinkiang. Ibid., d. 25, ll. 16+ob. Kuropatkin's inquiry came shortly after Major General Przhevalskii's third *puteshestvie*, the results of which appeared as *Iz Zaisana cherez Khami v Tibet i na verkhovia Zheltoi reki* (St. Petersburg, 1883).

70. *RGVIA*, F. 402, op. II, d. 25, ll. 18–20ob: "On Continuing Work on Strengthening the Provisioning of Force of the Frontier Districts in the Event of War," 14 May 1885.

71. Ibid., d. 25, ll. 21+ob, 16 May 1885.

72. Ibid., d. 25, ll. 25: "On the Continuation in the Main Staff in 1886 and 1887 of Work Preparatory to War."

73. Ibid., d. 25, ll. 25+ob.

74. All standard diplomatic histories of the period deal with Russia's "loss" of Bulgaria. See, e.g., Langer, *European Alliances and Alignments*, 334–338.

75. *RGVIA*, F. 402, op. I, d. 290, ll. 1–8: mobilization committee report dated 1 April 1885, annotated "Agreed" by Alexander III.

76. Ibid., d. 291, ll. 33–55, for letters of notification. The measures the commanders were to take included call-up of specialists (medical personnel, clerks, etc.), acquisition of horses, and coastal fortress reserve call-up.

77. Ibid., ll 78+ob.

78. Ibid., ll. 99–101.

79. *GP*, vol. 6: 19–28 (Reuss to Bismarck, 6 and 8 December 1887; Bismarck to Reuss, 15 December 1887). Schmerfeld, *Die deutsche Aufmarschpläne*, 137–142.

80. See his article on Russia's, Germany's, and Austria-Hungary's army deployments in *Russkii invalid*, 3 December 1887; this was the Russian government's official response to the press campaign.

81. *RGVIA*, F. 402, op. 2, d. 25, ll. 23–44ob: "Concerning Work Preparatory to War Completed in 1886 and 1887 by the Main Staff," Section C: "On the Formation of the 'Mobilization Commission of the Main Staff' for Preparation in the Event of War of Plans, Considerations and Estimates, Organized in the War Ministry in Accordance with the *Regulation on Field Authority of Forces in Wartime*" (ll. 35+ob).

82. Ibid., d. 15, ll. 60–61ob: correspondence between Fel'dman (head of Main Staff chancery) and Lieutenant General N. Ia. Zverev (chief of staff, Warsaw military district). Zverev had earlier served as a department head on the Main Staff, and as chief of staff in both Orenberg and Vilna districts.

83. Ibid., d. 15, ll. 78+ob: Letter from Kuropatkin to Naglovskii, 4 October 1885.

84. *RGVIA*, F. 400, op. 4, d. 445, ll. 72–77ob: "Historical Sketch of the Development of the Question of Strategic Deployment of Russian Forces on the Western Border" (typewritten), undated [early 1900s]; the discovery was made during the 1883–1884 winter work season: l. 77ob.

85. *RGVIA*, F. 402, op. 2, d. 25, ll. 27+ob.

86. These would constitute parts of a new "Regulation on Field Authority for Forces in Wartime" [*Polozhenie o polevom upravlenii voiskami v voennoe vremia*] (pt. 1, chaps. 1, 2), discussed below.

87. *RGVIA*, F. 402, op. 2, d. 25, l. 27ob.

88. Fuller, *Strategy and Power*, 347–349.

89. *RGVIA*, F. 402, op. 2, d. 25, ll. 28ob–30.

90. Fuller, *Strategy and Power*, 343. The problem of field authority dated to 1877: Miliutin argued that the 1877 war had increased staff specialization and dictated that wartime control of field forces "required rearrangement." *Vsepoddanneishchii doklad po Voennomy ministerstvy 1880 g.* (St. Petersburg, 1880), 37. Also Menning, *Bayonets before Bullets*, 98–100, for a sketch of the commission's work on the new regulation.

91. *RGVIA*, F. 402, op. 2, d. 25, ll. 28+ob.

92. On the German yardstick, embodied in values of *Leistung* and *Selbständigkeit*: Macgregor Knox, "The 'Prussian Idea of Freedom' and the Career Open to Talent: Battlefield Initiative and Social Ascent from Prussian Reform to Nazi Revolution, 1807–1944," *Foreign Policy and War in Fascist Italy and Nazi Germany* (Cambridge: Cambridge University Press, 1999).

93. *Voennyi sbornik*, throughout 1878 and after, was full of articles critical of tactical doctrine (particularly the tight column advances and rigid fire discipline imposed on attacking units); memoirs of participants likewise (though sometimes subtly) pointed to the same shortcomings of Russian combat leadership (e.g., P. P. Kartsov, *Iz proshlogo. Lichnye i sluzhebnye vospominaniia*, vol. 2, *1876–1878 gg.* (St. Petersburg, 1888), 619–630). Among the few really critical analyses are: A. Kersnovskii, *Istoriia russkoi armii*, vol. 2, *Ot vziatiia Parizha do pokoreniia Srednei Azii* (Belgrade, 1934), 416–418, and Greene, *Report on the Russian Army*. On casualties, estimated at seven hundred thousand in the official history, see: *Opisanie russko-turetskoi voiny*, vol. 9, pt. 2: Appendix 2.

94. The causes of military setback in East Asia lay more with the loss of the fleet and lagging capacity of the Siberian railroad: Marks, *Road to Power*, 200–205. Nonetheless, at the time, public and governmental sentiment searched for individual culpability and found Kuropatkin, the battlefield commander.

95. Carl von Clausewitz, *On War*, ed. and trans. Michael Howard and Peter Paret (Princeton, N.J.: Princeton University Press, 1976), bk. 1.

96. Beyond extensive anecdotal evidence in émigré literature and historical fiction, there is no systematic evidence of this problem. It has animated in part the investigation of a number of authors; see Steinberg, "Education and Training," which focuses mainly on the 1905 disaster and its aftermath in educational reform. Menning, *Bayonets before Bullets*, 15–18, takes a narrow view of Prusso-German innovation, restricted to infrastructural matters.

7. *Progress and Stalemate*

1. Thus, Fuller, *Strategy and Power*, 346–347, in relation to Russian intelligence collection, although it applies to the rest of the war planning apparatus as well.

2. Ibid., 362.

3. Evaluation of combat effectiveness: Martin van Crevald, *Fighting Power: German and U.S. Army Performance, 1939–1945* (Westport, Conn.: Greenwood, 1982), chap. 1. He calls this aspect of an army's combat excellence its "fighting power" and explicitly excludes "the quantity and quality of its equipment."

4. Menning, *Bayonets before Bullets*, 278. The four "Young Turks" of the imperial general staff who became *voenspetsy* (military specialists) in the 1920s were A. M. Zaionchkovskii, A. A. Svechin, A. A. Neznamov, and M. P. Mikhnevich.

5. "Transportation and Military Freight Section" [*Otdel po peredvizheniiu i voennykh gruzov*] and the "Special Conference to the Chief of Main Staff on Force and Military Freight Transportation" [*Osoboe soveshchanie pri nachal'nike Glavnogo shtaba po peredvizheniiu voisk i voennykh gruzov*]: War Department Prikaz No. 4, 5 January 1886. Kuropatkin's initiative: RGVIA, F. 402, op. 2, d. 25, ll. 23–41ob: "Concerning Work Completed in the Main Staff in 1886 and 1887, Preparatory to War," Section 3(C), ll. 35–37.

6. Bucholz, *Prussian War Planning*, 66–67. On the German General Staff's revolt against its minister: Craig, *Politics of the Prussian Army*, 227–231.

7. RGVIA, F. 402, op. 3, d. 25, l. 35.

8. RGVIA, F. 401, op. 4, d. 56–1887, l. 65: annotated Appendix 2—"Current Sequence for the Drafting of a Mobilization Timetable," Colonel [P. A.] Smorodskii.

9. Ibid., d. 56–1887, l. 65: "Schematic: The Proposed Procedure for Composition of the Mobilization Timetable." Colonel Smorodskii (the General Staff register indicates) was not a member of the General Staff Corps; despite academy graduation, he had not been inducted into the Corps, as half of each class were not. Because of his work he was authorized to use the title "of the General Staff" (*General'nogo shtaba*).

10. *RGVIA*, F. 402, op. 1, d. 313: "Journal #88, Committee for Force Mobilization," and correspondence, ll. 42–45.

11. Ibid., d. 266a: "Mobilization Schedule No. 10"; and ibid., d. 281a: "Mobilization Schedule No. 11," both typeset.

12. In Guards cadre sections the numbers increased from three to six remounts, and in all other reserve cadre sections, from four to nine remounts. *Prikaz 1892 No. 141*, in *Dopolnenie k Sistematicheskomu sborniku prikazov po Voennamu Vedomostvu i tsirkuliarov Glavnogo Shtaba* (St. Petersburg, 1893), 1.

13. *RGVIA*, F. 400, op. 3 Part I: "Historical Sketch."

14. *RGVIA*, F. 402, op. 2, dd. 79–97a: "Materials Concerning Mobilization Schedule No. 12"; railroad timetables (in printed, ledger form) occupy the ten sequential *dela* numbered: dd. 92–97a.

15. Ibid., d. 76, ll. 7ob.–8: "Imperial Memorandum of the War Minister," signed by Vannovskii, countersigned by Obruchev, 12 June 1887.

16. Fuller, *Strategy and Power*, 347–348. Obruchev used the terms "a defense of waiting" [*oboronitel'no vyzhidatel'nyi*] and "a defense of action" [*oboronitel'no nastupatel'nyi*]: *RGVIA*, F. 402, op. 2, d. 76, l. 1ob.

17. *RGVIA*, F. 402, op. 2, d. 76, l. 7.

18. Obruchev to Giers, 27 October 1883, quoted in Fuller, *Strategy and Power*, 339.

19. Thirty-three-year-old artillerist; promoted to lieutenant colonel while junior secretary on the chancellery staff of VUK, and adjunct professor of military administration at the academy during the early-1880s. Military attaché in Vienna 1886–1890 (colonel, April 1888).

20. Fuller, *Strategy and Power*, 336–337.

21. *RGVIA*, F. 402, op. 2, d. 76, l. 8 n. Attendees included: General-Adjutant Dragomirov; Lieutenant Generals Leer, Kosich, Bobrikov, Baron Vrevskii, Mirkovich, Naglovskii, and Bunakov; Major Generals. Fel'dman, Giubbenet, Lobko I, Kuropatkin, Golovin, Gudim-Levkovich, Puzyrevskii; and Colonels Sukhotin, Shcherbov, Nefedovich and Sollugub. On the middecade war scares, inter alia: Francis Roy Bridge, "Österreich-Ungarn unter den Grossmächten," *Die Habsburgermonarchie im System der internationalen Beziehungen*, pt. 1 [*Die Habsburgermonarchie 1848–1918*, vol. 6/1] (Vienna: Austrian Academy of Sciences, 1989), 270–279; G. P. Morozov, "Russko-frantsuzskie otnosheniia vo vremia voennoi trevogi 1887 g.," *Frantsuzskii ezhegodnik 1959* (Moscow: AN-SSSR, 1960); and I. S. Rybachenok, "Raznoglasiia v praviashchikh krugakh o napravlenii vneshnei politike v 1886–1887 gg.," *Vestnik Moskovskogo Universiteta* (Seriia IX, Istoriia), 1973: 5.

22. *RGVIA*, F. 402, op. 2, d. 76, ll. 1–39: "Imperial Memorandum of the War Minister on Allocation of Russian Forces to Operational Armies in the Event of War with Germany and Austria-Hungary, and Their Operations," signed by Vannovskii, countersigned by Obruchev, dated 12 June 1887. This report should be read in conjunction with Major General Kuropatkin's memorandum, "On the Or-

ganization, Strength, and Concentration of the Russian and Austro-German Armies": *RGVIA*, F. 402, op. 2, d. 115, ll. 1–13, 30 April 1887.

23. Bucholz, *Prussian War Planning*, 52, 125–126.

24. *RGVIA*, F. 402, op. 2, d. 76, l. 21.

25. *Obzor deiatel'nost' Ministerstva Putei soobshcheniia v tsarstvovanie Imperatora Aleksandra III 1881–1894* (St. Petersburg, 1903), 8–9.

26. *RGVIA*, F. 402, op. 2, d. 76, ll. 27ob–38. This document (June 1887) contains the earliest evidence that Russian war planners had developed their plans for parallel mobilization options plan beyond a mere conceptualization.

27. A. M. Zaionchkovskii, *Podgotovka Rossii*, chap. 14. Also Fuller, *Strategy and Power*, 442–445; and Menning, *Bayonets before Bullets*, 242–247.

28. Fuller, *Strategy and Power*, 349.

29. *RGVIA*, F. 402, op. 2, d. 25, ll. 27ob–29: "Concerning Work Completed in 1886 and 1887 by the Main Staff in Preparation for War."

30. Ibid., d. 76, ll. 8ob–9.

31. Ibid., d. 76, ll. 11ob.–12.

32. Pertti Luntinen, *French Information on the Russian War Plans 1880–1914*, Studia Historica 17 (Helsinki: SHS, 1984), 14. In mid-1879 Obruchev discussed an arrangement with his French counterparts, apparently without St. Petersburg's knowledge or sanction. When Bismarck learned of the contact, the Russian foreign ministry quickly disavowed Obruchev's moves, but that did not ruin the general's rise to head of the Main Staff less than two years later. See *GP*, vol. 3:141–143; Waller, *Bismarck at the Crossroads*, 239–243; Hans Lothar von Schweinitz, *Denkwurdigkeiten*, vol. 2: 83 (5 December 1879), 92–100 (8–12 February 1880).

33. *RGVIA*, F. 402, op. 2, d. 76, ll. 12+ob.

34. Austrian file: *RGVIA*, F. 401, op. 5, d. 461, April 1890; an example of frontier field intelligence work: *RGVIA*, F. 401, op. 4, d. 6–1882, ll. 1–2, February 1882, on German regiments around Thorn (East Prussia); the handbook prepared by the general staff's topographic section: *RGVIA*, F. 401, op. 5, d. 408: "Reference Concerning Topographical Characteristics of East Prussia and along the Route of Attack through Kovno to Gumbinen and Karshen." The report "Plan of Mobilization of the German Army *(General Instruction for Mobilization),*" *RGVIA*, F. 401, op. 5, d. 407, marked *"Ves'ma sekretno"* from German documents, October 1899 and updated in 1900 (i.e., precisely the moment when Schlieffen's famous plan was first taking shape); also the report "General Basis for Mobilization and Concentration of the German Army per the Mobilization Plan of 1900," *RGVIA*, F. 401, op. 5, d. 325, with details of Germany's two-track plan for "normal" and "accelerated" mobilization. Most of the data apparently came from Russia's attaché in Vienna, Colonel D. N. Voronets. St. Petersburg considered the intelligence the "best information on German mobilization plans" for five year in a row: *RGVIA*, F. 400, op. 4, d. 3, ll. 15–57 (quote from l. 23). From 1891, the Main Staff had access to some of the most sensitive German strategic documents. In October 1893, Obrachev gave foreign minister Griers a copy of Chief of the Great General Staff Waldersee's memorandum, "General Ideas that Pertain in the Event of Operations of the Allied Armies against France and Russia" (in French). AVPR, F. 138 op. 467, d. 128: 133, ll. 13–33.

35. *RGVIA*, F. 400, op. 3, d. 4787, l. 1, 23 May 1877.

36. *RGVIA*, F. 402, op. I, d. 302, ll. 68+ob. The Riga-Pskov line continued under construction, as did three other nonstrategic lines.

37. Ibid., d. 302, ll. 63–67: "Extract from Mobilization Committee Journal #103, 25 January 1889"; the committee's composition in 1889 was Obruchev (chair), Lieutenant Generals V. M. Shul'gin (topographer), F. K. Velichko (Asst. Chief of Main Staff; VUK), M. F. Mirkovich II (Asst. Chief of Main Staff; VUK), F. A. Fel'dman (Permanent Secretary of VUK; Miliutin's son-in-law), M. A. Narbut (Cossacks), O. Ia. Giubbenet (past chief, II Department, and twelve-year member of mobilization committee); Major Generals N. M. Golovin (head of force and freight transportation commissions; ministry representative to MPS), D. A. Tsikel'n (Sanitary Committee), A. K. Puzyrevskii (war ministry assistant chief of chancellery, adjunct professor at the academy); and Privy Councillor Beliaev. Secretary: Colonel E. E. Ussakovskii (chancellery secretary of the mobilization committee).

38. Ibid., d. 391, ll. 26–35ob, undated [mid-1888].

39. Ibid., d. 391, ll. 32ob–34.

40. Ibid., d. 391, ll. 36–43; the confusing use of terms for reserve *(zapasnye)* units resulted from Russia's three categories of reserves, and its jettisoning of militia, which the Germans continued to use. Consult Allan K. Wildman's clear summary: *The End of the Russian Imperial Army: The Old Army and the Soldiers' Revolt (March–April 1917)* (Princeton, N.J.: Princeton University Press, 1980), 25–29.

41. *RGVIA*, F. 402, op. I, d. 391, ll. 42–43. In fact, Germany's rail system—on which reservists overwhelmingly relied to reach their units—would not be fully mobilized until about M + 3, which also contributed to delays in reserve mobilization.

42. Fuller, "The Russian Empire," 98–126.

43. *RGVIA*, F. 402, op. 2, d. 25, ll. 53+ob., June 1888.

44. Ibid., d. 25, ll. 42–49ob: "Program for War Preparations in 1889," 10 January 1889, signed by Kuropatkin.

45. Ibid., d. 25, ll. 44–46. Among the other questions, Kuropatkin focused principally on tabulation of comparative information on differences between the old plan (No. 12) and the new one.

46. But as German analysts observed, by the end of the decade only half of *all* infantry and cavalry divisions in European Russia (including Finland) were more than two week's *march* from the theater of war. "Militärische Beurteilung der russischen Westgrenze für den Fall eines Krieges zwischen Deutschland und Russland," *Internationale Revue über die gesammten Armeen und Flotten*, 10, no. 1 (October–December 1891): 240–251.

47. *RGVIA*, F. 402, op. I, d. 313, ll. 187–199: "Examination of Readiness for Mobilization within the 19th Dragoon Regiment, 18 March 1888." Korf also inspected the 25th Dragoon Regiment, Romny (report: ll. 201–211) and the 3rd Cossack Regiment, Kiev (ll. 212–225), with similarly depressing results.

48. This observation is axiomatic to every study of Russian military performance, and particularly of the regimental culture. See especially the studies by Bushnell, "Tsarist Officer Corps," and Kenez "Prerevolutionary Officer Corps."

49. It was assigned to the 10th Cavalry Division of X Corps, per Schedule No. 13): *RGVIA*, F. 402, op. 2, d. 192: "Schedule of Forces in European Russia per Plan A to [Mobilization] Schedule No. 13", 12 May 1889.

50. *Vsepoddanneishchii doklad*, War Minister D. A. Miliutin, 15 January 1862, in *Stoletie voennogo ministerstva*, vol. 1, Appendix p. 90.

51. *Stoletie Voennogo ministerstva*, vol. 4, pt. II, bk. 2/sect. 1, 380.

52. "Die russischen Herbstmanöver des Jahres 1890 im Wolhynien," *Internationale Revue über die gesammten Armeen und Flotten*, 9, no. 1 (October/December, 1890): 544.

53. A. M. Zaionchkovskii, *Nastupatel'nyi boi po opytu deistvii generala Skobeleva v srazheniiakh pod Lovchei, Plevnoi (27 i 30 avg.) i Sheinovo* (St. Petersburg, 1893). See also comments on A. M. Zaionchkovskii in Menning, *Bayonets before Bullets*, 134, 215–216.

54. A. M. Zaionchkovskii, *Samostoiatel'nost' chastnykh nachal'nikov. Uvlecheniia i granitsy* (St. Petersburg, 1894), and *Initsiativa chastnykh nachal'nikov v oblasti ikh strategicheskoi raboty* (St. Petersburg, 1896), first appearing in: *Voennye besedy ispolnenniia v shtabe voisk Gvardii i Peterburgskogo voennogo okruga v 1895–1896 gg*, No. 17 (St. Petersburg, 1896). This officer had identified the key stone of doctrine that in fact rendered German military performance so lethal between 1860 and 1945.

55. Menning, *Bayonets before Bullets*, 259. Zaionchkovskii later concluded that blame for the rigidity of Russia's war-fighting doctrine lay squarely on the general staff, and only introduction of a new Field Regulation in 1912 rekindled some "audacity and maneuver" among small units during the last years of peace. A. M. Zaionchkovskii, *Mirovaia voina 1914–1918 gg.* (Leningrad, 1929).

56. I am powerfully attracted by Fritz Fischer's thesis of an accelerating social-economic spiral toward belligerency that enveloped imperial Germany's elites and leaders after Bismarck's time (if not earlier). Within that schema, Russia's alternatives were subordination, if not virtual vassalage, to Germany; war without allies; or war with allies. France's choices were homologous.

57. Fuller, *Strategy and Power*, 350–362.

58. *RGVIA*, F. 401, op. 5, d. 478, ll. 41–44, for the Russian- and French-language versions.

59. Luntinen, *French Information on the Russian War Plans*, 31–32.

8. Conclusion

1. Vitte, *Vospominaniia*, vol. 2:142–145.

2. *Glavnoe Upravlenie General'nogo shtaba*, which was a significantly different organization than its 1860s namesake. Menning, *Bayonets before Bullets*, 220–221.

3. Fuller notes a drift among *genshtabisty* toward greater eastern orientation, first expressed by Palitsyn. That shift found an advocate in Kuropatkin, demonstrating the extent to which Obruchev's strategic paradigm had been abandoned (at least, until 1912). *Strategy and Power*, 415–418, 456–458.

4. Rediger (war minister, 1905–1908) had repeated assignments as an action officer in the ministry chancellery; Zhilinskii (chief of GUGSh, 1911–1915), was raised through VUK's *deloproizvoditel'* ranks, and was the first general quartermaster following the 1902 reorganization; and Ianushkevich (chief of GUGSh, 1915–1917), had earlier duty in the ministry, the forward military districts, and in a GlavShtab planning section.

5. There is sharp disagreement among specialists over the impetus behind the strategic "reverse marches" (the revised 1910 deployment of the army in Europe): Fuller, *Strategy and Power*, chap. 9, suggests a new view of the significance of 1910;

and Menning, *Bayonets before Bullets,* 221–227, 230 and passim, articulates the more traditional view of its meaning.

6. Cited from Zhilin, ed., *Russkaia voennaia mysl'*, 146, in Menning, *Bayonets before Bullets,* 216.

7. Sukhomlinov justified his abandonment of the "Germany first" strategy by reference to a conversation between Kuropatkin and Obruchev in 1902. The retired chief of Main Staff told his protégé of a discussion he had had with Wilhelm II during the 1896 or 1897 German summer field maneuvers. They had exchanged thoughts on a Franco-Russo-German alliance against England. This chimerical delusion comforted Sukhomlinov as he shifted one hundred thousand troops out of Warsaw and Vilna districts eastward. V. A. Sukhomlinov, *Vospominaniia* (Berlin, 1924), 221–226; on his rationalization of the eastern threat: chaps. 17–21. Menning argues that concern for *logistical* problems—moving reservists from the center to the west during either mobilization or summer training in peacetime—had distorted the original territorial basis for conscription because of a disproportionate *dislokatsiia* of corps to Vilna, Warsaw, and Kiev Military Districts. *Bayonets before Bullets,* 222–226. However, peacetime reserve training did not increase or improve, and mobilization against Germany was not simplified through concentration of more units between Moscow and Kazan.

8. Fuller, *Strategy and Power,* 411.

9. Anton I. Denikin, *The Career of a Tsarist Officer: Memoirs 1872–1916,* trans. Margaret Patoski (Minneapolis: University of Minnesota Press, 1975), 60. Kenez, "Prerevolutionary Officer Corps," uncritically noted these claims.

10. "Sluzhba v Glavnom shtabe i v Glavnom upravlenii General'nogo shtaba (1903–1908 gg.)," ms., Hoover Institution archives, cited in Menning, *Bayonets before Bullets,* 292 n. 127.

11. Cited in Zaionchkovskii, *Samoderzhavie i russkaia armiia,* 149; also 153–154.

Bibliography

Principal Archival Sources

Rossisskyi Gosudarstvennyi Voenno-istoricheskii Arkhiv (RGVIA), Moscow:
Fond 400, *Glavnyi shtab*
    Opis' 2: *"I Otdelenie (po ustroistvu voisk), 1866–1910"*
    Opis' 3: *"II Otdelenie"*:
Pt. 1—*I & II stol*
Pt. 2—*II, III & IV stol*
Fond 401, *Voenno-Uchenyi komitet Glavnogo shtaba*
    Opisi 2–5: *"Kantseliariia"*
    Opis' 6: *"Vremennye komissi, obrazovannye pri Voenno-Uchenoi komitete Glavnogo shtaba (1882–1894)"*
Fond 402, *Kantseliariia Komiteta po mobilizatsii voisk Glavnogo shtaba (1873–1903)*
    Opis' 1: *"Komitet dlia podgotovki dannykh k mobilizatsii voisk 1875–1879 gg."*
    Opis' 2: *"Komitet po mobilizatsim voisk 1880–1903 gg."*
Fond 485, *Kollektsii voenno-uchenogo arkhiva No. 485: Russko-turetskaia voina 1877–1878 gg.*

Arkhiv vneshnei politiki Rossii (AVPR), Moscow:
Fond 133, *"Kantseliariia ministra"*:
    Opis' 470 (1870–1917)
Fond 138, Opis' 467: *"Sekretnyi arkhiv ministra (XII.1858–X.1917)"*
Fond 141, *"Shifroval'nyi otdel' 1731–1917 gg."*
    Opisi 1–3
Fond 151, *"Politarkiv"*
    Opis' 482 (1841–1917)
Fond 340, *"Kolektsiia dokumental'nykh materialov iz lichnykh arkhivov chinovnikov MID 1743–1933 gg."*

Published Primary Sources

Adamov, E. "K voprosu o podgotovke mirovoi voiny." *Krasnyi arkhiv*, 64, 1934 no. 3.

"Antisarmatikus" [P. A. Geisman]. *Ot Berlina i Veny k Peterburgu i Moskve i obratno. Otvet voinstvuiushchim tevtonam-russofobam.* Elisavetgrad, 1891.

"*Bessmertnyi.*" "Iz vospominanii o general-ad'iutante M. I. Dragomirove." *Russkii arkhiv*, 1912, bk. 2, 6: 226–227.

Bobrikov, G. I. "Vospominanie o Berlinskom kongresse." *Russkii vestnik*, 205, no. 12 (1889): 3–43.

———. *Zapiski.* Vol. 1, *Epokha voiny 1877–78 gg.* St. Petersburg, 1913.

Borisov, V. *Strategicheskie voprosy.* Warsaw, 1897.

Buinitskii, N. *Zablagovremennoe usilenie strategicheskikh punktov.* St. Petersburg, 1893.

D. L. L. [Drake, Liudvig L.]. "Nabroski iz proshlogo (Otryvochnye vospominaniia 1868–74 g.)." *Voenno-istoricheskii sbornik*, 1912/1: 61–74.

Deutschland und Russland. Ein französische Anschauung über den deutsch-russischen Zukunftkrieg. Von Major Z. Hannover, 1883/1886.

Die Internationalen Beziehungen im Zeitalter des Imperialismus. Dokumente aus der Archiven des zarischen und der provisorischen Regierung 1878–1898. Berlin, 1931–1943. [See also *Komissiia po izdanie . . .*, below.]

Dnevnik E. A. Perettsa (gosudarstvennogo sekretariia) (1880–1883). Edited by A. E. Presniakov. Moscow/Leningrad, 1927.

Dnevnik gosudarstvennogo sekretaria A.A. Polovtsova. 2 vols. (1883–1892). Edited by P. A. Zaionchkovskii. Moscow: Nauka, 1966.

Dnevnik P. A. Valueva. 2 vols. Edited by P. A. Zaionchkovskii. Moscow: AN–SSSR, 1961.

Dragomirov, M. *Opyt rukovodstva dlia podgotovki chastei k boiu.* Kiev, 1871/1885/1896.

[Dragomirov, M.] *Sbornik statei M. Dragomirova.* Vol. 1, *1858–1872 gg.* St. Petersburg, 1891.

[Dragomirov, M. I.] *Chetyrnadtsat' let. 1881–1895 gg. Sbornik original'nykh i perevodnykh statei M. Dragomirova.* St. Petersburg, 1895.

Dragomirova, S. A. "Radetskii, Skobelev, Dragomirov. (Iz vospominanii)." *Istoricheskii vestnik*, 139, no. 2 (1915): 432–437; no. 3: 796–803; 140 no. 4 (1916): 88–96; no. 6: 901–907.

Gazenkampf, M. *Ustroistvo General'nogo shtaba v pervostepennykh evropeiskikh armiiakh.* St. Petersburg, 1884.

Geisman, P. A. *Kratkii kurs istorii voennogo iskusstva v srednikh i novykh veka.* 3 vols. St. Petersburg, 1893–1896.

———. *Neskol'ko myslei po voprosu ob otnosheniiakh strategii k politike. Po povodu rechi V. I. Lamanskogo v obshchem sobranii chlenov.* St. Petersburg, 1895.

Golovachov, A. A. "Zheleznyia dorogi v Rossii. Istoriia postroiki dorog." 2 parts. *Sbornik gosudarstvennykh znanii*, 4/5. St. Petersburg, 1877/1878.

Griaznov, F. *Podvizhnost' konnitsy i ee znachenie.* St. Petersburg, 1885.

———. *Manevry na dve storony. Ofitsial'naia storona etogo dela v Germanii, Avstrii i Frantsii.* St. Petersburg, 1886.

Istoricheskii ocherk razvitiia zheleznykh dorog v Rossii s ikh osnovaniia po 1897 g., vkliuchitel'no. 2 vols. St. Petersburg, 1898.

Izvlechenie iz otchetov generalov, sostoiavshikh posrednikami na bol'shom manevre voisk Odesskogo i Khar'kovskogo okrugov 1888 g. Vol. 2, *4 i 5 dni (29/31 Avgusta) i obshchaia zakliucheniia.* St. Petersburg, 1889.

"K istorii vozniknoveniia mirovoi voiny s predisloviem." Edited by E. Adamova. *Krasnyi arkhiv,* 34 (1929 no. 3): 166–183.

Kislinskii, N. A. *Nasha zheleznodorozhnaia politika po dokumentam arkhiva komiteta ministrov.* 4 vols. Edited by A. N. Kulomzin. St. Petersburg, 1902.

Komissiia po izdaniiu dokumentov epokhi imperializma. Mezhdunarodnye otnosheniia v epokhu imperializma: Dokumenty iz arkhivov tsarskogo i vremennogo pravitelstv, 1878–1917 gg. 12 vols. Moscow/Leningrad, 1931–1938.

Konspekt strategii. Sost. ofitserami starshogo kursa Nikolaevskoi akademii General'nogo shtaba v 1883 g. St. Petersburg, 1883.

Konspekt II, III i IV otdelov kursa istorii voennogo iskusstva. Po lektsiiam ordinarnogo professora Nikolaevskoi akademii General'nogo shtaba Polkovnika Geismana. St. Petersburg, 1897.

Lebedev, V. T. *Veroiatnye operatsionnye linii v sluchae voiny franko-russkogo soiuza s germano-avstro-ital'ianskim.* St. Petersburg, 1896.

Leer, G. A. *Publichnyia lektsii o voine 1870–1871 gg.* St. Petersburg, 1873.

———. *Zapiski strategii.* 2 vols. St. Petersburg, 1877–1880.

———. *Znachenie printsipa deiatel'nosti na voine.* St. Petersburg, 1883.

———. *Strategicheskie etiudy.* St. Petersburg, 1885.

———. *Slozhnye operatsii.* St. Petersburg, 1892.

———. *Metod voennykh nauk (strategii, taktiki i voennoi istorii).* St. Petersburg, 1894.

Mau, N. I. *Pekhota, konnitsa i artilleriia v boiu vrozn' i vmeste. Opyt taktiki dlia unter-ofitserov. Besedy, schitannye s razresheniia nachal'stva v polkovoi uchebnoi komande 101 pekhotnogo Permskogo polka.* Vilna, 1880.

Mazhnyi, D. *Bol'shie manevry. Takticheskii ocherk.* St. Petersburg, 1887.

Mikhnevich, N. P. *Osnovy russkogo voennogo iskusstva. Sravnitel'nyi ocherk sostoianiia voennogo iskusstva v Rossii i zapadnoi Evrope v vazhneishie istoricheskie epokhi.* St. Petersburg, 1898.

———. *Vliianie noveishikh tekhnicheskikh; izobretenii na taktiku voisk.* St. Petersburg, 1893.

———. *Strategiia.* 2 vols. St. Petersburg, 1899–1901.

Mikulin, I. A. *Zamechaniia po strategicheskim temam dopolnitel'nogo kursa Nikolaevskoi akademii General'nogo shtaba v 1889 g.* St. Petersburg, 1909.

Nelidov, A. K. "K dvadtsatipiatiletiiu osvobozhdeniia Bolgarii. Zakliuchenie pere-miriia v Adrianopole 19-go ianv. 1878." *Istoricheskii vestnik,* 91, no. 1 (1903): 66–81.

Opisanie Narvsko-krasnosel'skikh manevrov 1890 goda. Sost. po neposredstvennym ukazaniiam Ego Imperatorskogo Vysochestva Glavnokomanduiushchogo voiskami Gvardii i Peterburgskogo voennogo okruga. St. Petersburg, 1891.

Prezhentsov, Ia. *Kavaleriia vperedi fronta armii.* St. Petersburg, 1887.

Rossiia i natsional'no-osvoboditel'naia bor'ba na Balkanakh 1875–1878. Edited by A. L. Narochnitskii. Moscow: Nauka, 1978.

Semenov, N. I. *Strategicheskaia zadacha. Deistviia I Armeiskogo korpusa v raione mezhdu rekami Visliiu, Pilitseiu i severnoi polosoiu Zapadnoi Galitsii.* St. Petersburg, 1894.

Simanskii, P. N. *Otvet g. Bliokhu na ego trud «Budushchaia voina v tekhnicheskom, ekonomicheskom i politicheskom otnosheniiakh».* Moscow, 1898.

Skhemy k sborniku sochinenii ofitserov Nikolaevskoi akademii General'nogo shtaba. St. Petersburg, 1907.

Skugarevskii, A. P. *O polevoi sluzhbe General'nogo shtaba.* St. Petersburg, 1885.

———. "M. N. Annenkov." *Razvedchik,* 1204 (1913): 726–728.

———. "Vospominaniia ob A. N. Vitmere." *Razvedchik,* 1363 (1916): 806–807.

Spisok general'nogo shtaba . . . [1874, 1882, 1889, 1895, 1902]. St. Petersburg, [1875, 1882, 1889, 1895, 1902].

Strategicheskye issledovaniia avstriiskikh voennykh liudei o voine Avstrii s Rossiiu. Sbornik izvlechenii i perevodov s nemetskogo s kartiiu. St. Petersburg, 1873.

Stremoukhov, P. D. "Iz moikh vospominanii o kniaze Bismarke." *Russkaia starina,* 96, no. 10 (1898): 65–68.

Sukhomlinov, V. *Sbornik statei po 1896 g.* St. Petersburg, 1896.

Sukhotin, N. N. *Zametki po predmetu istorii voennogo iskusstva: Predislovie.* St. Petersburg, 1881.

Uchenie o voine Klauzevitsa. Osnovnye polozheniia. Translated from German by M. Dragomirov. St. Petersburg, 1888.

Ustav o stroevoi pekhotnoi sluzhbe. St. Petersburg, 1881.

Voide, K. *Samostoiatel'nost' chastnykh nachal'nikov na voine.* St. Petersburg, 1892.

Wertheimer E. von. "Ein k. und k. Militärattaché über das politische Leben in Berlin (1880–1895)." *Preussische Jahrbücher,* 201 no. 3 (1925): 264–282.

Zeddeler, L. L. "Dvadtsat' piat' let tomu nazad. (Otryvok iz dnevnika)." *Istoricheskii vestnik,* 64, no. 4 (1896): 114–129; no. 5: 480–508.

———. "Otryvki iz vospominanii." *Istoricheskii vestnik,* 115, no. 3 (1909): 918–941.

Secondary Sources

Alksnis, Ia. Ia. "Podgotovka k voine i voprosy komplektovaniia armii." *Voina i revoliutsiia,* 1927, no. 6.

———. "Nachal'nyi period voiny." 2 pts. *Voina i revoliutsiia* 1929, no. 9: 3–22, no. 10: 3–15.

Askew, William C. "Russian Military Strength on the Eve of the Franco-Prussian War." *Slavonic and East European Review* 30 (1951): 185–205.

Bradley, Joseph. *Guns for the Tsar: American Technology and the Small Arms Industry in Nineteenth-Century Russia.* DeKalb: Northern Illinois University Press, 1990.

Brennan, W. H. "The Russian Foreign Ministry and the Alliance with Germany." *Russian History,* 1 (1974): 18–30.

Campion, L. K. "Behind the *Drang nach Osten:* Baltic Emigres and Russophobia in 19th Century Germany." Ph.D. diss., Indiana University, 1966.

Chernov, S. L. "K voprosu o San-Stefanovskom dogovore 1878 g." *Istoriia SSSR,* 6 (1975): 133–147.

Craig, G. "Military Diplomats in the Prussian and German Service: The Attachés, 1816–1914." *Political Science Quarterly,* 64 no. 1 (1949): 65–94.

Crean, E. M. "The Governor-Generalship of Turkestan under K. P. von Kaufmann, 1867–1882." Ph.D. diss., Yale University, 1970.

Deutschland und Russland im Zeitalter des Kapitalismus, 1871–1914. Edited by K. O. von Aretin and W. Conze. Wiesbaden: F. Steiner, 1977.

Dorpalen, A. "Alexander III and the Boulanger Crisis in France." *Journal of Modern History,* 23 (1951): 122–136.

Filosofiia i voennaia istoriia. Edited by E. I. Rybkin et al. Moscow: Nauka, 1979.

Fleischhauer, E. *Bismarcks Russlandpolitik im Jahrzehnt vor der Reichsgründung und ihre Darstellung in der sowjetischen Historiographie*. Cologne: Bohlau, 1976.

Frank, G., and E. Schüle. "Graf Pavel Andreevich Shuvalov, russischer Botschafter in Berlin, 1885–1894." *Zeitschrift zür Osteuropäischen Geschichte*, 7 (1933): 525–559.

Zur Geschichte und Problematik des deutsch–russischen Rückversicherungsvertrags von 1887. Edited by H. Hallmann. Darmstadt, Wissenschaftliche Buchgesellschaft, 1968.

Geschichtliche Kräfte und Entscheidungen. Festschrift zum 65. Geburtstage von Otto Becker. Edited by M. Gohring. Wiesbaden: F. Steiner, 1954.

Golovin, N.[N.]. *Sluzhba General'nogo shtaba*. St. Petersburg, 1912.

Grabau, A. *Das Festungsproblem in Deutschland und seine Auswirkung auf die strategische Lage 1870 bis 1914*. Berlin, 1935.

Groener, W. *Das Testament des Grafen Schlieffen*. Berlin, 1927.

Grosser Generalstab. Moltke in der Vorbereitung und Durchführung der Operationen (Kriegsgeschichtliche Einzelschriften, pt. 6, no. 36). Berlin, 1905.

Grundzüge der militärischen Kriegführung (Handbuch zur deutschen Militärgeschichte, no. 9). Munich: Bernard and Gräfe, 1979.

Hasselmayr, F. *Bismarcks Reichssicherung gegen Russland (1879–84). Der Erwerb der deutschen Kolonialbesitzes (1884–85)*. Munich, 1956.

Herzfeld, H. *Die deutsche-französische Kriegsgefahr vom 1875 (Forschungen und Darstellungen aus dem Reichsarchiv, III)*. Berlin, 1922.

Holborn, Hajo. *Bismarcks europäische Politik zu Beginn der Siebziger Jahre und die Mission Radowitz*. Berlin, 1925.

Jeismann, K.-E. *Das Problem des Präventivkreiges im europäischen Staatensystem mit besonderen Blick auf die Bismarckzeit*. Freiburg: K. Alber, 1957.

Jelavich, Barbara. "British Means of Offence against Russia in the 19th Century." *Russian History*, 1 (1974): 119–135.

———. *St. Petersburg and Moscow. Tsarist and Soviet Foreign Policy, 1814–1974*. Bloomington: Indiana University Press, 1974.

Jones, David R. *The Advanced Guard and Mobility in Russian and Soviet Military Thought and Practice (SAFRA Papers No. 1)*. Gulf Breeze, Fla.,: Academic Press International, 1985.

Kamon. "Istoricheskoe razvitie germanskogo plana voiny." *Voennyi zarubezhnik* 8/9 (1922): 404–410.

Kessel, Eberhard. "Zur Genesis der modernen Kriegslehre." *Wehrwissenschaftliche Rundschau*, 3 no. 9 (1953): 405–423.

———. "Die Tätigkeit des Grafen Waldersee als Quartiermeister und Chef des Generalstabes der Armee." *Der Welt als Geschichte*, 14 (1954): 192–221.

Khvostov, V. M. "Rossiia i germanskaia agressiia v dni evropeiskogo krizisa 1887 g. (k predistorii franko-russkogo soiuza.).". *Istoricheskie zapiski*, 18 (1946): 201–254.

Kirchner, W. "The Industrialization of Russia and the Siemans Firm, 1853–1890." *Jahrbuch für Geschichte Osteuropa*, 20 (1974): 321–357.

Klein-Wuttig, A. *Politik und Kriegführung in den deutschen Einigungskriegen (Abhandlungen zur mittleren und neueren Geschichte, 75)*. Berlin, 1934.

Kloster, W. *Der deutsche Generalstab und der Präventivkriegsgedanke*. Stuttgart, 1932.

Krasnov, P. N. "Pamiati imperatorskoi russkoi armii." *Russkaia letopis'*, [Paris] 5 (1923): 5–65.

Kresnovskii, A. *Istoriia russkoi armii.* 4 vols. Belgrade, 1933–1934.

Kultur und Kulturwissenschaft um 1900. Krise der Moderne und Glaube an die Wissenschaft. Stuttgart: F. Steiner, 1989.

Mayr, K. "Kriegsplan und staatsmännische Voraussicht. Kriegsgeschichtliche Betrachtungen über die Schlieffenschule." *Zeitschrift für Politik*, 14 no. 5 (1925): 385–411.

Meissner, H. O. "Briefwechsel zwischen Waldersee und Yorck von Wartenburg, 1885–94." *Historisch-Politisches Archiv*, 1 (1930).

———. "Graf Waldersees Pariser Informationen 1887." *Preussische Jahrbücher*, 224 no. 2 (1931): 125–149.

———. *Militärattachés und Militärbevollmächtigte in Preussen und im Deutschen Reich. Ein Beitrag zur Geschichte der Militärdiplomatie.* Berlin, Rutten and Loening 1957.

Müller-Link, H. *Industrialisierung und Aussenpolitik. Preussen-Deutschland und das Zarenreich, 1860–1890.* Göttingen: Vandenhoeck and Ruprecht, 1977.

Narochnitskaia, L. I. *Rossiia i voiny Prussii v 60-kh godakh XIX v. za ob"edinenie Germanii «sverkhu».* Moscow: Politicheskie literatury, 1960.

———. *Rossiia i otmena neitralizatsii Chernogo moria 1856–1877gg. K istorii Vostochnogo voprosa.* Moscow: Nauka, 1989.

Novotny, A. *Quellen und Studien zur Geschichte des Berliner Kongresses 1878.* Graz: H. Böhlaus.

Ob osobennostiakh imperializma v Rossii. Moscow, 1963.

Ocherki sovetskoi voennoi istoriografii. Edited by P. A. Zhilin, Moscow: Voenizdat, 1974.

Polvinen, T. *Die finnischen Eisenbahnen in den militärischen und politischen Plänen Russlands vor dem ersten Weltkrieg. (Studia Historica 4).* Helsinki: SHS, 1962.

Rassow, P. *Der Plan Moltkes für den Zweifrontenkrieg, 1871–1890.* Breslau, 1938.

Ritchie, G. B. "The Asiatic Department during the Reign of Alexander II, 1855–1881." Ph.D. diss., Columbia University, 1975.

Rosinski, Hubert. "Scharnhorst to Schlieffen: The Rise and Decline of German Military Thought." *U.S. Naval War College Review*, 24 no. 1 (1976): 83–103.

Rutkowski, E. R. von. "General Skobelew, die Krise des Jahres 1882 und die Anfänge der militärischen Vereinbarungen zwischen Österreich-Ungern und Deutschland." *Ostdeutsche Wissenschaft*, 10 (1963): 81–151.

Ryzhak, S. A. *Vydaiushchiesia inzhenery i uchenye zheleznodorozhnogo transporta.* Moscow: Transport, 1990.

Shneerson, L. M. *Avstro-prusskaia voina i diplomatiia velikikh evropeiskikh derzhav.* Minsk: Min. obrazovanii BSSR, 1962.

———. *V preddverii franko-prusskoi voiny. Franko-Germanskii konflikt 13–39 Liuksemburga v 1867g.* Minsk: BGU, 1969.

Skazkin, S. D. *Konets avstro-russko-germanskogo soiuza. Issledovanie po istorii russko-germanskikh i russko-avstriiskikh otnoshenii v sviazi s vostochnym voprosom v 80-e gody XIX stoletiia.* Moscow: Nauka, 1974.

Staabs, H. von. *Aufmarsch nach Zwei Fronten, auf Grund der Operatsionspläne von 1871–1914.* [Berlin]: E. S. Mittler, 1925.

Stadelmann, R. *Moltke und der Staat.* Krefeld: Scherpe-Verlag, 1950.

Svechin, A. "Evoliutsiia operativnogo razvertyvaniia." *Voina i revoliutsiia*. 1926, no. 5: 3–26.

Trutzschler, H. von. "Bismarcks Stellung zum Präventivkrieg." *Europäische Gespräche*, 1 (1923).

Wehler, Hans-Ulrich "'Absoluter' und 'totaler' Krieg von Clausewitz zu Ludendorff." *Politische Vierteljahresschrift*, 10 (1969).

―――. "Bismarcks späte Russlandspolitik, 1879–1890." *Krisenherde des Kaiserreiches 1871–1918*. Göttingen: Vandenhoeck and Ruprecht, 1970.

Wittram, R. "Bismarcks Russlandpolitik nach der Reichsgründung." *Russland, Europa und der deutsche Osten*. Munich: R. Oldenbourg, 1960.

Zaionchkovskii, A. M. *Podgotovka Rossii k mirovoi voine v mezhdunarodnom otnoshenii*. Leningrad, 1926.

Index